Hispanic Perspectives on Student Support and Community Empowerment

Angello Villarreal
Freehold Regional High School District, USA

Vice President of Editorial	Melissa Wagner
Managing Editor of Acquisitions	Mikaela Felty
Managing Editor of Book Development	Jocelynn Hessler
Production Manager	Mike Brehm
Cover Design	Phillip Shickler

Published in the United States of America by
    IGI Global Scientific Publishing
    701 East Chocolate Avenue
    Hershey, PA, 17033, USA
    Tel: 717-533-8845
    Fax: 717-533-8661
    E-mail: cust@igi-global.com
    Website: https://www.igi-global.com

Copyright © 2025 by IGI Global Scientific Publishing. All rights reserved. No part of this publication may be reproduced, stored or distributed in any form or by any means, electronic or mechanical, including photocopying, without written permission from the publisher.
Product or company names used in this set are for identification purposes only. Inclusion of the names of the products or companies does not indicate a claim of ownership by IGI Global Scientific Publishing of the trademark or registered trademark.

Library of Congress Cataloging-in-Publication Data

CIP Data Pending
ISBN:979-8-3373-1340-5
eISBN:979-8-3373-1342-9

British Cataloguing in Publication Data
A Cataloguing in Publication record for this book is available from the British Library.

All work contributed to this book is new, previously-unpublished material.
The views expressed in this book are those of the authors, but not necessarily of the publisher.
This book contains information sourced from authentic and highly regarded references, with reasonable efforts made to ensure the reliability of the data and information presented. The authors, editors, and publisher believe the information in this book to be accurate and true as of the date of publication. Every effort has been made to trace and credit the copyright holders of all materials included. However, the authors, editors, and publisher cannot assume responsibility for the validity of all materials or the consequences of their use. Should any copyright material be found unacknowledged, please inform the publisher so that corrections may be made in future reprints.

To my son, Ricardo (Ricky). You have inspired me to never give up and to always keep pushing forward. Seeing you smile has been my spark every day to continue with this journey and I hope I make you proud as your father.

To my twins, Elliana & Alejandro. You have challenged me in every single way, but you have made me a better person and father. Your smile, hugs and laughs are what keeps me moving forward.

To my students (former, current, and future). You have made me see life through a different lens, you have made me smile and sometimes even cry. Each one of you makes me a better educator and person, and I hope my achievements and failures inspire you to become your best.

Table of Contents

Preface xi

Chapter 1
Cross-Cultural Storytelling Project: Curiosity Creates Connection 1
    Melissa A. Campesi, Cross-Cultural Storytelling Project, USA

Chapter 2
The Power of Storytelling and the Positive Impact They Have on Students of
Color 33
    Lee Perez, Omaha Benson High School, USA
    Autumn Rivera, Glenwood Springs Middle School, USA
    Ramon Benavides, Del Valle High School, USA

Chapter 3
The Impact of Male Mentorship on Latino Immigrant Young Men 55
    Juan Andrés Ouviña, Montclair State University, USA

Chapter 4
#Latino Mentors/Teachers Needed 75
    Alex Guzman, Kean University, USA

Chapter 5
Centering Communities in Spanish Language Education: Pathways to an
Inclusive Approach for Heritage Learners 105
    Dorie Conlon, Glastonbury Public Schools, USA
    Marta Adán, Capitol Region Education Council, USA

Chapter 6
Community Cultural Wealth and Successful College Navigation Within New
Latinx Destinations 145
    Anthony Villarreal, San Diego State University, USA

Chapter 7
Breaking Down Barriers: Nurturing Our Resistance, Reclaiming Our Space,
and Calling for Shared Responsibility 175
    Françoise Thenoux, Independent Researcher, Chile

Chapter 8
Leveraging Identity and Positional Power in Service of Latinx Youth: The
Journey of Two Latina Doctoras in Pursuit of Community Advancement........ 197
    Fabiola Bagula, University of San Diego, USA
    Haydee Zavala, University of California, San Diego, USA

Chapter 9
The Critical Work of the Blue-Collar Scholar: Latinx Educators Working
Towards the Heteroglossic and Liberated English Language Development
Class.. 231
    David De La Cruz Rosales, California State University, Fullerton, USA

Chapter 10
Understanding Dyslexia in Multilingual Environments 257
    Concepción Moncada Cummings, University of Florida, USA
    Norma Gómez-Fuentes, Independent Researcher, USA
    Vivian Gonsalves, University of Florida, USA

Chapter 11
Integrating Reproductive Justice in Social Work Education: Empowering
Hispanic Communities Through Holistic Practice 289
    Caelin Elizabeth McCallum, Monmouth University, USA
    Amanda Marie Goodwin, Monmouth University, USA

Compilation of References 327

About the Contributors 369

Index... 375

Detailed Table of Contents

Preface xi

Chapter 1
Cross-Cultural Storytelling Project: Curiosity Creates Connection 1
 Melissa A. Campesi, Cross-Cultural Storytelling Project, USA

In this chapter you will meet Melissa Campesi, an entrepreneur, creator, author, and educator of Hispanic heritage. Her bilingual upbringing, varied teaching experiences, and appreciation of culture have shaped her unique approach to honoring the identities and interests of students with diverse linguistic and cultural backgrounds. She has found that celebrating individuality in the learning environment gives students a sense of inclusion and empowerment which leads to learning success. As the Founder of the Cross-Cultural Storytelling Project, the author shares the seeds of inspiration for this global project and how it continues to grow cultural connections through the power of storytelling.

Chapter 2
The Power of Storytelling and the Positive Impact They Have on Students of Color 33
 Lee Perez, Omaha Benson High School, USA
 Autumn Rivera, Glenwood Springs Middle School, USA
 Ramon Benavides, Del Valle High School, USA

Storytelling through the perspective of teachers of color can have a positive impact on students of color. With immigrant, migrant, and refugee populations increasing in classrooms across the United States of America, storytelling is a powerful vessel to assist students with their social and emotional needs during instruction and learning. Moreover, storytelling can teach culturally diverse populations empathy through the powerful lens of their teachers. This is essentially more powerful if their teachers look like the diverse students that they serve daily. This chapter aims to tell the stories of three prominent Latinx teachers and how they have used their respective stories to inspire and empower their students of color to be the best versions of themselves culturally, emotionally, linguistically, and academically.

Chapter 3
The Impact of Male Mentorship on Latino Immigrant Young Men 55
Juan Andrés Ouviña, Montclair State University, USA

This chapter examines the transformative potential of male mentorship in supporting Latino immigrant young men's academic success and identity development. Drawing from empirical research and first-hand experience as an educator and researcher, the author analyzes the implementation of culturally responsive mentorship programs for this population. The discussion explores Latino immigrant youth experiences through demographic trends and cultural transitions, examining identity development through theoretical frameworks like the Selection, Optimization, and Compensation Model. Through case studies and practical strategies, the chapter provides educators and community leaders with evidence-based approaches for effective mentorship initiatives. The author's perspective as both a former Latino first generation student and current educator offers unique insights while presenting a framework for sustainable mentorship programs that emphasize family engagement, community partnerships, and comprehensive support.

Chapter 4
#Latino Mentors/Teachers Needed 75
Alex Guzman, Kean University, USA

This chapter emphasizes the critical role of mentorship in promoting professional growth and leadership within the Latinx community, with a focus on increasing the recruitment and retention of Latinx educators. Through a servant leadership lens and personal counter-storytelling, it highlights the challenges faced by Latinx educators and proposes actionable solutions. The chapter underscores the importance of diversity in the teaching workforce and how mentorship supports the well-being of future Latinx educators.

Chapter 5
Centering Communities in Spanish Language Education: Pathways to an
Inclusive Approach for Heritage Learners.. 105
Dorie Conlon, Glastonbury Public Schools, USA
Marta Adán, Capitol Region Education Council, USA

Many Spanish language education programs in the US focus heavily on second language acquisition, often prioritizing communicative competence over intercultural competence (IC) and intercultural citizenship (iCit). This narrow emphasis on language development can overlook the unique needs of heritage speakers, leading to feelings of marginalization and potential attrition from programs. The authors argue that by centering the Communities goal area of the World-Readiness Standards for Learning Languages, educators can create inclusive Spanish language programs that better serve both heritage and non-heritage students. The chapter begins with an overview of heritage language learners followed by how the theoretical frameworks of IC and iCit can be used to center the Communities standards. The chapter then provides practical examples from the authors' classrooms, illustrating effective implementation strategies at elementary and high school levels. Finally, the authors offer reflective questions for teachers and program directors interested in centering the Communities standards.

Chapter 6
Community Cultural Wealth and Successful College Navigation Within New
Latinx Destinations 145
Anthony Villarreal, San Diego State University, USA

With dramatic population growth and redistribution, Latinx are becoming increasingly dispersed across the country. There is a need for educational research that does not attempt to operate under the same assumptions within regions where the Latinx presence is long-standing but rather carefully examines educational outcomes and experiences within the new Latinx destination context. This study explores the college access experiences of 20 Mexican American students through a Community Cultural Wealth framework (Yosso, 2005), an asset-based perspective that allowed for the identification of participants' strengths across six forms of capital—aspirational, familial, linguistic, navigational, social, and resistance forms of capital. Their reflections provide unique insights for enacting culturally affirming/sustaining practices for educators and counselors in new destination contexts.

Chapter 7
Breaking Down Barriers: Nurturing Our Resistance, Reclaiming Our Space,
and Calling for Shared Responsibility 175
Françoise Thenoux, Independent Researcher, Chile

This chapter examines the systemic inequities faced by Latinx teachers in the predominantly white U.S. education system. It explores the evolving concept of self-care, originally coined by Audre Lorde, which has become commodified and stripped of its radical roots. For Latinx educators, self-care transcends wellness trends; it is a survival strategy against anti-immigrant policies, tokenism, accentism, and the devaluation of their assets. My experience as an immigrant teacher highlights the burnout from visa renewals and institutional bias. The emotional and economic strain underscores the abusive conditions Latinx teachers often endure. Dismantling these oppressive systems requires shared responsibility from school leaders and administrators in reforming hiring practices and policies. By sharing our stories this chapter reveals collective experiences shaping our identities and the need for transformation. True self-care is rooted in resistance, community building, and advocacy, empowering Latinx educators to reclaim their narratives and become advocates for change.

Chapter 8

Leveraging Identity and Positional Power in Service of Latinx Youth: The Journey of Two Latina Doctoras in Pursuit of Community Advancement 197
Fabiola Bagula, University of San Diego, USA
Haydee Zavala, University of California, San Diego, USA

This paper explores the intersection of Latina leadership and the development of equitable educational systems that foster Latinx student success. It examines initiatives within a large Southern California school district to create more diverse leadership, particularly by elevating Latina voices, building transnational partnerships, and developing student-centered strategies. These include the Latinx Student Success Plan and efforts to designate the district as a Hispanic-Serving School District (HSSD). The paper highlights the unique challenges faced by first-generation Latinx students and leaders, while also celebrating the transformative power of representation, community, and identity in education. This paper will be written by two Latina doctoras in new leadership spaces in a very large urban school district in the United States. Our district educates close to 100,000 students and is situated very close to the large international border with Mexico. Almost half of our student population is Latinx.

Chapter 9

The Critical Work of the Blue-Collar Scholar: Latinx Educators Working Towards the Heteroglossic and Liberated English Language Development Class 231
David De La Cruz Rosales, California State University, Fullerton, USA

This chapter explores the essential role of Latinx educators in nurturing critical linguistic and literacy awareness among English Learners, referred to as Emergent Bilinguals. Specifically, the focus will be on the impact of Latinx educators in the English Language Development (ELD) classroom. This chapter asserts that the work of a Latinx ELD educator is based on a critical understanding of the oppressive systemic structures of assimilation policies, linguistic dominance, and constructed academic challenges and labels imposed on Emergent Bilinguals due to historical marginalization and oppressive systems, often exacerbated by political agendas and anti-immigrant sentiments. Despite the challenges posed by the monoglossic and hegemonic nature of ELD policies, Latinx educators can employ culturally relevant practices to amplify the voices of their students and communities within the framework of the ELD classroom.

Chapter 10
Understanding Dyslexia in Multilingual Environments 257
  Concepción Moncada Cummings, University of Florida, USA
  Norma Gómez-Fuentes, Independent Researcher, USA
  Vivian Gonsalves, University of Florida, USA

Given its prevalence, most teachers across the U.S. are likely to have students with dyslexia in their classrooms, and many of them may come from homes where English is not the primary language of communication. This chapter aims to provide insights, methods, and strategies for addressing dyslexia within multilingual environments, which often complicates identification and intervention. The chapter has three main sections. First, it begins with multilingual students' unique challenges, including language dominance, cross-linguistic transfer, and distinguishing between language differences and disorders. Then, it provides an overview of implications for literacy instruction for multilingual students with dyslexia, like the importance of culturally responsive teaching practices and evidence-based instructional strategies, such as including the Science of Reading, tailored to support the literacy development of multilingual students with dyslexia. The final section summarizes the recommended strategies across the literature discussed throughout the chapter.

Chapter 11
Integrating Reproductive Justice in Social Work Education: Empowering
Hispanic Communities Through Holistic Practice 289
  Caelin Elizabeth McCallum, Monmouth University, USA
  Amanda Marie Goodwin, Monmouth University, USA

This chapter examines the integration of reproductive justice into social work education, focusing on its importance for empowering Hispanic communities. Rooted in a framework developed by women of color, reproductive justice addresses not only reproductive rights, but also the social, economic, and political conditions that influence autonomy. The chapter highlights how Hispanic populations face unique barriers, such as limited healthcare access, cultural stigmas, and legal challenges. It advocates for embedding reproductive justice in MSW-level curricula to prepare social workers for culturally competent practice and policy advocacy. Through interdisciplinary education and systemic reforms, social workers can help dismantle barriers and promote reproductive autonomy for marginalized groups.

Compilation of References 327

About the Contributors 369

Index 375

Preface

Education serves as the cornerstone for growth, resilience, and empowerment in diverse societies. Within this context, the Hispanic and Latino communities have shown remarkable perseverance and potential in addressing challenges and capitalizing on opportunities in educational and communal spaces. It is my privilege to present *Hispanic Perspectives on Student Support and Community Empowerment*, a collaborative endeavor that seeks to amplify the narratives and insights of Hispanic and Latino scholars, educators, and advocates.

This book was conceived with a clear and resolute mission: to illuminate strategies that enhance the academic, social, and emotional well-being of Hispanic and Latino students across their educational journey. From PreK classrooms to institutions of higher learning, our contributors delve into pressing topics, such as curriculum and instruction tailored to culturally diverse learners, effective recruitment and retention practices for Hispanic educators, and the pivotal role of superintendents and supervisors in creating inclusive learning environments.

The mental health of Hispanic students and communities also occupies a central focus of this work. Recognizing the unique challenges faced by this demographic, the book highlights the voices of practicing counselors and mental health professionals dedicated to fostering resilience and holistic well-being. By addressing these critical areas, we aim to provide both theoretical insights and practical tools to educators, administrators, and community leaders alike.

This publication is not merely an academic collection; it is a call to action for collaboration and innovation. It underscores the importance of connecting Hispanic and Latino students with multi-ethnic communities and leveraging the unique strengths of Hispanic Serving Institutions (HSIs). Through diverse perspectives, research findings, and lived experiences, the chapters in this book present actionable approaches to empower not only students but also their families, educators, and the broader community.

Our target audience spans a wide range of professionals and advocates, including PreK to 12 teachers, school administrators, curriculum designers, mental health counselors, higher education leaders, and community organizers. The collective wisdom contained in these pages offers invaluable guidance for those committed to fostering equity, inclusion, and excellence within educational systems and beyond.

I extend my heartfelt gratitude to the contributing authors, whose expertise and dedication have brought this vision to life. Their work represents a vital step forward in understanding and addressing the unique needs of Hispanic and Latino communities.

As you navigate the chapters of this book, I hope you will find inspiration, practical strategies, and a renewed commitment to equity in education and community empowerment. Together, we can create a future where every student is supported, every voice is heard, and every community thrives.

ORGANIZATION OF THE BOOK

Chapter 1: Cross-Cultural Storytelling Project: Curiosity Creates Connection

Melissa Campesi shares her inspiring journey as an entrepreneur, educator, and advocate for cultural inclusivity. Shaped by her bilingual heritage and diverse teaching experiences, Campesi founded the Cross-Cultural Storytelling Project to empower students by celebrating their unique identities and cultural backgrounds. This chapter delves into the transformative potential of storytelling as a tool for fostering inclusion, enhancing student well-being, and building global cultural connections.

Chapter 2: The Power of Storytelling and the Positive Impact They Have on Students of Color

This chapter explores the role of storytelling in shaping the educational experiences of students of color. Through the narratives of three prominent Latinx educators, it demonstrates how personal stories can foster empathy, address social-emotional needs, and inspire academic and cultural growth among diverse student populations. The chapter underscores the profound impact of teachers who share their cultural backgrounds with their students, creating connections that resonate deeply on emotional and academic levels.

Chapter 3: The Impact of Male Mentorship on Latino Immigrant Young Men

This chapter highlights the importance of mentorship in supporting Latino immigrant young men as they navigate academic and cultural challenges. Through case studies and theoretical frameworks, it examines how culturally responsive mentorship programs can foster identity development and academic success. The author's personal perspective as a first-generation Latino student and educator enriches the discussion, offering practical strategies for creating sustainable mentorship initiatives grounded in community engagement and familial support.

Chapter 4: #Latino Mentors/Teachers Needed

Focusing on mentorship as a catalyst for professional growth, this chapter addresses the challenges Latinx educators face in recruitment and retention. Using a servant leadership lens, it advocates for mentorship as a means of promoting diversity in the teaching workforce and supporting future Latinx educators. Personal counter-storytelling reveals the systemic barriers and proposes actionable solutions to enhance leadership and inclusivity in education.

Chapter 5: Centering Communities in Spanish Language Education: Pathways to an Inclusive Approach for Heritage Learners

This chapter calls for a paradigm shift in Spanish language education, advocating for a focus on intercultural competence and citizenship for heritage learners. By centering the "Communities" standard of the World-Readiness Standards for Learning Languages, the authors present inclusive strategies that address the unique needs of heritage speakers. Practical classroom examples and reflective questions guide educators in creating programs that affirm the identities of both heritage and non-heritage learners.

Chapter 6: Community Cultural Wealth and Successful College Navigation within New Latinx Destinations

Drawing on the Community Cultural Wealth framework, this chapter examines the college navigation experiences of Mexican American students in emerging Latinx destination areas. Through their reflections, it identifies the aspirational, familial, linguistic, social, and resistance capitals that empower these students. This research provides actionable insights for educators and counselors to implement culturally sustaining practices tailored to these new contexts.

Chapter 7: Breaking Down Barriers: Nurturing Our Resistance, Reclaiming Our Space, and Calling for Shared Responsibility in Enacting Change

Through the lens of self-care as a form of resistance, this chapter explores the systemic inequities Latinx educators face in predominantly white educational institutions. It emphasizes the need for collective action in dismantling oppressive structures, advocating for shared responsibility in reforming policies and hiring practices. The chapter redefines self-care as an act of community building and advocacy, essential for fostering resilience and empowerment among Latinx educators.

Chapter 8: Leveraging Identity and Positional Power in Service of Latinx Youth

Two Latina leaders share their experiences in advancing equitable educational systems in a large urban district near the U.S.-Mexico border. They explore initiatives such as the Latinx Student Success Plan and efforts to designate the district as a Hispanic-Serving School District. The chapter celebrates the transformative power of representation and leadership while addressing the unique challenges faced by first-generation Latinx students and leaders.

Chapter 9: The Critical Work of the Blue-Collar Scholar

This chapter examines the essential role of Latinx educators in English Language Development classrooms, emphasizing their critical understanding of systemic challenges faced by Emergent Bilinguals. It explores how culturally relevant teaching practices can counteract oppressive policies and amplify students' voices. The chapter highlights the vital contributions of Latinx educators in fostering linguistic and cultural liberation for their communities.

Chapter 10: Understanding Dyslexia in Multilingual Environments

This chapter addresses the complexities of identifying and supporting multilingual students with dyslexia. It offers a comprehensive overview of challenges such as language dominance and cross-linguistic transfer, as well as evidence-based instructional strategies tailored to multilingual contexts. The chapter advocates for culturally responsive teaching practices to bridge the gap between language differences and disorders, ensuring equitable literacy development.

Chapter 11: Integrating Reproductive Justice in Social Work Education

Focusing on reproductive justice, this chapter highlights the unique barriers Hispanic communities face in accessing reproductive healthcare. It proposes integrating this framework into social work education to empower practitioners with culturally competent tools for advocacy and systemic reform. By addressing social, economic, and political conditions, the chapter outlines a holistic approach to advancing reproductive autonomy and equity.

CONCLUSION

As we embark on this journey through the pages of this edited reference book, we are reminded of the profound interconnectedness of education, identity, and cultural representation. Each chapter, meticulously crafted by our esteemed contributors, weaves a tapestry of resilience, innovation, and transformation that underscores the critical importance of empowering diverse voices in education and leadership. Together, these narratives illuminate pathways for fostering equity, celebrating individuality, and cultivating inclusive practices that inspire meaningful change.

This book is more than a collection of insights; it is a call to action for educators, researchers, and policymakers to challenge systemic inequities and reimagine educational spaces as catalysts for social justice. By centering the experiences of Latinx educators, students, and communities, we are reminded of the transformative power of representation and the enduring strength of cultural heritage.

May this work serve as a source of inspiration and a foundation for continued dialogue, ensuring that the stories and experiences within these pages ignite a collective commitment to creating a more just and inclusive future.

Acknowledged Reviewers

Dr. Danielle Frith
Ms. Elizabeth Giron
Dr. Denise Furlong
Dr. Amanda Guarino-Waggoner
Ms. Samantha Shane
Mr. Frank Torres

Chapter 1
Cross-Cultural Storytelling Project:
Curiosity Creates Connection

Melissa A. Campesi
Cross-Cultural Storytelling Project, USA

ABSTRACT

In this chapter you will meet Melissa Campesi, an entrepreneur, creator, author, and educator of Hispanic heritage. Her bilingual upbringing, varied teaching experiences, and appreciation of culture have shaped her unique approach to honoring the identities and interests of students with diverse linguistic and cultural backgrounds. She has found that celebrating individuality in the learning environment gives students a sense of inclusion and empowerment which leads to learning success. As the Founder of the Cross-Cultural Storytelling Project, the author shares the seeds of inspiration for this global project and how it continues to grow cultural connections through the power of storytelling.

INTRODUCTION: ONE WOMAN, MANY HATS

"I would like to be known as an intelligent woman, a courageous woman, a loving woman, a woman who teaches by being." – Maya Angelou

DOI: 10.4018/979-8-3373-1340-5.ch001

Copyright © 2025, IGI Global Scientific Publishing. Copying or distributing in print or electronic forms without written permission of IGI Global Scientific Publishing is prohibited.

Figure 1. Author in a bookstore with balloons

Life Roles

This chapter will take you through the journey of my life as an entrepreneurial woman, creator, author, and educator of Hispanic heritage. After reading this chapter you will have a better understanding of those multiple roles I play and the reason I chose to play them. Yet, all these roles are subordinate to my primary roles as wife to a supportive husband, mother to two charismatic sons, and daughter and granddaughter to my devoted family.

Like many others, family is my source of strength for confronting life's challenges, facing new and unknown adventures, and staying loyal to my roots. The admiration and passion I have for language, culture, and storytelling stem from my family's extraordinary influence. My childhood was filled with the sounds of blended languages, the powerful aroma of my grandmother's homemade sofrito, and the warmth of unconditional love. This cherished upbringing shaped me into who I am today and led me to all the destined roles I chose to play.

As the saying goes, we all wear different hats in this world. Some hats we choose to wear, such as our profession. Other hats we are blessed to wear like becoming a mother. Still others were handed down to us through our heritage. Whatever the source, for many of us life gets hectic when we have a lot of different hats accumulated in our closet. It can be overwhelming at times. I am still learning when the right time is to wear each hat. The trick is not to wear more than one hat at a time; unfortunately, it doesn't always work out that way. Some days the hat is on my head; other days I have multiple hats hanging off my arms and legs! This is all part of living a chaotic life. I find it can be a beautiful thing, as long as I roll and flow with it as it comes.

Nevertheless, some days and weeks can become overwhelming with all the juggling of different roles. This is when I look at myself in the mirror, breathe deeply, and hit "pause". To have pauses in life is to regain your power. Pauses restore energy that may have been depleted while taking care of others or being overly committed to work. When I know it's time to press pause, I look for a tranquil space that does not require wearing a hat. I'll find a cozy bookstore or coffee shop and lounge by a window and just observe. No thinking, no analyzing, just complete brain rest. This brain rest is critical if I want to be my best at orchestrating all my roles. It gives my mind time to heal, refocus, and organize my priorities. Everyone's pause time may look different. Some may need more active pauses like running or working out at the gym. Depending on what your body, mind, and spirit long for at the time, be mindful of your internal alert messages when life becomes overwhelming. When you get that message, pause to recharge.

Though having an assortment of hats can take its toll once in a while, I would not trade my hats for the world. They are an essential part of who I am and what I am meant to do on Earth. These hats represent many passions in my life, big and small. They fulfill me in ways I never imagined. For example, being a children's author stirs a childlike excitement within me. I feel exhilarated to share my love for literacy with enthusiastic children from all parts of the world. During author visits, in person or virtual, I feel I transform into a child myself because their positive vibes are contagious! I believe when children see an adult being passionate about something, they typically mimic that same energetic emotion and become automatically engaged. Just like the positive vibes children give off, passion is also contagious. True passionate leaders have the power to easily inspire and influence others to ignite their own passions. It is all in how they stand in their authenticity and allow others to not only believe them but believe in themselves. You cannot fake your passion. What we are passionate about lingers around us like a vibrant aura. It seldom leaves us.

Figure 2. Speaking in front of students

    Genius is the source of purpose and the seed of destiny in each of us. Despite modern confusions about individual purpose and meaning in life, the genius has destinations and destinies in mind for us. A true calling is aimed at the genius qualities already set within each person. In this old way of seeing, each person has some form of genius, each also has a calling or vocation and a purpose in life. On the outside it is felt as a calling and on the inside it is felt as the awakening of one's own way of seeing and of truly being in the world (Meade, 2016).

    Our passions, talents, gifts, and genius begin to become evident when we are young. As adults, we have to make a conscious effort to go back to those innocent childhood times and reflect on what satisfied our soul and made our heart happy. When those blissful feelings come to the surface and stay afloat, we will then know they are our treasured passions.

ESL Educator

When I decided to become an educator for multilingual learners, I knew my bilingual upbringing and admiration for literacy were a match made in heaven for this role. Working with diverse linguistic populations has molded me into the eclectic and adaptable woman I am today. My multilingual students taught me more about life and education than four years of college ever could. The stories of their home life brought to a foreign country were inspiring. Some faced trauma, others sought refuge, and most were here to start a new chapter of opportunity with their family. Whatever the reason, they were brave, resilient little souls navigating a new world. Through their influence, I became more responsive and compassionate as an educator and a human.

Over the years, I have collected meaningful and unconventional strategies for reaching students and identifying their individual capabilities to enhance their unique assets. Diverse languages and cultures, I have learned, are actually not roadblocks to learning but opportunities for innovation and growth. However, I have also learned that many different bridges must be built to reach all children. We have to be creative in our own practices and explore different pedagogical pathways to find the best fit for each individual child. Thus, one of our tasks as educators should be to know and understand our children in depth. By getting to know the intricate elements of each child's cultural identity and the interests that spark their curiosity, we can better engage with them. This requires a lot of time and effort, but for long-term success it is imperative not to rush.

The first few weeks of school are crucial to understanding our students on a personal level. If we do not learn their interests and how they identify as a person, then how will we know which strategies might benefit their learning style? One way is to choose strategies that support their cultural background:

Culturally responsive information processing techniques grow out of the learning traditions of oral cultures where knowledge is taught and processed through story, song, movement, repetitious chants, rituals, and dialogic talk. They are all forms of elaboration and rely heavily on the brain's memory system (Hammond, 2015).

The bottom line: becoming familiar with your students' family and background will lead to more success and achievement in the classroom.

As educators of multilingual learners, we must possess the virtue of patience. We know from years of research the process of acquiring a new language takes time, exposure, and application. Our mission in knowing this is to pass along these pieces of wisdom to educators who are not trained in multilingual and multicultural education. Personally, the most important role I have played for my multilingual students is as their advocate. Since many mainstream educators are not fully trained to address the needs of this specialized population, I encourage consistent collaboration to model and explain strategies that would benefit our multilingual students. Working together at the right pace from the beginning will increase the chances that our multilingual students will accomplish their language goals.

Many factors go into learning a new language. Second language acquisition is about vocabulary and grammar lessons, but it is also about creating a positive classroom atmosphere that encourages risk-taking. A critical concept in second language acquisition called the "Affective Filter Theory" (coined by American linguist and educational researcher Dr. Stephen D. Krashen) explains how emotional factors can impact acquiring a new language. Krashen & Terrell (1983) stated it best, "There are **affective** prerequisites to acquisition, as every teacher and language student knows. Briefly, the acquirer has to be "open" to the input in order to fully utilize it for acquisition. According to research, factors that contribute to a *low affective filter* include positive orientation to speakers of the language, acquiring in a low anxiety situation, and at least some degree of acquirer self-confidence" (p. 19). This theory implies negative emotions and lack of motivation develops an invisible psychological barrier which can impede language acquisition. Furthermore, dull textbooks, unpleasant classroom surroundings, or an exhausting schedule of study and/or work can also contribute to negative emotional reactions (Yule, 2010). To mentally and emotionally prepare a student for language learning, educators must foster positive emotions by forming a supportive environment, embracing linguistic and cultural identities through classroom activities, and building student self-confidence consistently. Through these responsive approaches, students will obtain a low affective filter resulting in processing language input adequately in the brain.

Another strategy I have used to make students feel supported, comfortable, and safe in their new surroundings is to provide lessons that elicit natural conversations where they are eager to contribute and connect with their classmates and teacher. Some ways educators can accomplish this is by implementing engaging board/card games, role play activities, and project based-learning.

If people focus on acquiring language through interactions with others, the results are much more effective. These language producing opportunities are authentic and provide all students with the chance to interact with peers in the target language. Not only are these students acquiring language, but they are also forming relationships with peers. Teachers with a communicative focus provide opportunities for students to use and understand language at a level appropriate for their language proficiency (Furlong, 2022).

A warm and inviting atmosphere with fun and interesting conversation prompts will set the tone for multilingual students to practice their new language without fear of feeling ashamed if they make mistakes. As educators, we should encourage our students to possess a sense of freedom to communicate their minds and needs without repercussions.

Every newcomer arriving to a new school must be evaluated by professionals for their English language level and academic skills. Most multilingual learners will have learning gaps depending on their prior schooling experience.

Some Newcomers come to us with solid and consistent foundations in education and others do not. Those who do not are considered to be SLIFE (sometimes referred to as SIFE), who are Students with Limited or Interrupted Formal Education. By classification (in some states), SLIFE have missed 2+ years of education in their native country (or the country in which they live while of educational age) or are 2+ years behind in academic levels where they should be according to their age. This can happen for a variety of reasons, all of which have a clear and visible effect on these children. They may have experienced trauma or loss in their lives, during which school may not have been the priority or their struggles absolutely inhibited their attendance (Furlong, 2022).

Our initial response to learning gaps in education tend to be addressed with quick fixes and rushed approaches. It is hard for any child that requires both linguistic and emotional support to board the runaway curriculum train. Unfortunately, many children are left behind to chase down that proverbial train, and they run out of breath. It may be satisfying to achieve short-term goals for data collecting purposes, but not lifelong ones. I think most educators want to educate for the long haul and will jump on the opportunity to do just that.

Furthermore, educators and other professionals that work with children want to see students feel successful not only in class, but in life. In this age of outside influencers such as TikTok and YouTube, educators must be the real-life influencers of our students. Our role is to shape their minds to think critically, interpret new perspectives, and simply be respectful members of society. We cannot rush our children's education because knowledge does not have an expiration date. Everyone goes on learning until their last breath! The majority of our learning comes in the form of new interactions and exploring different environments.

Student Voice

As responsive educators, we must explore the assets and knowledge foundation our students already bring to the classroom. They enter our classrooms (no matter the age, socioeconomic status, race, ethnicity, religion, etc.) with abundant life skills and experiences that shaped who they are at that moment in time.

All children bring a set of talents to the educational enterprise, and these need to be accepted as a basis for further learning. For instance, instead of viewing students for whom English is second language as 'non-English speakers,' why not consider them fluent speakers of another language? We can say the same about cultural and experiential differences, which have often been considered a deprivation rather than a resource that can be affirmed in the school. An alternative approach is to accept student differences as valid and valuable and build on them. In fact, a number of studies have demonstrated that students who are encouraged to retain close ties to their ethnic cultures while adapting to mainstream U.S. culture are not only more academically successful but also more emotionally secure (for a review of these studies, see Portes & Rumbaut, 2006) (Nieto, 2018).

Learning these essential pieces of our students is our homework. Yet, because of outside constraints, we often skip over the part of truly knowing our students. We must take the time to know and understand them. Give them the microphone and let them use their voice.

If I were to sum up my life's mission in one sentence, it would be to inspire and guide children in discovering who they are and help them develop their authentic voice in this world. Whether I do this as an educator, author, or consultant, the objective and outcome remains the same: to have our children be emotionally, socially, and academically competent and confident learners.

Voice is power. Power to express oneself, power to control what people know about oneself, power to have a record of one's feelings and experiences. Our students have lived through experiences that are unique to them and they have stories to be told. As others read their words, their bit of history is being shared. They are empowered by what they choose to share and what they decide to write (and what not to write!). We can learn much from them by just giving them the opportunity to use their Voice (Furlong, 2022).

Growing up, finding and developing my authentic voice took time. I was not confident in many areas of my life, both personally and professionally. Through writing, I learned to fine tune my thoughts, ideas, and perspectives. This therapeutic process helped me extinguish any negative notions and replaced them with clarity. Consequently, I began to unfold the different layers of myself through writing and discovered who I am in depth. My goal is to inspire and encourage students to do the same and build self-confidence by developing their authentic voice through storytelling and writing.

Figure 3. Author's family picture

My Family's Immigrant Story: "Cuando Sali de Cuba"

*"When opportunity presents itself, grab it.
Hold on tight and don't let go." – Celia Cruz*

I grew up in a three-family home in Queens, New York, with my parents, Lisa and Bill, and younger brother, Frank. My maternal grandmother, Marina, who spoke limited English, lived downstairs from us.

My maternal grandparents, along with my mother and an aunt, had left Cuba in 1961 shortly after Castro overthrew the Batista government and installed a communist regime. As a child growing up in Cuba in the 1940s and early 1950s, my grandfather lived a middle-class lifestyle. He had access to everything we think a first world country would have today: clean water, plentiful food, safe housing, and formal education. Sadly, his dream of raising a family there abruptly changed once communism crept in. Heartbroken and distraught at having to leave his country, my grandfather nevertheless felt he had no choice once the government began to overtake properties and businesses.

He and his family first emigrated to Spain where my grandmother's family lived. After only a few months, however, my grandfather set his sights on settling long-term in New York City, a place he had visited a few times as a child. He thought the United States would have more opportunities for his family. Thankfully, a family he had known in Cuba offered to put them up in their home until they were stable enough to be on their own. Thereafter, my grandparents began to slowly earn the lifestyle and upbringing for their children they had once envisioned in Cuba, and eventually they were able to pay it forward by helping other newly arrived Cuban families.

My grandparents' determination to live the American Dream came to fruition through hard work and selfless sacrifice. Because of this, my mother and aunt were able to achieve their own version of the American Dream. One of the main reasons I became an English language educator was to honor my family's immigrant story and pay my good fortune forward the way my grandparents did. My family's story exemplifies the unwavering devotion of so many immigrant families to their adopted country, and the success that can be achieved through hard work and a little encouragement.

Professional Background: A Life Purpose of Student Service

"Education needs to address the world around our learners but also the world within our learners." – Sir Ken Robinson

Figure 4. Students raising their hands

As a child, I remember playing "school" with my brother and cousins in our tiny playroom. As the oldest, I always played the teacher. I loved it! Especially writing on the chalkboard. I felt like I was in my natural element, even though I was only pretending. Imparting new knowledge to my brother and cousins gave me a feeling of confidence and empowerment.

This stemmed from the times I had observed my own mother teach her students. Earlier in her career, my mother served as a Bilingual Special Educator at an elementary school in Queens, and then as the Coordinator of Special Services at an intermediate school in Washington Heights, New York. As both a mother and teacher, she exuded compassion and kindness from the softness of her eyes and smile. My mother made sure all her students felt welcomed and belonged. I remember thinking that her students must consider her their second mother. She did not treat them any differently than she treated my brother and myself.

My mother was a true and fierce advocate for her students, even the students with behavioral challenges. She knew how to calmly soothe them and defuse any situation immediately. She spoke up for her students when needed, especially since the majority of them and their families spoke limited English. It was evident that the parents had full trust in my mother because she made it a priority to solidify the school-home relationship from the very beginning. They knew it was safe to contact her at any time, even during after-school hours. The mutual respect she had with all her students was obvious based on their willingness to engage in her lessons. Her students had full trust in my mother as an educator, and they knew she always had their back.

In hindsight, my mother was my first mentor as an aspiring educator. I wanted to be just like her in the classroom. The classroom atmosphere she created was consistently warm and inviting, and she made learning fun, not intimidating. She encouraged each individual student to reach their next level. Every child worked at their own pace. Student goals were achieved in baby steps, not long sprints. Her approach to teaching was to employ soft skills, as they are imperative for building trust, fostering collaboration, and ultimately, achieving success.

After many years of "shadowing" my mother and her work of "heart", I decided to also become an educator. I felt confident about my decision since I was equipped with the same values and wisdom I had absorbed from her. While in the field, I learned to reflect on the challenges and build upon the achievements. In the beginning, the learning process was not easy. However, I never gave up on developing myself to be my best for my students.

Like my mother, a priority of mine was to make my classroom feel like a safe space for new students. I made sure my students' cultural identities were represented in the classroom. Students had access to books in their language, story characters that accurately represented them, and visual art that displayed a positive sense of familiarity. These seemingly simple things are important ancillary aids to the learning environment, as I had come to know:

> *"In many collectivist cultures, beauty and harmony are important values that extend to the environment. An environment that is crowded or cluttered may obscure the values you have in mind. Think carefully about what visuals are displayed on the walls. They send a nonverbal message about what and who is valued in the classroom. Unconsciously, we pick up clues about affirmation and validation from our surroundings. Remember that our RAS continually scans the*

environment and takes in millions of bits of information and evaluates it almost instantaneously. Just below consciousness, our brain is determining if there is anything in the environment that creates a sense of well-being based on what we recognize from our home and community environment" (Hammond, 2015).

Our classrooms, in reality, are our students' second home. We have to accommodate our learning spaces to reflect who our students are, especially for students of linguistically diverse backgrounds. They rely on their surroundings to feel they belong in that learning community.

Another way I made certain my multilingual students felt welcome and invited in my class was in the way I spoke to them. When communicating to children whose first language is not English, there are simple communication techniques that can support their understanding and sense of belonging. Since our voice is a powerful instrument, it is capable of giving a child a boost of confidence or breaking down their self-esteem. The words we use to address children are important. If a student has limited vocabulary in their English repertoire, we must be sure to slowly use one word or two- and three-word phrases. Repetition helps at times, along with a visual aid or body language (physical prompting). However, even before a multilingual student can process a word, they will hear and interpret the teacher's tone of voice. Loud, fast, and abrupt speech will send a negative message to the child even without knowing the words spoken. Educators of multilingual learners must be aware of their tone, word choice, and rate of speech. Implementing these simple tips will allow your student to feel comfortable learning with you. It certainly made a difference in building my relationship with my own students.

Knowing the different worlds inside our individual students – what motivates them, what sparks their curiosity – is a beautiful blessing. Getting to know students on a personal level is the key to their transformation in school. One of the aspects I loved about being an educator of multilingual students was witnessing their substantial growth and development over the course of the school year. It is fascinating how children learn and flourish at their own speed, in their own time. It truly is magic that unravels before our eyes. Everything positive we implement in our lessons and activities does pay off. We usually do not see the payoff right away, but with patience it will come. There is no feeling like seeing your student with limited English proficiency go from quiet and uncertain at the beginning of the year to a more confident speaker toward the end of the year, no matter what English proficiency level they have reached. If we instill the love of learning in our students early, they will have the power to learn on their own each day for the rest of their lives.

Authentic Approaches to Supporting Hispanic/Latino Students, Parents, and Multiethnic Communities

"If you have a chance to accomplish something that will make things better for people coming behind you, and you don't do that, you are wasting your time on this Earth."
– Roberto Clemente

Figure 5. Picture collage

To manifest real transformational change in education today, I believe we need to focus on collaborating with: (1) the students, (2) the educators, (3) the parents/family, and (4) the community. Bringing these four groups together will generate a colossal tidal wave of educational transformation.

As a starting point, research must be conducted regarding each party's desired values, goals, and outcomes in education. If a school district and community are of diverse ethnic and linguistic backgrounds, the curriculum and standards should reflect the unique communities being served:

"...[G]iven the so-called education reform movement of the past three decades, it has been difficult for schools and teachers to implement a multicultural perspective to any great extent in most public schools. With calls for more accountability and more rigidly standardized curriculum, the situation has worsened in the past decade. And although scholars such as Christine Sleeter have made the important point that high standards are compatible with multicultural education (Sleeter, 2005), the suffocating presence of high-stakes testing and other standardizing policies have made this a difficult sell" (Nieto, 2018).

A society in which education is mostly driven by national standardized learning and testing, limited room is left to honor and validate the cultural identities of our students in the classroom. For each student to feel they have a place in their school, the lessons, activities, and literature must be inclusive.

This brings me to the next step. After acknowledging the problem, how should we approach a solution? My proposal is to hear those involved and give them the stage to amplify their voice for change:

"If we want people to fully show up, to bring their whole selves including their unarmored, whole hearts – so we can innovate, solve problems, and serve people – we have to be vigilant about creating a culture in which people feel safe, seen, heard, and respected" (Brown, 2018).

No one person holds the right answer to designing a sustainable, diverse, and inclusive learning system; however, in collaboration with stakeholders, we all hold possible solutions. The best educational leaders are the ones who understand we must come together as a whole system.

One idea might be for schools to host small and intimate gatherings to personally connect with each group of stakeholders. Holding meetings where the leaders stand at a podium "talking at" the crowd and referring to a slideshow presentation could come across as intimidating and not welcoming new ideas. Sending out email polls to stakeholders to gather data is efficient and time effective. However, real conversations should occur as well if we want a sustainable outcome. Conversations bring a deeper understanding of perspective and reason. In other words, to address problems regarding people we need to alter our mindset and keep it human centered – eye to eye, heart to heart. If we want to strive for an inclusive learning atmosphere for all students and educators, we must solve the problem with a comprehensive approach. All voices must be heard and understood, no matter how long it takes to hear them. These voices speak in many languages and bring the experience of many cultures, ethnicities, races, nationalities, religions, etc. They provide diverse ideas that can make for positive and everlasting change. The ones in charge need to trust that all those involved and affected have sincere intentions.

Monumental challenges like educational transformation will take years. However, if addressed correctly from the beginning, such transformation can create a positive difference for generations to come. It is critical that we listen and reflect the words of those who come to classrooms each day to learn, who teach in those classrooms, who nurture the children, and who support our schools.

"Teachers' roles in the school also need to be redefined, because empowered teachers help to create learner environments in which students are empowered. Also, the role of families needs to be expanded so that the insights and values of the community can be accurately reflected in the school" (Nieto, 2018).

Those in a position to navigate change should be prepared with questions and prompts in order to provoke reflection and responses from the stakeholders. Everything should be recorded and analyzed. This will take time and a lot of data collection, but the most reliable data to collect is straight from the source – and that includes ALL voices involved.

As an educator and author, I support our Hispanic/Latino communities in different ways. Through my author presentations on cultural awareness and identity, I bring to light the significance and value of the background, language, and lifestyle of students using my children's book, *I Am an English Language Learner*, as a mentor text. I also present workshops to seasoned and aspiring educators of multilingual and multicultural students to expand their perspective on their students' identities and how to apply responsive strategies for academic engagement and success. Another fun way I connect with children and the community is during interactive story time at local bookstores and libraries. I love the intimacy of reading a book to children and hearing their real-time reactions. Meeting children and adults from all walks of life at author venues and expos is another wonderful way I engage with the community and learn about lives and aspirations. Just this year, I started a weekly after school program on creative writing at a local middle school. It has been so exciting to see all the different ways children can creatively express themselves and develop their authentic voice. The bilingual students in this program are encouraged to write and share in their native language. Nothing brings me more joy than seeing children's faces illuminated with confidence and pride after creating something unique on their own. I have been blessed to connect with a variety of children and adults so far on this journey. Learning about who they are, how they see the world, and the significant roles they play reminds me that we all carry a bit of personal magic to make our schools, communities, and world an extraordinary place.

Children's Author: Writing to Inspire Curiosity and Creativity in Children

"If there is a book that you want to read, but it hasn't been written yet, then you must write it." -Toni Morrison

Figure 6. Writing

    Writing has been one of the most natural ways I know to express myself, along with songwriting. I have learned that we all have our innate ways to communicate and express our thoughts, ideas, and feelings.
    My father was a significant and positive influence on my interest in writing at a young age. Growing up, I was surrounded by different types of books, stories, poetry, and music. When my father introduced me to Shakespeare and Robert Frost in grammar school, I was instantly captivated by the sounds of the words themselves. The alliteration and intrinsic beauty of the English language with its hidden and intelligent designs overwhelmed me. Where some of my peers saw accident, serendipity, and chance, I saw structure, divinity, and mind.
    Sonically, the words were beautifully strung together like the melody of a transcendental hymn. As a child I remember watching Shakespeare's plays such as *Henry V* and *Hamlet*. This opened up a whole new realm of self-expression for me. The language of poetry ignited a spark of wonder internally, and I was inspired to write my own poems at a young age. I would play and manipulate words to form

poems, fabricate short stories, and compose musical plays on the piano. The poet, the writer, and the composer all see the world like everyone else. The difference is that they are better able to emotionally express those realities in succinct, elegant, and compact ways. Words enabled me to escape reality, at least for a little while, and gave me the ability to craft my own universes, to exchange the existential for the transcendental. I became acquainted with Whitman, Emerson, and Thoreau. This was transforming. It offered me a metamorphosis, like a butterfly emerging from its chrysalis. I was changed, no doubt, yet nothing (at least nothing visible) was added. This opened up my spirit, my soul, and my mind to the art of not only writing but writing with emotional depth.

I did not accept, or would I ever accept, anything with nonsensical constraints or rules when it came to creative writing. Such hindrances simply had no place in my art. I wrote exactly what I felt and loved the satisfaction of finding the perfect words to put on paper. This gave me a sense of self-validation and freedom to be who I am and perceive the world in my own unique way without fear of judgment. I am still learning that I can magically make any idea come to life using only the combined powers of mind, pen, and paper! As an adult writer, I still remind myself every day to carve out this playful time and escape to a place of wonder.

Writing was, and still is, an outlet for me to reflect on my authentic experiences and unique choices. What type of artist would I be if I lived the same routine repeatedly? The most impactful storytellers are the ones who want exposure to different worlds then live to tell about them. As my father often mentioned to me, the way in which I navigate through life is symbolized best by the words of Robert Frost's poem, "The Road Not Taken." My father believed this poem is a metaphor for my choice of unconventional routes and distinctive outlooks on everyday occurrences. I gravitate toward these paths because they're unique and provide fulfilling experiences rather than striving for traditional success. As Frost said so eloquently, "I shall be telling this with a sigh - Somewhere ages and ages hence; Two roads diverged in a wood, and - I took the one less traveled by, And that has made all the difference" (Frost, 2017). Being drawn to these "roads not taken" has gifted me more opportunities for personal growth, creativity for my work, and interpreting the world through multiple perspectives. This curious mindset I've had since childhood motivates and excites me to explore life's unknown possibilities with no regrets. I subconsciously gather and store these amusing experiences to one day spill on the empty spaces of my journal.

Figure 7. Author with books

I Am an English-Language Learner, 2019

First Children's Book

As a child and adolescent who was passionate about writing, I never thought about becoming a published author. It seemed like an unattainable dream. I always imagined authors as prestigious scholars who were automatically chosen to write stories for the world to read. But then came two nudges from the universe that gave me the vision to write my first book. The first nudge I felt in the fall of 2015 when I was an ESL teacher in Edison, New Jersey. At the beginning of the year I intentionally chose books that would reflect my students' cultural backgrounds and identities. I believed that reading books representing my multilingual students helped establish a trusting foundation by allowing them to feel seen, welcomed, and understood. I am not the only one with this belief:

> *Representing all cultures is crucial for the wellbeing of all students. Through the representation of their culture in literature (and within the school community) students can see themselves in other situations and other places and this can plant the seeds for where they see themselves in the world and in their future. This can also help foster a sense of belonging within the group and pride in one's own culture"* (Furlong, 2022) *(emphasis added.)*

The challenge I faced was finding *one* book that represented *many* students from different ethnicities and backgrounds. In the back of my mind, I knew I must write a book about children from different cultural backgrounds coming to the United States. I envisioned one book with a page dedicated to each immigrant child and their individual culture.

I loved hearing the students speak about their home countries, traditions, and significant holidays. We would honor different cultural festivals, such as Diwali or Lunar New Year, by celebrating them with enriching activities in the classroom and school. Parents and families were invited to participate and were eager to be involved because they had the chance to teach us in more detail about their cultural rituals and traditions. I remember thinking how valuable their stories were. They became catalysts for cultural conversations—as important as any autobiography on the shelves of prestigious libraries or bookstores. Authentic stories and personal narratives do not have a hierarchy. Our society as a whole needs to grasp that, no matter which corner of the world an individual comes from, they have the potential to provide others with inspiration and new knowledge drawn from their story's compelling universal themes. In this way we learn from one another. We are interchangeably each other's teacher and student.

I kept the concept of the book secretly stored in the back of my mind. Two years later, I began to teach adult multilingual learners for the same district in the evening. I grew very close to these students because I felt my grandparents' immigrant story present in my heart when I taught them. I taught my adult multilingual students in the same compassionate manner as I did my Spanish grandmother. With this specific group of multilingual students, teaching English needed to include an extra dose of patience and empathy because acquiring a new language after adolescence becomes more difficult. "After the critical period for language acquisition has passed, around the time of puberty, it becomes very difficult to acquire another language fully" (Yule, 2010). These students demonstrated the same determination and resilience as my grandparents while working full time jobs and tending to their families. I respected their bravery and dedication to learning English and the American way of life. Unlike children who acquire another language more easily, adults are more conscientious and take fewer risks because they are afraid to use an incorrect word or mispronounce. Children, on the other hand, are less self-conscious and more likely to take risks. The adult multilingual students' English levels ranged across the board. Some students were stronger in speaking and writing skills, while other students had some mastery of listening and reading skills. Although the classes had a variety of English levels, we all supported one another to learn something new in each class.

My favorite times were when my students responded to personal prompts to practice speaking. This speaking warm-up we called "Conversation Café," and it involved using universal prompts and conversation starters to elicit natural, friendly dialogue. These interactive, low stress activities (which were also differentiated and scaffolded), allowed me to know my students on a personal and human level. I was able to get a stronger understanding of their culture, their family, their way of life at home, and the rich lived experiences they had in their country. The students were appreciative that others were interested in their stories. Hearing all their stories was powerful, and it empowered them. We focused much less on grammar correction than content and meaning. Each story was very different, yet all were inspiring. These immigrant stories were not only about struggles but about pride; pride in who they were and where they had come from. They were enthusiastic about sharing because they were the experts about themselves and their culture. My observation as the ESL teacher was that the students were eager to speak about where they came from regardless of their English proficiency level.

Listening to my adult multilingual students speak about their cultures gave me my second nudge, and in 2017 I finally began putting together a children's book comprised of authentic and unique stories to share with the world. My hope in publishing that book, *I am an English Language Learner, was* to promote cultural awareness, celebrate diverse perspectives, and develop empathy. I slowly collected eight beautiful stories from family, friends, and some of my adult multilingual students. I am grateful that they entrusted me to publish their stories with dignity. I pieced together the structure of the book; designing the storytelling, adding vibrant illustrations, and providing a map and a glossary of new terms to guide educators in the classroom when reading aloud.

There was no urgency to publish until a life-changing event pushed me to publish the book quickly. The heartbreaking news of my mother's cancer diagnosis in 2018 left me and my family shaken up and feeling helpless. As time progressed, we learned her cancer was terminal. I focused on transforming my overwhelming feeling of helplessness to hopefulness. That sense of hope never left me. I made sure my mother sensed that promise of never giving up whenever we were together, for hope is contagious. With this hope ingrained in my bones, I knew I had to publish this book with my mother's immigrant story from Cuba as soon as I could. I was determined to see her physically hold this book, which would include her true life story, in her hands. Between the horrors of chemo treatments, blood infusions and transfusions, and unexpected hospital stays, I made publishing my book a priority to honor my mother's story and life while she was still alive.

Figure 8. Author's mother with book

In the fall of 2019, *I Am an English Language Learner* was published. The experience of having my mother hold the book in her hand and read aloud her own words was one of the most emotionally fulfilling moments of my life. I knew that one day when she was gone her story would live on. At the time, this was the only thing that mattered. My mother passed away in the winter of 2021. She was with us much longer than the doctors expected. I still believe it was her daily dose of medicinal hope that lengthened our time together. As intended, her spirit now stays alive through her immigrant story. My mother's story is the one I read aloud as a mentor text during classroom visits and workshops. In this way, my mother's legacy continues to breathe through my children's book and my mission to encourage students to tell their stories. Her words will be an inspiration to me and my family, as well as others around the world, for generations to come. Experiencing this tragedy has humbly taught me that the power of words is immortal. We as humans possess divine capabilities to become alchemists with our art, transforming grief into inspiration.

Figure 9. CCSP mentor text sample

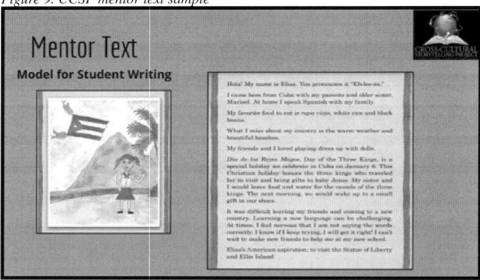

Not only does my mother's immigrant story inspire, but so do all of the eight immigrant voices in my children's book. I often wonder how many children out in the world were able to connect to at least one part of a story in the book. This becomes transparent during author visits at schools when I read aloud each story and discuss how important language and culture are to our daily lives. These multicultural stories support the concept of "Mirrors, Windows, and Sliding Glass Doors" introduced by Dr. Rudine Sims Bishop, which emphasizes the importance of diversity in literature. It suggests that books can serve as *mirrors* (reflecting readers' own experiences) *windows* (views into others' lives), and *sliding glass doors* (exposure to different worlds). This framework encourages young readers to develop empathy and broaden their world view through diverse books (McNair & Edwards, 2021).

When students hear parts of their culture highlighted in a story, they light up and raise their hand to express how their family does the same thing or something similar. Hearing elements of their culture in a printed book makes students feel validated. They also learn that this world holds space for other cultures to live life a little differently, and that coexisting in this way is okay. As the saying goes, there is strength in diversity. Schools need to embrace and expose children to the fact that other cultures will not only be tolerated but lovingly accepted.

Almost immediately after I published my book, Covid-19 sprung up across the world leaving me to do author visits virtually. Despite all the hardships caused by isolation, as a new author this brave new virtual world turned out to be a blessing in disguise. It gave me the opportunity to connect with global educators and students from California, Ohio, Colorado, New York, Rhode Island, Canada, India, and Honduras. I was able to share my message and mission of the book on a much larger scale. We even took things a step further with some of our online classes. I collaborated with some like-minded global educators via Zoom and crafted lessons following the book's storytelling structure in combination with their content standards. In partnership, I was able to support these educators in organizing and structuring their students' cultural stories.

Another positive part of this unique experience was that many of the children's families were home to help teach their children about their cultures and the reasoning behind religious rituals and traditions. One school in Ohio published their own book of inspiring student cultural stories. These students felt empowered as "authors." We also connected classes virtually to read and share their stories in online breakout rooms. At times, technological difficulties would get in the way or delay lessons. However, overall it was exciting to reach and teach students in ways that helped them deeply understand their culture.

Figure 10. Remote teaching

Participating in this cross-cultural learning experience became the launching pad for The Cross-Cultural Storytelling Project. This project I designed as an interactive online platform where students can write and publish their cultural stories. My goal for this inclusive online community was for students to share who they are and where they come from while simultaneously reading about other students' cultures across the world. I encourage positive comments and/or respectful questions under each story. I have also invited educators I've collaborated with globally to publish blogs on my site supporting multicultural education and sharing best practices. Examples of some of the blog titles educators wrote about are, "How Can You Use a Culturally and Linguistically Responsive Approach in your School?", "Translanguaging Like an Artist", and "Four Ways to Celebrate Hispanic Heritage Month." This philosophy of sharing cultural stories spotlights the importance of learning about different perspectives, values, and life experiences. My hope is that global educators will use The Cross-Cultural Storytelling Project as another resource to meet the multicultural goals in their classroom.

Figure 11. Picture collage

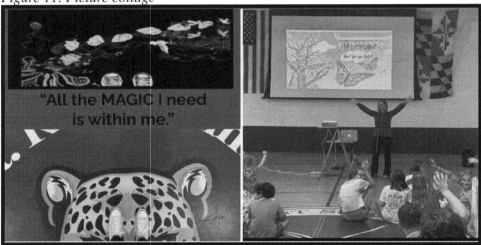

Imagine Song, 2022

Second Children's Book

Just as culture and storytelling are important to me, so is imagination and creativity. As an avid daydreamer (then and now), I felt a calling to write about its advantages from the perspective of a young girl (me). My second children's book, *Imagine Song*, was a tribute to my love of music, songwriting, creativity, and imagination. It is about a young girl named Melody who was formally trained in piano but unexpectedly discovers her natural talent for songwriting. This fictional story is based on true events in my life. As a child, one of my favorite pastimes when I found myself alone was playing the piano my Cuban grandfather purchased for his daughters (my mother and aunt). I would play the piano freely with no structure. This allowed me to daydream and craft imaginary stories in my head, like plays or musicals. This "alone" time proved critical to my creativity. As a writer, I feel that connecting to one's creativity is a vital part of a child's development. Consequently, I decided to condense this message into *Imagine Song*, a bite-sized fictional story wherein I used components of my childhood to unravel creative themes.

The story of *Imagine Song* follows the protagonist, Melody, on her creative journey as she gains the courage to share her songwriting gift with the world. The story aims to inspire children to explore their creative potential and embrace their talents. "If each person has natural gifts and innate talents, then the true nature of education must involve the awakening, inviting, and blessing of the inner genius and unique life spirit of each young person" (Meade, 2016). The book is a soft whisper to pursue your passions and be proud of your unique abilities. I participate in author visits at schools to spread the book's positive message about imagination and creativity. Students connect with the book by sharing their special gifts and talents and how they can use them to impact our world now and in the future. This is another reminder for students to believe in themselves and never lose hold of the things about which they are passionate.

Figure 12. Student cultural stories & self portraits

Cross-Cultural Storytelling Project:
Curiosity Creates Connection

"We are all storytellers. We all live in a network of stories. There isn't a stronger connection between people than storytelling." -Jimmy Neil Smith

As previously mentioned, The Cross-Cultural Storytelling Project was inspired by my first children's book, *I Am an English Language Learner*. The Project is an online platform for global students and educators to learn more about one another. Students are encouraged to share their cultural stories and experiences. Educators, in turn, share these culturally responsive teaching resources and ideas with their own students. It's a healthy and exciting mutualistic relationship that enhances the learning experience:

> *Students have many reasons for creating stories in their personal lives, which are generally tied to identity, trying to make sense of the world, and creating a sense of belonging. When we embrace storytelling in academic settings, we acknowledge the desire for students to consume and create stories and provide the professional support students need to develop a healthy relationship to the tools and processes they're already exploring beyond the classroom (Hernandez, 2024).*

Students participate in the Cross-Cultural Storytelling Project by sharing their unique stories with themes such as lifestyles, experiences, and passions. The project fosters an environment where students can develop a deeper understanding of global diversity. Further, the Project addresses the United Nation's 2030 Sustainable Development (SDG) Goal 4.7 which focuses on ensuring all learners acquire the knowledge and skills needed to promote sustainable development and global citizenship.

Since my mission has been to collect cultural stories from as many parts of the world as I can, my *I Am an English-Language Learner* book proved too limiting. Instead of writing and publishing more books, I decided to create one space that could accommodate multiple diverse narratives on an ongoing basis with no limit. The best part of pulling the pieces together for the Cross-Cultural Storytelling Project was receiving support from all around the globe. Implementing project-based learning techniques, such as those shared in the Cross-Cultural Storytelling Project, is a productive way to modernize and improve student skills in the 21st century.

> *"Storytelling projects are often treated as a reward for students once their "real work" has been completed. Somehow we've developed a mindset that project-based learning experiences like nonfiction storytelling are a lower form of learning than traditional assignments, perhaps because they can be fun and rewarding, rather than tedious or painful. But rigor and hard work can be synonymous with passion and purpose—we can and should enjoy working hard to achieve goals that are meaningful and for causes we care about. This is really the most important lesson we need to teach our students. For nearly a quarter century, I've witnessed the power of storytelling projects to elevate learning and invigorate students' sense of curiosity and provide meaning and purpose for school" (Hernandez, 2024).*

Figure 13. CCSP mission, vision & goals

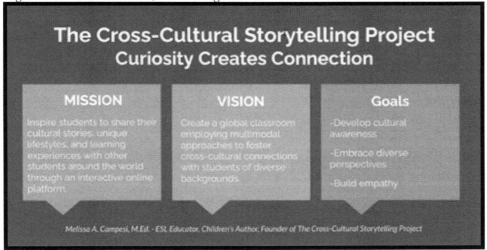

As educators, if we think beyond traditional approaches to learning, we'll uncover numerous methods which intersect multicultural education with literacy and content standards. We should attempt to readjust our reliance on rote information consumption to connect with others globally who have expertise in a particular subject area or content matter.

Imagine joining forces with students or educators from across different parts of the world to work as a team for educational purposes on global research topics, environmental solutions, or interdisciplinary projects? A system like this broadens and heightens our learning spectrum to attain exclusive and diverse resources. This new-age, progressive, and forward-thinking mindset thrives on building cross-cultural relationships with others around the world to enhance learning outcomes for long-term goals. Interacting with others online and recognizing their diverse backgrounds can give us more opportunities to gain new knowledge in an ever-changing world.

Envisioning the Future of Student Cultural Storytelling

"Curiosity is essential for progress. Only when we look to worlds beyond our own can we really know if there's room for improvement." – Simon Sinek

Figure 14. Cross-cultural storytelling project

The concluding paragraph of my children's book, *I Am an English-Language Learner,* is,

> *"The best education comes from learning about one another. Be curious about the people you meet. I guarantee you will discover something fascinating from a new friend. All you have to do is start a conversation with a sweet hello and warm smile."*

This statement not only encapsulates my philosophy about education but about life. Ultimately, education is about guiding, supporting, and teaching children various ways to navigate life's journey. Learning not only happens in our classrooms, but around us every day through human interaction on the streets, at social gatherings, and in any new environment. Our greatest teachers are one another. Engaging in deep and meaningful dialogue, especially with people from backgrounds different than our own, expands our minds intellectually and spiritually. People are walking and talking encyclopedias of experiential knowledge and real-life inspiration. Once we burn the boundaries of judgement and bias, we can walk through the ashes into a beautiful world of understanding and respect. Only then will we reach across to one another and open a kindhearted conversation. Let's embrace each other with genuine sincerity and care. Perhaps we will even become real muses in one another's lives.

Not only is the Cross-Cultural Storytelling Project an online platform to interact with each other's stories and share culturally responsive resources, it is a visible model to reimagine education. The Project symbolizes a utopian world so many of us would like to make a reality. My wish is to see children express the love and pride of their identity and interests for others to read and learn about. This will bring a better understanding to humankind. Much of our hate and exclusion stems from not having the curiosity to see things from different points of view. That doesn't mean we must agree with everything a culture does, but at least we should respectfully comprehend that it exists in someone else's life.

Our history of international and intercultural conflicts is in desperate need of resolve, not repetition. This ominous cycle of indifference and division stops with us. Next to parents, educators are the ones who hold the key to this change. Let my voice encourage you to be the change, act the change, and never give up on the change. Every day our children look to us as positive influencers to shape them into their best selves. This happens over time by addressing everyday situations with emotional intelligence, empathy, and respect. We are models for our students; let us be the kind and caring humans we want them to be.

As discussed earlier in this chapter, diversity and inclusion books are an effective way to introduce these soft skills through storytelling. Since stories were the dominant way our ancestors communicated and exchanged knowledge, we tend to grasp lessons easier through stories. Our brains are hardwired to retain long-term information through storytelling. A powerful and impactful story is hard to forget, especially when you can personally connect with it. Words hold this power. They are capable of making us think in ways we never thought before.

"Protecting our democracy begins with a respect for the power of words. And where better to develop that respect than in a good book? If the thinking one does while reading that book disrupts complacency, encourages compassion for others around us, both near and far, and a willingness to at least hear their stories or arguments, then we will be closer to creating the participants in our society that our democracy not only deserves but demands (Beers & Probst, 2017).

Since launching the Cross-Cultural Storytelling Project a few years ago, I've come to believe our authentic stories could be the main solution to some of our societal problems. Hence, the Project's slogan, "Curiosity creates connection."

Let's imagine for a moment the type of world we want our children to flourish in. What do you see in your mind's eye? If you are reading this book, I am almost certain your vision includes no discrimination, violence, neglect, abuse, conflict, self-esteem issues, or anything negative that could hinder a child's potential growth. I am guessing the scene you have painted is a colorful and inviting page, such as one in a children's book, with images of inspirational symbols and good-hearted narratives. One where children humbly love themselves and treat others, the earth, and the earth's creatures with dignity and kindness. Let this be our collective dream and make it happen. We all need to play a part. What hat will you wear? Which role will you play in this dream? My hope is that you will add to your hat collection and make a difference for yourself, our children, and the future generations to come. Be sure to make your imprint in this world; we need you for positive, practical, and sustainable change. But first, let's hear your story…

REFERENCES

Beers, K., & Probst, R. (2017). Disrupting thinking. Scholastic. https://scholastic.com/beersandprobst

Brown, B. (2018). Dare to lead. Penguin Random House LLC. https://www.BreneBrown.com

Campesi, M. (2019). I am an english-language learner: The real and unique stories of immigrant children in america. LuLu Publishing. https://www.melissacampesi.com

Campesi, M. (2022). Imagine Song: A story about the kindred connection between a child, an instrument, and an imagination. ReadersMagnet. https://www.melissacampesi.com

Frost, R. (2017). Selected poems of Robert Frost. Fall Rivers Press. https://www.sterlingpublishing.com

Furlong, D. (2022). Voices of newcomers: Experiences of multilingual learners. EduMatch Publishing. https://www.edumatch.org

Hammond, Z. (2015). Culturally responsive teaching & the brain. Corwin a Sage Company. https://www.corwin.com

Hernandez, M. (2024). Storytelling with purpose. ISTE. https://iste.org

Krashen, S. D., & Terrell, T. D. (1983). *The natural approach (Language acquisition in the classroom).* Alemany Press. https://www.sdkrashen.com

McNair, J. C., & Edwards, P. A. (2021). The Lasting Legacy of Rudine Sims Bishop: Mirrors, Windows, Sliding Glass Doors, and More. *Literacy Research: Theory, Method, and Practice*, 70(1), 202–212. DOI: 10.1177/23813377211028256

Meade, M. (2016). The genius myth. GreenFire Press. https://www.mosaicvoices.org

Nieto, S. (2018). Language, culture, and teaching. Routledge. https://www.routledge.com/education

Sleeter, C. E. (1995). An analysis of the critiques of multicultural education. In J.A. Banks & C. A. M. Banks (Eds.), Handbook of research on multicultural education Macmillan. https://www.christinesleeter.org

Sleeter, C. E. (2005). Un-standardizing curriculum: Multicultural teaching in standards-based classroom. Teachers College Press. https://www.christinesleeter.org

Yule, G. (2010). *The study of language* (4th ed.). Cambridge University Press., https://www.cambridge.org

Chapter 2
The Power of Storytelling and the Positive Impact They Have on Students of Color

Lee Perez
Omaha Benson High School, USA

Autumn Rivera
https://orcid.org/0009-0002-5009-9486
Glenwood Springs Middle School, USA

Ramon Benavides
https://orcid.org/0009-0004-8446-1943
Del Valle High School, USA

ABSTRACT

Storytelling through the perspective of teachers of color can have a positive impact on students of color. With immigrant, migrant, and refugee populations increasing in classrooms across the United States of America, storytelling is a powerful vessel to assist students with their social and emotional needs during instruction and learning. Moreover, storytelling can teach culturally diverse populations empathy through the powerful lens of their teachers. This is essentially more powerful if their teachers look like the diverse students that they serve daily. This chapter aims to tell the stories of three prominent Latinx teachers and how they have used their respective stories to inspire and empower their students of color to be the best versions of themselves culturally, emotionally, linguistically, and academically.

DOI: 10.4018/979-8-3373-1340-5.ch002

Copyright © 2025, IGI Global Scientific Publishing. Copying or distributing in print or electronic forms without written permission of IGI Global is prohibited.

INTRODUCTION:

How Storytelling is a Powerful Resource to use with Students of Color:

There is no doubt that storytelling can be used as a prominent resource in all classrooms regardless of curriculum. This is because stories have the power to inspire, unite, and teach about different cultural and historical viewpoints, thus creating a positive classroom environment (Boris, 2023). Moreover, when those stories are told by teachers of color to students of color, the results are much more beneficial. Studies confirm that when students of color have teachers of color more educational opportunities are presented when they learn from a teacher from the same ethnic and racial group (Blazar, 2021). Additionally, developing awareness and appreciation for all student's cultures can create and breed an environment optimal for higher academic achievements (Salva & Matis, 2017). Each section of this chapter will outline how storytelling by three teachers of color has had a profound impact on students of color, both inside and outside their respective classrooms.

Section One: Lee Perez's Story

Educational Background:

My name is Lee Perez, and I teach English as a Second Language (ESL) in Omaha, Nebraska. I have been a teacher for 18 years in a very diverse urban public-school setting. I have taught in both a Dual Language program and in sheltered ESL programs in Omaha. Professionally, I have received several recognitions for my work as an ESL teacher. In 2022, I was named the Nebraska Teacher of the Year (TOY). I was the first male, person of color, and ESL teacher to receive this recognition in Nebraska's history.

In 2023, I received the prestigious national Horace Mann Teaching Excellence award. As a Horace Mann Awardee, I was featured in a mini-documentary and was recognized in Washington D.C. as one of the top five best educators in the country. Like TOY, I was the first teacher in Nebraska history to be recognized for this honor. Predictably, this inspired me to bring more awareness to Nebraska's and the nation's growing English Language Learner (ELL) populations.

Over my tenure, I discovered that content-area classroom teachers struggle with the rapidly growing ELL populations in their classrooms. However, this is not the fault of classroom teachers, rather it is a lack of training and preparation by teacher preparation programs nationwide. Teacher preparation programs only tend to focus more on content-area pedagogy, rather than language development for ELLs

(Rubinstein-Avila & Lee, 2014). Therefore, through my advocacy, speeches, and professional development workshops I used my state and national platform to inform education majors on the fundamentals of ESL training and how to apply effective research-based ESL strategies for ELLs in all mainstream classrooms. Furthermore, I told my father's story of how he tragically suffered from language loss and the traumatic effects that had on his linguistic and cultural upbringing as a child.

My Father's Story:

My father, Martin "Marty" Perez suffered from language loss during his upbringing in San Marcos, Texas. Language loss occurs when a person's native language (L1) is lost due to minimal support of that native language in a particular environment (Goldstein, 2022). Like many families seeking better opportunities, my father and his family immigrated to the United States of America from Mexico.

When they arrived, they settled in San Marcos, Texas and they came here working as migrant farm workers. They worked in the fields from sunup to sundown and picked beets, potatoes, and even cotton. Eventually, they left San Marcos, Texas, and migrated North and settled in Wellington, Kansas continuing to do migrant fieldwork. Eventually, they went North to North Platte, Nebraska, where my father would eventually settle and call home. My father's first language was Spanish and he and his siblings spoke it regularly. Unfortunately, my father attended school in the 1950s and he experienced racism and discrimination no matter what state he lived in.

During this period in American history, the linguistic viewpoint was trending toward English-only initiatives. This was extremely harmful to Latino populations as favoring English as an official language created racist attitudes and anti-immigration viewpoints (Crawford & Krashen, 2015). One evening, my father confided in me that when he attended school all the students would speak Spanish to each other. However, once the teacher entered the classroom all students were required to only speak English. He went on to explain that if any students were caught speaking Spanish, they would be disciplined.

I asked my father what he meant by "disciplined?" He clarified by describing that the teacher would stand him in front of the room and hit his hands and knuckles until they became bloody. This type of corporal punishment happened every time a student was caught speaking Spanish by the teacher according to my father. These experiences left my father traumatized and this is how language loss occurred with his native language of Spanish. Hence, English became his dominant native language due to these racist and discriminatory educational practices in Texas in the 1950s.

Tragically, because of this painful trauma that my father endured, he and many of my family turned to substance abuse to cope with these horrible experiences. Alcohol abuse ran through my father's side of the family and he was an alcoholic for over two decades. Research confirms that alcoholism can affect families genetically and genes are responsible for over half the risk of those individuals developing alcoholism (Edenburg & Foroud, 2013).

Unfortunately, I did develop alcoholism in my younger years since it occurred on my father's side of the family. Little did I realize that there was a direct correlation between my father's trauma due to language loss and his alcoholism. I never fully comprehended this until my father told me these painful experiences that led to his alcoholism. Moreover, it also explains why I developed the tendency to become an alcoholic myself. I do not blame my father for turning to substance abuse for dealing with these terrible experiences. He, like so many who have suffered from language loss turned to substance abuse to deal with their emotions.

How I use this Story to Empower my Students and Others:

One might be wondering as they read this section of this book, does he tell this story to his students? Did he present this tragic story when he spoke as the 2022 Nebraska Teacher of the Year? Did he mention this in his documentary as a Horace Mann Awardee? The answer to these complex questions is, yes, and I use this story to empower, inspire, and give hope to all who hear it in their lives. I can often relate to the difficulties that some of my students face because of the challenges I have overcome in my own life.

For example, when I see students whom I know are dealing with alcohol or substance abuse issues, I tell them I understand what they are trying to deal with because I have been there. Again, I am a longtime recovering alcoholic; my problems started when I was their age. In my experience, the key to making a difference in the lives of young people is embracing a student-first philosophy. I embrace that ideology and build trust with my students by being transparent with them about my journey and creating lessons that are relevant to their lives. I do not shy away from my father or my story of alcoholism and substance abuse. In fact, many of my students have confided in me that their families faced similar issues when immigrating to the United States.

For example, a student of mine from Honduras years ago explained to me that my father's immigration story was like hers. She told me that her family made the perilous journey from Honduras to the United States by foot, train, and even the assistance of coyotes in Mexico. Coyotes are organizations that assist immigrants and migrants by smuggling them into the United States (Ortmeyer & Quinn, 2012). She arrived in Mexico and she told me that in 2017, things were not much different than the 1950s. She explained that Americans would hurl racist insults at her, tell her family to go back to where they came from, and only speak English and not Spanish. Consequently, her family turned to alcoholism to deal with these traumatic events they were experiencing. I remember telling her that I understood where she was coming from and that I could empathize with her family's trauma. I recall telling her in detail what had happened to my father's side of the family when he was growing up and how language loss occurred with him and his siblings. Luckily, this student of mine did not suffer from language loss. In fact, she was enrolled in a Dual Language Program that celebrated bilingualism. I asked her if telling my father's story helped to empower her to keep her bilingual and cultural identity and to do well academically in school. I remember she very confidently told me yes; my story did uplift her. Furthermore, she pushed me to continue to tell this story as it can resonate with many more individuals than just her.

Thus, I continued to tell my father's story to give students hope, inspiration, and empowerment. My objective was to build strong relationships with my students through that powerful lens of storytelling. When I began my journey as a teacher, I made the mistake of focusing on the curriculum first and then trying to build positive rapport with my students second. It was around my fifth year of teaching that I realized I had to start with making personal connections before moving onto the curriculum. Storytelling is a powerful way that I build positive relationships with my students and it is something that I continue to this day. Hence, good storytelling in the classroom creates a sense of connection and trust and allows the listener to enter one's story, making them more willing to engage and learn (Boris, 2023).

Over the course of my tenure, many of my students have explained to me that my father's story gave them hope in my classroom. Another former student explained to me that my father's story helped them to realize the importance of not losing their first language and cultural identity. They went on to explain that they wanted to use their bilingualism to advance their educational opportunities in their professional career. Statistically, those who are bilingual, as opposed to monolingual are more likely to offer future employers more potential resources in a competitive United States labor market (Callahan & Gándara, 2014).

Moreover, this student confined in me that my story helped to inspire them to not take a free public education for granted. My father's side of the family was not very educated. They either did not go to school, dropped out, or had only a high school level education. Notably, this was due to language loss and the trauma they endured during their time in San Marcos, Texas. However, this student hearing this story said that it gave her a different perspective on the importance of school. As a result, she was more engaged in class and took her academics very seriously. She appreciated me telling this story and it built a bridge of hope for her she never knew that was there. Eventually, this student went on to graduate high-school and to this day, we still keep in touch. She recently graduated with a bachelor's degree from the University of Nebraska at Omaha (UNO) in Omaha, Nebraska. Why is this milestone so important for her? Because she was the first person to graduate from college in her family, breaking generational curses.

When I was named the 2022 Nebraska Teacher of the Year, my father's story and mine were central to my message to new teachers entering the field. During my year of service, I gave over one hundred speeches, that included keynotes, presentations, professional developments, and workshops. In each instance, I told my father's story and mine hoping to teach future educators the power of storytelling in the classroom. I recall one time after I gave a keynote speech to education majors at the University of Nebraska at Kearney (UNK) in Kearney, Nebraska. Afterwards, a student approached me and told me that my family's story was meaningful to her. She went on to inform me that she was a refugee from Cuba and when she and her family arrived in Nebraska, they were met with harsh attitudes towards their language and culture. She told me that some of her teachers, like my father, would not allow her to speak Spanish in the classroom. She went on to describe in painful detail that she did not feel accepted, seen, and even safe because of this. As she told me this, I could see tears coming out of her eyes. I remember comforting her and telling her that it was my goal to tell my father's story as it could impact so many, who could tragically empathize with it. To this day, it still is my goal to tell this story and the power it can have.

Why Teachers should tell Stories in their Classrooms:

Every year all teachers across the United States go back to their classrooms and welcome their students back after summer. Naturally, they begin with icebreaker activities, rules, procedures, and the day-to-day procedural things the first week of school requires. However, I challenge teachers who are reading me, Ramon, and Autumn's story to use storytelling in their classrooms to create a sense of community and inclusiveness. When teachers share stories, particularly stories that their students can empathize with, their students are more willing to be engaged in lessons, attend school, and even graduate from high school.

All teachers need to use storytelling, but also show why storytelling can teach our students to learn from their failures. Statistically, chronic absenteeism is a big problem in the United States currently. Post-COVID-19 pandemic, more students are missing school and falling behind in their education. I have witnessed this in my career and I would often ask myself, "How can I get my students motivated to come to school?" I found the answer in telling my father's story, but also telling my own story of failure. Over my 18-year career, I have told my story to thousands of my students. I serve a very diverse immigrant, migrant, and refugee population, so my story was relatable to almost all of them. So many of them found hope, inspiration, motivation, and empowerment in my father's story and mine. By telling these stories I noticed that two things happened, academic achievement increased and so did my attendance rates.

Academically, my students, whose first language was not English started to thrive. Why? Because in me, they say a successful person of color, whose family overcame many terrible obstacles. Their willingness to learn and be engaged was thriving in my classroom. Thus, all teachers who are reading this chapter, tell your stories to your students and be fully transparent about it. Teach your students that obstacles and even failure can be overcome in their lives. Moreover, educate them what failure looks like and more importantly describe to them on how to overcome failure and learn from it. After all, all of us will fail in life, so we must be intentional in how we teach our students to recover from failure to ultimately be successful. Once I started using storytelling in my classroom, student's grades and their test scores went up and they took a direct interest in their learning.

I also started to see an increase in my attendance due to telling and using stories in my classroom. Suddenly, students who were having chronic absenteeism issues were coming to school and my classes. Some of my students confided in me that telling my family's story gave them the push they needed to come to school. They thought that they could never recover from failure or even their own trauma. Hearing how my family overcame so much, proved that they too could overcome any obstacles in their lives. After all, I was in jail for a few days due to alcohol-level offenses, you do not get any more rock bottom than that. So, educators reading this section of this chapter, use stories to help shape the foundations in your classroom. Not only will storytelling help you improve grades, test scores, engagement, and attendance rates, but it will help you build strong personal relationships with your students. Finally, it will make you look humble and it will display a human side to you that your students need to see. All of us have a story, tell them and use them to uplift students who are struggling and need to hear and learn from them.

Storytelling Teaching Strategies:

Now the questions becomes, how do I infuse storytelling instructional strategies into my classroom instruction? There are two specific ways that I use storytelling with my students during instructional time. The first way I use this in my instruction is what I call a story circle with my students. Essentially, I get all my students and we form a circle and I sit in the middle of that circle and I tell my story. Think of it as a good old fashion storytelling where I tell the story while the students are listening actively. In each respective classroom, one can structure this however they want, but the objective is to tell stories and have the students actively listen.

Additionally, you can provide reflection questions to answer or even have students write and ask questions once the story is told. For example, in the past I have had a question-and-answer session, where the students would ask me questions and I would provide clarity on my story. Or, I would give my students opportunities to make direct parallels with my story and share their own experiences. Moreover, story circles help my English Learners develop critical thinking skills that they need to be successful in all content areas. Story circles assist ELLs with engaging in a degree of deep reflection of their second language learning which can lead to higher academic achievement through critical thinking (Fast, 2023). Additionally, I also saw a rise in my state test scores once I started to implement story circles into my classroom. For example, each year in the state of Nebraska all ELLs across the state are required to take the English Proficiency for the 21st century summative assessment (ELPA 21). This is a very rigorous test in the areas of reading, writing, speaking, and listening. To exit ESL services, all students must score proficient or advanced in all four areas of this statewide assessment. In the spring of 2020, 42% of my ELLs scored proficient or advanced in all four areas, exiting ESL services. This was a 31% increase from the previous school year. Thus, showing the power of story circles to engage, motivated, and prompt critical thinking into classroom instruction.

The second way I use storytelling in my classrooms is an extension of the first strategy, but in this instance, I have my students share their stories with other students. This accomplishes two very critical things in my classroom. One, it gives my students a sense of ownership of their learning and storytelling abilities, thus giving them multiple chances to practice their speaking skills. Second, through their respective stories, they are helping me to create a collectivist positive culture, where they feel safe telling their stories. Hence, they are building on one another's story to create an inclusive language learning environment. This method of oral storytelling is used to increase cultural and linguistic awareness of one's own culture, but also a simultaneous understanding of the existence of other cultures (Hanson, 2018). When students feel comfortable around other different cultures, they are more willing to share their stories because of the sense of community and belonging that storytelling can create. Predictably, this will lead to higher student engagement and the wiliness to take more risks in their academic and language learning.

Section Two: Autumn Rivera's Story

My Hispanic Roots:

My grandfather's family has lived in the same area in New Mexico for generations. The country of 'ownership' has changed, first Indigenous land, then Spain, Mexico, and now the United States, but the area has stayed the same. My ancestors used the land to farm beans and raise sheep among the pinon and sagebrush. However, it is hard for a bean farm to support a family of 11 kids. When my grandfather turned 15, he set out to find work. He ended up three hundred miles north, in the Rocky Mountains of Colorado. There, he lied about his age to get a job working on the railroad as a section laborer. A few years later, he married his childhood sweetheart, and they began a family in Colorado.

My father is the fourth of seven children and the first boy in a large Hispanic family. The stories the siblings have of growing up together always make me smile. For instance, digging up and selling worms to local fishermen at one penny a worm. Or, on the day of the big high school football game, my grandfather's truck broke down, and my dad and uncle, the offensive and defensive captains of the game, would miss the bus. So, the school bus drove 14 miles out of its way to pick them up so they could play in the game. They had a childhood full of adventure and love.

I have a painting my dad made when he was a kid sitting on a shelf in my living room. It shows a bookshelf filled with mundane things. An old radio, a fly swatter, and a few books are on the shelves. A red fishing pole with two sinkers and a worm on the hook leans against the shelf while a mouse climbs into one of the lower drawers. The shelf sits in front of a window with one of the panes cracked. It is such a simple painting, but one I treasure because it is a picture of what life was like for my dad's family.

Raising seven children and two adults on a railroad laborer's salary was difficult. My dad did not have running water until he was in elementary school and did not have hot running water until he was in middle school. Each morning, my aunts would help my grandmother make a set of tortillas for the family to eat for the day. Cutting down wood to heat the house and boil water was a big chore. Working together as a team, the family provided for each other.

Spanish was my dad's first language; however, when he went to school, he was surrounded by people who only spoke English. No one spoke his language at school, so sadly, my father's Spanish began to change. Pieces exist, but not enough to pass on to my brothers or me. As a Hispanic female, it has been difficult not to share my father's home language with him. Language is a huge part of identity, and I felt I was missing out on a part of myself. Still, to this day, I struggle with feeling like I cannot fully call myself Hispanic or belong in those circles because I cannot speak Spanish.

Growing up, I never thought about myself as a minority. I was one of the only families of color in my small mountain town, but we had been there for so long that we were accepted as one of the locals. It was not until I went to college that I was treated differently. On one college tour, I remember a tour guide smiling excitedly as she told me about their extra support for their Hispanic students. I was confused as to why I needed extra help because I was Hispanic. It was the first time I remember feeling othered.

Finding My Own Identity:

I have been a teacher now for over twenty years. While getting my teaching degree, I was taught to keep my personal story separate from my classroom. There was Ms. Rivera and Autumn, and they were very separate. For the first few years, I tried to follow this method. However, I found it made teaching very difficult. Who I am as a teacher is shaped by who I am. Not sharing that part with my students, I was dehumanizing myself and dehumanizing them. I slowly began to shift from two separate worlds to one.

After seven years of teaching, I decided the big city was too much, and I longed for my hometown. I took a job at a school close to my home. In my home community, I truly began to feel like I could share who I was with my students. The school community I currently teach is 65% Hispanic and Latino students. However, I am one of four Hispanic teachers in the building. At first, I struggled to relate to being a teacher of color. Yes, we shared a similar skin color, but I did not speak the language. My family story is not about running away from home to keep a family safe, looking for a better future.

As an adjunct college professor, a Latino student once stayed after class to talk to me. He asked what my background was. When I told him my short story, he looked disappointed. He said, 'Oh, I thought you were one of us." Again, I felt othered, but from a different group this time. I looked at the part on the outside, but it was a fraud inside. There was no place for me to belong.

For a few years, I avoided sharing my story. Better to let others assume my background over being disappointed in who I was. However, in October of 2021, everything changed. One day, I was teaching my students when my principal walked into my classroom to invite us down to the library. This was during the end of strict restrictions with COVID, and it was weird to have him bring us out of class. The students lined up, and we walked down to the library. When I walked in, I was surprised to see flowers and balloons waiting. My parents, brothers, nieces, and nephews were all there. My students sat in the provided chairs while the president of our state teacher's union and the commissioner of education were waiting on the side. They were here to announce that I was named the 2022 Colorado State Teacher of the Year. It was a shocking experience and one that has completely changed my life. I was pushed further out of my comfort zone when I was named a National Teacher of the Year Finalist the following January.

Each recognition brought me into new circles with new people. Latin and Hispanic groups were reaching out to me to speak with them about what it meant to be a Latina teacher; however, I didn't feel like I had an answer. I wanted to pull people aside and tell them I wasn't a real Hispanic; they had the wrong person. This was until I met my 2022 State Teacher of the Year Cohort. It was with this amazing group of educators that I finally began to accept who I truly was. Through talks with other teachers from around the nation, I learned that I wasn't the only one who felt the way I did. I began to accept my story as something beautiful, and now take pride in my history and believe it is something to be shared.

Sharing My Story with My Students:

As I was learning who I was, I looked around and realized that many things I thought separated me from my students instead brought us together. For example, a former student, Angeline (a pseudonym), did not share her parents' home language. Therefore, when an interpreter came to support her during her student-led conference, I could tell that this was one of the only times Angeline and her parents could fully communicate. This lack of communication can lead to stress within a household (Moule, 2012).

Another time, I was taking a group of students to present at a conference in Chicago. While waiting to check in at the airport, Eddie's (a pseudonym) mom pulled me aside with a worried look in her eyes. This was the first time Eddie would leave home with no family members going along. She was very concerned. It reminded me of when I left for college. I was going to a school four hours away, and my aunts and grandma were worried because I would be so far away. I understood the importance of being close to family.

As children begin to take on new cultures, they separate from their household culture, isolating themselves even more from their roots, but not entirely fitting into their new environment (Moule, 2012). The isolation they experienced was like the one I experienced. While the background of the stories is different, the basic feeling of isolation is the same.

I began to share my feelings and experiences with my students. I wanted them to see and understand that they were not alone. I encouraged them not to lose their home languages, as being bilingual is a beautiful gift. I take safe risks in my classroom by speaking limited Spanish to them and encouraging them to do the same with me in their English. The human in me celebrates the human in them.

While getting to know many of my students, I realized we have more in common than I had imagined. Yes, I do not speak the language, but I get them. I understand that a family gathering will always involve over fifty people. Massive amounts of food will always be served, and leaving the gathering needs a thirty-minute goodbye period to ensure you have hugged everyone at least once before you leave. Siblings are not hidden off to the side but are included in everything. I cannot tell you the number of wrestling matches and football games I have watched with my brothers and cousins growing up. When it is time for student-led conferences, I always ensure my students' siblings have something to do so they feel included. I get to know the families because I know that getting to know the families is getting to know the students.

In sharing my story of not being able to speak my father's home language I can celebrate those who can speak the language. I build off my limited Spanish and my students' limited English to come together to learn a new language, science. Benavides and Medina-Jerez (2017) described the importance of identifying key vocabulary words and making connections between languages when working with multilingual students in content areas. While science involves many new words, I can use students' home language and science cognates to make needed connections.

Sharing my background with my students helps them to feel more understood. Things that may seem different to other teachers, such as always having the entire family show up to an event, make sense to me. I have leveraged this love of family in my classroom by inviting the families into the work. Each Friday I text home to parents a question to ask their student about our learning for the week. Families are invited to learn what their student knows and share their background with the topic. Allowing families to be a part of the learning not just at school, but also at home increases the connection between family, student, and the classroom (Kim, Kim, & Barnett, 2021). Providing talking points between student and family allows everyone to feel more invested in the student learning.

In my travels as Teacher of the Year, I continued celebrating my story with those around me. It is not just my story in isolation that I am sharing, but the stories of my students. In sharing and learning together, our stories began to intertwine. In speeches, interviews, and panels, I shared our struggles and successes with those listening. I shared pictures and experiences with my students when I returned to class. They became a part of the awards, the celebrations, and the recognition. In honoring them, they were able to celebrate themselves.

In their book *Language of Identify, Language of Access,* Benegas and Benjamin name the importance of finding identity within oneself and how crucial it is for one to explore the identity of one's ancestors and share that identity with current connections (2024). In finding out who I am within my own story, I have learned from my students. Celebrating similarities and laughing at differences, such as the best way to make a homemade tortilla or which chile, red or green, is best, gives me a new connection to them. We continue to learn from and with each other. Sharing stories has become such a precious gift.

Looking Forward:

It was at one specific speech I gave for a college graduation that I realized my next steps. A colleague approached me to take a picture with her and two other Latina professors. The four of us were the only female Latina people in the room. Dressed in our regalia, getting ready to walk out and celebrate our graduating students, we smiled for the camera. Two of us have Masters degrees, and two have Doctoral degrees. The professor who asked to take the photo mailed me a framed copy of the photo a few weeks later. Looking at this picture, the words 'you cannot be what you cannot see' were never truer. I realized in that photo that I had a new role. Yes, it was important for me to share the story of my past with my students, but it was also important to share examples of possible futures with them.

I decided that showing examples of Hispanic and Latine scientists to help celebrate diversity in my class was not enough. I needed my students to not just see some stranger who looked like them on the internet doing something cool; they needed to know someone. So, I decided to join my fellow college professors in earning my doctorate. I enrolled in a program the next semester and am pursuing a doctorate in Curriculum, Instruction, and Assessment. When asked why I am getting this degree, I always answer that it is not for me. This is not something I am doing to better myself, though it is making me a better teacher. My real reason is twofold. First, I think of my grandfather, who loved to learn but did not have the same educational opportunities I had. Second, I think of my students, who are getting to see someone who shares a similar story and earns a higher degree. While not all of them will pursue higher education, I want them to at least see it as an available option.

I look forward to the day when I can celebrate student achievements with them and their families as they grow up. With aunts, uncles, and children running around in the background, a mix of Spanish and English surrounds us, delicious food is piled on tables, and a shared smile of celebration is passed between us.

Section Three: Ramon Benavides Story:

Doors of Opportunity:

Life often presents doors of opportunity, some of which we walk through, while others may go unnoticed or bypassed. Opportunities can emerge from our actions or outside influences. Being cognizant of when these opportunities arise played a significant role in my parents' journey and in mine. Many of us, people of color, specifically Latino/a/x, are predisposed to statistics that seem to work against us, yet opportunities are presented, enabling us to challenge those odds. In some cases, these moments are rare and should be embraced. Achieving success through these opportunities necessitates willingness—fueled by confidence and determination—to take advantage of these opportunities. This commitment to walk through these doors of opportunity involves acknowledging and welcoming the support from those we meet and who provide direction throughout our journey.

These doors of opportunity shaped my personal and professional journey as a public-school educator, the 2022 Texas Teacher of the Year, and now high school administrator. The journeys through these doors resulted in narratives I shared in various roles, specifically as a teacher. These stories made an impact in and out of the classroom. It is important to know that storytelling is a constructive instructional instrument that captures students' attention and promotes participation, sharing, and collaboration (Maharaj-Sharma, R., 2022). Its engaging nature makes it an effective instructional strategy, as highlighted in various studies (Maharaj-Sharma, R., 2022). To honor my parents, wife, sons, and other important individuals compelled me to share our stories filled with resilience, legacy, and impact.

These critical narratives shaped who I am today through an array of opportunities and where I was able to share with my students via content lessons or life lessons: the opportunities my parents and I encountered, utilizing these opportunities to carry my parents' legacy, how these opportunities influenced my educational values and philosophy, and their impact in all that I have done. The instructional practice of storytelling helps students learn by engaging and immersing them at a personal level via the phenomenon of narrative transportation (Andrews et al.; K., 2010). The following three narratives played an important role in my teaching when creating the essential teacher-student relationships.

Taking These Doors of Opportunity:

My parents, Ramon and Gloria Benavides were generational migrant farmworkers who encountered many hardships associated with this line of work, which encompassed dropping out of school to support their families. Yet, their determination to seek better opportunities led them back to school, where they eventually became educators themselves. Their resilience demonstrated that perseverance could overcome any obstacle, and education is the key to breaking the cycle of poverty and all the other measures associated with it. It is imperative to recognize education affects individuals and groups by shaping the way they think, their social status, employment, and rewarding opportunities (Sadovnik & Coughlan, 2016).

My father dropped out of school in the sixth grade to work in the cotton fields of Lubbock, Texas. My mother dropped out of high school in the 11th grade to help her family as they traveled in search of work across the Midwest. Poverty, instability, and constant migration defined their lives, but they were determined to break that cycle. After years of fieldwork, they returned to school to earn their GEDs and later became educators. This transformation was made possible because of the fortunate opportunities that arose, and this is where my journey began.

I was born and raised in Brownsville, Texas. A small city at the southern tip of Texas along the US / Mexico border. My borderland neighborhood was marked by violence, drugs, and poverty. The borderlands, as stated by Anzaldua (1987), outlines an area intersection for the US and Mexico, but most importantly, it describes the emotional and cultural challenges of those living between different identities and languages.

Living in poverty most definitely had its challenges. Students from low-income, high-crime areas often struggle academically due to environmental stressors and lack of resources (Ferguson, 2019). The existence of illegal drug activity and especially violence made its impact. One of the most traumatic events I encountered was witnessing a drug deal that had gone bad, which resulted in a gruesome murder. This dreadful encounter, along with the others associated with our circumstances, created its challenges, especially mental health obstacles.

Nevertheless, these stressors and the lack of having were not roadblocks but detours to success. Despite these troubles, several doors of opportunity arose and allowed me and my family to rise above those barriers. it allowed me to understand that success entailed "ganas y poder". I have earned multiple degrees, including a Ph.D.; each milestone wasn't just personal success but a testament to the opportunities seized along the way.

The importance of my parents' journey is immeasurable, from migrant farm workers to educators, remains a perpetual source of inspiration, reminding me that education is a transformative tool and extends opportunity. Their resilience, dedication, and emphasis on education are principles I cherish in all aspects of my life. This legacy is one I aim to impart to others and especially with students who share a similar upbringing in hopes of empowering them to overcome the obstacles of hardship and limited resources.

Continuing My Parents' Legacy as the 2022 Texas Teacher of the Year:

Being named the 2022 Texas Teacher of the Year was a pivotal moment in my career. It represented not just a personal milestone but also a continuation of the legacy my parents established when they chose to pursue education against all odds. As the child of migrant farmworkers who became educators, I deeply understand the importance of using this platform to advocate for students from underserved communities.

My parents instilled in me the conviction that education is not solely about individual achievement but also about giving back to others. These values shaped my function as an educator, and I view my role as Texas Teacher of the Year as a chance to further advocate for equity and access in education. Research by Gándara and Contreras (2009) highlights that Latino students often encounter significant obstacles to academic success, such as language barriers, insufficient resources, and institutional biases (Gándara and Contreras, 2009). As an advocate, I am dedicated to dismantling these barriers and ensuring that all students have access to the opportunities they rightfully deserve.

As Texas Teacher of the Year, I have had the privilege of mentoring fellow teachers, sharing my experiences across various platforms, and advocating for policies that support students from low-income, minority, and immigrant families. My journey and my parents' story resonate with many educators who have faced similar challenges. By sharing these narratives, I hope to inspire others to keep fighting for educational equity and to create more opportunities for the students who need them the most.

Mentorship plays a vital role in my work as an educator. I've been lucky to have mentors throughout my career who have guided and supported me, and I strive to give back in the same way. Whether it's mentoring new teachers, helping students as they navigate their educational paths, or advocating for policies that uplift underserved communities, I am dedicated to creating opportunities for others. Hudson (2013) notes that effective mentoring in education can significantly benefit both the mentor and the mentee, resulting in enhanced teaching practices and improved student outcomes.

Continuing my parents' legacy means not just achieving success in my own career but also paving the way for others to thrive. It involves advocating for students and educators who, like me, come from backgrounds where opportunities may be scarce, yet their potential is boundless. It's about keeping the doors and windows of opportunity open for future generations. By nurturing environments where every student can succeed, my goal is to ensure that education remains a transformative force. This commitment to equity and empowerment is at the core of my educational philosophy, which drives my work as an administrator and shapes how I approach educational leadership in the field.

My Educational Philosophy and Its Impact on My Journey:

My teaching journey followed the path my parents took many years ago. The profession has been a significant part of my family, and it continues with both me and my youngest sister. I am deeply passionate about teaching, a love that has always been evident in everything I do. My dedication to education extends far beyond the four walls of the classroom, driven by a desire to make a lasting impact on student's lives, thus shaping my educational philosophy.

I began my teaching career in El Paso, Texas, in a borderland community that closely mirrors my upbringing. My educational philosophy, shaped by my personal and academic experiences, was grounded in the belief that education should support students academically and nurture their individual growth. Although I am no longer in the classroom, I carry these same values as an administrator. My approach to education, like the example set by my parents and many of my teachers, is rooted in love, compassion, and empathy.

The challenges I've encountered, along with the insights gained from my family and students, have significantly shaped my educational philosophy. Education goes beyond simply sharing knowledge; it's about fostering opportunities that can genuinely transform lives. I strived to cultivate an environment where students felt acknowledged, valued, and motivated to achieve their fullest potential.

Many of the students that came into my classroom encountered comparable obstacles. I faced poverty, language barriers, lack of resources, and a problematic neighborhood. Nevertheless, I am convinced the classroom is a place where these challenges are recognized and addressed. As noted by Ladson-Billings (1995), culturally relevant pedagogy empowers students intellectually, socially, and emotionally by incorporating cultural references into the teaching of knowledge, skills, and attitudes. This is precisely what I aimed to achieve in my classroom.

At the heart of my *modus operandi* is the importance of building authentic, caring relationships with my students. I believe that when students sense their teacher genuinely cares about their well-being, they are more likely to excel academically. Positive teacher-student relationships contribute to better student outcomes, such as increased engagement, improved attendance, and enhanced academic performance (Roorda et al., 2011). I focused on establishing trust with my students by sharing my own stories of triumph and struggle, demonstrating that I, too, have faced and overcome challenges.

One of the most impactful ways I connected with my students is through storytelling. I share my individual experiences—growing up with limited means, witnessing violence, and facing academic difficulties. Using this I was able to create a safe environment where my students felt encouraged to share their stories. This connection nurtures a sense of community in the classroom, leading to a more supportive and empowering learning atmosphere.

However, my educational philosophy transcended beyond the classroom especially through my work outside the classroom. Research indicates that being involved in extracurricular activities can lead to positive educational outcomes, especially for students from disadvantaged backgrounds (Mahoney, Cairns, & Farmer, 2003). I sponsored several extracurricular student clubs, such as the Medical Sciences Club, the Environmental Stewardship Club, and the Anime Club. Through these clubs, I strived to create doors of opportunities for my students to explore their interests, acquire new skills, and envision a future that extends beyond their current situations.

My educational philosophy is fastened in the belief that students should see themselves reflected in the curriculum and in the classroom as a form of authenticity. I made it a priority to include culturally relevant materials and stories from my upbringing in my classroom. This method not only facilitated students to feel connected to the content but also highlighted the value of their culture and experiences. According to Nieto (2010), culturally responsive teaching involves recognizing the significance of incorporating students' cultural references in all aspects of learning (Nieto, 2010). By doing so, I enabled my students to take pride in their culture and background while supporting them with the knowledge and skills necessary for academic success beyond my classroom.

As One Door Closes, Then Many Others Open:

One thing is sure: our journeys are filled with opportunities, whether created or passed on by others. What we do with these opportunities determines our ultimate placement in life. The accounts shared here are grounded in the lived and academic experiences of my parents and myself. My parents came from migrant farm workers who overcame adversity and persevered by firmly believing that education is the equalizer and powerful enough to break poverty and hardships. Their resilience taught me to never let any great opportunity pass by.

As a public-school educator, administrator, and the 2022 Texas Teacher of the Year, my goal has been to continue the work my parents started: to fight for equity and access. I know that education can change lives and generational hardships just as they did. This drives my work: a philosophical belief that students from all walks of life have the right to achieve their goals. Through mentorship, advocacy, and teaching, I have made a career commitment to removing those barriers that too often stand between success for underserved students like me, which turns into a professional commitment.

Sharing these narratives as part of my pedagogical practice allowed students' perspectives to be shaped by engaging them with a model that integrated their imagination and brought forth understanding at a personal level (Andrews et al.; K., 2010). Just this past summer I ran into one of my former students. After exchanging pleasantries, the student recalled the story of my parents. He mentioned how inspiring and motivating it was and allowed him to see there is hope when there is motivation and resiliency. This alone validated the instructional practice of storytelling in the classroom, which I adamantly share with all.

A key component of education is to take notice of the spaces where students would feel seen, valued, and empowered to prosper amid challenges. It has been my objective, whether in the classroom or via extracurricular activities, to enable them to have a future full of opportunities for themselves. Through culturally relevant pedagogy, authentically building relationships, and specifically, I have brought opportunities to our students, allowing them to see that success is not beyond reach. Out of this philosophy of love and compassion, my work as an educator and administrator has guided me in opening doors of opportunity to future generations through the practice of storytelling.

REFERENCES

Andrews, D. H., Hull, T. D., & DeMeester, K. (2010). Storytelling as an instructional method: Research perspectives.

Anzaldúa, G. (1987). *Borderlands/La frontera: The new mestiza*. Aunt Lute Books.

Benavides, R., & Medina-Jerez, W. (2017). No Puedo: "I don't get it"—Assisting Spanglish-speaking students in the science classroom. *Science Teacher (Normal, Ill.)*, 84(4), 30–35. DOI: 10.2505/4/tst17_084_04_30

Benegas, M., & Benjamin, N. (2024). *Language of Identity, Language of Access*. Corwin.

Blazar, D. (2021, November 30). *Teachers of color, culturally responsive teaching, and student outcomes: Experimental evidence from the random assignment of teachers to classes. edworkingpaper no. 21-501.* Annenberg Institute for School Reform at Brown University. https://eric.ed.gov/?id=ED616770

Boris, V. (2023, January 9). *What makes storytelling so effective for learning?* Harvard Business Publishing. https://www.harvardbusiness.org/what-makes-storytelling -so-effective-for-learning/

Callahan, R. M., & Gándara, P. C. (2014). *The bilingual advantage: Language, literacy and the US labor market*. Channel View Publications. DOI: 10.21832/9781783092437

Crawford, J., & Krashen, S. D. (2015). *English learners in American classrooms: 101 questions, 101 answers*. DiversityLearningK12.

Edenberg, H. J., & Foroud, T. (2013). Genetics and alcoholism. *Nature Reviews. Gastroenterology & Hepatology*, 10(8), 487–494. DOI: 10.1038/nrgastro.2013.86 PMID: 23712313

Fast, T. (2023). NESCO Story Circles in a TESOL Context. *International Forum of Teaching & Studies, 19*(1), 44–52.

Ferguson, R. (2019). The challenges of educating low-income students. *Educational Leadership*, 76(5), 30–35.

Gándara, P., & Contreras, F. (2009). *The Latino education crisis: The consequences of failed social policies*. Harvard University Press. DOI: 10.4159/9780674056367

Goldstein, B. A. (2022). *Bilingual Language Development & Disorders in Spanish– English Speakers* (3rd ed.). Brooks Publishing Co.

Hanson, S. L. (2018). *Building Understanding Among Students of Many Cultures: Story and Cultural Competence* [Master's thesis, Bethel University]. Spark Repository. https://spark.bethel.edu/etd/268

Hudson, P. (2013). Mentoring as professional development: 'Growth for both mentor and mentee'. *Professional Development in Education*, 39(5), 771–783. DOI: 10.1080/19415257.2012.749415

Kim, D., Kim, S. L., & Barnett, M. (2021). "That makes sense now!": Bicultural middle school students' learning in a culturally relevant science classroom. *International Journal of Multicultural Education*, 23(2), 145–172. DOI: 10.18251/ijme.v23i2.2595

Ladson-Billings, G. (1995). Toward a theory of culturally relevant pedagogy. *American Educational Research Journal*, 32(3), 465–491. DOI: 10.3102/00028312032003465

Maharaj-Sharma, R. (2022). Using storytelling to teach a topic in physics. *Education Inquiry*, 15(2), 227–246. DOI: 10.1080/20004508.2022.2092977

Mahoney, J. L., Cairns, B. D., & Farmer, T. W. (2003). Promoting interpersonal competence and educational success through extracurricular activity participation. *Journal of Educational Psychology*, 95(2), 409–418. DOI: 10.1037/0022-0663.95.2.409

Moule, J. (2012). *Cultural competence: A primer for educators* (2nd ed.). Wadsworth.

Nieto, S. (2010). *The light in their eyes: Creating multicultural learning communities*. Teachers College Press.

Ortmeyer, D. L., & Quinn, M. A. (2012). COYOTES, MIGRATION DURATION, AND REMITTANCES. *Journal of Developing Areas*, 46(2), 185–203. https://www.jstor.org/stable/23215369. DOI: 10.1353/jda.2012.0038

Roorda, D. L., Koomen, H. M., Spilt, J. L., & Oort, F. J. (2011). The influence of affective teacher–student relationships on students' school engagement and achievement: A meta-analytic approach. *Review of Educational Research*, 81(4), 493–529. DOI: 10.3102/0034654311421793

Rubinstein-Avila, E., & Lee, E. H. (2014). Secondary teachers and English language learners (ells): Attitudes, preparation, and implications. *The Clearing House: A Journal of Educational Strategies, Issues and Ideas*, 87(5), 187–191. DOI: 10.1080/00098655.2014.910162

Sadovnik, A. R., & Coughlan, R. W. (2016). *Sociology of education: A critical reader*. Routledge. DOI: 10.1007/978-94-6300-717-7

Salva, C., & Matis, A. (2017). *Boosting achievement: Reaching students with interrupted or minimal education.* Seidlitz Education.

Chapter 3
The Impact of Male Mentorship on Latino Immigrant Young Men

Juan Andrés Ouviña
Montclair State University, USA

ABSTRACT

This chapter examines the transformative potential of male mentorship in supporting Latino immigrant young men's academic success and identity development. Drawing from empirical research and first-hand experience as an educator and researcher, the author analyzes the implementation of culturally responsive mentorship programs for this population. The discussion explores Latino immigrant youth experiences through demographic trends and cultural transitions, examining identity development through theoretical frameworks like the Selection, Optimization, and Compensation Model. Through case studies and practical strategies, the chapter provides educators and community leaders with evidence-based approaches for effective mentorship initiatives. The author's perspective as both a former Latino first generation student and current educator offers unique insights while presenting a framework for sustainable mentorship programs that emphasize family engagement, community partnerships, and comprehensive support.

INTRODUCTION

As I stand before my high school English class, I'm inspired by the determination, curiosity, and intellectual depth I see in my students' eyes. As the son of immigrants, my journey from student to dedicated educator and doctoral researcher has been profoundly shaped by mentors who recognized and nurtured my potential along the

DOI: 10.4018/979-8-3373-1340-5.ch003

way. It is through this lens—having witnessed my parents' immigrant experience, now serving as a high school teacher in a vibrant multicultural community, and pursuing scholarship that explores the complexities of immigrant experiences—that I approach the critical topic of male mentorship for Latino immigrant young men.

The landscape of mentorship for Latino immigrant youth has evolved significantly over recent decades, moving beyond traditional academic support to embrace a holistic approach that honors cultural identity, promotes social-emotional development, and cultivates leadership potential. This evolution reflects a deeper understanding of how cultural wisdom, family connections, and community engagement intersect with academic achievement and personal growth.

This chapter examines how effective mentorship can create transformative spaces where Latino immigrant young men develop not only academic prowess but also strong cultural identities, emotional resilience, and leadership capabilities. Drawing from both empirical research and practitioner experience, we explore the multifaceted nature of meaningful mentorship, considering how translingual practices, cultural knowledge, and community connections contribute to student success.

This chapter aims to bridge the gap between academic research and lived experience, offering a comprehensive exploration of male mentorship as a catalyst for positive change in the lives of Latino immigrant youth. Drawing from my personal journey, my experiences in the classroom, and rigorous academic research, we will examine the multifaceted challenges faced by this population and the transformative potential of well-structured mentorship programs.At its core, this work is driven by a fundamental thesis that I've seen proven time and again: Male mentorship, when culturally responsive and strategically implemented, can play a pivotal role in supporting the academic, social, and emotional needs of Latino immigrant young men. By providing guidance, fostering a sense of belonging, and offering positive male role models, mentorship can help these young men develop strong, positive identities, overcome obstacles, and realize their full potential.

Throughout this chapter, we will explore the nuances of identity development among Latino immigrant young men, highlighting the intersections of culture, ethnicity, and masculinity that shape their experiences. I will share stories from my own classroom and community that illustrate these concepts, bringing theoretical frameworks to life through real-world examples. We will delve into the key components of effective mentorship programs, offering evidence-based strategies for educators, community leaders, and policymakers to implement and scale these initiatives.

Moreover, this chapter will address the challenges and ethical considerations inherent in mentorship programs, drawing on my firsthand experiences navigating cultural differences and addressing systemic inequities. We will look to the future, discussing emerging trends in mentorship, including the integration of technology and the development of cross-cultural mentorship networks—innovations I'm exploring in my doctoral research and beginning to implement in my own teaching practice.

As we embark on this exploration, I invite you to see through my eyes—the eyes of a once-struggling immigrant student, now a passionate educator and researcher. The challenges faced by Latino immigrant young men are not insurmountable barriers, but rather opportunities for growth, resilience, and transformation. Through effective mentorship and targeted support, we can empower these young men to not only overcome obstacles but to thrive, becoming leaders in their communities and contributors to the rich cultural fabric of American society.

This chapter is intended for a diverse audience of professionals committed to supporting Latino immigrant youth. To my fellow educators, I offer practical strategies born from classroom experience. To higher education professionals, I provide insights into supporting the transition and success of Latino immigrant students in post-secondary education. To counselors and mental health professionals, I share approaches to addressing the unique psychological and emotional needs of this population, informed by both research and real-world observation. To community organizations and advocates, I present valuable information on developing and scaling mentorship initiatives beyond the classroom. And to my colleagues in research, I offer a synthesis of current findings and directions for future study in this critical field.

Understanding the Latino Immigrant Youth Experience

For young Latino immigrants, the process of adapting to life in the United States often involves complex negotiations between their heritage culture and the norms of their new environment. This acculturation process can be particularly challenging for adolescents and young adults who are simultaneously navigating the typical developmental tasks of identity formation.

Key challenges in cultural transition include:

1. Family dynamics: The immigration process can disrupt traditional family structures, with children sometimes acculturating faster than their parents, leading to intergenerational conflicts and shifting family roles.
2. Peer relationships: Forming friendships and social connections across cultural lines can be difficult, potentially leading to feelings of isolation or pressure to assimilate at the expense of cultural identity.
3. Cultural identity development: Young Latino immigrants may struggle with questions of belonging, often feeling caught between two worlds.

For many Latino immigrant youth, language acquisition represents both a significant challenge and a critical pathway to success in their new environment. The impact of language barriers extends far beyond mere communication difficulties:

1. Academic performance: Limited English proficiency can hinder academic progress across all subject areas, potentially leading to lower grades, reduced engagement, and increased dropout rates.
2. Social integration: Language barriers can impede the formation of friendships and participation in extracurricular activities, essential components of a well-rounded educational experience.
3. Access to resources: Students with limited English skills may struggle to understand and access important educational resources, support services, and opportunities for advancement.
4. Standardized testing: High-stakes tests, often administered only in English, can place English language learners at a significant disadvantage, potentially impacting their educational and career trajectories.
5. Parent involvement: When parents have limited English proficiency, it can reduce their ability to engage with schools, support their children's learning, and advocate for their educational needs.

The family plays a central role in Latino cultures, and immigration can significantly impact family structures and dynamics:

Family separation: Many immigrant youth experience prolonged separation from family members, either due to staggered migration or deportation, leading to emotional stress and disrupted support systems.

Shifting roles: Young immigrants often take on adult responsibilities, such as translating for parents or contributing financially to the household, which can impact their educational focus and social development.

Academic expectations: While many immigrant families place a high value on education, they may lack familiarity with the U.S. educational system, leading to misaligned expectations or difficulties in providing academic support.

Cultural transmission: Young immigrants may feel pressure to maintain cultural traditions and language, even as they adapt to American society, creating potential internal conflicts.

The socioeconomic realities faced by many Latino immigrant families can significantly impact the experiences and opportunities available to young people:

1. Economic pressures: Financial strain may necessitate that young people work to contribute to family income, potentially interfering with educational pursuits.

2. Housing instability: Frequent moves due to economic factors can disrupt education and social connections.
3. Healthcare access: Limited access to healthcare, including mental health services, can impact overall well-being and academic performance.
4. Legal status: Undocumented status or mixed-status families face additional stressors, including limited access to higher education funding and fear of family separation due to deportation.

Understanding these multifaceted challenges is crucial for developing effective mentorship programs and support systems for Latino immigrant young men. By recognizing the complex interplay of cultural, linguistic, familial, and socioeconomic factors, mentors and educators can better tailor their approaches to meet the unique needs of this population. In the following sections, we will explore how targeted mentorship can address these challenges and support the positive development of Latino immigrant youth.

Historical Context of Latino Male Mentorship Programs

The evolution of mentorship programs for Latino immigrant young men mirrors broader societal transformations in how we understand identity, belonging, and success in American society. Early initiatives in the 1960s and 1970s emerged from the civil rights movement and growing awareness of educational inequities (Martinez & Fernández, 2021). While these initial programs focused primarily on academic support and English language acquisition, they laid important groundwork for more comprehensive approaches to student development.

The 1980s marked a pivotal shift in mentorship philosophy, as research began highlighting the intrinsic connection between cultural identity and academic success. Programs started moving beyond deficit-based models that had characterized early interventions, instead recognizing the rich cultural and linguistic resources that Latino students bring to their educational journeys. This period saw the emergence of what Vega and Martinez (2020) describe as "culturally sustaining mentorship"—approaches that actively value and build upon students' cultural knowledge and experiences.

The 1990s witnessed the development of pioneering programs like the Puente Project, which demonstrated the power of integrated approaches to student support. Through careful documentation and research, the project revealed how mentorship could simultaneously nurture academic achievement, cultural pride, and personal development. The Puente Project's success in increasing college enrollment and completion rates among Latino students highlighted the effectiveness of programs that engage families, honor cultural traditions, and create strong community partnerships (Laden, 2000).

This period also saw growing recognition of what researchers term "cultural synthesis" in mentorship approaches. Rather than viewing cultural adaptation as a linear process of assimilation, successful programs began recognizing the sophisticated ways in which Latino immigrant young men navigate multiple cultural contexts. This understanding led to more nuanced approaches that support what González et al. (2005) describe as "dynamic cultural identity development."

Theoretical Frameworks Understanding Latino Male Mentorship

The process of identity formation is a critical developmental task for all adolescents and young adults. For Latino immigrant young men, this process is further complicated by the need to navigate multiple cultural contexts, gender expectations, and societal pressures. This section explores the unique aspects of identity development for this population and strategies for fostering positive identity formation.

The complexity of supporting Latino immigrant male students requires a sophisticated theoretical foundation that moves beyond single-model approaches. Multiple theoretical frameworks, when integrated thoughtfully, provide comprehensive lenses for understanding and implementing effective mentorship programs.

Community Cultural Wealth Framework

Yosso's (2005) Community Cultural Wealth framework fundamentally reshapes how we understand the resources Latino immigrant young men bring to their educational journeys. Moving beyond traditional capital theories that often privileged dominant cultural norms, this framework identifies six forms of capital that exist within communities of color, each contributing uniquely to student success and development.

Aspirational Capital emerges through communities' ability to maintain hopes and dreams despite real and perceived barriers. For Latino immigrant young men, this often manifests in their capacity to envision future success while navigating present challenges. Mentorship programs that recognize and nurture this form of capital help students develop what researchers term "resilient aspirations" - goals that remain strong even in the face of obstacles.

Linguistic Capital encompasses the intellectual and social skills gained through experience with multiple languages and communication styles. This includes not only bilingual abilities but also the sophisticated translingual practices that emerge from moving between cultural contexts. Successful mentorship programs recognize these linguistic capabilities as cognitive assets rather than barriers to overcome.

The framework's recognition of Familial Capital has particular relevance for mentorship program design. This form of capital, which includes cultural knowledge nurtured within familia (family), carries a sense of community history, memory, and cultural intuition. Effective programs build upon these family connections rather than seeing them as separate from or in competition with mentorship relationships.

Social Capital, comprising networks of people and community resources, provides both instrumental and emotional support. Understanding these networks helps mentorship programs create more effective support systems that build upon existing community strengths. This often involves what Martinez and Fernández (2021) term "network amplification" - strengthening and expanding existing support systems rather than replacing them.

Navigational Capital and Resistant Capital complete Yosso's framework, addressing crucial aspects of how Latino immigrant young men move through institutional spaces and develop critical consciousness. Navigational Capital proves especially valuable when helping young men traverse educational systems and career pathways, while Resistant Capital fosters the knowledge and skills needed to challenge inequality while maintaining cultural pride.

The SOC Model in Cultural Context

The Selection, Optimization, and Compensation (SOC) Model (Baltes & Baltes, 1990) provides crucial insights into how Latino immigrant young men actively shape their development trajectories. Unlike passive models of acculturation, this framework reveals how young men strategically navigate cultural adaptation through conscious choices and deliberate actions.

Selection processes involve sophisticated decisions about which cultural practices and values to maintain or adopt. Rather than wholesale assimilation or rejection, young men actively select elements that support their growth while maintaining cultural integrity. This selective process creates what Torres (2003) calls "integrated cultural identities" - personalized syntheses of heritage and host culture elements.

The optimization process involves developing and refining resources needed for success in chosen domains. This might include enhancing translingual abilities, building cross-cultural communication skills, or strengthening academic capabilities. Successful mentorship programs support this optimization process by providing structured opportunities for skill development while honoring cultural knowledge.

Compensation strategies emerge when traditional pathways prove challenging, leading to the development of alternative approaches that draw on cultural strengths. For example, when direct academic support isn't available at home, students might leverage community networks or peer study groups. Effective programs help students recognize these adaptive strategies as strengths rather than deficits.

The Phenomenological Variant of Ecological Systems Theory (PVEST)

Spencer's (2006) PVEST framework builds upon Bronfenbrenner's ecological systems theory to explain how individuals actively construct meaning and identity within multiple environmental contexts. This framework proves particularly valuable for understanding Latino immigrant male development because it recognizes the dynamic interaction between individual identity formation and environmental influences.

The theory identifies five key components that interact dynamically in youth development:

1. Net Vulnerability Level encompasses both risk factors and protective factors affecting development. For Latino immigrant young men, risk factors might include discrimination or economic challenges, while protective factors often include strong family bonds and cultural pride.
2. Net Stress Engagement refers to actual experiences challenging an individual's well-being and the supports available to address these challenges. Successful mentorship programs help young men develop what researchers term "adaptive coping strategies" while strengthening support networks.
3. Reactive Coping Methods represent the strategies individuals develop to respond to challenges. For Latino immigrant young men, these strategies often blend traditional cultural approaches with new adaptations. Effective mentorship programs help students recognize and refine these coping methods while developing new ones as needed.
4. Emergent Identities form through self-appraisal processes that lead to stable coping responses and define how individuals view themselves. The development of these identities involves what Gándara and Mordechay (2022) term "cultural synthesis" - the active creation of self-understanding that incorporates both heritage and host culture elements.
5. Life-Stage Specific Outcomes represent the consequences of coping processes, which can be productive or adverse. Successful mentorship programs help ensure positive outcomes by providing appropriate support at crucial developmental stages while recognizing the unique challenges facing Latino immigrant young men.

Contemporary Challenges and Opportunities

The digital revolution has fundamentally transformed how Latino immigrant young men engage with both heritage and host cultures. Recent research by Cortez and Santiago (2023) reveals the complex ways digital tools intersect with cultural identity development and mentorship relationships, creating what they term "virtual cultural borderlands" - spaces where young men navigate multiple cultural identities simultaneously.

Digital Cultural Spaces and Technology Integration

Social media and online platforms create unprecedented opportunities for cultural connection while also presenting new challenges for identity development. Program director Elena Rodriguez explains, "Digital spaces allow our students to maintain connections with family and cultural communities across borders, but they also require sophisticated navigation skills to maintain authentic cultural expression."Recent Pew Research data indicates significant disparities in digital access and usage patterns among Latino youth. These differences create both opportunities and challenges for mentorship programs. While 95% of Latino teens have smartphone access, the digital divide remains significant regarding computer access and internet connectivity at home.

The technological landscape presents particular complexities for Latino immigrant young men. Beyond basic access issues, programs must address what Cortez and Santiago (2023) identify as "digital cultural navigation challenges" - the sophisticated ways young men must manage their cultural identities across multiple digital spaces.

Research reveals that many Latino immigrant young men serve as their families' primary technology navigators, creating what researchers term "digital responsibility stress." Successful programs recognize this challenge and provide what Martinez-Cola (2023) calls "digital mentorship support" - guidance that helps young men manage these responsibilities while maintaining healthy boundaries.

Successful programs have developed innovative approaches to addressing these challenges. The Conexiones Digitales initiative, for example, uses a hybrid model combining virtual mentoring sessions with in-person community gatherings. This approach maintains what Hernandez and Napierala (2023) call "high-touch, high-tech balance" - using technology to enhance rather than replace personal connections.

Mental Health and Well-being

Contemporary research highlights unique mental health challenges facing Latino immigrant young men. Traditional concepts of masculinity (machismo) often conflict with help-seeking behaviors, creating what Gándara and Mordechay (2022) describe as "cultural barriers to emotional support." Successful programs address these challenges through culturally responsive approaches that honor traditional values while promoting emotional well-being.

Immigration-related stress, whether experienced directly or through family members, creates unique challenges that affect mental well-being. Programs increasingly recognize what researchers term the "intergenerational echo" of immigration experiences - the ways immigration stress reverberates through families and across generations. Effective mentorship programs develop what Ramos and Chavez (2022) call "culturally syntonic healing spaces" - environments where mental health support aligns with cultural values and practices.

Professional Development and Mentor Support

The preparation and ongoing support of mentors represents a critical program component. Contemporary approaches recognize that effective mentor development extends far beyond basic cultural competency training to create what Laden (2000) terms "cultural humility practice." This approach emphasizes continuous learning, regular self-reflection, and deep engagement with community wisdom.

Successful programs implement what Martinez and Fernández (2021) call "recursive learning cycles" for mentor development. These cycles integrate theoretical understanding with practical experience, regular reflection, and community feedback. Through these cycles, mentors develop an increasingly sophisticated understanding of how to support Latino immigrant young men while maintaining cultural authenticity.

Trauma-informed practices have become increasingly central to mentor preparation. Given the complex experiences many Latino immigrant young men bring to mentoring relationships, programs increasingly incorporate understanding of immigration-related trauma, family separation issues, and acculturation stress. This preparation enables mentors to provide what Gloria et al. (2005) term "healing-centered engagement" - support that recognizes both challenges and resilience.

The preparation and ongoing support of mentors requires sophisticated approaches that recognize the complex nature of cultural mentorship. Recent research emphasizes the importance of what Laden (2000) terms "recursive cultural learning" - approaches that combine theoretical understanding with practical experience and regular reflection.

Successful programs implement multidimensional professional development models that address:

Cultural Competency Development: Programs utilize what researchers call "immersive learning approaches" - methods that combine theoretical understanding with direct community engagement. This might include:

1. Community-led cultural workshops
2. Family engagement activities
3. Cultural celebration participation
4. Community service projects

Implementation Strategies for Effective Programs

The translation of theoretical understanding into effective practice requires thoughtful program design that honors both research insights and community wisdom. Successful programs create what González et al. (2005) term "cultural sanctuary spaces" - environments that facilitate both individual reflection and community gathering while honoring the complex cultural identities of Latino immigrant young men.

Physical spaces in these programs reflect deep understanding of cultural values rather than superficial representation. Program director Maria Ramirez describes their approach: "We created flexible spaces that shift from individual mentoring corners to larger community gathering areas. Every element reinforces the message that cultural identity is a source of strength."

The implementation of effective mentorship programs requires attention to what González et al. (2005) term "cultural ecosystem development" - the creation of comprehensive support environments that address multiple dimensions of student experience. Successful programs create what researchers call "integrated support matrices" that connect various program elements:

1. Cultural Knowledge Integration: Programs systematically incorporate community cultural knowledge into mentorship practices. For example, the Senderos program in Chicago documents local community histories and traditions, using these as foundational elements in mentor training and program activities.
2. Language Practice Development: Successful programs create what Ramos and Chavez (2022) term "linguistic affirmation spaces" - environments where fluid movement between languages is recognized as a sophisticated skill rather than a deficit. These spaces support what researchers call "dynamic language development" - the ability to use language flexibly across different contexts while maintaining cultural authenticity.

Family and Community Engagement

Successful mentorship programs recognize that supporting Latino immigrant young men requires engaging their entire support network. Recent research by Ramos and Chavez (2022) identifies several effective strategies for what they term "collaborative mentorship ecosystems" - approaches that actively involve families and communities as essential partners rather than passive recipients of services.

Family engagement in these programs reflects deep understanding of Latino cultural values and family dynamics. Rather than imposing predetermined models of parent involvement, effective programs create what researchers call "cultural listening spaces" - opportunities for families to share their wisdom, concerns, and aspirations. This approach recognizes what González et al. (2005) term "funds of knowledge" - the rich cultural and intellectual resources that exist within Latino families.

Community partnerships extend program impact beyond immediate mentoring relationships. Successful programs build networks that include:

1. Cultural organizations providing additional programming and resources
2. Professional networks offering career exposure and internship opportunities
3. Faith-based organizations supporting spiritual and community connections
4. Social service agencies providing comprehensive family support

Assessment and Program Evolution

Contemporary assessment frameworks capture both quantitative outcomes and qualitative transformations. Moving beyond traditional academic metrics, these frameworks examine what Gándara and Mordechay (2022) term "holistic development indicators" - measures that reflect growth across multiple dimensions:

Identity Development:

Programs track student growth through multiple lenses including cultural identity formation, leadership development, and community engagement. This multidimensional assessment recognizes that successful mentorship influences not just academic achievement but broader aspects of personal development.

Family Impact:

Assessment includes examination of how mentorship influences family relationships and cultural transmission. Programs document what Torres (2003) calls "ripple effects" - ways in which mentorship benefits extend beyond individual participants to strengthen family systems.

Community Influence:

Evaluation frameworks capture broader community effects, including:

Enhanced institutional cultural competence
Strengthened community partnerships
Development of new cultural resources
Creation of sustainable support networks

The evaluation of mentorship program effectiveness requires sophisticated approaches that capture both quantitative and qualitative dimensions of impact. Recent research by Gándara and Mordechay (2022) emphasizes the importance of what they term "culturally responsive assessment matrices" - frameworks that examine program effects across multiple domains and timeframes.

Successful programs implement multi-level assessment strategies that examine:

Individual Development Trajectories: Programs track what Torres (2003) calls "cultural growth indicators" - markers of development that go beyond traditional academic metrics. These might include:

1. Cultural identity formation patterns
2. Leadership skill development
3. Community engagement levels
4. Family relationship evolutionProfessional aspiration development

The Puente Project's assessment model demonstrates the effectiveness of this comprehensive approach. Their longitudinal studies reveal what program evaluator Carmen Valdez describes as "cascading positive outcomes" - benefits that multiply over time and influence multiple life domains. For example, improvements in cultural identity confidence often lead to enhanced academic performance, which in turn strengthens family relationships and community engagement.

Cross-Cultural Communication and Identity Formation

The development of effective cross-cultural communication skills represents a crucial aspect of successful mentorship programs for Latino immigrant young men. Recent research by Martinez and Fernández (2021) reveals how sophisticated communication practices emerge through what they term "cultural navigation spaces" - environments where young men develop advanced capabilities in moving between different cultural contexts.

Communication Competencies and Cultural Navigation

Successful programs recognize what González et al. (2005) call "dynamic communication patterns" - the complex ways Latino immigrant young men adapt their communication styles across different contexts. These adaptations go far beyond simple code-switching to encompass what researchers term "cultural voice development" - the ability to maintain authentic cultural expression while navigating diverse social spaces. Research reveals several key dimensions of communication development: Cultural Code Navigation: Young men develop sophisticated abilities to read and respond to what Torres (2003) calls "cultural cues" - subtle signals that indicate appropriate communication styles in different contexts. Effective programs help students recognize these cues while maintaining cultural authenticity. Voice and Identity Expression: Programs support what Ramos and Chavez (2022) term "authentic voice development" - the ability to express oneself genuinely across cultural contexts. This involves understanding how to: - Maintain cultural integrity while adapting to new environments - Express cultural pride appropriately in different settings - Navigate cultural misunderstandings effectively - Build bridges between different cultural groups

Identity Formation in Multicultural Contexts

The process of identity formation for Latino immigrant young men involves what Gándara and Mordechay (2022) describe as "dynamic cultural synthesis" - the active creation of personal identity that draws from multiple cultural sources. Successful mentorship programs support this process by creating what researchers call "identity exploration spaces" - environments where young men can safely explore and develop their cultural identities. Recent studies identify several crucial aspects of identity development: Cultural Pride and Adaptation: Programs help students develop what Martinez-Cola (2023) terms "bicultural confidence" - the ability to maintain strong cultural pride while successfully adapting to new environments.

This involves understanding how to: - Honor cultural traditions while embracing new opportunities

- Build upon cultural strengths in academic and professional settings
- Navigate cultural tensions productively
- Create personal syntheses of different cultural elements

Future Directions and Emerging Trends

The field of Latino male mentorship continues to evolve, shaped by changing demographics, technological advances, and deepening understanding of identity development. Several key trends emerge as particularly significant for future program development:

Technology Integration

While digital tools transform mentorship possibilities, successful programs maintain what Hernandez and Napierala (2023) call "high-touch, high-tech balance." This approach recognizes technology as a tool for enhancing rather than replacing personal connections. Programs increasingly utilize digital platforms to:

Facilitate cross-generational connections
Document and share cultural knowledge
Support ongoing mentor-mentee communication
Enable broader community engagement

Leadership Development and Cultural Empowerment

Contemporary programs emphasize what Martinez and Fernández (2021) term "culturally grounded leadership pathways" - approaches that recognize and build upon participants' unique cultural strengths and experiences. This focus on leadership development extends beyond traditional models to embrace what researchers call "transformative cultural leadership" - preparing young men to serve as bridges between communities while maintaining strong cultural identities.

The Líderes del Futuro initiative exemplifies this approach, developing leadership capabilities through what program director Antonio Ramirez describes as "cultural asset activation." This process helps young men recognize their multicultural experiences and translingual abilities as leadership strengths rather than challenges to overcome.

Successful programs create what González et al. (2005) term "knowledge bridges" - systematic approaches to incorporating community wisdom into mentorship practice. This integration occurs through several key mechanisms:

1. Community Elder Engagement: Programs actively involve community elders in mentorship activities, creating what researchers call "intergenerational knowledge transfer spaces." These interactions provide opportunities for young men to develop deeper understanding of their cultural heritage while building connections with community leaders.
2. Cultural Practice Documentation: Effective programs systematically document local cultural practices and traditions, creating what Martinez and Fernández (2021) describe as "living cultural archives." These resources serve multiple purposes:
3. Informing mentor training and program development
4. Supporting cultural identity exploration
5. Strengthening community connections
6. Preserving cultural knowledge for future generations

Research Priorities and Evidence-Based Practice

Future research directions point toward several crucial areas of investigation:

Longitudinal Impact Studies:

Initial findings from Gándara and Contreras (2021) suggest significant long-term influences on:

> Career trajectories and professional development
> Community leadership roles
> Family relationships and cultural transmission
> Personal identity development and well-being
> Educational achievement and advancement

The role of translingual practices in mentorship deserves particular attention as programs increasingly recognize language as a tool for identity development and cognitive growth. Research suggests that fluid language practices enhance:

1. Academic learning and conceptual development
2. Cultural identity formation and expression
3. Family communication and connection

4. Professional skill development
5. Leadership capabilities

CONCLUSION

As the son of immigrants and now an educator and researcher, I have witnessed the transformative power of effective mentorship from multiple perspectives. The determination and potential I see in my high school English students daily reminds me of the crucial importance of creating mentorship spaces that honor both heritage and aspiration.

The research and practice outlined in this chapter demonstrate several key insights:

Effective mentorship must embrace both cultural preservation and adaptation, recognizing these as complementary rather than competing goals.

Support systems must engage families and communities as essential partners, drawing upon their wisdom while creating new opportunities for engagement.

Programs must address both academic and social-emotional development, recognizing these as intertwined aspects of student success.

Assessment should capture multiple dimensions of growth and impact, acknowledging the complex ways in which mentorship influences individual and community development.

Looking ahead, the growing presence of Latino immigrant young men in American educational institutions presents both challenges and opportunities. Successfully supporting these young men requires mentorship approaches that recognize their unique strengths while addressing real obstacles. It is my sincere hope that this research will contribute to the development of more effective mentorship programs, enabling future generations of Latino immigrant young men to realize their full potential while enriching our shared American story.

REFERENCES

Anderson, M., & Jiang, J. (2023). *Digital divide trends among Latino youth*. Pew Research Center.

Baltes, P. B., & Baltes, M. M. (1990). Psychological perspectives on successful aging: The model of selective optimization with compensation. In Baltes, P. B., & Baltes, M. M. (Eds.), *Successful aging: Perspectives from the behavioral sciences* (pp. 1–34). Cambridge University Press. DOI: 10.1017/CBO9780511665684.003

Bronfenbrenner, U. (1979). *The ecology of human development: Experiments by nature and design*. Harvard University Press. DOI: 10.4159/9780674028845

Cortez, R. M., & Santiago, A. M. (2023). Digital mentoring strategies for Latino youth: Emerging practices and outcomes. *Journal of Technology Education*, 45(3), 278–295.

Gándara, P., & Contreras, F. (2021). Latino educational opportunity in the post-pandemic era. *American Educational Research Journal*, 58(6), 1125–1159.

Gándara, P., & Mordechay, K. (2022). Post-pandemic educational recovery in Latino communities. *American Educational Research Journal*, 59(4), 1388–1422.

García, O., & Wei, L. (2014). *Translanguaging: Language, bilingualism and education*. Palgrave Macmillan. DOI: 10.1057/9781137385765

Gloria, A. M., Castellanos, J., Lopez, A. G., & Rosales, R. (2005). An examination of academic nonpersistence decisions of Latino undergraduates. *Hispanic Journal of Behavioral Sciences*, 27(2), 202–223. DOI: 10.1177/0739986305275098

González, N., Moll, L. C., & Amanti, C. (2005). *Funds of knowledge: Theorizing practices in households, communities, and classrooms*. Lawrence Erlbaum Associates.

Hernandez, D. J., & Napierala, J. S. (2023). Children of immigrants: Demographic patterns and educational attainment. *The Future of Children*, 33(1), 7–39.

Laden, B. V. (2000). The Puente Project: Socializing and mentoring Latino community college students. *Academic Exchange Quarterly*, 4(2), 90–99.

Martinez, R. A., & Fernández, E. (2021). The evolution of Latino education: Historical perspectives and current challenges. *Harvard Educational Review*, 91(3), 331–357.

Martinez-Cola, M. (2023). Understanding demographic shifts in Latino communities: Implications for education. *Demographic Research*, 48(2), 145–168.

Ramos, D., & Chavez, M. (2022). Family engagement strategies in Latino communities. *Hispanic Journal of Behavioral Sciences*, 44(2), 145–168.

Santos, S. J., & Reigadas, E. T. (2002). Latinos in higher education: An evaluation of a university faculty mentoring program. *Journal of Hispanic Higher Education*, 1(1), 40–50. DOI: 10.1177/1538192702001001004

Spencer, M. B. (2006). Phenomenological variant of ecological systems theory: Development of diverse groups. In Damon, W., & Lerner, R. M. (Eds.), *Theoretical models of human development* (pp. 829–893). Handbook of child psychology. John Wiley & Sons.

Torres, V. (2003). Influences on ethnic identity development of Latino college students in the first two years of college. *Journal of College Student Development*, 44(4), 532–547. DOI: 10.1353/csd.2003.0044

Vega, D., & Martinez, R. (2020). Latino male mentoring: A review of best practices and call to action. *Journal of Hispanic Higher Education*, 19(2), 164–182.

Yosso, T. J. (2005). Whose culture has capital? A critical race theory discussion of community cultural wealth. *Race, Ethnicity and Education*, 8(1), 69–91. DOI: 10.1080/1361332052000341006

Chapter 4
#Latino Mentors/ Teachers Needed

Alex Guzman

https://orcid.org/0000-0002-6766-3322

Kean University, USA

ABSTRACT

This chapter emphasizes the critical role of mentorship in promoting professional growth and leadership within the Latinx community, with a focus on increasing the recruitment and retention of Latinx educators. Through a servant leadership lens and personal counter-storytelling, it highlights the challenges faced by Latinx educators and proposes actionable solutions. The chapter underscores the importance of diversity in the teaching workforce and how mentorship supports the well-being of future Latinx educators.

INTRODUCTION

Embarking on my education path was a journey filled with passion, challenges, and a deep sense of purpose. For me, this journey began with a need for long-term stability to support and serve my mother and sister. As an Afro-Latino, I faced unique challenges and opportunities that shaped my perspective and fueled my desire to make a difference in students' lives and well-being. Through a servant leadership (Greenleaf, 2002) lens, I share the genesis of my career in education and educational leadership, blending personal counter-storytelling narrative (Solórzano & Yosso, 2002) with compelling research to paint a vivid picture of the need for diversity

DOI: 10.4018/979-8-3373-1340-5.ch004

Copyright © 2025, IGI Global Scientific Publishing. Copying or distributing in print or electronic forms without written permission of IGI Global Scientific Publishing is prohibited.

in our teaching workforce, mentors and integrating how all these experiences and possible supports impact the wellbeing of future Latinx educators.

My formative years in an urban setting, where I was keenly aware of the disparities in educational opportunities, played a significant role in shaping my career path. As a student in a low-income neighborhood made up of predominantly people of color, I experienced firsthand the stark contrast in resources and support compared to more affluent areas. These early observations sowed the seeds for my future in education. I realized that education is not a given, and I could be a catalyst for change by leveraging what I learn about the inequities and how to navigate the system that impacts my personal and, eventually, my professional well-being. This understanding, coupled with the belief that my presence in careers where Latinos are underrepresented and that presence in the classroom could inspire others who saw themselves in me, was the catalyst that set me on the path to becoming an educator.

The importance of diversity in education cannot be overstated. Currently, Latino representation among educators is significantly lower than that of the student population. According to recent NCES (2023), while Hispanic students make up approximately 28% of the student body in the United States, Hispanic educators constitute only about 9% of the teaching workforce. This significant disparity underscores the urgent need for a more diverse and representative teaching staff. Research consistently shows that having teachers who share their students' cultural and linguistic backgrounds can improve academic outcomes, higher graduation rates, and a greater sense of belonging among students (Goldhaber D. et al., 2015). The academic and social benefits of having teachers who share the racial or ethnic background of their students are well-documented. When students see teachers who share their background, it reinforces their identity and strengthens their connection to the school environment, making education more relevant and meaningful to their lived experiences and improving their social and emotional development (Bristol & Martin-Fernandez, 2019). Latino educators bring valuable cultural knowledge, understanding, and linguistic skills that enrich classrooms, enhancing cultural competence among both teachers and students. Their presence helps create more inclusive and responsive learning environments where students from all backgrounds feel understood and supported (Castro & Calzada, 2021). Teachers of color (TOC) tend to have higher expectations for students of color, which can improve student performance and reduce the likelihood of discipline disparities.

In addition to impacting academic achievement and social-emotional health, Latinx educators serve as essential role models, which also impacts students' well-being (Cholewa et al., 2014). These educators represent a tangible example of success for Latinx students, helping break underrepresentation cycles in higher education and professional careers. They offer mentorship and guidance that is both culturally relevant and personally resonant, encouraging more Latino students to pursue careers in education, which in turn places them on a path to more opportunities.

Finally, a more diverse teaching workforce is vital to challenging systemic biases and stereotypes. Latino educators play a crucial role in disrupting implicit biases that often shape the academic and social experiences of Latino students. Latino educators can challenge the system by helping others learn the language needed to refute and refuse racist procedures, processes, and policies. They can empower students and communities to advocate for change by giving them the tools and knowledge to articulate their experiences and demands. Their presence and support equips individuals to navigate and resist oppressive systems. They help foster a more equitable education system where diverse perspectives are included and celebrated. By prioritizing the recruitment and retention of Latino educators, we can significantly improve Latino students' educational experiences and enrich the learning environment for all students, fostering a more just and inclusive society. However, the practice of tokenism, where a few people of color are included in predominantly White spaces to give the appearance of diversity without addressing underlying systemic issues, is detrimental and perpetuates negative effects on diversifying the teacher workforce (Wright & Boese, 2015). Such practices increase the pressure on people of color to be representatives of their group and perform at a higher level. Furthermore, these practices divert time and focus away from addressing the racialized organizational culture of the learning institutions (Chávez-Moreno, 2022) and workplace (Stewart et. al., 2021).

Growing up, the absence of Latino role models was deeply felt. This lack of representation made it challenging to envision myself succeeding and recognizing opportunities for advancement. I remember my high school years when my aspirations to pursue a higher education degree in science were met with skepticism and microaggressions by some educators; "That's a lofty goal." "Are you sure you could handle the workload?" It is probable that they made negative assumptions regarding my potential based on my socioeconomic status, cultural background, and communication style. The subtle biases and lowered expectations were disheartening. "Did coming from a Puerto Rican and Honduran cultural background impact my chances at achieving my goals?" "Am I missing some information?" "Am I not being prepared to compete and achieve with those of more privileged backgrounds?" Who is here to help me understand the complexity of a system that I need but is simultaneously working against my efforts?" "Who is here to help me understand the financial requirements of attending higher education and look for resources to attend higher education?"

In this chapter, "*#LatinoMentorsNeeded,*" I aim to intertwine my experiences with research findings to highlight the critical need for diversity in education. By sharing my journey and challenges, I hope to provide a relatable narrative that underscores the importance of Latinx representation from the classroom to administrative positions. Additionally, this chapter sets the stage for exploring the recruitment process, early career challenges, the power of mentorship, cultural identity, retention, and educators' profound impact on their students and communities.

Mi Gente (Science Education Leaders)! Where are you?

"How many teachers of color did I have in my K-16 educational experience? Three. How many science teachers of color did I have in my K-16 educational experience? Just one. Was my preparation rigorous enough to compete? Can I compete with others from more prestigious and larger higher ed. institutions?"

Reflecting on my K-16 educational experience as I was learning to teach high school chemistry and physics, I learned that the habits of mind disposition for teaching science and science practices are attributed to Western thinking and values (Walls, 2016). However, my personal journey with science has been influenced by members of my family, the limited resources at home, and my own curiosity. As a child, I discovered a deep love for science, particularly figuring out how certain things works, and had an unconventional idea of growing plants using human hair. It was a "hair-raising" experience. This concept, learned from my Puerto Rican aunt, sparked my interest in scientific exploration. While passionate about science, I realized I needed a formal mentor or understanding of what science truly entailed. This personal experience highlights the importance of diverse perspectives and mentorship in fostering scientific exploration and understanding. Science education aims to prepare students to understand scientific concepts and engage meaningfully with the world through a scientific lens. However, what does this mean to a young Latino male entering the science education profession?

Science teachers who adopt a social justice identity are instrumental in creating inclusive and equitable learning environments. This identity guides their knowledge, decisions, advocacy, and practices, enabling them to challenge school norms and structures that perpetuate inequities (Chen & Mensah, 2021). By recognizing and addressing the social and historical contexts of science, these teachers can promote diversity, equity, and inclusivity in the classroom. A social justice identity empowers teachers to identify and challenge systemic inequities within their schools and communities. This includes addressing issues such as unequal access to resources, biased curriculum, and discriminatory practices.

A social justice identity can help create a classroom environment where all students feel valued, respected, and included. By addressing students' needs and experiences, teachers can foster a sense of belonging and empower students to reach their full potential. Promoting diverse perspectives and incorporating diverse experiences into their teaching, science teachers can help students develop a more nuanced understanding of the world. This includes acknowledging the contributions of marginalized scientists and scientists of color, as well as exploring the intersection of science with social issues. Furthermore, fostering a sense of belonging and developing critical thinking skills, a social justice lens encourages students to think critically about scientific knowledge's social and historical implications. By examining how science has been used to marginalize or exploit certain groups, students can develop a more nuanced understanding of the relationship between science and society.

While I may not have had a fully developed social justice identity then, I recognized that something needed to be done. My innate sense of fairness and equity was slowly being uncovered and my desire to create a more inclusive and equitable learning environment became a valuable asset, and my experiences served as a foundation for further growth and development.

The importance of representation in the teaching profession is not a new topic in education. Representation goes beyond having a TOC in front of the class because it impacts the level of engagement of students of color, leading to higher academic performance and a greater sense of belonging. More problematic is the representation of TOCs in science education, where the voices and contributions of marginalized groups have not been recognized and shared. As Walls (2016) asked in their study of the representation of TOCs in science research, is an equitable approach to research being pursued? Is race and racism preventing K-12 students from benefiting from ongoing science education research? Walls(2016) explains the concept of structural barriers to equity, particularly in the context of structural racism in education and science education. The structural barriers to equity, such as the obstacles (i.e., curriculum tracking, prioritizing standardized test prep, non-lab science courses) embedded within social and institutional systems, prevent marginalized groups from achieving fairness and equal access to science learning opportunities. These barriers are often deeply ingrained in society and not easily visible or changeable by those directly affected (the oppressed), in my case, a young Latino male (Griffin, 2018).

Additionally, even people who benefit from these structures (those in privileged groups, i.e., white educators) may be unaware of their existence because they are so normalized. Furthermore, structural racism, such as the systems, practices, and policies that perpetuate racial inequality, often without individuals or groups consciously intending to be discriminatory. This kind of racism functions independently of people's personal beliefs or actions, meaning that it persists through societal structures, not just through overt racist behavior or intent, for example, the structures that act as gatekeepers to more rigorous science curricula and resources. These systems collectively create and maintain racial disparities over time, making it difficult for racial and ethnic groups to achieve equity. In science education, the notion of "science as white property" reflects how specific ways of knowing and practicing science, often tied to Western, Eurocentric traditions, are privileged. At the same time, other perspectives or approaches are devalued (Mensah & Jackson, 2018). This phenomenon is deeply rooted in systemic biases, where anything outside the dominant narrative is considered less legitimate. Furthermore, scientist "are convinced that objectivit prevents an oppressive culture because discoveries are independent of identity" (Le and Matias, 2019,22), which suggests that the belief in objectivity, the idea that knowledge, facts, or discoveries exist independently of personal biases, perspectives, or identities, is seen as a safeguard against oppression. The underlying argument is that if discoveries or truths are not influenced by the identity (e.g., race, gender, or cultural background) of the individual making them, then these truths should be fair and equitable, and thus less likely to perpetuate an oppressive culture. However, this perspective has been critiqued by scholars, particularly in critical theory and social justice fields. Critics argue that objectivity itself can be shaped by dominant cultural and societal norms, meaning what is deemed "objective" often reflects the perspectives of those in power, thereby perpetuating oppression. Furthermore, people's identities and lived experiences influence how they perceive and understand the world. Ignoring this can marginalize voices that challenge the dominant narrative. Even if a discovery is "independent" of an individual's identity, the systems within which discoveries are validated, shared, and implemented might still be shaped by oppressive norms (e.g., racism, sexism).

In the context of science education, the belief that objectivity prevents oppression might overlook how systemic inequities are embedded in the production, validation, dissemination of knowledge and the development of science educators and leaders of color. For a more inclusive and equitable approach, it's essential to critically examine whose perspectives are considered and valued in the process of discovery.

My experience as a science educator in a predominantly white suburban district exemplifies this dynamic.

Research indicates that the presence of STEM instructors who share the same racial or ethnic background as these students can significantly encourage their involvement in these subjects (Price 2010). However, during the 2017–18 school year, the demographic makeup of middle and high school mathematics and science teachers did not reflect the diversity of the U.S. student population. Approximately 80% of these teachers were White, while only about 7% were Black, and 8% were Hispanic. In comparison, the U.S. public school student population in 2019 was more diverse, with 48% White, 15% Black, and 27% Hispanic students (National Science Board, National Science Foundation, 2021)

When students see themselves reflected in their teachers, school leaders, and curriculum, it can lead to several positive outcomes. Increased engagement is one significant effect, as students are more likely to participate actively in class discussions and activities when they feel understood and valued. This connection fosters a more profound interest in learning and helps students relate more personally to the material. Furthermore, representation contributes to a greater sense of belonging in the school environment. When students see their identities and experiences acknowledged and respected, they feel they are an integral part of the school community. This sense of belonging is crucial for their social and emotional well-being, reducing feelings of isolation and alienation. It can decrease dropout rates and encourage students to pursue further education, knowing their voices and experiences matter. Latino students, especially English language learners (ELLs), often find themselves in learning environments where teachers have lower academic expectations for them due to assumptions about their language abilities or perceived academic struggles. When teachers assume that students who struggle with English are less capable of handling rigorous coursework, especially in subjects like science, they inadvertently limit these students' educational opportunities. This creates a cycle where students are not challenged or supported to reach their full potential (Atwater et al., 2013).

In terms of students' sense of belonging, such environments can be alienating. When students feel that their teachers expect less from them based on assumptions tied to their ethnicity or language proficiency, they may internalize these low expectations, leading to disengagement, a diminished sense of self-worth, and a feeling that they do not fully belong in the academic space. A lack of academic rigor or support signals to students that they are not seen as capable or valued in the same way as their peers, undermining their sense of inclusion in the classroom community. This dynamic negatively impacts their educational experience and limits their ability to fully participate, thrive, and feel a sense of belonging in the school environment.

Barriers to entry to the science and science education field present themselves as students needing more access to quality science education, financial constraints, and limited mentorship opportunities. In my case, I attended urban schools with low academic achievement ratings, and the coursework was a traditional comprehensive high school science program with labs. However, it lacked the tools and resources to provide rigorous science preparation. How do I know it could have been more rigorous? When I compared my preparation with that of other students in the science and math classes, I observed that I did not use the more sophisticated vocabulary. Compared to my peers from more affluent communities, I was not exposed to an elevated level of science-based literature and did not have access to more advanced math and science courses in middle school. The difference was noticeable. I am not saying that my teachers were unprepared or qualified, but could they have had higher expectations for me? Did they have the resources and support to provide us with more rigorous science learning experiences?

One of the barriers research consistently identifies is the unequal access to rigorous science education programs, especially at higher education institutions. Despite being accepted to several prestigious R1 institutions known for their rigorous science program, I could not attend due to financial constraints. Instead, I enrolled at a university that had evolved from a teaching college, offering science programs, including my bachelor's degree in chemistry.

While this institution provided me with personalized attention, particularly as one of the few students in the chemistry and secondary education track, it raises important questions about the trade-offs I faced. What academic opportunities were less available to me? How might my experience have differed in a more resource-rich, research-intensive environment?

As a young college student learning to navigate the complexities of higher education, balancing work, a rigorous chemistry degree, and the demands of teacher preparation, I did not always know what questions to ask. Should I have sought more external research opportunities? Could I have explored other pathways that combined my interests in science and education? More critically, how might my trajectory have shifted if financial barriers had not limited my choices?

Reardon et al. (2022) report, *"Is Separate Still Unequal? New Evidence on School Segregation"* argues that racial segregation in U.S. public schools continues to contribute significantly to racial achievement gaps. It highlights that racial economic segregation, where minority students are concentrated in high-poverty schools, drives these disparities, as such schools tend to be less effective than lower-poverty schools. Differences in teacher characteristics, such as experience and absenteeism, account for a notable portion of this inequality, contributing to unequal learning outcomes. The study suggests that segregation affects educational outcomes through mechanisms like disparities in school resources, teacher quality, and funding. It emphasizes the need for comprehensive policies to address educational inequalities and broader socioeconomic issues exacerbating school segregation. While contemporary segregation is no longer legally mandated, its effects remain significant, underscoring the need for further research to understand and address these dynamics better.

Despite earning a degree in chemistry and completing honors-level coursework, I was still questioned about my qualifications to teach chemistry and physics. It was not enough that I had the academic background; I felt I had to prove that I belonged in the science classroom by sharing my educational credentials to ease concerns from parents who might otherwise have complained. This questioning was not rooted in my actual competence but in underlying assumptions about who "belongs" in STEM. There were indeed some complaints, but fortunately, my supervisor supported me, recognizing my expertise and the unfair scrutiny I was facing.

This experience reflects the subtle, often unspoken cues encountered by people of color in STEM fields, cues that suggest we do not belong. Microaggressions, racial stereotypes, and the devaluation of our capabilities are perpetuated not only in K-12 classrooms but also in higher education. These microaggressions, like questioning whether I knew my content, serve as constant reminders that we are outsiders in spaces traditionally reserved for white students and educators. This is within-class segregation, where some expertise is valued, and others are under undue scrutiny.

The experiences I've shared highlight the concept of "whiteness as property," a term coined by scholars like Cheryl Harris (1993). This concept refers to the often unacknowledged privileges and advantages associated with being white. In the context of education, whiteness as property manifests in various ways. A curriculum that primarily centers on European and white perspectives, excluding or marginalizing the contributions of people of color. Furthermore, as students of color enter teacher preparation programs for science, they often encounter a persistent cycle of alienation, exclusion, and inequity rooted in the historical perception of science as a predominantly White domain (Mensha & Jackson, 2018).

As a Latinx educator, I often felt like an imposter, constantly questioning my qualifications and belonging in predominantly white spaces. This phenomenon, imposter syndrome (Clance, 1985) is particularly prevalent among people of color in STEM fields (Chrousos & Mentis, 2020). It can lead to debilitating feelings of self-doubt, anxiety, and a fear of failure. However, as Ramos & Wright-Mair (2021) argue, the issue is not inherent to individuals but rather systemic. Systemic barriers, such as implicit bias, microaggressions, and a lack of representation, contribute to the perpetuation of imposter syndrome among marginalized groups. *"It's not me, it's the system!"*

My personal journey, marked by both adversity and resilience, offers a unique perspective on the challenges faced by people of color in STEM. My story counters this dominant narrative by challenging the notion that there is only one legitimate way to "know" and "do" science. It calls attention to how people of color in STEM must continually prove themselves in unwelcoming or outright hostile spaces. If we do not challenge these dynamics, we allow a system to persist that limits access to scientific knowledge and perpetuates inequity, keeping students and educators of color on the margins. Le and Matias (2019) argue that *"If we continue to ignore whiteness and its operation within science, we essentially, regardless to whether or not we intend to do so, dehumanize our students of Color and choose to uphold a system that maintains White supremacy"* (p. 18-19). My experience demonstrates the resilience required to succeed in these spaces, but it also highlights the need for systemic changes that dismantle these harmful practices and biases in science education (Wilson-Lopez & Hasbún, 2023).

This analysis supports my earlier reflection on the barriers to accessing rigorous academic programs, especially for underrepresented students, and the systemic inequalities that limit their opportunities to thrive in more resource-rich environments. Just as segregation affects student outcomes, financial and institutional barriers create similar limitations in higher education, shaping the academic paths students can pursue. These reflections highlight my journey and the broader systemic challenges many students face, particularly those from underrepresented backgrounds, in accessing and thriving within the most rigorous academic environments. During my junior year of high school, I was fortunate to build a relationship with an "ally," a white male science teacher who believed in my potential and encouraged me to pursue my dreams relentlessly. This experience profoundly impacted me. This teacher reinforced the idea of representation's crucial role in motivating and inspiring students from underrepresented backgrounds. He made me observe and start questioning why I did not see anyone who looked or sounded like me. This ignited my belief in the transformative power of mentorship, a belief that has guided my career and this chapter.

Te veo! I hear you!! Me ves? Can you hear me??

"Who am I? An Afro-Latino of Puerto Rican and Honduran descent? American? Spanish, Spanglish, English speaking learner? Educator? Science educator? Leader? Educational Leaders? Son, Hombre, Brother, Primo, Father, Husband, Friend? A decent, vulnerable human being? Yes, Si, and Yes!!! To all of it!!!!"

These questions, which I have asked myself for as long as I can remember, served both to clarify and complicate my understanding of my personal and professional identity. Moreover, they played out throughout my personal and professional life, helping and confusing me. These questions helped me come to an understanding that my identity is multifaceted. This holistic self-recognition helped me embrace my ethnic, linguistic, and professional identities rather than classifying them. I have a combination of many roles—Afro-Latino, American, multilingual learner, educator, father, and more. In my personal and professional life, asking these questions helped me foster a deeper sense of belonging and purpose. However, it took me time to recognize parts of my identity and acknowledge the complexity of it and how it impacts and how to integrate my identity in all aspects of myself into my work, relationships, and leadership style.

Reflecting on my identity encouraged vulnerability and authenticity. I learned to embrace my identity as a "vulnerable human being," which added authenticity as a leader. It helps me develop a leadership style rooted in empathy and openness, which are crucial when guiding others, especially students and colleagues navigating similar struggles around identity and belonging. This awareness enhanced my ability to mentor others, as it fosters trust and deeper connections. Continuous reflection strengthened my sense of purpose and reinforced my role as an educator and leader in the context of my cultural and personal background. I continuously reminded myself that my experiences as an Afro-Latino in science and education have shaped my journey, giving me the strength to push boundaries and support others who share similar struggles. It sharpened my awareness of the unique perspectives and contributions I bring to my work, enabling me to advocate for greater inclusivity in education.

On the flip side, navigating multiple identities was overwhelming. In some contexts, certain aspects of my identity felt more valued than others, leading to internal conflict. For example, in predominantly white academic or professional spaces, my identity as an Afro-Latino science educator was underappreciated or questioned, while in other parts, such as a male teacher with a strong discipline approach, was leveraged more. The pressure to fit into certain boxes created confusion about how to bring all aspects of yourself into different environments authentically.

As someone who speaks Spanish, Spanglish, and English and comes from a rich, prideful cultural background, I experienced tension between navigating the expectations of different communities—whether within my family, work, or society at large. Questions of language, heritage, and cultural belonging created ambiguity around how to position myself in spaces where my experiences are not fully understood or acknowledged. Juggling multiple roles—son, brother, father, husband—alongside my professional identity as an educator and leader created tension. Each role comes with its own set of responsibilities and expectations, and finding a balance can be confusing. How much of my personal life should influence my professional life? And vice versa? How do I navigate being a nurturing family member while maintaining the authoritative stance that leadership sometimes requires?

Research on teacher identity development emphasizes the dynamic and evolving nature of how educators come to understand themselves as teachers, shaped by personal experiences, professional interactions, and sociocultural contexts. For science teacher identity development specifically, the process includes the general aspects of teacher identity formation and the unique challenges and influences that come from engaging with science content, pedagogy, and the broader educational system and scientific community.

Teacher identity is shaped by the social and cultural contexts in which teachers work and live. This includes their experiences with students, colleagues, and the larger educational community. Teachers draw on their backgrounds, i.e., ethnicity, linguistic, cultural, and education, to navigate their roles, which can influence their teaching philosophy and approach (Suarez & McGrath, 2022). Furthermore, the role of critical reflection on teaching practices, values, and experiences plays a significant role in identity development. Teachers who regularly engage in reflective practice often develop a stronger sense of self and purpose as educators. This type of reflection centers on challenging the individual to consider how their positionalities in the education system influence their actions and thoughts, which may lead to tension and conflict in identities (Gorski & Dalton, 2020).

Teachers often experience tensions between their personal beliefs and the expectations of the school or education system. Identity conflict can arise when individuals strongly identify with multiple identities with incompatible values, goals, or norms (Horton et al., 2014). These conflicts can spur identity development as teachers reconcile or negotiate these tensions to form a coherent professional identity. For instance, teachers may feel conflicted between student-centered teaching and the demands of standardized testing. More deeply, conflict may be the tension between the goal of the school, the curriculum program, the need to serve the whole child, and how to go about it. Teachers' identities are also influenced by their membership in professional communities. Collegial relationships, mentorship, and participation in professional organizations help teachers shape their identities, providing support, models, and feedback that guide their growth.

Teacher identity is not static. It evolves as teachers encounter new challenges, gain experience, and develop new understandings of their roles and practices. The interaction between their personal values, the changing educational landscape, and the professional environment shapes this continual process of development. While the general principles of teacher identity development apply to all educators, science teachers face distinct challenges and opportunities that shape their professional identity. Building on our understanding of general teacher identity, I now delve into the unique aspects of science teacher identity development.

Science teacher identity is shaped by various factors, including their pedagogical approach, content knowledge, and the broader educational context. A key aspect of science teacher identity is their perceived competence in both content knowledge and pedagogical strategies. Teachers who successfully integrate these two elements often feel more connected to their role as facilitators of scientific thinking rather than simply transmitters of knowledge (Puente *et al, 2021*).

Teachers who embrace a student-centered, inquiry-driven approach to science teaching may feel more empowered and connected to their identity as educators. This approach fosters critical thinking, problem-solving, and a deeper understanding of scientific concepts. Adopting an inquiry-based approach can represent a significant shift in teaching style, moving away from traditional lecture-based methods. This shift can lead to a stronger sense of purpose and fulfillment as educators. A strong foundation in science content knowledge is essential for effective teaching. Teachers who feel confident in their understanding of the subject matter are more likely to inspire student interest and engagement.

Successfully integrating content knowledge with effective teaching strategies is crucial for creating meaningful learning experiences. Teachers who connect abstract concepts to real-world examples and engage students in inquiry-based activities are more likely to foster a positive learning environment. However, new science teachers often adopt the teaching practices and norms prevalent in their specific school environment, even if these practices do not fully align with the values and experiences they learned during their teacher preparation programs. This could be due to factors such as the school culture, peer pressure to conform to the practices of their colleagues in order to fit in and be successful, and administrative expectations for teaching practices that may not always align with the values and experiences promoted in teacher preparation programs (Marco-Bujosa et. a., 2020).

Research on the intersection of race, identity, and science education highlights that teachers of color often face additional challenges in developing their science teacher identity. The perception of science as "white property" marginalizes alternative ways of knowing and doing science, reinforcing stereotypes that can undermine the identities of science teachers from underrepresented groups (Wilson-Lopez & Hasbún, 2023). These teachers may feel more pressure to prove their competence than their white counterparts, affecting their self-efficacy and sense of belonging in the field.

Science teachers, like all teachers, must navigate multiple, intersecting identities. For example, a teacher might identify as a scientist, an educator, and a person of color, each of which brings its own set of expectations and challenges. These multiple identities can sometimes be in conflict, especially in educational environments where there are stereotypes about who is "fit" to teach science, leading teachers to constantly negotiate their identity to align with their personal values and professional goals (Chen et al., 2021).

Research also indicates that strong mentorship and targeted professional development can play critical roles in science teacher identity development (Atkins et al., 2020). Opportunities to engage with other science teachers, participate in collaborative inquiry, and reflect on science teaching practices help teachers strengthen their professional identity. For teachers of color, culturally responsive mentorship (Han & Onchwari, 2018) can be crucial for navigating biases and challenges in predominantly white spaces. Furthermore, teachers of color are more likely to teach in high-poverty schools with limited resources, which significantly impacts science teacher identity. Teachers in schools with limited resources may struggle to enact the kind of engaging, inquiry-based science instruction they envision, leading to frustration and challenges in forming a strong professional identity. Conversely, supportive environments that promote innovation and collaboration reinforce positive identity development for science teachers.

From the perspective of a teacher of color, legitimacy and a sense of belonging play an important role. Many science teachers, especially those from marginalized groups, struggle with feeling a sense of legitimacy and belonging in science education. This is tied to the broader perception of who can be a scientist or a science educator. Teachers from underrepresented backgrounds may feel pressure to prove their worth in ways their peers do not. Teachers of color recognize the need to make science education culturally relevant, especially for students from diverse backgrounds. Those who successfully integrate culturally responsive teaching practices into their science curriculum feel a stronger connection to their role as educators who bridge scientific knowledge with students' lived experiences.

Research on general teacher identity and science teacher identity development highlights the importance of personal, social, and professional factors in shaping educators' sense of self. For science teachers, integrating content knowledge, pedagogical strategies, and the negotiation of belonging in the field of STEM are crucial to their identity development. Teachers' racial, cultural, and linguistic backgrounds also play a significant role, particularly for those underrepresented in science education. Addressing these factors through mentorship, professional development, and institutional support is key to fostering strong, confident science teacher identities. This can be both empowering and challenging, particularly when white males traditionally dominate STEM fields. For women and teachers of color, the journey to develop a STEM identity is often complicated by systemic biases and stereotypes about who "belongs" in STEM.

Recognizing identity development's complexity, What do Latino mentors need to do? In this next section, I will explain the crucial role mentors play in the personal and professional development of Latinx educators through a *testimonio*. I explore the cultural relevance of mentorship, demonstrating how community cultural wealth (Yosso, 2005) and shared cultural backgrounds can strengthen mentor-mentee relationships, disrupt whiteness as property, and support navigation through challenges and opportunities in higher education, teacher education, and the teaching profession (Burciaga & Kohli, 2018). Leveraging the work of Morales, A. R. et al. (2022), I will review the current research on mentorship for Latino educators while identifying gaps that need further investigation.

The Power of Mentorship: Supporting Latino Science Teachers

Mentorship plays a pivotal role in fostering Latino science teachers' professional growth and development. By offering guidance, support, and a sense of belonging, mentors can empower these educators to overcome challenges, develop their leadership skills, and make a lasting impact on their students and communities.

A supportive network is essential for encouraging Latino students to pursue science teaching as a career. Mentorship programs, scholarships, targeted recruitment initiatives, and community support can provide the necessary resources and encouragement. Mentors can guide the pathway to the profession, including coursework, certifications, and job search strategies. Additionally, discussing the financial realities of teaching, such as the cost of education, entry-level pay, and potential avenues for financial support, is crucial for helping aspiring Latino science teachers make informed decisions.

Sharing personal stories of overcoming challenges can inspire and motivate Latino students to pursue science teaching. By highlighting the resilience and determination of successful Latino science teachers, mentors can demonstrate that it is possible to achieve one's goals with hard work and perseverance. Mentorship for preservice teachers is a collaborative partnership between an experienced educator and a teacher candidate. The mentor serves as a guide, advisor, and supporter, helping the preservice teacher develop teaching skills, understand classroom management, and apply educational theory to practice. Beyond these core functions, effective mentorship also recognizes and leverages the preservice teacher's unique strengths and experiences. Understanding the novice's community cultural wealth (CCW) (Yosso, 2005), including aspirational, linguistic, familial, social, navigational, and resistant capital, is a valuable resource for preservice teachers to leverage throughout their personal and professional experience. Mentors can help them identify and harness these strengths to enhance their teaching practice. By reflecting on their experiences and navigating challenges both inside and outside the classroom, preservice teachers can develop a more holistic understanding of their role as educators.

Healing and community support are essential for Latino science teachers to navigate the emotional and psychological toll of working in a racially charged environment. Racial affinity groups can provide a safe space for educators to share experiences, support one another, and address common challenges. Building strong relationships with community organizations can also provide resources, advocacy, and a sense of belonging. Mentors can support preservice teachers in navigating the complexities of the education system, building relationships with diverse school communities, and addressing systemic barriers. Through mentorship, preservice teachers can develop the skills, knowledge, and confidence needed to become effective and culturally responsive educators.

Empowering Latino Educators Through Awareness and Action

Raising awareness is crucial for individuals to comprehend the intricate interplay of ethics, power, and values that shape complex societal issues. As a person of color, leader, mentor, educator, and father, I am dedicated to assisting others in recognizing the pervasive influence of class privilege and the stubborn persistence of racism.

The class privilege extends beyond mere financial wealth. It encompasses social and cultural capital, including access to power and authority, influential networks, and a nuanced understanding of how societal systems function to maintain the status quo. Those who are privileged often unconsciously benefit from these advantages. Racism is a deeply entrenched system of prejudice and discrimination rooted in race.

Its intransigence, or stubborn resistance to change, stems from a complex interplay of various factors. Overcoming the intransigence of racism necessitates a multifaceted approach that includes education, advocacy, policy reform, and individual action. By actively challenging our own biases, promoting diversity and inclusion, and striving for a more equitable society, we can contribute to dismantling the structures that perpetuate racism. What does this conversation about such tough concepts look and sound like in a mentor-mentee relationship? Let's explore how this conversation about such challenging concepts might unfold within a mentor-mentee relationship.

Remember, a mentor-mentee relationship should be a safe space for open dialogue and learning. The conversation between the mentor and mentee needs to focus on understanding the complexities of racism and developing strategies to address it. They should discuss various aspects of racism, including its historical roots, the role of implicit bias, structural inequalities, fear and uncertainty, and socialization. The mentor should provide a framework for understanding these issues and encourage the mentees to reflect on their experiences and beliefs. The conversation should aim to create a safe and open space for dialogue and learning, ultimately fostering empathy, understanding, and a commitment to social justice. By acknowledging the existence of class privilege and the intransigence of racism, we can develop knowledge, skills, practices, and dispositions to challenge harmful stereotypes, promote empathy, and work towards dismantling systems that perpetuate inequality.

Here, I propose some initial steps individuals could take to raise awareness in others, which I learned by making observations, asking questions, and through experience (some good experiences, some not so great). Individuals can take several proactive steps to support Latino educators in developing their leadership skills. These actions, informed by observation, questioning, and personal experience, can foster a more inclusive and equitable educational environment.

1. Seek Out Diverse Perspectives:
   - *Expand Your Reading List:* Read books, biographies, research, and articles that explore the struggles and contributions of marginalized groups, including Latinos, to broaden your understanding of diverse experiences and perspectives.
   - *Engage with Different Voices:* Seek out opportunities to interact with individuals from diverse backgrounds, such as conferences, joining professional organizations, or participating in online communities.
2. Practice Critical Self-Reflection:
   - *Examine Your Privilege:* Reflect on your position within the class structure and how privilege may have impacted your life experiences. Understanding your own privilege can help you recognize and challenge systemic inequalities.

- *Identify Implicit Biases*: Be aware of your own implicit biases and work to overcome them. Challenge assumptions and stereotypes that may perpetuate discrimination.
3. Amplify Marginalized Voices:
   - *Share Diverse Stories:* Use your platform to share the stories and perspectives of marginalized individuals, including Latino educators to raise awareness and challenge stereotypes.
   - *Advocate for Equity:* Speak out against discriminatory policies and practices that affect Latino educators and students. Use your voice to advocate for a more equitable and inclusive educational system.
4. Foster Inclusive Communities:
   - *Create Safe Spaces:* Work to create inclusive and welcoming environments for Latino educators and students. This can involve challenging discriminatory behavior, promoting diversity, and fostering a sense of belonging.
   - *Build Relationships*: Develop strong relationships with Latino educators and community members. These connections can provide support, mentorship, and opportunities for collaboration.

By raising awareness of their own cultural identity, power, and privilege, educators can understand the factors impacting their daily personal and professional lives and seek a mentor to support their growth as they navigate the system.

Creating a Plan to Find a Mentor

Finding a mentor involves a combination of self-awareness of your own needs, a proactive approach, and learning how to network. Although I was never taught how to find a mentor, I was able to use my observational skills to acquire one. Here are steps to help you identify and connect with a potential mentor.

1. Define Your Goals
   a. *Clarify what you need:* Are you seeking career advice, personal development, or help with a specific skill? Knowing your specific needs will help you identify the right mentor. When considering a mentor, remember that some may specialize in specific projects, while others offer more general, long-term guidance.
   b. *Consider long-term versus short-term goals*: For short-term goals, think about day-to-day tasks and set achievable objectives. While this may have been challenging for my family and I due to financial constraints, it's important to focus on progress, even if it's incremental. Long-term goals

should align with your dreams and aspirations. These could be monthly, semesterly, or yearly objectives. Keep track of your accomplishments to celebrate your progress and learn from setbacks or failures. Don't let guilt about past mistakes hinder your ability to take action in the present.

2. Identify Potential Mentors
   a. *Look within your network:* Start by considering people you already know, colleagues, professors, leaders in your organization, or industry contacts.
   b. *Expand your search:* If you need someone in your immediate network to be more suitable, attend industry events, seminars, or conferences where you can meet experienced professionals. In New Jersey, organizations like *New Jersey Association for Supervision and Curriculum Development* (NJASCD), *New Jersey Education Association* (NJEA), *New Jersey Science Teachers Associations* (NJSTA), and the *New Jersey Teachers of English to Speakers of Other Languages/New Jersey Bilingual Educators* (NJTESOL/ NJBE) offer opportunities to connect pre-service and novice teachers with resources, other professionals, and networking opportunities. These organizations often provide professional development, sometimes for free.
   c. *Join professional organizations:* Many industries have mentorship programs through associations or networking groups. Consider joining relevant organizations to expand your potential mentor pool and access valuable resources.

3. Research Their Background
   a. Once you've identified potential mentors, learn more about them. Review their work, career history, and contributions to the field. Make sure their experience aligns with your goals. When I started in the profession, social media did not exist, and finding out about someone and connecting most likely happened at events or sometimes by chance. Therefore, always be ready with an elevator pitch to introduce yourself, explain your goals, and explain how that person could support you. Don't forget to ask them a question to keep them engaged. If you have more time, try to establish some type of connection. Reach out to potential mentors for advice or feedback. You don't have to ask for mentorship immediately; let the relationship develop naturally. Be genuine and express why you admire their work and how their experience aligns with your goals. Show that you're eager to learn.
   b. Leverage Online Platforms like LinkedIn, Meetup, and specialized mentorship sites (Latinos for Education) offer ways to connect with mentors in your industry. While social media and online conversations are helpful, face-to-face conversations are just as effective.

4. Ask for Mentorship

a.   Once you've established rapport, you can make a formal request. Be clear about what you're looking for (e.g., regular meetings, advice on specific projects) and respect their time.

b.   Be specific: Share how you think they can help, and outline the commitment you're looking for (e.g., monthly check-ins, a few hours per quarter).

5.   Use Formal Mentorship Programs

a.   Many schools and professional organizations have formal mentorship programs that pair mentees with mentors. Research opportunities in your field.

6.   Be Prepared to Give Back.

a.   This is your opportunity to serve and be a leader yourself. Mentorship is a two-way street. Be prepared to offer something in return, whether it is helping your mentor with a task, providing feedback, or simply showing gratitude for their time.

Finding a mentor can be a valuable investment in your professional development. Be proactive and persistent in your search, and don't be afraid to ask for guidance and support. Remember, finding a mentor is a journey. Be patient, persistent, and open to new opportunities.

The Role of Support Systems in Nurturing Latinx Science Teachers

It is essential to provide robust support systems tailored to their unique needs to encourage more Latinx students to pursue careers in science education. These systems should address various challenges, including financial barriers, cultural isolation, and the lack of role models. As shared above, there is an immense, well-documented need to increase the number of Hispanic/other underrepresented groups of teachers in STEM disciplines. How do we start them on the path to becoming science teachers? First, start by asking the question, How can we best engage the Latino community? Begin by raising awareness of opportunities in the field of science. Work with them to provide exposure to science resources. Build an "inquiry community" centered on collaboration with mentors and colleagues. Help them identify and understand the issues involving power and accessibility to science education. Awaken them to the possibilities and inequities that lie ahead. Make them aware of the financial challenges and available resources. Help them set short and long-term career goals. Empower them to think beyond the day-to-day and to consider the long-term impact they may have in our scientific and technological society.

Mentorship Programs can be pivotal in guiding Latinx students toward science teaching. Mentors can offer invaluable advice, support, and insights into the profession. They can also help students navigate the complexities of higher education and develop the necessary skills for success. (Brown et al., 2018). Targeted recruitment initiatives are crucial for reaching out to Latinx students early in their academic careers. These initiatives can involve outreach programs, workshops, and partnerships with schools and community organizations. By highlighting the importance of science education and the opportunities available to Latinx students, we can inspire them to pursue this path.

Scholarships and financial aid are essential to alleviate the financial burden many Latinx students face. By providing scholarships and financial assistance, we help ensure that talented students have the opportunity to pursue higher education and specialize in science education. Community support is also vital. Latinx communities can play a significant role in encouraging and supporting students who aspire to become science teachers. This can involve providing mentorship, networking opportunities, and emotional support. Examples of communities that may be able to support the recruitment of potential Latinx science educators are:

- Hispanic Serving Institutions (HSIs)- institutions which have been instrumental in increasing the number of Latinx students in STEM fields, including science education (Turner et al., 2017)
- Grow Your Own (GYO) programs- programs that aim in adding to the teacher pipeline and have successfully guided students of color through the teacher preparation process, both formal and informal (Jones, et al., 2019)

RETAINING LATINO SCIENCE EDUCATORS: A CRITICAL IMPERATIVE

Retaining Latinx science educators is crucial for fostering equitable access to high-quality science education for all students. Latino educators bring invaluable cultural perspectives, lived experiences, and linguistic expertise to the classroom, which can significantly benefit students from diverse backgrounds. To effectively retain these educators, it is essential to provide ongoing, culturally relevant professional development opportunities that address their unique needs and challenges. These opportunities should focus on navigating systemic inequities, cultivating culturally responsive classrooms, and engaging with diverse student populations (Carter Andrews et al., 2019).

Morales (2018) presents several key ideas regarding the recruitment, preparation, and support of culturally and linguistically diverse (CLD) teachers, emphasizing their unique needs and contributions. They can bring invaluable cultural intuition and funds of knowledge to their classrooms however their success is not automatic. Institutions must implement intentional, informed, context-specific pedagogical practices and mentorship to help CLD teachers thrive, especially within systems rooted in predominantly white norms. This calls for a rethinking of teacher preparation programs to better meet the needs of diverse teacher candidates.

While in service, Pour-Khorshid (2018) underscores the necessity of supporting teachers of color through intentional practices and spaces that address their unique experiences with systemic oppression. The study highlights the importance of racial affinity groups for healing, critical reflection, and solidarity in overcoming the emotional and professional challenges imposed by white supremacy, patriarchy, and other intersecting systems of oppression. Such efforts are crucial for enabling educators to thrive both personally and professionally while breaking cycles of harm in education.

Call to Action: Creating the Next Generation of Latino Science Teachers and Leaders

Imagine a world where every Latino student has access to a dedicated science teacher who understands their unique experiences and can inspire them to pursue their dreams. By volunteering as a mentor, advocating for equity, supporting community initiatives, and sharing inspiring stories, you can play a vital role in making this vision a reality. Your actions can make a tangible difference in the lives of young Latinx educators. You can offer guidance, support, and a sense of belonging by providing mentorship and advocating for equity. You can help to dismantle systemic barriers that limit opportunities for Latino teachers. You can foster a more inclusive and supportive environment for all by supporting community initiatives and creating a future where Latinx science teachers are celebrated, empowered, and equipped to inspire the next generation of scientists.

CONCLUSION

The purpose of the chapter was to emphasize the necessity of mentorship in fostering professional growth and leadership among the Latinx community and to increase the recruitment and retention of Latinx educators, highlighting the challenges and proposing actionable solutions. I conclude this chapter by sharing some personal history. This year, I have had the opportunity to serve others in various ways. I've interacted with individuals from different races, ethnicities, genders, sexual orientations, veterans, family members, and friends. While I may not have had a formal mentor, I've always been surrounded by family and friends who offered valuable advice and support.

My journey into education was shaped by a deep-seated desire to make a positive impact on the lives of others, particularly within the Latinx community. Growing up in a predominantly minority neighborhood, I witnessed firsthand the disparities in educational opportunities that often hinder the aspirations of students from under-represented backgrounds. These experiences ignited a passion for education and a commitment to serving my community and creating more equitable opportunities for student's personal and professional growth. As a Latino educator, I believe that my presence in the classroom can serve as a powerful catalyst for change. By sharing my personal experiences and cultural perspectives, I hope to inspire students to reach their full potential and break down barriers that may limit their aspirations and opportunities.

The hashtag *#LatinoMentors/TeachersNeeded* highlights the urgent need for Latino educators and mentors in our schools. It calls attention to the underrepresentation of Latinx teachers in the education system, stressing the importance of role models who reflect students' cultural and linguistic backgrounds. By advocating for more Latino mentors and teachers, the hashtag encourages efforts to recruit, support, and retain Latinx professionals who can guide the next generation and promote diversity in the classroom.

I want to express my gratitude to Linda Murphy for guiding me on my leadership journey from the very beginning. From day one she told me that she was training me to be a LEADER. Her faith, service and mentorship has helped me grow as a person, a leader, a father, and a husband. Despite facing doubts and disagreements from others, Linda remained steadfast in her leadership, always prioritizing service and integrity.

A Tale of Resilience and Triumph

In the heart of the city, nestled amidst economically, racially, and ethnically divided neighborhoods, lived a young Afro-Latino named Alex. Alex, a first-generation Latino with immigrant parents, had always yearned for a mentor, someone who could guide him through the labyrinthine corridors of his possible future. Yet, despite his fervent search, he found himself adrift, a solitary figure navigating the unfamiliar waters of an urban American society.

Alex's journey was one of relentless pursuit of knowledge and opportunity. He possessed a linguistic capital that allowed him to bridge the gap between his native Spanish and the English language, opening doors to new worlds and experiences. His familial capital, rooted in the rich tapestry of his family's history, provided him with a strong foundation of values and traditions. It was a source of comfort and strength, a constant reminder of his heritage and the sacrifices made by his ancestors.

Despite his challenges, Alex refused to let his aspirational capital dwindle. He embraced a resilient outlook, refusing to succumb to the obstacles often confronting people of color. His dreams, his hopes, were an anchor in the stormy seas of adversity.

Alex's social capital was a network of diverse individuals he had cultivated over the years. These connections, forged through shared experiences and mutual support, proved invaluable in navigating the complex landscape of dominant institutions. Through his social network, Alex found mentors, opportunities, and a sense of belonging.

His navigational capital, honed through years of overcoming adversity, equipped him with the skills to adapt, persevere, and thrive in challenging environments. He learned to navigate the subtle currents of racism and discrimination, using his experiences as a source of strength and resilience.

Alex's resistant capital was a testament to his unwavering spirit. He had learned to resist oppression, to challenge injustice, and to stand up for what he believed in. His experiences had taught him the power of collective action and the importance of sharing knowledge and skills with marginalized communities.

His spiritual capital, rooted in his ancestral beliefs, provided him with a deep sense of purpose and meaning. It was a source of strength, inspiration, and support, guiding him through the most difficult times.

Though Alex had never found a formal mentor, he had discovered that his own resilience, determination, and the support of his community were the most valuable forms of mentorship. He had cultivated a rich tapestry of capital, a resource that would continue to sustain him and empower him to shape his own destiny. *

*This story was developed with the assistance of ChatGPT (OpenAI, 2024) and subsequently edited by the author.

REFERENCES

Atkins, K., Dougan, B. M., Dromgold-Sermen, M. S., Potter, H., Sathy, V., & Panter, A. T. (2020). "Looking at Myself in the Future": How mentoring shapes scientific identity for STEM students from underrepresented groups. *International Journal of STEM Education*, 7(1), 1–15. DOI: 10.1186/s40594-020-00242-3 PMID: 32850287

Atwater, M. M., Lance, J., Woodard, U., & Johnson, N. H. (2013). Race and ethnicity: Powerful cultural forecasters of science learning and performance. *Theory into Practice*, 52(1), 6–13. DOI: 10.1080/07351690.2013.743757

Bristol, T. J., & Martin-Fernandez, J. (2019). The added value of latinx and black teachers for latinx and black students: Implications for policy. *Policy Insights from the Behavioral and Brain Sciences*, 6(2), 147–153. DOI: 10.1177/2372732219862573

Brooms, D. R., Franklin, W., Clark, J. S., & Smith, M. (2018). 'It's more than just mentoring': Critical mentoring black and latino males from college to the community. *Race, Ethnicity and Education*, 24(2), 210–228. DOI: 10.1080/13613324.2018.1538125

Burciaga, R., & Kohli, R. (2018). Disrupting whitestream measures of quality teaching: The community cultural wealth of teachers of color. *Multicultural Perspectives*, 20(1), 5–12. DOI: 10.1080/15210960.2017.1400915

Carter Andrews, D. J., Castro, E., Cho, C. L., Petchauer, E., Richmond, G., & Floden, R. (2019). Changing the narrative on diversifying the teaching workforce: A look at historical and contemporary factors that inform recruitment and retention of teachers of color. *Journal of Teacher Education*, 70(1), 6–12. DOI: 10.1177/0022487118812418

Castro, A. S., & Calzada, E. J. (2021). Teaching Latinx students: Do teacher ethnicity and bilingualism matter? *Contemporary Educational Psychology*, 66, 101994. DOI: 10.1016/j.cedpsych.2021.101994 PMID: 34393328

Chávez-Moreno, L. C., Villegas, A. M., & Cochran-Smith, M. (2022). The experiences and preparation of teacher candidates of color: A literature review. *Handbook of research on teachers of color and indigenous teachers, 165.*

Chen, S., Binning, K. R., Manke, K. J., Brady, S. T., McGreevy, E. M., Betancur, L., Limeri, L. B., & Kaufmann, N. (2021). Am I a science person? A strong science identity bolsters minority students' sense of belonging and performance in college. *Personality and Social Psychology Bulletin*, 47(4), 593–606. DOI: 10.1177/0146167220936480 PMID: 32659167

Cholewa, B., Goodman, R. D., West-Olatunji, C., & Amatea, E. (2014). A qualitative examination of the impact of culturally responsive educational practices on the psychological well-being of students of color. *The Urban Review*, 46(4), 574–596. DOI: 10.1007/s11256-014-0272-y

Chrousos, G. P., & Mentis, A.-F. A. (2020). Imposter syndrome threatens diversity. *Science*, 367(6479), 749–750. DOI: 10.1126/science.aba8039 PMID: 32054753

Clance, P. R. (1985). *The impostor phenomenon: Overcoming the fear that haunts your success*. Peachtree Pub Limited.

Coffey, H., Putman, S. M., Handler, L. K., & Leach, W. (2019). Growing them early: Recruiting and preparing future urban teachers through an early college collaboration between a college of education and an urban school district. *Teacher Education Quarterly*, 46(1), 35–54. https://www.jstor.org/stable/26558181

Gándara, P. C., & Contreras, F. (2010). *The Latino education crisis: The consequences of failed social policies*. Harvard University Press. DOI: 10.2307/j.ctv13qftm4

Garza, R. (2019). Paving the way for Latinx teachers: Recruitment and preparation to promote educator diversity. newamerica.org/education-policy/reports/paving-way-latinx.teachers/.

Gist, C. D. (2019). Special issue: Grow your own programs and teachers of color: Taking inventory of an emerging field. *Teacher Education Quarterly*, 46(1), 5–8. https://www.jstor.org/stable/26558178

Gist, C. D. (2019). For what purpose?: Making sense of the various projects driving grow your own program development. *Teacher Education Quarterly*, 46(1), 9–22. https://www.jstor.org/stable/26558179

Goldhaber, D., Theobald, R., & Tien, C. (2015). The theoretical and empirical arguments for diversifying the teacher workforce: A review of the evidence. *The Center for Education Data & Research, University of Washington Bothell*, 202015-9.

Gorski, P. C., & Dalton, K. (2020). Striving for critical reflection in multicultural and social justice teacher education: Introducing a typology of reflection approaches. *Journal of Teacher Education*, 71(3), 357–368. DOI: 10.1177/0022487119883545

Greenleaf, R. (2002). *Servant leadership: A journey into the nature of legitimate power & greatness*. Paulist Press.

Griffin, A. (2018). *Our stories, our struggles, our strengths: Perspectives and reflections from Latino Teachers*. Education Trust.

Han, I., & Onchwari, A. J. (2018). Development and implementation of a culturally responsive mentoring program for faculty and staff of color. *Interdisciplinary Journal of Partnership Studies*, 5(2), 3. Advance online publication. DOI: 10.24926/ijps.v5i2.1006

Harris, C. (1993). Whiteness as property. *Harvard Law Review*, 106(8), 1709–1791. DOI: 10.2307/1341787

Horton, K. E., Bayerl, P. S., & Jacobs, G. (2014). Identity conflicts at work: An integrative framework. *Journal of Organizational Behavior*, 35(S1), S6–S22. https://www.jstor.org/stable/26610872. DOI: 10.1002/job.1893

Jones, R., Holton, W., & Joseph, M. (2019). Call me MiSTER: Black male grow your own program. *Teacher Education Quarterly*, 46(1), 55–68. https://www.jstor.org/stable/26558182

Kirmaci, M. (2022). Examining Latinx teacher resistance: From margins to empowerment. *Journal of Latinos and Education*, 22(5), 2102–2115. DOI: 10.1080/15348431.2022.2092108

Marco-Bujosa, L. M., McNeill, K. L., & Friedman, A. A. (2020). Becoming an urban science teacher: How beginning teachers negotiate contradictory school contexts. *Journal of Research in Science Teaching*, 57(1), 3–32. DOI: 10.1002/tea.21583

Martinez, J., & Santiago, D. (2020). *Tapping Latino talent: How HSIs are preparing Latino students for the workforce — Covid-19 Update*. Excelencia in Education.

Mensah, F. M., & Jackson, I. (2018). Whiteness as property in science teacher education. *Teachers College Record*, 120(1), 1–38. DOI: 10.1177/016146811812000108

Moje, E. B., Ciechanowski, K. M., Kramer, K., Ellis, L., Carrillo, R., & Collazo, T. (2004). Working toward third space in content area literacy: An examination of everyday funds of knowledge and discourse. *Reading Research Quarterly*, 39(1), 38–70. DOI: 10.1598/RRQ.39.1.4

Morales, A. R. (2018). Within and beyond a grow-your-own-teacher program: Documenting the contextualized preparation and professional development experiences of critically conscious Latina teachers. *Teaching Education*, 29(4), 357–369. DOI: 10.1080/10476210.2018.1510483

Morales, A. R., Espinoza, P. S., & Duke, K. B. (2022). What exists and "What I need ": In search of critical, empowering, and race-conscious approaches to mentoring from the perspective of Latina/o/x teachers. *Handbook of research on teachers of color and indigenous teachers*, 441-458.

National Center for Education Statistics. (2023). Characteristics of public school teachers. *Condition of Education*. U.S. Department of Education, Institute of Education Sciences. Retrieved [date], from https://nces.ed.gov/programs/coe/indicator/clr

National Science Board, National Science Foundation. (2021). *Elementary and Secondary STEM Education. Science and Engineering Indicators 2022*. NSB-2021-1. https://ncses.nsf.gov/pubs/nsb20211/

Ocasio, K. M. (2019). Nuestro camino: A review of literature surrounding the Latino teacher pipeline. *Critical readings on Latinos and education*, 95-116.

Open, A. I. (2024). Story generated by ChatGPT in response to a prompt provided by author. Retrieved [August 29, 2024], from https://chat.openai.com/

Pedraza, P., & Rivera, M. (Eds.). (2005). *Latino education: An agenda for community action research*. Taylor & Francis Group.

Pour-Khorshid, F. (2018). Cultivating sacred spaces: A racial affinity group approach to support critical educators of color. *Teaching Education*, 29(4), 318–329. DOI: 10.1080/10476210.2018.1512092

Price, J. (2010). The fffect of instructor race and gender on student persistence in STEM Fields. *Economics of Education Review*, 29(6), 901–910. DOI: 10.1016/j.econedurev.2010.07.009

Puente, K., Starr, C. R., Eccles, J. S., & Simpkins, S. D. (2021). Developmental trajectories of science identity beliefs: Within-group differences among Black, Latinx, Asian, and White students. *Journal of Youth and Adolescence*, 50(12), 2394–2411. DOI: 10.1007/s10964-021-01493-1 PMID: 34518982

Ramos, D., & Wright-Mair, R. (2021). Imposter syndrome: A buzzword with damaging consequences. *Diverse Issues in Higher Education*. https://www.diverseeducation.com/tenure/article/15109066/imposter-syndrome-a-buzzword-with-damaging-consequences

Reardon, S. F., Weathers, E. S., Fahle, E. M., Jang, H., & Kalogrides, D. (2019). Is separate still unequal? New evidence on school segregation and racial academic achievement gaps (*CEPA Working Paper No. 19-06*). Retrieved from Stanford Center for Education Policy Analysis: https://cepa.stanford.edu/wp19-06

Rogers-Ard, R., Knaus, C., Bianco, M., Brandehoff, R., & Gist, C. D. (2019). The grow your own collective: A critical race movement to transform education. *Teacher Education Quarterly*, 46(1), 23–34. https://www.jstor.org/stable/26558180

Solari, M., & Martín Ortega, E. (2022). Teachers' professional identity construction: A sociocultural approach to its definition and research. *Journal of Constructivist Psychology*, 35(2), 626–655. DOI: 10.1080/10720537.2020.1852987

Solórzano, D. G., & Yosso, T. J. (2002). Critical race methodology: Counter-storytelling as an analytical framework for education research. *Qualitative Inquiry*, 8(1), 23–44. DOI: 10.1177/107780040200800103

Stewart, M. D., García, A., & Petersen, H. (2021). Schools as racialized organizations in policy and practice. *Sociology Compass*, 15(12), 1–13. https://doi-org.kean.idm .oclc.org/10.1111/soc4.12940. DOI: 10.1111/soc4.12940

Suarez, V., & McGrath, J. (2022), Teacher professional identity: How to develop and support it in times of change, *OECD Education Working Papers*, No. 267, OECD Publishing, Paris, DOI: 10.1787/19939019

Turner, C. S., Cosmé, P. X., Dinehart, L., Martí, R., McDonald, D., Ramirez, M., & Zamora, J. (2017). Hispanic-serving institution scholars and administrators on improving Latina/Latino/Latinx/Hispanic teacher pipelines: Critical junctures along career pathways. *Association of Mexican American Educators Journal*, 11(3), 251–275. DOI: 10.24974/amae.11.3.369

Varelas, M., Segura, D., Bernal-Munera, M., & Mitchener, C. (2023). Embracing equity and excellence while constructing science teacher identities in urban schools: Voices of new Teachers of Color. *Journal of Research in Science Teaching*, 60(1), 196–233. DOI: 10.1002/tea.21795

Walls, L. (2016). Awakening a dialogue: A critical race theory analysis of U. S. nature of science research from 1967 to 2013. *Journal of Research in Science Teaching*, 53(10), 1546–1570. DOI: 10.1002/tea.21266

Wilson-Lopez, A., & Hasbún, I. M. (2023). Countering science as White property through linguistic justice. *Journal of Research in Science Teaching*, 60(3), 675–677. DOI: 10.1002/tea.21838

Wright, S. C., & Boese, G. D. B. (2015). Meritocracy and tokenism. In James, D. W. (Ed.), *International Encyclopedia of the Social & Behavioral Sciences* (2nd ed., pp. 239–245). Elsevier., https://doi.org/https://doi.org/10.1016/B978-0-08-097086 -8.24074-9 DOI: 10.1016/B978-0-08-097086-8.24074-9

Wright-Mair, R., Ramos, D., & Passano, B. (2024). Latinx college students' strategies for resisting imposter syndrome at predominantly white institutions. *Journal of Latinos and Education*, 23(2), 725–743. DOI: 10.1080/15348431.2023.2180366

Yosso, T. J. (2005). Whose culture has capital? A critical race theory discussion of community cultural wealth. *Race, Ethnicity and Education*, 1(8), 69–91. DOI: 10.1080/1361332052000341006

Zhai, Y., Tripp, J., & Liu, X. (2024). Science teacher identity research: A scoping literature review. *International Journal of STEM Education*, 11(1), 20. DOI: 10.1186/s40594-024-00481-8

Chapter 5
Centering Communities in Spanish Language Education:
Pathways to an Inclusive Approach for Heritage Learners

Dorie Conlon
https://orcid.org/0009-0001-5568-7482
Glastonbury Public Schools, USA

Marta Adán
Capitol Region Education Council, USA

ABSTRACT

Many Spanish language education programs in the US focus heavily on second language acquisition, often prioritizing communicative competence over intercultural competence (IC) and intercultural citizenship (iCit). This narrow emphasis on language development can overlook the unique needs of heritage speakers, leading to feelings of marginalization and potential attrition from programs. The authors argue that by centering the Communities goal area of the World-Readiness Standards for Learning Languages, educators can create inclusive Spanish language programs that better serve both heritage and non-heritage students. The chapter begins with an overview of heritage language learners followed by how the theoretical frameworks of IC and iCit can be used to center the Communities standards. The chapter then provides practical examples from the authors' classrooms, illustrating effective implementation strategies at elementary and high school levels. Finally, the authors offer reflective questions for teachers and program directors interested in centering the Communities standards.

DOI: 10.4018/979-8-3373-1340-5.ch005

Copyright © 2025, IGI Global Scientific Publishing. Copying or distributing in print or electronic forms without written permission of IGI Global Scientific Publishing is prohibited.

INTRODUCTION

Although the goals of Spanish language education are diverse, many programs—particularly those in the United States—tend to place a heavy emphasis on second language acquisition (Conlon & Wagner, 2022; Magnan et al., 2012; Magnan, 2008; ACTFL Task Force on Decade of Standards Project, 2011; and Darhower, 2006). This emphasis on communication over other goals can be seen in language teacher preparation, language program pathways (elementary through college), and materials available, such as textbooks, leveled readers, and online resources. Traditional programs that emphasize communication goals over other goals of language education, such as intercultural competence (IC), or intercultural citizenship (iCit), often ignore the unique needs of heritage speakers of the language which can lead to heritage speakers feeling othered and, ultimately exiting the program. In this chapter, we will argue that by centering the Communtines standards of the World-Readiness Standards for Learning Languages (The National Standards Collaborative Board, 2015), educators can design Spanish language courses and programs that are not only inclusive of their heritage students, but also better serve the non-Latinx and heritage students in their Spanish language programs through the development of IC and iCit. The chapter will begin with a description of heritage language learners within the context of the United States along with an overview of the theoretical models of IC and iCit. We will then describe how centering the Communities standards can serve heritage learners along with their non-heritage counterparts by helping all students develop IC and iCit. Finally, the chapter will conclude with practical examples from the author's own classrooms on how this theory can be put into practice at both the elementary school and high school levels.

HERITAGE LANGUAGE LEARNERS IN SPANISH EDUCATION IN THE UNITED STATES

Heritage languages can be referred to as home languages precisely because of their active usage in communities, making them far from foreign in the United States. In the case of Spanish, the language is arguably within the fabric of this country and should thus be treated as local by students and their teachers (Pascual y Cabo & Prada, 2018). Although once limited to predictable geographies, (im)migration trends put Spanish heritage language learners (SHLLs) in school districts across the map (Potowski, 2005). However, most World Language education programs—and thus teachers—lack the training to address Spanish as a heritage language rather than as a second language. Previous studies call attention to the greater need for an integrated Spanish teacher preparation model as well as professional development that includes SHLLs (Gironzetti & Belpoliti, 2021; Beaudrie, 2020; Carreira, 2018; Randolph, 2017). Historically, heritage language courses or programs emerge from educator-led efforts after noticing the differences between second language and heritage learners in terms of both their linguistic and affective features. In addition, approval from stakeholders is needed to run these courses deemed necessary for the allocation of resources. Although it is ideal to offer Spanish heritage courses, due to these nuances, it is far more common to have mixed heritage language learner (HLL) and L2 classrooms where teachers typically teach with the second language learner majority in mind.

Definitions vary regarding HLLs since it depends on how the learner is being evaluated. Oftentimes a broad definition is preferred where ethnic membership takes precedence over proficiency level, and the learner is an individual "raised in a home where a non-English language is spoken. The students may speak or merely understand the heritage language and be, to some degree, bilingual in English and the heritage language" (Valdés, 2001, cited by Beaudrie, 2020, p.417). However, in practice, a heritage learner is usually referred to as a heritage *speaker* that has a personal experience with the heritage language and this has led to some amount of language proficiency on a biliteracy continuum (Polinsky, 2014; Zyzik, 2016).

It is important to note that heritage language learners at times share traits with second language learners and other times with native speakers (Carriera & Chik, 2018). In comparison with their L2 counterparts, heritage learners have had a natural exposure to the language, granting them advantage in terms of pronunciation, syntax, and vocabulary (Montrul 2010). Recommended approaches such as learning from different entry points and utilizing purposeful grouping to avoid intimidation between students can lead to heterogeneous collaboration through students' strengths (Carreira, 2018; Walls, 2018; Henshaw, 2015; Bowles 2011). Since HLLs have had exposure to the target language outside of the classroom, they benefit from starting from their experiential knowledge, which requires macro-based instruction (Carriera & Chik, 2018). On the other hand, micro-based instruction which highlights discrete aspects of language, vocabulary, and metacognitive grammar concepts, can anchor most second language learners before focusing on their application. We will argue further that all students need both types of instruction but with a greater emphasis on the macro in order to connect to real life usage of language within communities.

Language gains in HLLs then must work in tandem with more personal or individualized instruction that views the whole student and their motivations, attitudes, and identity (Bowles, 2018). Moving past focusing on language use itself, HLL and L2 have different affective needs regarding group-membership that need to be addressed even when they are in the same course with similar proficiency (Carriera & Potowski, 2011). Prioritizing group-membership which Carriera (2018) links to identity work allows students to benefit from separate conversations that, when they come together, allow students to learn and hear from different perspectives. This aspect of prioritizing group membership is central to our argument in favor of prioritizing the Communities goal areas of the World-Readiness Standards for Learning Languages to benefit both HLLs and L2 learners in Spanish language programs as we will expand upon in the following section. At the same time, it is also important to note that many HLLs come to the classroom carrying the weight of feeling like they do not fit in perfectly with either group. Validating this feeling is as important to explore with students as it is to use as a motivator to continue to create space for and value the HLLs experience in tangible ways, such as allowing students to express themselves using their entire language repertoire in the case of translanguaging, which challenges monolingualism (García, 2009; Bucholtz, et al., 2017; Rosa & Flores, 2017).

As educators, our job is to distinguish HLLs' traits and focus on growing their assets, which have strong ties to the active use of *languaging* in their communities. Since students also have internalized ideologies that affect their concept of self as multilingual learners, there is a growing need to become conscious of these ideologies through critical language awareness (CLA) in order to respond to them (Beauderie & Loza, 2022; Holguín Mendoza, 2018; Leeman, 2018; Leeman & Serafini, 2016; Beaudrie, et al., 2014). This framework is defined as a theoretical and pedagogical framework that examines "how ideologies, politics, and social hierarchies are embodied, reproduced, and naturalized through language" (Leeman & Serafini, 2016). CLA, based on sociolinguistic principles, is needed in order to rewrite and erase the deficit mindset that both teachers and students can carry. Even when teachers view SHLLs through an additive lens, their practices can still carry a deficit mindset when perpetuating standard dialect while limiting nonstandard forms of language. Ultimately, students need a sociolinguistic and critical understanding of language and power to build healthy linguistic identities that honor language varieties (Leeman, 2005; Martínez, 2003), and they need teachers that work through this lens by maintaining critical self-reflection (Randolph, 2017, p. 283).

When making curricular decisions, it is essential to start with heritage learners first and build that bridge from home to school life whether those students are in a heritage or mixed (heritage and L2) classroom. Because heritage language learners' experience with language has been within the community outside of school, it is especially important to connect the two. Students need to be empowered within the classroom to strengthen and value their heritage community rather than see these entities as separate. Failing to address these dynamics can leave students accepting their "less than" monolingual selves and avoid language and culture maintenance and propagation. Identity is thus crucial to heritage language research (Leeman, et.al, 2011).

The latest iteration of goals for the HLL curriculum, as seen below, now include CLA, but it is still essential for instructors to address all of the goal areas and realize which are truly a priority when considering students' goals and motivations:

- the development of Critical Language Awareness in HL learning communities
- maintenance of the heritage language
- acquisition of a standard language variety
- expansion of bilingual range (i.e., building upon background knowledge)
- transfer of literacy skills (ie. writing genres)
- acquisition of academic skills in the heritage language
- cultivation of positive attitudes toward the heritage language
- acquisition or development of cultural awareness

(Beauderie, et al., 2021; Beaudrie & Wilson, 2022).

As a guiding principle, "Identifying goals and priorities should stem from this identity work that honors the affordances heritage students bring to the classroom. Thus, the established goals of heritage language courses only disrupt heritage language marginalization as far as they integrate and honor students' sense of self and community" (Adán, 2023).

Aligning with critical pedagogies (Hines-Gaither & Accilien, 2023; Anya, 2021; Byram, 2021; Glynn & Spenader, 2020; Dover, 2013) in the larger World Language field, heritage language education has the potential to address authentic conversations that uncover societal and personal injustice to create changemakers. Course goals and instruction that focus on inquiry and creativity, such as project-based learning and service learning are at the center of HLLs' agency especially because it connects learners to their cultural awareness and immediate communities in real ways (Beauderie, 2020; Burgo, 2017; Correa, 2011). These activities help implement a curriculum that emphasizes the cultural study of various Latinx community-based groups in the U.S. which matters most to HLLs (Potowski, 2012; 2018). Linking activities to student identities makes work for the class contextual, community-based, and uses meaning-making to further develop evolving identities within a critical framework. Ultimately, the goal is for students to act within their communities, exercising their critical agency which is defined as "the recognition of one's ability to act, together with purposeful action or activity" (Leeman, et al., 2011, p.484). Furthermore, critical agency involves one's own ability to take action, measuring its possible implications in one's context (p.485). Exercising one's agency to sustain communities has lasting effects on the learner and their environment. As such, in the following section, we will describe how these critical pedagogies can be enacted in order to center the Communities goal areas of the World-Readiness Standards for

Learning Languages and, as a result, create Spanish language education experiences that better serve our HLL students.

STRENGTHENING HERITAGE LEARNERS' CLASSROOM EXPERIENCES THROUGH THE CENTERING OF THE COMMUNITIES STANDARDS

As previously described, the unique needs and individual contexts of SHLLs in Spanish classrooms must be considered in order to make curricular decisions that help these students strengthen bonds with the language communities to which they belong. To accomplish this, Spanish teachers can look to the World-Readiness Standards for Learning Languages (The National Standards Collaborative Board, 2015; referred to hereafter as the Standards) for guidance. These Standards, which demonstrate that the goals of language learning go well beyond the developing language proficiency, include social and academic goals such as the exploration of one's own and other cultures, development of intercultural competence and critical thinking, and even finding enjoyment in the study of language.

First developed as the National Standards for Foreign Language Learning in 1996 and revised in 2015, the World-Readiness Standards for Learning Languages emphasize that language education can and should extend beyond mere communicative competence. In addition to the Communications goal area, four other areas—Cultures, Connections, Comparisons, and Communities—are integral to fostering a holistic language education. While the Communication goal area often receives the most emphasis in world language programs by both teachers and stakeholders (ACTFL Task Force on the Decade of Standards Project, 2011; Magnan, 2008; Conlon, 2024), research indicates that the Communities goal area is the aspect of the Standards that most strongly aligns with students' own goals for language education (Magnan, 2008). This misalignment between teacher priorities and student aspirations highlights the need for a more community-focused approach to language education and we argue that this is especially true for teachers of HLLs in order to design programs and curriculum that recognize and prioritize the unique experiences and needs of SHLLs in the Spanish Classroom. In order to accomplish this, we look at how Intercultural Citizenship (iCit) and Culturally Sustaining Pedagogies (CSP) can be used as guiding frameworks for teachers looking to create a more community-focused curriculum that is more responsive to the needs of HLLs.

As the Standards have evolved, so too has the understanding of culture and communities. The shift from teaching culture as static knowledge and cultural factoids to emphasizing the development of intercultural competence (IC) reflects an understanding that effective language education must prepare students to engage meaningfully with diverse communities. The 2015 revision of the Standards explicitly encourages students to interact with intercultural competence, rather than merely gaining knowledge about the cultures being studied. This evolution in the approaches to teaching culture underscores the potential for language learning to facilitate deeper intercultural connections, preferably within the communities of the languages being studied, which is especially true for HLLs who navigate multiple cultural landscapes both within and beyond the classroom walls.

In order to assist language teachers in teaching intercultural competence within their classrooms, the National Council of State Supervisors for Languages (NCSSFL) and ACTFL (the national professional organization for world language teachers in the United States, formerly named the American Council on the Teaching of Foreign Languages) introduced the Can-Do Statements for Intercultural Communication (ACTFL, 2017a) and an accompanying Intercultural Reflection Tool (ACTFL, 2017b). These frameworks offer actionable guidelines for assessing students' abilities to interact effectively with individuals from various cultural backgrounds and emphasize the importance of critical reflection in the development of intercultural communicative competence. However, while these statements provide useful benchmarks, they do not inherently address the complexities of identity formation, critical cultural awareness nor meaningful engagement within communities that are essential for all learners including HLLs. For that, we suggest language teachers can look to Byram's (2008) model of intercultural citizenship (iCit).

Using Intercultural Citizenship to reach
the Communities Standards

In introducing iCit, Byram (2008) calls into question the very purpose of language education and argues it should go beyond the acquisition of a new language. Byram cautions that when language education is taken in a narrow sense, in other words reduced to a focus on simply learning to communicate in a new language, then "it does not and cannot lead to a reduction in isolationism and can increase in internationalism" (pp. 28-29). With this in mind, in addition to developing language skills, Byram's model of iCit emphasizes the development of intercultural attitudes, knowledge, and skills in real-world contexts. Wagner et al. (2019) describe iCit as "being active in one's community—local or beyond the local—using one's linguistic and intercultural competences to realize and enrich discussions, relationships and activities with people of varied linguistic and cultural backgrounds" (p. XV). Thus, the iCit framework emphasizes that language learners should not only understand cultural nuances, but also actively engage in problems-solving within their communities, addressing social justice issues and fostering inclusion.

In addition, Byram (2008) stresses the importance of differentiating teaching methods to meet the diverse backgrounds and individual experiences of students, particularly acknowledging the power dynamics that affect intercultural interactions. Therefore, this approach is particularly relevant for HLLs who often grapple with their identities and cultural affiliations as described in the previous section. In describing what Byram's iCit model might look like within the context of world language education, Wagner et al. (2019) state

The significant characteristics of intercultural citizenship include:

- A concern about social justice and a belief in the values of humanistic thought and action;
- a readiness to encourage a questioning attitude that recognizes the positive and negative in a social group's beliefs, values and behaviors when evaluated against humanistic standards;
- a willingness to promote social action in the world and the creation of identification with others beyond the limits of national boundaries. (p. 24)

They also outline what that might involve in practice including 1) the "inclusion of students in decisions about the focus of their learning" 2) "learning activities that lead to engagement with people from outside the classroom" and 3) "taking decisions to participate in community life outside the classroom by drawing on competences acquired within the classroom" (p. 25). These elements of iCit have a strong overlap with the Communities goal area of the Standards which is defined as "communicate and interact with cultural competence in order to participate in multilingual communities at home and around the world" (The National Standards Collective Board, 2015, p. 99). The Communities goal area is further broken down into two individual standards: 1) school and global communities—defined as "learners use the language both within and beyond the classroom to interact and collaborate in their community and the globalized world" (p. 101) and 2) lifelong learning—defined as "learners set goals and reflect on their progress in using language for enjoyment, enrichment, and advancement" (p. 106). As we can see, this goal area of the Standards overlaps with iCit as it encourages language education that leads to students using the language to collaborate with communities within and beyond classroom walls as well as encouraging students to take ownership of their own language learning journeys. We argue, therefore, that teachers can use Byram's iCit framework in order to center the Communities goal area of the Standards in order to create Spanish language programs and curriculum that is more inclusive to the needs of the HLLs in our classrooms.

Approaching communities through Culturally Sustaining Pedagogies

While Byram's (2008) iCit model can provide language educators with a roadmap to approaching the Communities goal area of the standards, Spanish language educators must also consider how this can be done in a way that intentionally sustains the various cultural backgrounds and communities represented in their classroom. For this, teachers can look to Culturally Sustaining Pedagogies (Paris & Alim, 2017) to provide a critical lens on how cultural competence can be developed while simultaneously ensuring students remain firmly grounded in their home culture and communities.

Based on the work of its predecessor, Culturally Responsive Pedagogies (Ladson-Billings, 1995), CSP is a framework for teaching that "seeks to perpetuate and foster—to sustain—linguistic, literate, and cultural pluralism as part of schooling for positive social transformation" (Paris & Alim, 2017, p. 1). Essential to CSP, Paris and Alim call for sustaining dynamic community practices which recognizes and honors the ways in which students fashion new linguistically and culturally dexterous ways of enacting their cultural practices within the communities they belong. In other words, Paris and Alim caution teachers against viewing our students' cultures and communities as static and fixed, but instead enact pedagogies that "address the well-understood fact that what it means to be Black or Latinx or Pacific Islander (as examples) both remains rooted *and* continues to shift in the ways culture always has." (p. 9, emphasis in the original). CSP also sets itself apart from its predecessors by moving beyond the established asset-based mindset by creating a space of transformation for students and their impact on their own communities (Paris & Alim, 2014). This recognition that the cultures and communities of the HLLs in our Spanish language classrooms are transformative and ever-evolving is essential for designing curriculum inclusive of our HLLs' needs and personal goals. We believe, in the context of Spanish language education for HLLs, this requires educators to ensure students remain rooted in their rich cultural histories and practices while simultaneously equipping and encouraging them to participate in emerging cultural practices and communities.

CLASSROOM EXAMPLES

In this section, we will share two examples from the authors' own classrooms to exemplify how using ICit to center the Communities standards can create language learning experiences that help heritage learners not only develop their communication skills but connect to their own communities, as well as build new language communities with the non-heritage students within their school. These examples fall under practitioner inquiry, in which the authors were also the instructors seeking to theorize their practice and improve their classrooms by responding to their unique contexts (Gilchrist, 2018; Cochran-Smith & Lytle, 2009). The inclusion of these classroom examples is not so that the reader has lessons they can replicate in their own settings, but rather serve as an example of how the previously mentioned theoretical concepts can be applied in practice within our individual contexts. Therefore, readers are encouraged to critically reflect on the examples given and use them as potential sources of inspiration for their own instruction, while at the same time acknowledging that your students' needs will inevitably vary greatly from our own. We also remind the reader that the lessons and activities presented here are but a snapshot in time from our dynamic classrooms which shift and evolve not only as our learners' unique needs change each year, but also as we as educators grow and improve our own practice.

The first example comes from [author 1's name]'s elementary school classroom in which her fifth grade Spanish students explore how art has been used for protest within Latinx communities at home and abroad. Within this unit, students first learn what protest means and then discuss examples of how *arpilleras*—brightly colored burlap collages—were used in Chile to protest the Pinochet dictatorship. Students then explore a wide variety of protest art from the Spanish-Speaking world including music, graffiti, fashion and more. The unit concludes with a community-building activity in which students critically examine their own communities and create their own protest art designed to make positive change. This classroom example will demonstrate how students were able to reach the goals of the Communities standards with their limited, novice-level language skills. In addition, an analysis of how this activity had benefits for the heterogeneous group of heritage and non-heritage language students within the classroom.

The second example comes from [author 2]'s high school classroom in which most students are upperclassmen, heritage language learners. Students in this advanced course explore critical topics that affect global and local Latinx populations throughout the school year, while allowing students to layer their self and community-based reflections as they design their own inquiry projects that interact with the units of study. During this process, students make their own connections by applying and enacting their critical lens to explore a passion topic that affects them individually but also as a member of a larger community. In one sample project, students explore the topics of colorism to design their multimodal research project with the intention of advocacy. Student reflections through a multi-unit project reveal not just the depth of their understanding of said societal issues but the development of self-efficacy needed to see themselves as agents of change.

Strengthening Communities through the Art of Protest with Elementary Spanish Students

The following section is a description of how I redesigned a unit that I, [author 1's name], have implemented over the course of several years in my fifth grade Spanish classes at [school name], a kindergarten through fifth grade elementary school in [Town, State]. Students in the [town] language program begin studying Spanish in school in first grade with two classes a week, each lasting 25 minutes. In second grade, Spanish classes increase to three times a week and continue with this frequency until the students reach fifth grade. At [Name] School, approximately 20% of the student population in the school describe themselves as Hispanic or Latino according to data collected by the Connecticut State Department of Education (Connecticut State Department of Education, n.d.). In addition, approximately 25 students' families report speaking Spanish as their primary language at home with additional students speaking Spanish at home in addition to another primary language. These students whose home language is primarily Spanish are enrolled in the same Spanish language classes as the general population at the school. Therefore, a typical Spanish class consists of L2 students with novice-level Spanish language proficiency alongside SHLL students whose language skills are at significantly higher proficiency level, often at the intermediate high level as measured by the ACTFL Assessment of Performance toward Proficiency in Languages (AAPPL). In this chapter, I will describe how I redesigned a unit on arpilleras—a traditional artform from Chile—into a unit on protest art. This new unit was designed and implemented with the goal of reaching the Communities goal area of the Standards and will emphasize the outcomes for the HLL students who participated in the project.

My Positionality

I am a third generation white Puerto Rican who began learning Spanish in the public school system in sixth grade. When I first began studying Spanish, I was very excited to learn the language that had been lost by my grandfather's strong desire for his family, especially his children, to assimilate into U.S. American culture. My mother had always communicated to me her regret about not being able to speak the language, so when the opportunity to learn Spanish finally arose in my life, I was eager to learn with hopes of connecting to my own Puerto Rican heritage. Instead, I found Spanish class to be rife with stereotypical, and sometimes even racist, representations of the Spanish-speaking cultures being studied. Learning Spanish, therefore, did not bring me closer to my family heritage or help connect me to the Latinx communities in my local areas. This experience, however, inspired me to approach my own journey as a Spanish teacher with a critical lens, leading to me becoming particularly interested in how we can teach Spanish in ways that will lead to equity, anti-racism, and social justice. It is now my desire to help students see the varieties of Spanish-speaking cultures not as static stereotypes, but as dynamic and, most importantly, alive within our own communities. This is especially true for my Latinx students consisting of both SHHs and L2 learners of Spanish.

Critical Reflection

In the [District] Spanish curriculum for 5th grade, the students explore the year-long essential questions "who am I?" and "who are the people of the Americas?" with a particular cultural focus on the people of Perú and Chile. Through these overarching essential questions, students develop proficiency in the Spanish language alongside exploring cultures through different thematic units including topics such as daily routines, descriptions of personalities, and school schedules and subjects. The academic year concludes with a unit on *arpilleras,* a type of artwork described as "brightly-colored patchwork pictures stitched onto sacking [which chronicle] the life of the poor and oppressed in Chile in the 1970s and 1980s during the totalitarian military regime of General Augusto Pinochet Ugarte." (The William Benton Museum of Art, n.d. a, para. 2).

The unit on arpilleras as it is currently written as part of the district curriculum serves as a way to help students advance their Spanish language skills by describing examples of this artwork in detail. Because this form of art depicts different aspects of life, students are able to use vocabulary they have already acquired in previous years—such as animals, descriptions of houses and communities, fruits and landscapes, and the clothing people are wearing—as well as learn new vocabulary related to the specific cultural context of the arpilleras—such as animals and vegetables specific to the geographical region. Although a strength of this unit as written in the district curriculum is that it draws on students' previous knowledge and skills while offering new opportunities for language development within a cultural context, upon reflecting critically on this unit, I felt students were tasked with simply describing an arpillera without understanding its true origins and purpose: to "document and denounce oppression in a country where all normal channels of free expression were closed" (The William Benton Museum of Art, n.d. a, para. 4). In addition, the arpilleras chosen for the curriculum and published in the district common assessments and the student notebooks given to all fifth graders largely depict seemingly happy farming villages, which could be either non-political arpilleras or arpilleras created by the government for propaganda purposes (see The William Benton Museum of Art, n.d. b, Propaganda section for an example).

In addition to the lack of cultural origins of the arpillera itself, another critique I had of this unit is the heavy focus on language development over the other goals of Spanish language education. The unit itself is based in a cultural context and can provide opportunities for students to explore Chilean and Peruvian culture, however, the expectations and common assessments designed for this unit are largely for students to simply name and describe cultural products. In no way were students truly reaching the Cultures goal areas of the Standards which requires students to be "an explorer, using language to investigate, explain, and reflect on how perspectives are exhibited in the practices and products of a culture" (National Standards Collaborative Board, 2015, p. 68-69) Furthermore, the unit falls short of helping students meet the Communities goal area of the standards as it does not provide students to opportunities for engagement with or meaningful connection to Chilean and Peruvian cultures and communities nor students' own cultures and communities.

My overall reflection on this unit was that it flattened a complex cultural product that originated as a form of protest against a cruel dictatorship and presented it to students as an opportunity to do little more than name the cultural products they can see depicted in the artwork. By the end of the unit, students could use their novice level language skills to name and describe objects found within an arpillera (e.g. *En la arpillera, hay tres llamas blancas. Hay dos mujeres en un jardín con papas y zanahorias.* [In the arpillera, there are three white llamas. There are two women in a garden with potatoes and carrots]), but they could not tell you how or why arpilleras were used by Chilean women to spark change within their communities. Therefore, in reimagining what this unit could look like if I used iCit to center the Communities goal area of the Standards, I decided to redesign the unit as one in which students could explore the essential question "How can art be used as protest?"

Implementation

Rather than beginning with my traditional approach of presenting facts about arpilleras to my students, I started the revised unit with an inquiry-based approach, engaging students on the first day by exploring the question "What is art?" This broad question provided an entry point for students to brainstorm and discuss art using basic language these students have already acquired. To guide their conversations, I projected photos of different forms of art—such as paintings, music graffiti, poetry, fashion and more—from a variety of Spanish-Speaking communities including those abroad, but also examples from our local communities, including those from Latinx artists. During this initial introduction to art, the students discussed their opinions on the different artwork shared and began to consider what messages the artists were trying to send within their artwork. This initial discussion allowed students to begin to make connections between art forms and cultural expression and also served as a way to review where in the world Spanish is spoken as we would work together to identify the individual communities where the art was created.

On the second day, I introduced students to arpilleras by presenting students with authentic examples of arpilleras created during the Pinochet dictatorship as we began to explore the question "how can art be used as protest?" I encouraged the students to use their language skills to describe what they observed, including the familiar such as houses, cars, trees, mountains, and women, as well as the unfamiliar such as a sign reading "*¿Dónde están?*" (Where are they?) Once the students had listed and described everything they saw in the tapestry, I then asked them to consider what they *couldn't* see, leading to a discussion about the absence of men in this particular arpillera. This crucial, yet simple, observation set the stage for the following day's lesson in which students revisited the same arpillera but discussed the meaning behind the phrase "*¿Dónde están?*" and its connection to the disappearance of men during the dictatorship. This led to an exploration of how Chilean women used this artform that they had created to protest human rights violations, giving voice to their experiences under an oppressive regime which was hostile towards free speech. In the following classes, I brought in additional examples of arpilleras, and we continued in the same pattern of describing each one, what we saw, what we didn't see, and finally determining the message the artist was trying to portray within the arpillera. Through these linguistically simple, yet cognitively and emotionally complex discussions, students began to understand the importance the arpilleras had in documenting the atrocities committed during the Pinochet dictatorship, but also the resilience, strength and ingenuity of the women who invented this artform.

The final phase of this unit shifted to student-led projects in which students were asked to collaborate in small groups or work independently to identify a problem within their own communities and create a piece of protest art—in the style of an arpillera—that aimed at raising awareness and fostering change. This task encouraged students to apply their understanding of arpilleras while using their developing Spanish language skills to identify and describe social issues within their communities that were personally meaningful to them. At the end of the unit, students engaged in a presentational speaking activity where they formally presented their protest artwork to the class and described what they had created. In this way, students were still working towards the linguistic goals set by the district in which they describe what they see in an arpillera, but did so in a way that was meaningful to them and helped them develop the skills of intercultural citizenship.

The artwork the students created varied greatly between the groups and included messages such as students should be given less homework, our community needs to work together to recycle more, adults and children should develop habits to decrease their screentime on mobile devices, adding recess to the schedule for students in grades seven through twelve, greater acceptance of LGBTQIA+ students at school, banning TikTok for reasons of national security, having more access to healthcare in the United States, combating racism within our community, and increasing social support systems for the homeless. In addition to the student work focusing on primarily issues facing the United States, there were also several pieces of artwork based on Latinx communities abroad. For example, one student who was born and raised in Perú until age five, decided to create a work of art titled "*para*" (stop) which protested the current president of Perú. In reflecting on her artwork, this student commented that she cares about her home country and worries about the path the current president is on, especially since much of her family still lives there. She encouraged her classmates to care for her country and "hope for the best" because she did "not want my home country to be in a bad condition". In presenting her work to the class, she not only described her arpillera-style art, but she also gave students additional background information about Perú and brought family photos to share with her classmates.

After presenting their artwork to the class, students were encouraged to upload photos of their finished projects to our online workspace in which students could view and comment on each other's work. Although the majority of the comments were written in English, it was evident that students were reflecting deeply on the social issues and messages found within the art. For example, one student commenting on the artwork protesting the current president of Perú wrote "Peru is such an amazing country and I hope the best for it" and "your drawing is amazing and goes right with your statement!!!" On another project in which students encouraged fellow fifth graders to get more sleep at night, one student commented "I completely agree that us 5th graders need more sleep because when I get up, I can barely open my eyes because it's so early and I'm exhausted. Also, because it's important to get sleep so that we can pay attention in class. I love this idea!" and another student suggested they work together to write a letter to the Board of Education to petition for later school start times in order to ensure students get enough rest. Through these comments, students are building a sense of community through working together to solve real problems in their lives, aligning with the critical cultural awareness aspect of Byram's (2008) model of iCit and aligning with the Communities goal areas of the Standards. These—and additional—outcomes will be discussed in detail in the following section.

Outcomes

The revised unit had several notable outcomes in creating more inclusive Spanish language educational experiences for SHLLs in an elementary aged classroom along with their L2 peers. These outcomes were the direct result centering the Communities goal area of the Standards through the guiding frameworks of iCit and CSP. This new unit was intentionally designed to be more closely aligned with the Communities goal area of the Standards which emphasize using the language both within and beyond the classroom to participate in multilingual communities within and beyond the classroom walls as well as using language for personal enjoyment. By connecting students' Spanish language development to their lived experiences and encouraging them to address real-world problems through art, this unit attempted to bridge the gap between academic learning and community engagement.

One significant outcome was that students began to see the role of Spanish language education to develop skills beyond solely the acquisition of language. The project encouraged students to recognize the connection between their studies in Spanish class and the communities they are a part of, enabling them to use skills they learn in class for social engagement. By designing and describing their own pieces of protest art, the language classroom became a place where students learn to particulate their perspectives on local problems, positioning students as agents of change. In addition, the process encouraged students to reflect on and critique their own communities through a social justice lens. In this newly revised unit, students used Spanish not only to describe cultural products, but to actively participate in a broader conversation about social justice, reflecting the shift from a passive student acquiring language to an active learner using language for real world purposes as emphasized in the Communities goal area of the Standards.

Although the focus of the unit shifted to prioritize the Communities standards, students continued to develop the language skills necessary to meet the district's performance standards on common assessments. In reviewing results from their assessments, students still performed at the same level as peers across the district in their ability to describe arpilleras, but the classroom experience was more meaningful, especially to HLLs who had already mastered the linguistic components of this unit. Rather than being bored as they were required to practice using vocabulary and language structures they already knew, the HLL students in my classroom experienced the ability to put their language to use, drawing on historical cultural practices while adapting them to their current contexts resulting in a more equitable Spanish education.

In addition, the inclusion of SHLLs in a more meaningful capacity by allowing them to reflect critically on the different communities to which they belong, had a positive impact on engagement. In the past, the SHLLs in my classroom would often find themselves bored when using simple vocabulary to describe the propaganda-style arpilleras presented in class, but this new approach allowed the students to utilize their language skills to address community issues, thereby making their classroom experience more relevant and engaging. In this way, the SHLLs experienced a form of cultural participation and community involvement by drawing on the historical practice of creating protest arpilleras while, at the same time, adapting them to their current contexts in a meaningful way.

Future Steps

While the implementation of the redesigned unit was successful in many ways, I continue to critically reflect on how to improve this unit for future years. One glaring opportunity for improvement is for greater involvement with communities beyond the classroom walls. While this is an important aspect of the Communities standards, within Byram's (2008) model of iCit, and within CSP, I struggle to fully engage my young students with outside communities. This is partly due to the restrictions my district places on community engagement for the safety of my young students. Within the context of their education my students, for example, have limited access to field trips, strict protections preventing them from online communication with individuals outside of our school district, and restrictions on bringing outside community members inside the school. While these restrictions are necessary for the protection of my students at such a young age, they do pose significant barriers for creating a curriculum that truly centers community. Although these barriers exist, I remain committed to finding creative solutions for more community involvement in my curriculum.

In addition, while my students sharing their protest artwork with one another in the classroom was an engaging activity, in future years I would like to look for additional opportunities for the students to share their art with audiences beyond the classroom. For example, as described in the previous section, one student suggested they write a letter to the Board of Education regarding changing school start times in order to ensure students get an adequate amount of sleep. While writing this letter would have the most benefit if it were written in English, as all of our school Board members speak English as their primary language, in future years I would like to seek out opportunities for cross-disciplinary collaboration in which the students can write these letters as part of their English Language Arts classwork.

Finally, I continue to look for ways in which the students themselves can take ownership of the curriculum and influence the objectives and learning opportunities found within. One step towards that goal was allowing students to choose their own issue to protest that was meaningful to them, although this aspect of the unit occurred very late within the sequence of lessons. For future years, I would like for students—especially SHLL students—to have more autonomy from the beginning of the unit when exploring different forms of art and how they can be used to protest. I believe that together, these changes will help students invest more in their Spanish language education and find personal fulfillment in their language learning journeys.

Empowering Student Identities and Communities through Activism

This section describes a course that I, [author 2's name], have taught for eight years and redesigned the last two years at CREC's (Capitol Region Education Council) [School Name]. Although the course takes place at a 6-12 public magnet school, the classroom example offered takes place specifically in an 11th-12th grade classroom of mixed heritage language and second language learners. These students are in the highest level of Spanish available in our district referred to as ECE (Early College Experience) Spanish through the University of Connecticut. Spanish 3178, Intermediate Composition in Spanish, is run concurrently at the secondary and collegiate levels; therefore, students receive both a university grade and a high school grade at the end of the course.

The school and district has an approximate 35% self-identifying Latino/ Hispanic population (as indicated on school forms and reported by Connecticut State Department of Education). It is important to note that this population is not homogenous and breaks down into different nationalities, races, and socioeconomic backgrounds. They also come from different regions, such as Puerto Rico, Perú, Colombia, la República Dominicana, Ecuador, México, Guatemala, Honduras, Chile, Argentina, and Cuba (roughly in respective order). Within this demographic the Spanish heritage language learners (SHLLs) that take this course vary in language proficiency and from students who are recent (im)migrants to others whose families reside in Connecticut for two or three generations. Not all the heritage students in the school are able to take part in this class or even in the pathway designed for Spanish heritage learners due to the resources available and scheduling conflicts. For this reason, the study is bounded by a narrow definition (Valdés, 2001) of what it means to be a heritage learner, which requires language output in addition to input comprehension (albeit of a variety of proficiency levels).

Since Spanish is the only World Language offered at the school, Spanish heritage students were usually placed in higher-level Spanish courses (typically starting at level 3). However, even at a higher level, most of the existing courses follow a second language acquisition curriculum that is not tailored to the heritage learner. Over the course of the last five years, SHLLs are now placed in a new pathway of courses before taking the dual-enrollment courses in writing and conversation through the University of Connecticut. It is within this culminating course level that heritage and second language learners meet. As a prerequisite, most students in the course either took Spanish II- IV as second language learners or have taken Spanish for Heritage Speakers I and II before being admitted during their junior or senior year to take this course. A few students blended these two pathways due to being language learners of varying proficiency levels.

The students at this level are also familiar with the school and district requirement of a capstone project that entails a research element. Although students can complete their own research in any discipline, they currently complete and present original research during their senior year. Students in this course are either juniors enticed by the idea of exploring a capstone project before their official one the following school year or seniors who can add to their research interests with a language component.

My Positionality

I am a first generation white Cuban-American who primarily spoke Spanish until I entered the school system in Pre-K where I grew up in New Jersey. Although I quickly became bilingual, I became English dominant through my education as I spent less time with my parents and grandparents during the day. Thankfully, I was able to maintain my Spanish due to the adults in my home life who not only required me to speak in Spanish, but also instilled in me the importance of preserving my culture through my bilingualism and believed my linguistic assets would also benefit my future career. As I went through school, I felt a desire to access a multilingual education, but unfortunately did not have access to one. World languages at the time were not offered at my parochial elementary and middle school. The first time I had access to taking a Spanish course was in High School where I was unfortunately placed in Spanish I, with students who never spoke Spanish, due to a placement test that apparently did not portray my fluency. I spent most of my time bored in class, repeating basic vocabulary words and writing skits along with the rest of the class. Even though these courses were taught through a grammar based curriculum, I remained motivated to "perfect" my Spanish and gain the metacognition of verb tenses. Ironically, this experience was the impetus that led me to the desire of becoming a Spanish teacher and later furthering my studies in Latin American history, literature, and education at the collegiate level to continue learning about my heritage and other Latinx experiences both in and out of the US. As an educator, my goal is to offer a more equitable learning experience than the one I had to both HLL and L2 learners by applying student-centered and critical pedagogies to work towards social justice.

Course Overview

The curriculum of this course was revamped in two significant ways: (1) units were not just cumulative but also interconnected and (2) each unit guided students to follow a personal passion project that stemmed from the units' content. The course was redesigned by adding strategic layers to the communicative and language skills needed to retain the integrity of a Spanish intermediate writing course at the postsecondary level while extending its impact on the learner and their community. The previous course syllabus prioritized connecting writing genres to a variety of topics and not explicitly connecting those topics through the students' own final project. Although College Board's six themes of Spanish Language and Culture related to families and communities, beauty and aesthetics, global challenges, science and technology, contemporary life, and personal/ public identities were still present, the student and instructor goals now surpassed focusing on these themes throughout the units of the course by anchoring them with a purpose. Instead, these topics were embedded within four quarters, with each quarter adding a piece to students' individual research journey throughout the year. The vision for the entire course was introduced from the beginning of the year but also reiterated throughout each unit in order to tie communicative objectives with their application in students' communities.

Table 1 below outlines the sequence of writing genres used to conduct research in order to root those genres in units that allow students to start with themselves (their identity and experiences in education) and then progress from this starting point to the topic of activism, where students can begin to reflect on themselves as researchers and activists as they move on to topics that impact greater society, such as environment, and health. Ultimately, these changes were made with heritage language learners in mind without ignoring that L2 learners also benefit from identity work that continues throughout the course, making the learning process not only student-centered but also authentically generated. As stated in the previous section, heritage language education needs to emphasize identity (Leeman, et.al, 2011), however, this approach also aligns with critical pedagogies leading world language education. By enacting a critical lens as educators with students by questioning the normalized, hierarchical, and intersecting features of oppression (Bell, 2016), we are gaining understanding or making progress in social equity (Randolph & Johnson, 2017). In fact, by incorporating the social justice standards of Identity, Diversity, Justice, and Action with the 5 C's, the community standards can be accomplished while making World Language less foreign and centralize the Spanish-speaking world locally and globally while learners also learn more about themselves through language learning (Randolph & Wang, 2022). In the sections that follow, the logistics of this course is also used to understand how facilitating units where students can make their own connections locally and globally can lead not only to action as an end product but rather as a way to empower students' overall socio-emotional well-being by strengthening their self-efficacy and leading them to enact their own agency in response to valued personal experiences and research.

Table 1. Units' writing genres linked to final project

Unit	Writing Genre	Personal Project
Education and Identity	Personal Narrative	Problem; Positionality
Waves of Activism in Latin America and the US	Argumentative	Research Questions; Literature Review
The Environment and Technology	Argumentative: Comparative	Literature Review; Methodology
Physical and Emotional Health	Description and Analysis	Data Collection; Analysis of data

Within these units, I developed assessments aligned with unit topics that adhere to the district's shift toward standards-based grading, categorized into practice, formative, and summative assessments linked to specific skills. Practice assignments, which had minimal stakes, primarily included participatory activities such as notebook entries), small group discussions, and homework focused on grammatical structures. Digital notebooks encompassed unit content, featuring multimodal texts that addressed key issues. Some slides were designated as practice, while others included rubrics for formative assessments, culminating in application slides that contributed to summative assessments. These summative evaluations were integrated into students' year-long projects, facilitating connections between their work and the thematic content of the units.

Implementation

In this section, I highlight the aforementioned course units through one student project, which involved two students. I will refer to the students with the pseudonyms Dania and Gabby for their privacy. At the time of the course, both students were juniors and although they worked independently towards their final project; for most of the course, they decided to work in a complementary fashion during the last quarter since they were interested in the same topic of colorism in Latin America and the US but for different personal connections. I argue that their process of learning and researching needed to be different since their personal connection to the Spanish language and the various communities in which the language is present is distinct. Both students are heritage language learners and highly proficient in Spanish, proven in their daily interactions using the language and its varieties both inside and outside of the classroom. In addition, both students surpassed the requirements to achieve their Biliteracy Seal through a proficiency exam taken in the final weeks of the school year that documented their intermediate - advanced proficiency in the skills of writing, speaking, listening, and reading in accordance with ACTFL.

Dania is a SHLL in the narrow sense as described previously in the section offering a synthesized definition of HLLs in this chapter. She can also represent most of the HLLs in the course as she is first generation born in the U.S but has strong linguistic and cultural ties to her parents' country, in her case the Dominican Republic. Gabby is a HLL but of Portuguese and has gained comparable proficiency in Spanish through her schooling and contact with the Spanish-speaking community. Most of Gabby's close friends are Spanish speakers and she often hears and uses her Spanish in Hartford in addition to her Brazilian Portuguese. Although I closely follow Dania's process through the course, Gabby's experience also offers unique insight as both a HLL and L2 learner, especially when she joins forces with Dania. In addition, it is important to disclose that I am selecting this student project in efforts to highlight how their learning process most closely reveals how HLLs (and their L2 counterparts) can access their own critical awareness through their diverse experiences centered on social justice themes that affect Latinx communities.

Centering Language Experiences. The first unit centers students in their own identity and relationship to their languages. Even though HLLs in the course could easily relate to the topic, L2 students were also asked to reflect on the language varieties they use in addition to their own perceptions of Spanish-speakers in their own communities, including of course our diverse school community. Since languages exist within communities, it is essential to establish how linguistic abilities such as code-switching and translanguaging are active ways of using language to access not only information but connections with others. Identifying the "appropriateness" (Flores & Rosa, 2015; Rosa & Flores, 2017) and prestige given to particular language varieties puts into question what truly gives value to languages and how communities actively use them. By creating linguistic autobiographies all students in the course had to validate what languages they had access to in a multimodal presentation that visually represented the student's languages throughout their life. Dania chose to represent her languages of English, Spanish, and Spanglish as kingdoms–separate castles. As seen below in Figure 1, each castle represents the text over it where each of her languages has a formal and informal varieties however, the last castle of Spanglish mixes all forms of Spanish and English and "En nuestra comunidad, el idioma Spanglish nos une porque es algo que creamos para el idioma estándar" (In our community, the Spanglish language unites us because it is something we created to be the standard language). Although she shows inconsistencies in developing her critical language awareness, such as placing her Caribbean Spanish below other varieties as informal, Dania starts to question this status quo by placing quotes around phrases such as "español correcto" (correct Spanish) or "hablarlo correctamente" (speak it correctly). She also places herself in a position of knowledge and describes herself as someone who can code switch and refers to this as "una habilidad" (a skill). Similarly Gabby represented English, Spanish, Brazilian Portuguese, and her own mix of languages Portu-English and Portuñol. Her mapping did not include a metaphor of representation as Dania's poster, but she included examples not just of what these varieties sound like or mix but also where she uses them. Similar to Dania, she cannot use her languages or their varieties in any context but can identify where they are welcomed and offer her access to communicating with different communities.

Figure 1. Linguistic Autobiography

The culmination of the first unit was to write a personal narrative with writing techniques such as a "hook," dialogue, and vivid description. Without making a conscious decision at the time, Dania's personal narrative would thread through all of her coursework. It not only led her to her research topic for her final project, but also became a piece of writing she would polish during the last quarter and submit to a writing competition on language and identity for Hartford secondary students. Her narrative retells a personal event when she was in first grade that made her wrestle with her identity. She hooks the reader with the question "¿Eres adoptada?" from a peer in her elementary school who asked her bluntly if she was adopted when the student saw Dania's mother when she came to the classroom that day as a volunteer because the mother had much darker skin than her daughter. This incident ultimately gets Dania, along with her mother, escorted to the principal's office after Dania left a mark across her peer's face in anger for such a remark. She links both her language use and her physical appearance at times validating her as being dominicana and other times not "dominicana enough." She describes this position at school as "vivía entre dos mundos–dos idiomas, uno de la escuela y el otro el de mis padres, pero nunca pensé realmente en el color de mi piel ni de mi familia." Even though she knew of the divide between her home language and her school language, she looked at "la variedad del color de piel en mi familia como simplemente normal". In her analysis of this event now in 2024, she says that this event "fue la lección más valiosa en mi vida" (was the most valuable lesson of her life) and "La experiencia fue necesaria para que yo realmente conociera quién soy como una persona y como puedo valorar mis idiomas, mis experiencias y las raíces que llevo en la sangre" (The experience was necessary for me to know who I am as a person and how I can value my languages, my experiences, and the races that I carry in my blood). Her other realization in the present is that her peer was also "Latina" and thus the lack of understanding of language and race existed within our community–even in a place like our diverse capital city of Hartford. Instead of succumbing to this event and to the larger issues it uncovered, she feels empowered towards the end of the essay to apply and put into action what she believes about herself and not let others judge or "categorize" her. In the final version of the essay, she adds a poem that affirms no one gets to decide who she is and how she identifies by outward appearances.

¿Quién define lo que es actuar dominicana?

O ¿Cómo lucir dominicana?

Hierve mi sangre cada vez que escucho a alguien decir algo sobre mi apariencia o mi familia porque puede ser que no nos parezcamos, pero siguen siendo míos.

Yo soy fuerte,(no scratch that), somos fuertes.

Rechazamos estas observaciones.

Her courage is felt particularly in the line where translanguaging is present "Yo soy fuerte, (no scratch that), somos fuertes" referring to how her family and perhaps also those who also stand up against racial and linguistic generalizations are strong in their act of resistance to narratives that question their identities and the subjective authenticity of these identities.

Instead of writing a traditional narrative, Gabby wrote a letter to her future self. She hopes that the future Gabby would be able to tell her of events where she no longer worried about how others thought of her and thus did not hold back from accomplishing all of her dreams. Her dialogue was between present and future Gabby highlighting a duality within the same person. She did not delve into her language use in this piece, however, in her journal entries for the course she speaks to language variety by defining Portuguese from Portugal instead of Brazil as "extraño" (weird) and supporting this by noting the difference in pronunciation, which she also demonstrated for the class. A debate ensued in the classroom as to whether or not the official peninsular languages of Castilian Spanish and Portuguese are perceived as more formal and ultimately where did that idea of formality come from if we apply what we know about colonialism, particularly in Latin America. Seeing Gabby retract her previous statement in preference for Brazilian Portuguese only as far as admitting that her preference had to do with her contact and experience with the language itself can give insights into how critical language awareness can work to balance language resistance with cultural competence through a contextual understanding (based on sociolinguistic principles). Both Dania and Gabby wrestle with how their languages and their varieties represent their identities. They value the skill associated with reading a crowd and acting "appropriately" in that given context, but they are also building a new narrative for themselves that rejects the power found in the listeners rather than the speakers–who actively and continuously shape language and their own identities.

Taking on an Activist Lens. The second unit on waves of activism sought to awaken a sense of urgency to respond to an issue and allow students to search for role models who have fought for their issue of personal interest. Unit content serves as examples to encourage students to define activism for themselves and see how they can take on the empowering role as activists within a social justice paradigm. Reviewing concepts such as inclusivity, empathy, solidarity, advocacy, and action and how they are interconnected to work towards social justice offered different lenses within activism that students could relate to and see in tangible historical examples, regardless of their topic of choice. By providing students with choices and liberty of topics, they could be encouraged to focus on their purpose and truly care, blurring the line between the personal from academics or the learning process itself. Offering choice with this end can unite "los dos mundos" (the two words) that Dania refers to in her personal narrative. Looking towards role models in greater society allows for students to see themselves in those that may seem out of reach that have laid the groundwork for the student's passion. After all, the point of exposing students to activism is to inspire and empower them to respond in their circles of influence. To see themselves as capable actors in their communities, students need to understand the work of those before them as they take on their own stance against injustice.

Advocating for a cause often leads to interacting with a multilingual audience and towards the end of this unit, students wrote a letter to an activist related to their cause or someone they believed could help them understand their chosen cause better. Secondly, students presented a digital or handmade poster that could convince an audience to support their cause through argumentative and persuasive methods such as pathos, logos, and ethos, as outlined in Figure 2 below. In the process of preparing these projects, students began collecting and annotating a mix of texts (such as articles, videos, podcasts, and social media posts) on a research log provided.

Figure 2. Argumentative poster

Dania and Gabby both worked on the same topic of colorism and its impact in Latin American communities (both abroad and in the US) during this unit. Since their personal experience with the topic differed, so did their research questions and ultimately the work they presented in the form of a letter and poster. Dania wrote to Amara la Negra, a young Dominican singer and actress that openly used her platform in both Spanish and English to work against colorism and instead celebrate blackness in Dominican American culture as well as in the Latinx community. In a reflection about writing this letter, Dania says "Cuando leí la entrevista con Amara la Negra pensé...esa soy yo!" Even though Amara is Dominican- American like Dania, there is an element of surprise in her reflection. Finding and identifying with someone from her background that went beyond her local community created feelings of validation especially considering that Amara la Negra is a public figure.

Through Dania's research she also expanded the extension of her community by citing an article of the effects of colorism in Peru and internationally through social media, specifically focusing on the use of filters. During a portion of class time dedicated to finding sources, it was a conversation with Gabby that led Dania to find an article on the impact of filters. Since the students knew they were researching the same topic, I would catch a glimpse of collaboration like this. Dania was most interested in how colorism infiltrated the perception of beauty in different contexts, yet she had not thought about the impact of filters making a person lighter skinned and the impacts it had on the person posting and viewing these posts. When I conferenced with their table, Dania and Gabby's faces lit up as they recounted their conversation in Spanish with words like "filter," "post," and "story" inserted in English. Until then, they did not have sources to prove what they had observed in social media, but quickly they began to find them, which fit best with Dania's project. This moment was pivotal for the students to begin working more closely together and ultimately, as seen further, decide to work together on their final project. Student led research, as seen in this example, not only validates students' experiences but widens their awareness of social issues in different contexts.

Gabby wrote her letter to congresswoman Llhan Omar since the representative has fought for stricter laws in the US to prohibit whitening products due to its negative impact on consumers' health. Gabby cites how these products are found around the world, proving colorism impacts the concepts of beauty in contexts of power, coloniality, and in this case capitalistic opportunity through products that sell whitening at a high cost. Gabby spent her downtime from finding articles to cite the danger of these products by looking at ads and false promises that she said, "honestly make me sad." The marketing aspect would prove to be complementary to Dania's personal experience, driven by the questioning of her identity. In Gabby's reflection in preparation for her final project, she goes beyond the physical health issues caused by these products for capitalistic gains by connecting to their impact on "el estándar de belleza y felicidad de las personas" (beauty standards and the happiness of people). Ultimately, this addition is the result of collaborating and working with Dania who realized in the transition to Unit 4, on physical and emotional health, that by affecting beauty standards, colorism also impacts the socio-emotional well-being of individuals.

Connecting the Local with the Global. As Dania and Gabby continued to collaborate, they also expanded the reach of their communities by making global connections. The fight against colorism existed within them through unique personal experiences however, it was further developing as they built a wider perspective of how iterations of their experiences are found in different contexts. Dania and Gabby already had a connection between their experiences in the US and the countries their families emigrated from, Dominican Republic and Brazil, respectively. Their first point of contact that expanded their experience of "the local" came precisely from their interaction. Soon through more research, they found that colorism existed in a colonial context–something all of their examples of Latin America shared, along with the US. Gabby in particular found that the whiting products she was researching existed in other continents. Although the students first thought of skin whiting in terms of denying Black ancestry, this generalization was debunked as they were reminded through products in Asia for instance.

Simultaneously, Unit 3 focuses on the environment and indigenous movements in the Mesoamerican region, specifically in Guatemala. Although there are students with families from Guatemala in the school, there are none in this particular class. The unit concludes with a guest speaker, who also happened to be a mother of students in the school. Although she was born in Connecticut, she worked through the Peace Corps in Guatemala, where she later met her husband, and developed and maintains strong ties to K'iche women that were protecting their textile designs from being patented by cheap labor, often found on their dress, güipiles, that had been passed down for generations. She worked specifically with the group AFEDES (Asociación Femenina para el Desarrollo de Sacatepéquez) and now continues to support their artisan work through her own non-for-profit. In preparation for her attendance, students explored questions about tradition preservation in their physical notebooks, watched a video and read social media content from "El Movimento Nacional de Tejedoras," learned specific vocabulary to discuss Guatemalan textiles in context through visual content, and created questions for our visitor that were first drafted and then submitted on a class Google document. Their challenge was to ask questions that were also somehow linked to their research interests. I challenged them to think that their passion project was their lens from which to analyze and connect to other experiences. Although our guest focused on the preservation of ancestral textile making, this issue did not stand alone. Since textile making has been mainly practiced by indigenous women, this topic brought up women's rights, fair trade economics, access to education, cultural appropriation, effects on the environment, language preservation, as well as racial and linguistic discrimination. Perhaps more so than focusing on the issues, this example offered students an example of resilience and of sincere allyship.

In a collaborative effort, students were asked to work in groups to write thank you letters to our speaker while also explicitly connecting their own interests in activism. Students were placed in groups according to their project topic in order to foster the collaboration needed to make strong connections between what they knew and what they learned. Once the drafted letters were completed, groups were formed again to become editors of one section of the letter or email format. This time, groups had to synthesize the class' ideas that were pertinent for their part of the letter. The learning goals related to the writing genre were still accomplished but with an end task that pushed beyond the hypothetical by replying to someone in the school community.

The connections between the presenter's topic and students' projects was, for most, challenging. It was through class discussions and workshop time with the smaller groups that students built the confidence to reach their own connections and conclusions. For instance, in a reflection, a student noted that even though we had discussed discrimination in terms of how a person speaks in the first unit, "También hay países latinos donde la gente discrimina a los demás por hablar un lenguaje nativo o indígena." Thus, students were beginning to not only connect their projects to larger global issues, but they were also doing so through the continuous and interconnected nature of the course.

Dania and Gabby worked in the same group for the collaborative thank you letter to our presenter. In line with their project, they focused on the larger topic of beauty standards and this time made connections to the indigenous context, which had been ignored in their project until this point. During a class discussion, Dania was particularly taken aback by the speaker's examples that showed white Latina models appropriating traditional K'iche clothing and designs that were mass produced. In their letter, they chose to compare the commercial and capitalistic gains of colorism through whitening products with the appropriation and mass production of ancestral textiles:

> "...específicamente, un proyecto que hicimos habla de cómo las empresas se benefician del colorismo vendiendo productos para blanquear. Estos productos hacen mucho daño a la salud de las personas, pero generan mucho dinero a las empresas por eso lo siguen haciendo. Esto nos recordó lo que usted dijo a nuestra clase sobre cómo las empresas más grandes estafan a los artesanos indígenas, tomando su trabajo y vendiéndolo más barato, lo que afecta a estos artistas indígenas porque su arte es su fuente principal de dinero."

The comparison poignantly ends on a positive note, revealing that the students felt inspired to learn from beacons of hope. They state: "Muchas veces hay gente que se aprovecha de personas en otros países. Usted ha tenido un impacto positivo en las vidas de esas personas. Especialmente en las vidas de las jóvenes. Su historia nos inspira aprender más sobre otras culturas y brindar ayuda a quienes lo necesitan."

Thus, focusing on resilience in others, in this case both the guest speaker and the tejedoras (weavers) from Guatemala, allows students to imagine an alternative reality and feel empowered in the process of acting in response to the current state of the world.

Applied Learning. During the last unit, students were able to plan their own research through qualitative and/or quantitative data collection and proposals for action in response to what they learned throughout the year. The traditional research paper genre was not completely lost but built its momentum in a portfolio style that required editing. The act of learning was an on-going, dynamic process. Some students built upon the intention of developing previous work each unit as was the case with Dania, whose topic remained the same and a steady evolution occurred as the course content shaped her ideas in an organic way. Other students shifted interests in the process of moving through the year and its units. Instead of ending the course with a traditional research paper, students were prompted to (re)-write four short documents (introduction, literature review, methodology, and analysis/conclusions) and then present their research and their personal growth through the study of their topic in a multimodal presentation.

Dania and Gabby decided that their action project would be to interview three staff members about how beauty standards, particularly those influenced by colorism, affected self-esteem, happiness, and well-being. They would record their interviews and code the major themes. They chose two Latinx teachers and one African-American male to gather a different perspective within our school community. Their questions were previously drafted and approved to make sure that they aligned with their research questions. The workshop process allowed them to take ownership of their project without just emphasizing the finished product. Ultimately, their presentation to the class consisted in a slide deck that synthesized their process through the course, from independent work to working in partnership and deciding what to do within their school community to address their issue.

When they reflected on how their project could impact their future, Dania said that "Nos gustaría crear conciencia en nuestra escuela para enseñar a otros sobre el colorismo y ayudar a evitar que esto suceda o ayudar a alguien que esté pasando por este problema" (We would like to raise awareness in our school to educate others about colorism and help prevent this from happening or assist someone who is experiencing this issue). Gabby complemented this reflection adding that colorism should be addressed in school and that their presentation could be used to discuss experiences of people "en la vida real" (in real life). Dania states that others can become aware that "esto no le está sucediendo solo a un grupo de personas, sino a todos nosotros" (this is not just happening to a group of people but to all of us) and Gabby sees the impact that changing opinions of other students could produce a change in generations to come after them. Both students also saw the impact of their research as significant to their community due to the vast impact that colorism has on both those actively hurt by it or those who perpetuate its existence. Their project could also propel the change of mindsets in their school and ripple outward.

Outcomes

The revision of this course incorporated the 5 C's, particularly the Communities goals of the Standards, which allowed HLLs and their L2 counterparts to deepen their critical awareness while empowering them to advocate for themselves and others. Students embarked on a journey of self-discovery that valued their experiences throughout the learning process, which allowed students to add to their funds of knowledge (Moll, et al., 1992) in a culturally sustaining classroom environment (Paris & Alim, 2017). It is from this space that students could critically analyze their surroundings, make connections that extend their sense of community, and create new knowledge that adds to who they are without subtracting or erasing. Approaching language and identity work through Critical Language Awareness (CLA) also allowed students to identify the power communities possess as dynamic and live creators of what continuously become social norms. Having this awareness allows students to make more conscious decisions with their language use, giving them more agency to participate in different social contexts.

Without losing sight of the language and research skills that were working side-by-side, students began to see language as a tool that connected them to more intricate communities rather than a means to an end. Students could use their languages and their varieties in different contexts to reach a wider audience even in more private conversations. By applying and reflecting on course material, they were able to then self-direct their own projects to continue learning with a personal purpose that exceeded the acquisition of language itself. Instead, there was an emphasis for language acquisition to align with the purpose of communication. Students were able to start from an issue that had personal significance to them and their local community, which enabled them to connect with and learn from contexts that would otherwise seem foreign. This was particularly evident when students were challenged to link the context of our guest speaker and that of the K'iche community in Guatemala with their projects. This process allowed students to widen their cultural perspectives by ironically both honoring and decentering students' experiences but without devaluing them.

Although this course has always been designed with HLLs in mind first, the reality of it being a mixed classroom offered both challenges and benefits for students at similar proficiencies but with different experiences. One of the challenges was still needing to address language acquisition, related to the assignments at hand, but differentiation proved to be essential. Offering resources where students could choose their aids or practice outside of the classroom allowed for this flexibility and individualization, as long as students were at the intermediate range. To achieve the benefits of this mixed classroom setting, required special planning and grouping from their instructor. As seen in the example of Dania and Gabby, the students shared a passion topic but from different vantage points. Being able to collaborate and gain from the variation of experiences is what truly made this course more equitable than it was before for both HLLs and L2 learners.

Future Steps

The implementation of this redesigned course offered improvements, particularly in the continuity of the learning process for both SHLLs and L2 learners alike. However, there is always room for reflection and growth when a course is repeated or if this project-based activism is applied in another context. Since the end of the school year tends to have many interruptions due to testing and events, it would be beneficial for students to collect data earlier in the year so that an action project can be executed from this data. Nearly all of the projects still made suggestive actions rather than concrete and tangible ones, including the example from Dania and Gabby. I realize now that this struggle of achieving "action" is rooted in three tensions: (1) adjusting the learning process to expected school year milestones, (2) striving for individualized learning within a class community, and (3) valuing the learning process over its product. Admittedly, as their teacher, I repeatedly encouraged students through our conferencing and coaching to apply their research and data analysis in the community, but I too struggled with the action piece. I learned that this last product also needs the time and guidance that other steps of the project received. By embedding more experiences, such as critical service learning outside of the classroom or school building, can lead to more meaningful student engagement and in turn more actionable projects at the end of the course. Although students had research practice throughout the units, there was a need for more experiences that interacted within the local community to also serve as examples of *action*. With that said, it would be remiss to underestimate the act of reflection and personal growth that students had through the exploration of a social issue that mattered to them.

AN INVITATION

In this chapter, we argue that centering the Communities goal area of the World-Readiness Standards for Learning Languages (The National Standards Collaborative Board, 2015) through the guiding frameworks of iCit (Byram, 2008) and CSP (Paris & Alim, 2017) can lead to a more equitable Spanish language education for heritage students. Through the theory and practical examples we described, it is our hope that our colleagues will consider joining us in our journeys in critically reflecting on our current curriculum and practices and take steps towards a more inclusive approach to language education for HLLs. It is our belief that when educators take a systematic approach in prioritizing the Communities goal area of the Standards, all students including both SHLLs and L2 learners will benefit. To help with this goal, we offer the following questions which have helped us reflect critically about the ways in which we center communities, implement iCit, and design and implement curriculum using CSP.

- In what ways do I already provide my students with opportunities to engage with multilingual communities both at home and abroad?
- How do I help my students use Spanish for personal enjoyment?
- What opportunities do I give my students to use their language skills to solve real-world problems that are meaningful to them?
- How do I consider my students' varied cultural backgrounds when designing and implementing curriculum?

- How do I help my students engage with various Spanish-Speaking communities without losing or replacing their own cultural heritage?
- What do I do to help my students sustain their own various cultures?

REFERENCES

ACTFL. (2017a). *NCSSFL-ACTFL can-do-statements for intercultural communication*. Available from, https://www.actfl.org/publications/guidelines-and-manuals/ncssfl-actfl-can-do-statements

ACTFL. (2017b). *Intercultural reflection tool*. Available from, https://www.actfl.org/publications/guidelines-and-manuals/ncssfl-actfl-can-do-statements

ACTFL Task Force on Decade of Standards Project. (2011, April). *A decade of foreign language standards: influence, impact, and future directions*. Survey results [Electronic report]. Retrieved February 24, 2024, from https://www.actfl.org/sites/default/files/publications/standards/NationalStandards2011.pd

Adán, M. (2023). Sustaining the Empoderamiento of Spanish Heritage Learners at the Secondary Level through Critical Pedagogies. [Doctoral dissertation, Indiana University]. Thesis and Dissertations Collection, Indiana University Library. https://hdl.handle.net/2022/29668

Anya, U. (2021). Critical race pedagogy for more effective and inclusive world language teaching. *Applied Linguistics*, 42(6), 1055–1069. DOI: 10.1093/applin/amab068

Beaudrie, S., & Wilson, D. V. (2022). Reimagining the Goals of HL Pedagogy through Critical Language Awareness. In S. Loza & S. Beaudrie (Eds.) (2022) Heritage Language Teaching: Critical Language Awareness Perspectives for Research and Pedagogy (pp. 63-79). New York, NY: Routledge

Beaudrie, S. M. (2020). Towards Growth for Spanish Heritage Programs in the United States: Key Markers of Success. *Foreign Language Annals*, 53(3), 416–437. DOI: 10.1111/flan.12476

Beaudrie, S. M., Amenzua, A., & Loza, S. (2021). Critical language awareness in the heritage language classroom: Design, implementation, and evaluation of a curricular intervention. *International Multilingual Research Journal*, 15(1), 61–81. DOI: 10.1080/19313152.2020.1753931

Beaudrie, S. M., Ducar, C., & Potowski, K. (2014). *Heritage language teaching: research and practice*. McGraw-Hill Education Create.

Beaudrie, S. M., & Loza, S. (2022). The Central Role of Critical Language Awareness in Spanish Heritage Language Education in the United States: An Introduction. In Loza, S., & Beaudrie, S. M. (Eds.), *Heritage Language Teaching: Critical Language Awareness Perspectives for Research and Pedagogy* (pp. 1–20). Routledge.

Bell, L. (2016). Theoretical foundation social justice education. In M. Adam & L. Bell with D. Goodman & K. Joshi (Eds.), Teaching for diversity and social justice (3rd ed.) (pp. 3-26). New York: Routledge.

Bowles, M. (2018). Outcomes of classroom Spanish heritage language instruction. In *The Routledge Handbook of Spanish as a Heritage Language*. Routledge Taylor & Francis Group. DOI: 10.4324/9781315735139-21

Bowles, M. A. (2011). Exploring the Role of Modality: L2-Heritage Learner Interactions in the Spanish Language Classroom. In Heritage Language Journal (Vol. 8, Issue 1).

Bucholtz, M., Casillas, D. I., & Lee, J. S. (2017). Language and Culture as Sustenance. In *Paris, D., & Alim, H. S. (2017). Culturally sustaining pedagogies : teaching and learning for justice in a changing world* (pp. 43–59). Teachers College Press.

Burgo, C. (2017). *Culture and Instruction in the Spanish Heritage Language Classroom*. Philologica Canariensia., DOI: 10.20420/PhilCan.2017.145

Byram, M. (2008). *From foreign language education to education for intercultural citizenship: Essays and reflections*. Multilingual Matters. DOI: 10.21832/9781847690807

Byram, M. (2021). *Teaching and assessing intercultural communicative competence –Revisited*. Multilingual Matters. DOI: 10.21832/9781800410251

Carreira, M. (2018). *Strategies for Teaching Mixed Classes: Meeting the Needs of Heritage and Second Language Learners of Spanish*. In Webinar Series Center for Language Instruction and Coordination.

Carreira, M., & Chik, C. (2018). *Differentiated Teaching: A primer for heritage and mixed classes. The Routledge Handbook of Spanish as a Heritage Language*. Routledge Taylor & Francis Group. DOI: 10.4324/9781315735139-23

Carreira, M., & Potowski, K. (2011). Commentary: Pedagogical Implications of Experimental SNS Research. In Heritage Language Journal (Vol. 8, Issue 1).

Cochran-Smith, M., & Lytle, S. (2009). Teacher research as stance. In Somekh, B., & Noffke, S. (Eds.), *The Sage handbook of educational action research* (pp. 39–49). Sage. DOI: 10.4135/9780857021021.n5

Conlon, D. (2024). Meeting the World-Readiness Standards for Learning Languages through Comprehensible Input Readers in Level 1 Spanish, A Comparative Analysis of Teachers' Perceptions [Doctoral dissertation, University of Connecticut]. Archives & Special Collections, University of Connecticut Library. https://ctdigitalarchive .org/node/3768402

Conlon, D., & Wagner, M. (2022). Enacting Social Justice in World Language Education through Intercultural Citizenship. In Wassell, B., & Glynn, C. (Eds.), *Transforming World Language Teaching and Teacher Education for Equity and Justice: Pushing Boundaries in US Contexts*. Multilingual Matters.

Connecticut State Department of Education. (n.d.). Naubuc School Report. Connecticut Report Cards. https://edsight.ct.gov/SASStoredProcess/guest?_district= Glastonbury+School+

Correa, M. (2011). Advocating for Critical Pedagogical Approaches to Teaching Spanish as a Heritage Language: Some Considerations. *Foreign Language Annals*, 44(2), 308–320. DOI: 10.1111/j.1944-9720.2011.01132.x

Darhower, M. (2006). Where's the community? Bilingual Internet chat and the fifth C of the National Standards. *Hispania, 89*,1. 84-98

District&_school=Naubuc+School&_program=%2FCTDOE%2FEdSight%2FRelease%2FReporting%2FPublic%2FReports%2FStoredProcesses%2FConnecticutReportCard&_select=Submit

Dover, A. (2013). Teaching for social justice: From conceptual frameworks to classroom practices. *Multicultural Perspectives*, 15(1), 3–11. DOI: 10.1080/15210960.2013.754285

Flores, N., & Rosa, J. (2015). Undoing appropriateness: Raciolinguistic ideologies and language diversity in education. *Harvard Educational Review*, 85(2), 149–171. DOI: 10.17763/0017-8055.85.2.149

García, O. (2009). *Multilingualism and Language Education*. The Routledge Companion to English Studies., DOI: 10.4324/9781315852515.ch6

Gilchrist, G. (2018). *Practitioner Enquiry: Professional Development with Impact for Teachers, Schools and Systems*. Routledge. DOI: 10.4324/9781315232270

Gironzetti, E., & Belpoliti, F. (2021). The other side of heritage language education: Understanding Spanish heritage language teachers in the United States. *Foreign Language Annals*, 54(4), 1189–1213. DOI: 10.1111/flan.12591

Glynn, C., & Spenader, A. (2020). Critical Content Based Instruction for the Transformation of World Language Classrooms. *Journal of Linguistics and Language Teaching*, 12(2). Advance online publication. DOI: 10.5070/L212246307

Henshaw, F. G. (2015). Learning Outcomes of L2–Heritage Learner Interaction: The Proof Is In the Posttests. *Heritage Language Journal*, 12(3), 245–270. DOI: 10.46538/hlj.12.3.2

Hines-Gaither, K., & Accilien, C. (2023). *The Antiracist World language classroom*. Routledge.

Holguín Mendoza, C. (2018). Critical Language Awareness (CLA) for Spanish Heritage Language Programs: Implementing a Complete Curriculum. *International Multilingual Research Journal*, 12(2), 65–79. DOI: 10.1080/19313152.2017.1401445

Ladson-Billings, G. (1995, Summer). But That's Just Good Teaching! The Case for Culturally Relevant Pedagogy. *Theory into Practice*, 34(3), 159–165. DOI: 10.1080/00405849509543675

Leeman, J. (2005). Engaging critical pedagogy: Spanish for native speakers. *Foreign Language Annals*, 38(1), 35–45. DOI: 10.1111/j.1944-9720.2005.tb02451.x

Leeman, J. (2018). Critical language awareness in SHL: Challenging the linguistic subordination of US Latinxs. In Potowski, K. (Ed.), *Handbook of Spanish as a Minority/Heritage Language* (pp. 345–358). Routledge. DOI: 10.4324/9781315735139-22

Leeman, J., Rabin, L., & Román-Mendoza, E. (2011). Identity and Activism in Heritage Language Education. *Modern Language Journal*, 95(4), 481–495. DOI: 10.1111/j.1540-4781.2011.01237.x

Leeman, J., & Serafini, E. J. (2016). Sociolinguistics for Heritage Language Educators and Students: A Model for Critical Translingual Competence. In Fairclough, M., & Beaudrie, S. M. (Eds.), *Innovative Strategies for Heritage Language Teaching: A Practical Guide for the Classroom* (pp. 56–79). Georgetown University Press.

Magnan, S. S. (2008). Reexamining the priorities of the National Standards for Foreign Language Education. *Language Teaching*, 43(3), 349–366. DOI: 10.1017/S0261444808005041

Magnan, S. S., Dianna, M., Sahakyan, N., & Kim, S. (2012). Student Goals, Expectations, and the Standards for Foreign Language Learning. *Foreign Language Annals*, 45(2), 170–192. DOI: 10.1111/j.1944-9720.2012.01192.x

Martínez, G. (2003). Classroom based dialect awareness in heritage language instruction: A critical applied linguistic approach. *Heritage Language Journal*, 7(1), 1–14. DOI: 10.46538/hlj.1.1.3

Montrul, S. (2010). How similar are L2 learners and heritage speakers? Spanish clitics and word order. *Applied Psycholinguistics*, 31, 167–207. DOI: 10.1017/S014271640999021X

Paris, D., & Alim, H. S. (2014). What are we seeking to sustain through culturally sustaining pedagogy? A loving critique forward. *Harvard Educational Review*, 84(1), 85–100. https://doi-org.proxyiub.uits.iu.edu/10.17763/haer.84.1.982l873k2ht16m77. DOI: 10.17763/haer.84.1.982l873k2ht16m77

Paris, D., & Alim, H. S. (2017). *Culturally sustaining pedagogies: Teaching and learning for justice in a changing world*. Teachers College Press.

Pascual y Cabo, D., & Prada, J. (2018). Redefining Spanish teaching and learning in the United States. *Foreign Language Annals*, 51(3), 533–547. DOI: 10.1111/flan.12355

Polinsky, M. (2014). Heritage Languages and Their Speakers: Looking Ahead. In Fairclough, M., & Beaudrie, S. M. (Eds.), *Innovative Approaches to Heritage Languages: From Research to Practice*. Georgetown University Press.

Potowski, K. (2005). *Fundamentos de la enseñanza del español a hispanohablantes en los EE. UU*. Arco Libros.

Potowski, K. (2012). *Identity and Heritage Learners: Moving Beyond Essentializations. Spanish As a Heritage Language in the United States: The State of the Field*. Georgetown University Press.

Potowski, K. (2018). Virtual Q&A. In Webinar Series Center for Language Instruction and Coordination. University of Illinois at Urbana-Champaign. https://mediaspace.illinois.edu/media/t/1_uds5wrkd/90905681

Randolph, L. J. (2017). Heritage Language Learners in Mixed Spanish Classes: Subtractive Practices and Perceptions of High School Spanish Teachers. *Hispania*, 100(2), 274–288. DOI: 10.1353/hpn.2017.0040

Rosa, J., & Flores, N. (2017). *Paris, D., & Alim, H. S. (2017). Culturally sustaining pedagogies: teaching and learning for justice in a changing world*. Teachers College Press.

The National Standards Collaborative Board. (2015). *World-Readiness standards for learning languages* (4th ed.).

The William Benton Museum of Art. (n.d. a). What is an Arpillera? University of Connecticut William Benton Museum of Art. https://benton.uconn.edu/web-exhibitions-2/arpillera/what-is-an-arpillera/

The William Benton Museum of Art. (n.d. b). View Arpilleras. University of Connecticut William Benton Museum of Art. https://benton.uconn.edu/web-exhibitions-2/arpillera/images/

Valdés, G. (2001). Heritage language students: Profiles and possibilities. In Peyton, J. K., Ranard, D. A., & McGinnis, S. (Eds.), *Heritage languages in America: Preserving a national resource* (pp. 37–77). Delta Systems.

Wagner, M., Cardetti, F., & Byram, M. (2019). *Teaching intercultural citizenship across the curriculum: the role of language education*. ACTFL.

Walls, L. (2018). The Effect of Dyad Type on Collaboration: Interactions among Heritage and Second Language Learners. *Foreign Language Annals*, 51(3), 638–657. DOI: 10.1111/flan.12356

Zyzik, E. (2016). Toward a Prototype Model of the Heritage Language Learner: Understanding Strengths and Needs. In Fairclough, M., & Beaudrie, S. M. (Eds.), *Innovative Strategies for Heritage Language Teaching: A Practical Guide for the Classroom* (pp. 19–38). Georgetown University Press.

KEY TERMS AND DEFINITIONS

Communities: groups of people brought together by a common interest, goal, social group membership or other defining characteristic.

Critical language awareness: the understanding of how language is shaped by power dynamics, identity, and community values with the intention of empowering students to navigate their linguistic identities with confidence and critical insight

Critical Reflection: actively and intentionally reflecting on one's current situation and beliefs in order analyze our current deeply held assumptions and work towards positive change

Culturally sustaining pedagogies: an instructional approach that seeks to actively sustain students' cultural backgrounds, especially the cultural backgrounds of students belonging to marginalized populations

Heritage language learners: students that have a personal connection to a language other than the dominant language of their community with varying degrees of proficiency

Intercultural citizenship: applying the attitudes, knowledge, and skills of intercultural competence to solve a problem of relevance to students

Intercultural competence: the attitudes, knowledge, and skills of an intercultural speaker which include, but are not limited to, empathy, curiosity, and a willingness to suspend beliefs to consider alternative perspectives

Translanguaging: the flexible and dynamic use of multiple languages in communication and learning that allows multilingual students to use their entire linguistic repertoire to express themselves by mixing and switching between languages

Chapter 6
Community Cultural Wealth and Successful College Navigation Within New Latinx Destinations

Anthony Villarreal
San Diego State University, USA

ABSTRACT

With dramatic population growth and redistribution, Latinx are becoming increasingly dispersed across the country. There is a need for educational research that does not attempt to operate under the same assumptions within regions where the Latinx presence is long-standing but rather carefully examines educational outcomes and experiences within the new Latinx destination context. This study explores the college access experiences of 20 Mexican American students through a Community Cultural Wealth framework (Yosso, 2005), an asset-based perspective that allowed for the identification of participants' strengths across six forms of capital—aspirational, familial, linguistic, navigational, social, and resistance forms of capital. Their reflections provide unique insights for enacting culturally affirming/sustaining practices for educators and counselors in new destination contexts.

INTRODUCTION

The rapid growth of the Latinx population in the United States—referring to people and communities associated with the ethnic labels Latina, Latino, Latin@, Latine, and Hispanic— is well documented as the nation's second-fastest-growing racial or ethnic group (Flores, 2017). In 2023, there were 62.5 million Latinx in the

DOI: 10.4018/979-8-3373-1340-5.ch006

Copyright © 2025, IGI Global Scientific Publishing. Copying or distributing in print or electronic forms without written permission of IGI Global is prohibited.

United States compared to 1980, when there were 14.8 million Latinx, according to the Pew Research Center (Moslimani & Noe-Bustamante, 2023). Furthermore, the US Census population projections expect the number of Latinx in the nation to nearly double by 2060 (Vespa et al., 2018). Once concentrated in a handful of "established" Latinx settlement states such as California, Texas, and Florida, Latinx are now increasingly dispersed across the country in states that previously had very few Latinx residents (Fry, 2011). New Latinx destinations (NLDs) include "where increasing numbers of Latinx (many immigrants and some from elsewhere in the United States) are settling both temporarily and permanently in areas of the United States that have not traditionally been home to Latinx" (Murillo et al., 2002, p. 1). Examples include areas within the Pacific Northwest (PNW), such as Oregon, where the Latinx population increased 144% between 1990 and 2000 and 64% between 2000 and 2010 (US Census 2000, 2010). This dramatic population growth and redistribution has reshaped the racial and ethnic landscape in new destination communities and emphasizes the importance of understanding Latinx educational attainment, which will be essential to sustaining economic and social well-being in the US (Kelly, et al., 2010).

Postsecondary access has not kept pace with the overall growth of the population as Latinx continued to lag in college enrollment with a lower enrollment rate for 18-24-year-old Latinx (36%) in comparison to their Asian (59%), White (42%), and Black (37%) counterparts (Hussar et al., 2020). Latinx remain underrepresented in college (Gay, 2014) and are less likely to complete associate and bachelor's degrees (Krogstad, 2016). For example, as of 2019, only 21% of Latinx ages 25 to 29 have a bachelor's degree or higher in comparison to 71% of Asian Americans, 45% of Whites, and 29% of African Americans in the same age group (Hussar et al., 2020). Furthermore, empirical findings indicate that contrary to national trends, demographic growth is negatively associated with changes in college enrollment equity for Latinx students over the last decade (Hatch, et al., 2015). Thus, it is important to understand further how the contexts within new Latinx destinations impact two- and four-year college access and attainment for Latinx students.

The historical underrepresentation of Latinx in college stems from the structural inequities in K-12 education (Sólorzano, et al., 2005). Latinx often attend segregated school settings that are overcrowded and under-resourced (Yosso & Solórzano, 2006). Undertrained and under-resourced teachers and counselors work under racialized structures, policies, and practices that assume students come with a variety of deficits rather than acknowledging and nurturing students' cultural advantages (Valenzuela, 2010). Negative dominant narratives can impact Latinx educational trajectories as students internalize these narratives as explanations for their level of academic achievement rather than attributing challenges and lack of access to institutional and structural barriers (Nunez, 2017). Yosso's (2005) community cultural wealth is a useful framework that reframes and highlights the cultural assets that students possess. This is especially important in new Latinx destinations as education systems are encountering large student populations that were not previously present in such a capacity.

This study aims to examine the experiences of Latinx students' college access within new Latinx destinations through a community cultural lens. The research question addressed is:

- What role does community cultural wealth play in Latinx college students' higher education pursuits within "New Latinx Destinations"?

PRIOR LITERATURE

In reviewing the literature, four areas are highlighted: 1) educational pathways within new Latinx destinations, 2) immigrant students, 3) Latinx immigrant students of indigenous backgrounds and 4) undocumented students. I specifically focus on scholarship that utilizes asset-based perspectives, such as community cultural wealth (Yosso, 2005).

Education Pathways within New Latinx Destinations

The emerging literature focused specifically within new Latinx destinations has primarily focused on K-12 settings. The newness of the immigrant population within these areas presents both challenges and opportunities within community and educational contexts (Hamann, et al., 2015; Zúñiga & Hernández-León, 2005). Some scholars question the capacity of schools in new immigrant destinations to teach newcomer and non-English-speaking children (Lowenhaupt & Reeves, 2015) as they may lack the networks, resources, and established systems necessary to meet the new Latinx population's needs. The research focused on the new Latinx diaspora has highlighted the absence of trained bilingual teachers, counselors, and staff and adequate programing to address the needs of English language learners (Wortham, et al., 2002). ELL programs and services may be left up to teachers or paraprofessionals with limited credentials and little prior exposure to Latinx culture (Wortham, et al., 2013). Beyond the classroom, in general engagement and communication with parents and families is severely hindered when there is a dearth of bilingual and bicultural teachers, counselors, and staff (Gallo, & Wortham, 2012).

A few studies have begun to examine college access and completion in new Latinx destinations. Carrillo (2016a) examined working-class Latinx male college students in North Carolina who navigate multiple cultural worlds and excel academically.

This work counters anti-deficit notions by acknowledging that "intelligence is a social construct deeply tainted by the definitions of those in positions of power" (Carrillo, 2016a, pg. 159). Instead, it emphasizes the various forms of linguistic and cultural straddling that Latinx students engage in to ultimately produce academic excellence. Furthermore, the identity development of immigrant Latinx youth are being shaped within regional contexts where Latinx history, culture, and political landscapes are limited and provide little validation and empowerment of cultural assets and strengths (Carrillo, 2016b).

Immigrant Students

Immigrant families today face numerous barriers in pursuing higher education, securing employment, healthcare, housing, and other basic needs (Baum & Flores, 2011; Perez, et al., 2010). Immigrants come to the US from multiple backgrounds and for various reasons and may have left extreme poverty or violence in order to seek opportunities for their families (Suárez-Orozco & Todorova, 2003). Regardless of the reasons for immigration or country of origin, many immigrant families stay in the US and share the American dream to see their children live successful, well-educated lives, but are often confronted by prejudice, racism, and discrimination (Sánchez, & Machado-Casas, 2009). Many immigrants come to the US seeking educational opportunities (Baum & Flores, 2011; Perez, 2011) and postsecondary aspirations; however, many immigrant students are vulnerable due to legal and financial constraints (Guarneros, et al., 2009). Even if they do not know how to promote their children's educational success, these families value and encourage hard work and high academic achievement. Unfortunately, our educational system often views immigrant students' cultural norms as inferior and, subsequently, places less emphasis on pedagogical strategies that support cultural and linguistic diversity (Borjian & Padilla 2010) and instead seeks to replace immigrant youth's cultural norms with more "acceptable" ones (Valenzuela, 2010). This may be true with new Latinx destinations, where schools are not culturally informed on the best practices for supporting immigrant youth and may lead to more harmful social and psychological experiences with the education system.

Many of the psychological experiences that immigrant students in the US face are intertwined with identity and adjustment required to survive in a new context (Suárez-Orozco, 2004). Despite the optimism that is at the very heart of the immigrant experience, there is emotional and psychological stress associated with multiple losses of migration that may impact parents, families, and ultimately academics of immigrant youth (Suárez-Orozco, et al., 2008). For immigrant youth who are in the key identity developmental stage of adolescence, it can be difficult to maintain a positive ethnic identity in schools that may or may not promote multiculturalism and tolerance and within an anti-immigrant environment (Perreira, et al., 2010). Sustained contact within ethnic communities fosters a sense of affinity with one's culture of origin across generations (Suárez-Orozco, 2004), which is evident in large ethnic neighborhoods and enclaves often found in traditional Latinx areas. Within new Latinx destinations, where the population is just beginning to emerge, it may be more challenging to replicate the strength of the collective co-ethnic identity, the community's cohesiveness, and the availability of cultural role models, which is determined by the density of the local ethnic population. In addition, community support across the various Latinx sub-groups (i.e., countries of origin), intersectional identities (i.e., indigenous backgrounds), and unique situations (i.e., immigration status), may be even more rare within the new Latinx diaspora.

Latinx Immigrants of Indigenous Backgrounds

The growing trend of Latinx indigenous immigrants settling throughout the US is often ignored (Sánchez, & Machado-Casas, 2009); yet we need to acknowledge that indigenous exist within the label of Latinx as their cultures, languages, and lifestyles are considerably distinct (Machado-Casas, 2009). It is essential to consider this intersectional identity as the 2014 National Survey of Latinx (NSL) found that one-in-four (25%) Latinx adults consider themselves indigenous (Parker, et al., 2015) and Mixtec, Nahuas, Purepechas, Triques, and Otomi have been noted as the largest indigenous groups migrating to the US (Zabin, et al., 1993). Youth may face negative and racial stereotypes because of their immigrant or indigenous background, which may cause them to internalize low social and academic expectations (Fuligni, et al., 2005). Indigenous immigrant youth encounter structural barriers in accessing critical resources and deficit discourse that may even be perpetuated among their non-indigenous Latinx peers, which may lead to feelings of shame about their identity (Kovats, 2010). Machado-Casas' (2009) longitudinal qualitative study counters this deficit narrative and explores the ways in which Latinx indigenous immigrant parents transmit transnational funds of knowledge (Moll, et al., 1992). More research is needed that examines the intersectional identities of Latinx populations.

Undocumented College Students

Immigrants come to the United States for various reasons; many are seeking opportunities for their families. Significant driving forces behind many undocumented immigrants entering the US include failed US immigration policies and economic factors (Gonzalez, 2001). Many immigrants left extreme poverty or violence to seek opportunities in the United States; these appear to be circumstances that have rarely been addressed in the literature that exists about undocumented students

(Gildersleeve, et al., 2010). In addition, scholars cite that these students' parents make a decision for which the student cannot come willfully or fully to understand the legal ramifications (Contreras, 2009; Pérez, et al., 2009). Within the past decade, numerous research studies have been conducted focusing on access and retention of undocumented students in higher education and the lived experiences of undocumented students within those institutions, both public and private (i.e., Contreras, 2009; Pérez et al., 2010).

The research focused on undocumented students in higher education continues to grow since Pérez's (2009) seminal work examining the academic resilience of undocumented Latinx students. Three main indicators of academic success were investigated: 1) grade point average, 2) number of academic awards, and 3) number of academically rigorous, honors, and AP classes. The study hypothesized that, due to legal and social marginalization, undocumented students were at high risk of academic failure. The results from regression and cluster analyses (N = 110) indicated that undocumented students who have high levels of personal and environmental protective factors (e.g. supportive parents and participation in school activities) reported higher levels of academic success than did students sharing similar risk factors and lower levels of personal and environmental protective factors. Examples of the risk factors that undocumented students' overcame include low parental education and high employment hours during school. Furthermore, as a group, college-eligible undocumented students demonstrated academic achievement, high leadership participation, and civic engagement, with over 90% reported volunteer and community service participation, and 95% participated in extracurricular activities. The study found that undocumented students exhibited high levels of psychological resilience, perseverance, and optimism. The study also found that the participants reported high levels of community service and volunteering.

While there has been more recent literature focused on undocumented students, explicitly analyzing the effects of in-state tuition on education access of undocumented students (Frum, 2007; Gildersleeve, et al., 2010) and other studies examined the college experiences of undocumented students (e.g., Flores & Horn, 2009; Perez, et al., 2009; Montiel, 2017), only a few studies investigate the experience of undocumented students through asset-based perspectives. Most recently, Montiel (2017) examined the experiences of undocumented Mexican students at private universities through a funds of knowledge lens (Moll, et al., 1992). Her analysis identified the concept of hacerle la lucha (hard work; remaining in the struggle) as something students possessed as a skill and resource that helped them to succeed and how family, and in particular the parents of these Mexican students, served as examples of "hard work" motivate them in their pursuit of higher education. These findings support literature using a CCW lens that highlights parents and families as sources of support and inspiration for undocumented Latinx college students (Perez,

2009; Enriquez, 2011) and counters the myth often perpetuated in research that Latinx families, especially Mexican families, do not value school (Valencia & Black, 2002). Other vital relationships that serve as supports for undocumented Latinx are faculty and staff (Muñoz, 2008) and peers can serve as one of the greatest sources of support for students, particularly on campuses where there is an established culture that is supportive of undocumented students (Herrera & Chen, 2010). Research has emphasized the need for welcoming campus climates (Hurtado & Carter, 1997), particularly for undocumented students (Abrego & Gonzales, 2010; Pérez Huber, 2010). Within new Latinx destinations, there may be less awareness and support for undocumented students, and there is a need to fill the void of literature that examines the undocumented student population specifically within this context.

THEORETICAL PERSPECTIVE

Community cultural wealth is a useful framework that describes "an array of knowledge, skills, abilities, and contacts possessed and utilized by Communities of Color to survive and resist macro and micro-forms of oppression" (Yosso, 2005, pg. 77). Community cultural wealth stems from a Critical Race Theory (CRT), which posits that race and racism are central to understanding how the US society functions (Bell, 1992). This perspective can be used to examine the role of race and racism in implicitly and explicitly impacting social structures, practices, and discourses, particularly in education (Dixson & Rousseau, 2005). CRT can be used to explore how racism continues to permeate postsecondary institutions and the collegiate interactions for students of color, including Latinx students (Yosso, et al., 2009). Yosso's (2005) core assumptions are theorized through six categories of assets and resources found in communities of color, which have the potential to support students along their educational pathways—1) aspirational, 2) linguistic, 3) navigational, 4) resistant, 5) social, and 6) familial. Latinx navigating educational systems within "new Latinx destinations" are encountering systems unprepared to serve their new and growing communities. Schools must be cognizant of the power dynamics that may continue perpetuating inequities for new immigrant communities. Thus, community cultural wealth gives us different constructs of cultural value, knowledge, and wealth to reframe deficit discourse.

METHODOLOGY

Data Collection

Setting and context. This research is set within the context of new Latinx destinations, which are defined as states that have dramatically increased in the Latinx population since the 2000 census. Participants in this study were specifically located within the new Latinx destination of Oregon and completed their K-12 and college education within the context of growing Latinx populations in a predominately White state. Oregon was chosen specifically to explore their experiences with education systems that continue to need to adjust to large Latinx and immigrant student populations as they were not previously present in this state since the recent waves of immigration beginning in the early 90s. While the overall nation-wide growth of Latinx populations has slowed since the onset of the Great Recession in 2007 (Stepler & Lopez, 2016), Latinx numbers in the PNW have remained strong within Oregon, where 22 of the 36 counties experienced high Latinx growth (>25% increases). In fact, two Oregon counties are among the 3.6% of counties across the nation that have 100,000 or more Latino residents (Noe-Bustamante et al., 2020). The legacy of rapid growth and sustained Latinx presence over the last four decades marks Oregon as a key new Latinx destination to examine educational outcomes to inform efforts in states that have more recently shifted toward becoming new Latinx destinations. While Latinx made up 13.9% of the Oregon population in 2020 (US Census, 2020), Latinx are projected to make up over 23% of the high school graduating class by 2030 (Bransberger et al., 2020). Yet, according to a Higher Education Coordinating Commission (HECC) in 2019, only 31% of Latinx adults (25 and older) have an associate's degree or higher, compared to 55% of White adults in Oregon (HECC, 2021).

Recruitment. The required criteria for participation in the study included: 1) Have attended at least four years of K-12 in Oregon; 2) Racially/ethnically identify as Latinx, Hispanic, and/or Chicanx; 3) Have obtained a college degree in a New Latinx Destination. A purposeful sampling approach and snowball sampling were used to locate rich key informants (Patton, 2014). Through my networks of educators and professionals in Oregon, I identified a list of participants who might meet the study criteria. I then sent the recruitment email with the study information to this initial list of potential participants. This email invited them to participate in my study and/or forward the study information to potential participants. After completing interviews with these initial participants, I again asked them to identify individuals within their networks who might fit the study requirements and requested that they forward the recruitment and study information to potential participants.

Interview data. Utilizing a semi-structured approach, the interview protocol questions were open-ended to allow for the flow of conversation to be flexible and guided by the participant (Creswell, 2013). The interview protocol focused on participants' family history, educational background, bilingual and English language acquisition; educational experiences, students and interactions with educators; experiences with racism and/or discrimination; school and/or cultural barriers; and the role of family and community; and other questions informed by Community Cultural Wealth and the six forms of capital. Interviews ranged from 60-120 minutes and averaged 90 minutes. Interviews were recorded, transcribed, and reviewed for accuracy.

Participant Profiles. 20 Mexican American participants who successfully completed a college degree within a new Latinx destination. All participants identified Mexico as their country of origin, although most were born in the United States; only eight were born in Mexico. Most participants had parents who worked in agriculture and were part of the migrant program. Most identified Spanish as their first language (n=17), but all participants were fluent in both Spanish and English. A few participants also identified as indigenous, with their parents or themselves speaking an indigenous language (n=3). The overwhelming majority came from low-income, two-parent households, and most were first-generation college students (n=18). While I did not ask for their citizenship status in the questionnaire, a few participants in the study disclosed that they were undocumented students and navigated Deferred Action for Childhood Arrivals (DACA) policies. All participants had completed their baccalaureate from a public or private university in Oregon at the time of the interviews. The majority of the sample also pursued higher levels of education with 13 who earned master's degrees and three participates who earned doctoral degrees (2=PhDs & 1=JD). However, not all participants were traditional students. Some participants' paths were not straightforward, and they took more than four years to complete their baccalaureate degree, due to various circumstances such as navigating community college, working full-time and/or becoming parents early in their college years. Despite the broad age range among participants (Range=28-45; Mean=38.4), many similar experiences and patterns were identified across the narratives of their college trajectories.

Analysis

Narrative analysis perspective. A narrative approach places emphasis on stories, understanding lived experiences, and holistic narratives (Jones, et. al, 2014). Jones and colleagues (2014) propose four steps to narrative analysis. The first step is to discover general themes through an overall reading of each interview and returning to specific parts of each transcript to develop meaning, with an awareness of how these contribute to understanding the overarching narrative. Second, multiple readings of each transcript provide a deeper analysis of how the narratives relate to one another. The third step involves parsing out the emerging patterns across multiple narratives, while capturing the relationship to the overarching narrative. The final step is utilizing the theoretical research to deepen the researcher's interpretation of emerging stories. I reanalyzed the data using prior knowledge from the concepts outlined in the theoretical framework of Community Cultural Wealth with attentiveness to the intersections of race, class, and gender (Yosso, 2005).

Positionality. My positionality in this research is influenced by my professional and personal experience. My upbringing as the eldest son of immigrant parents from Nayarit, Mexican American, US citizen, low-income, first-generation college student, positions me as closely tied to my research topic. I am also bilingual and hold deep roots in my Latinx culture, traditions, and language, despite growing up in a new Latinx destination during my adolescent years. I have personal experience navigating the New Latinx context to successfully complete postsecondary education; therefore, I bring unique insights to this work, as I keenly understand the contexts and power dynamics. Not only do I have personal experience, but I also have a wealth of professional experience as an educator within schools that have a rapidly growing Latinx population. As a K-12 counselor and Outreach Coordinator, I focused on college access, working with low-income, first-generation student populations that were majority Latinx and collaborated with administrators, university representatives, and community organizations to develop programs to promote Latinx students in postsecondary education. Examining my dispositions, beliefs, and assumptions helped me to be transparent about my positionality and develop strategies to maintain a more unbiased focus on the research.

I recognize that while I have some similar experiences, I need to remain open to hearing and empowering the voices of my participants to share their unique experiences. As a US-born Mexican American, my experience and perspective may be significantly different from those of my participants, who are indigenous, multilingual, and grew up in Mexico, for example. I emphasize the importance of "bracketing" the beliefs and assumptions that stem from my own experience throughout the inquiry process to remain open-minded, look at different points of view, and be willing to change position when reason leads to doing so (Jones, et. al, 2014). Drawing from a critical perspective that values empowering my participants through the opportunity to give voice to the participants' stories (Merriam, 2009), I utilized member checking to further ensure accuracy, engage participants in the research, and to gain further clarity on the emerging themes (Jones, et. al, 2014). Applicants were provided an electronic copy of their transcribed interview for verification and an invitation for a follow-up conversation to gain their feedback on my interpretation and to ask clarifying questions

RESULTS

The New Latinx Destination Context

Latinx students navigate their personal and academic lives within the unique contexts of new Latinx destinations. For many current college students and alums within new Latinx destinations, the rapid demographic shifts happened during significant developmental stages of their youth. Oscar describes the community characteristics that have evolved since his initial arrival in Oregon.

"There's a lot of farms, vineyards, nurseries, canneries, and factories. There's a big Mixteco community here from my village, in this area, and there's also a big Hispanic community. It's one of the top three counties that has the most concentration of Latinx, Chicanos, in the state. And it's growing. It's the fastest growing county in the state. When we first arrived, there was not a lot of Mexican stores or radio stations. Those were barely coming up, so the new restaurants and radio stations were added. The local channels for Spanish televisions were available now. So it changed from the late '90s to now." ~ Oscar

These shifts were also evident within the educational system, which until recently had only served predominately White student populations. Deana reflects on her experience as an English language learner (ELL) and articulates how there was a lack of resources and trained bilingual teachers available to her during his school years.

"In K-12 the staff and teachers were all White, it wasn't until high school that I began to see some Latino staff, like the secretary, but they were mostly service staff and one Latino teacher and but there were a lot of Latino students [...] In college there was no representation in staff and faculty and I was the only student of color in all my classes. There were maybe 30 students of color somewhere on campus, but you never saw them. I knew I was different as a minority." ~Deana

While there have been some gains in addressing the needs of ELLs, changes have not kept pace with the changing demographics of new Latinx destination schools.

Themes Related to Community Cultural Wealth

The study findings describe in terms of how the six capitals defined through community cultural wealth (Yosso, 2005) emerged as part of the college access process for the participants in new Latinx destinations. In particular, this section explores how participants employed aspirational, familial, social, linguistic, navigational, and resistant capital to facilitate their achievement.

Aspirational Capital. Aspirational capital is parental transmission and maintenance of dreams and goals "beyond present circumstances" throughout the children's educational journeys despite real or perceived barriers and often without resources

(Yosso & Solorzano 2005). The desire for new avenues toward upward mobility in education, employment, and living often drives the aspiration of Latinx in new destinations. Despite having limited knowledge or no experience of how to reach these goals, Latinx frequently seek a "better life" for future generations, and education is one venue for achieving this goal.

> *"Dad didn't go to school; mom went up to 6th grade [...] they never made education optional and it was always a must. Even though they didn't understand their role or the system. There was never a doubt that education was important [...] they never wanted us to end up like them" ~ Luz*

Luz mentioned that her parents shared their own life stories about overcoming adversity and provided support and advice, emphasizing the importance of education and how perseverance would result in a better life. Thru these stories, her parents served as role models and instilled in her a sense of hopefulness, which fostered her aspirations. Similarly, Oscar and Leo's motivation for higher education was driven by his parent's life stories of overcoming adversity.

> *"They'd say as immigrant parents "Vas estudiar para que no termines como nosotros"[you're going to study so you don't end up like us]. So they didn't want me to be in the farm and to work and to labor from four o'clock in the morning 'til like six o'clock in the evening. They wanted me to go to college, and then envisioned me to be sitting in an office, with a little fan there, mas tranquelitos con cafecito[calm with a cup of coffee] and making some good money." ~Oscar*
>
> *"My abuelo [grandpa] always told me, everyday after work: 'Go to school so you are not working hard. You could be in comfortable chair in an air conditioned office'. My dad grew up in Zapotecas, where he had to take care of goats. He would tell me how he had to stay overnight with the goats in thunderstorms and here [in the US] working the fields and how hard that life was and how they didn't want that for us. So they used those stories to motivate us to want more in life." ~Leo*

Nearly all participants describe how their parents envisioned a better life for their children and wanted them to have careers that were not "in the fields" or manual labor. Participants found both purpose and strength in watching their parents and their personal resistance in their everyday lives. Their families clearly saw education as the key, aspired beyond their own current circumstances, and envisioned a "better life" and occupation for their children. Their parents dispel the myth that Latinx do not value education. Their advice emphasizes how highly they hold education and their belief that determination would result in a better life.

Linguistic Capital. Linguistic capital is the intellectual and social skills learned through communication experiences in more than one language and/or style. Bilingual Latinx youth can serve as language brokers for their families and build "connections between racialized cultural history and language" (Yosso, 2005, p. 132). These real-world communication skills are intellectual and social tools that are transferable and aid in navigating social settings across languages and linguistics styles.

Within new Latinx destinations, participants experienced predominately White educational contexts, which often did not value their emerging bilingual skills. Sergio and Oscar shared similar experiences:

"Initially learning English was difficult, I was held back in 2nd grade and thought it was a negative thing […] I grew up translating a lot for my parents and others my community and I learned not be ashamed of it. I was determined to succeed in education to continue to give back to my community" ~Sergio

"Facing the challenges of not understanding the language in a classroom, full of people that, they're all spoke English. I was the only one. So, the teacher had a major struggle with me of, sometimes trying to find a translator, sometimes studying, and then teaching me the class. Those who spoke a little bit of Spanish, there was a teacher, Miss Sandoval, who was a New Mexican teacher who, ella [she] spoke a little bit of Spanish, and she used to stop the class and teach me for 15 minutes. So everybody was staring at me. So that was another part of it that, it was a, that being conscious that I was a recent immigrant. I was an indigenous immigrant, and I was an immigrant who couldn't speak the language, couldn't communicate with the rest. So I always walked with that challenge every day, I was very conscious of that Now, I speak the language everywhere, but where I give my presentations. I care in my identity, my language as a point of pride, but as point of witnessing, and as a point for the other young Mixtecos". ~Oscar

Linguistic capital was also significant for Sergio and Oscar's and how they were able to give back to and inspire others. While participants were initially susceptible to accepting negative, deficit perceptions about their language skills, they eventually understood the significance of their bilingualism, as Luz further elaborates:

"Being bilingual had really helped me just navigate both of the two worlds that I'm from, help me make connections, help me think about things different, feel things differently and really help my community and meet them where they are at." ~Luz

Their Spanish and English skills helped them communicate, form relationships, and navigate multiple contexts requiring different forms of language expression. For most participants, linguistic capital was also particularly important for identity development and solidifying their aspirations to align life and career goals in a way that contributed to their communities.

Navigational Capital. Navigational capital is the set of social-psychological skills to maneuver through social institutions and dominant structures and acknowledges individual agency within structural constraints. Latinx students' navigational strategies to circumvent the system can be informed by a consciousness of resistance. (Yosso 2005).

"Navigating the K-12 system was very hard for me because my dad never went to school, and my mom finished second grade. So even if they wanted to help me, or even they wanted to do the best, they did everything that they could in their own way to help me, but I had to navigate and find the different resources and help also my siblings to navigate the K-12 system. It's a complex system for immigrants who are barely learning the system, but also, it is a system that's very full of racism. The biggest challenge for me to first learn the language, two, learn the system, and three, to understand on how to navigate the resources that are available, and then also to get ready to accomplish my tasks, my homework, and all the requirements that was expected of me. So, that was part of the journey of navigating." ~Oscar

Despite having no formal education, the navigational skills that Oscar's parents fostered through their overall immigration experience, translated to their family's ability to acquire personal, education, and economic resources. Similarly, Luz's family's navigational capital was fueled by the knowledge gained in certain locations, and dominant structures, and using it for mobility purposes to further obtain capital to enter a better school district, according to her family.

"Everything we ever did was to ... from like moving school districts, it was always like them talking to other people. We became really close friends with the Flight family, and she was the manager of an apartment complex where we lived when I was in elementary school, and they she moved to Wilsonville. She was like, "They have really great schools." ~Luz"

Part of navigating was socially engaging with others to know where to go or what to do. Luz's family moved around for employment purposes, but forged social networks that helped them to understand and investigate the best education fit for their children and made intentional life decisions based on this information.

Resistant Capital. Resistant capital is the awareness, knowledge, and skills developed in opposition to oppression and inequality. Resistant capital acknowledges agency or willingness to challenge and transform inequalities, which is grounded in the legacy of resistance to subordination exhibited by Communities of Color (Yosso, 2005).

"Coming here to this country as an indigenous immigrant, we faced discrimination by the Anglo community, and by our own Mexican-Americans second generation, Chicanos that were already living here. They look at me and they knew I was from an indigenous village and because we were indigenous, we were made fun of, were called " Oaxacaquitas, Oaxacos, indios, indio-paterajata, indio bajados de la sierra a tamborazos, VIP, vete indio pendejo .. [derogatory terms]. So there was a lot of that, those attacks and bullying and traumatized. Because of that sometimes, when they asked me, "Where are you from?" Sometimes I didn't

say. I just changed the subject." Oaxacaquitas, Oaxacos, indios, indio bajados de la sierra a tamborazos" ~Oscar

The day-to-day realities of Latinx youth in the US, particularly within new Latinx contexts, include constantly being scrutinized, ostracized and stereotyped within society. Oscar faced oppression as an immigrant in the US, but also experienced discrimination within the Latinx community. The experiences of racism among participants ranged from covert, subtle macroaggressions to overt and direct racist confrontations.

"I was born in Mexico and came here for 1st grade [...] I knew there was a difference in my upbringing in having overcome adversity [...] Third grade I was in a group project and I misspelled something and one of the White kids made fun and laughed at me [...] from that point on I was never going to let White people show me that I am not as good as them [...] I went to the library every day after school; read a lot of books; practiced my writing [...] and feeling that I had to prove that I was just as capable as my counterparts or people that were born here [...] I could push back against that white supremacist narrative by retaining my cultural and language" ~Sergio

Sergio acquired resistant capital by overcoming negative, discriminatory experiences and was inspired to challenge inequalities, which he would depend on when facing academic and social obstacles. Participants and their families faced many challenges coming to the US and through these experiences of oppression, they gained skills that were developed by opposing inequity. Luz described her parents emphasizing "doors only close if you allow them to". Thus, parents fostered resistance capital in their children by encouraging them to continue in their educational pathways despite other barriers they would encounter.

Social capital. Traditionally described, social capital emphasizes the networks of people and community resources that can help students and families draw instrumental and social support to navigate social structures (Liou, et al,, 2009).

"The Spanish department really took me under their wing. They just loved me. They just supported me for everything. I was able to reclaim my identity to start at the beginning of me starting to reclaim my identity. Opened my eyes a lot to Social justice, to what was happening in Latinx America the differences in Mexico. They encouraged me to study abroad." ~Luz

Luz utilized social networks to develop the social capital necessary to identify opportunities that aided her in successfully navigating college. Likewise, Deana was inspired by those from similar backgrounds and intentionally chose a college where she could find culturally relevant support systems.

" One was a person at the college who helped me with the financial aid process and provided a lot of guidance and mentoring in understanding all of those things that I didn't know. She was from Nayarit, where my parents are from, and I still go to her for mentoring in my career today" ~Deana

While there are many sources on campus that could have provided resources, participants relied especially on networks formed with other Latinx that they could relate to and could provide a sense of community. As Deana described, the individuals within these networks often became mentors and life-long relationships that provided education, career, personal, and culturally aligned support.

Familial Capital. Cultural knowledge, in the form of familial capital, is cultivated within families and nurtured through kinship networks that carry a sense of cultural identity, community history, memory and cultural intuition (Yosso, 2005)

"Yeah, they helped me with my books, and that was the biggest sacrifice that they could ever make for me, and they still remind me how they really supported me through my education. I'm like, "You only bought me books," but at the same time, I'm like, "Okay, I recognize that was a really huge sacrifice for them." ~Luz

Luz's family significantly contributed to her education by buying her books. This was extremely meaningful as a working-class community member because of the high cost. It has a large economic impact on parents working several jobs to maintain a stable living. Many participants describe how their parents greatly impacted and supported their educational goals. This commitment within the family structure fostered a sense of collective or communal goals rather than perceiving education as an individualistic goal. Cultural and family practices and traditions shaped participants' understanding of the world and what they sought out in terms of education and career goals. Oscar describes the advice and familial teachings critical to his successful navigation.

"The humility to understand that we all learn from someone and we also all can contribute teaching or wisdom to someone. That I learned that from my indigenous community."

"Si quieres comer por un año, sembrar maíz. Si quieres comer por diez anos, sembrar árboles. Pero si quieres comer para toda la vida, sembrar conocimiento, mi amigos"[If you want to eat for a year, plant corn. If you want to eat for ten years plant trees. But if you want to eat for the rest of your life plant knowledge, my friends.]." ~Oscar

Familial and community consejos, refranes y dichos served as intentional transmission of cultural knowledge that was just as valuable in Oscar's development as the mainstream knowledge prioritized and validated within our educational systems. All participants described strong familial and communal bonds and valued the importance of maintaining a healthy connection to the community and its resources, their positioning, and the opportunities for service with their communities.

CONCLUSION

Discussion of Findings

Community cultural wealth (CCW) provides useful concepts that highlight students' cultural assets. Through the framework of community culture wealth, we acknowledge the abilities, skills, and contacts obtained by communities of color. CRT is used to explore how oppression continues to perpetuate postsecondary institutions and the educational interactions for Latinx students. Through this lens, we can deconstruct the hypothesis that Latinx lack social and cultural capital and reframe understanding through anti-deficit perspectives. It is crucial to approach working with growing Latinx populations in new destinations from a critical perspective that focuses on critiquing the structures in our society that distribute power and how individuals experience and negotiate these structures. Within new Latinx destinations, there are power dynamics that maintain historic trends of inequality and put Latinx in disadvantaged scenarios. Yet, students' navigational strategies in moving through stratified educational systems can be informed by a consciousness of resistance and the legacy of resistance to subordination exhibited by communities of color (Yosso, 2005).

In the case of this study, participants talked about navigating academic curriculum requirements for college, financial aid, and emphasized how their community cultural wealth translated their college-going expectations into academic success. Participants encountered barriers that traditionally discourage first-generation Latinx college students from entering and finishing college. The strong emphasis on family reflecting aspirational capital was not surprising, given the vast college access scholarship on familismo (Alvarez, 2015; Martinez, 2013). While the significant role of the family in impacting the aspirations of Mexican American/Chicanx students is also well-documented (Acevedo-Gil, 2017; Ceja, 2004, 2006), the narratives described a direct connection to the family and community histories and journeys to new Latinx destinations. Immigration, familial, and community oral histories were tied to participants' values, morals, and work ethic and how they constructed college ideologies (Rios-Aguilar & Kiyama, 2019). Participants asserted that their aspirational cultural wealth was not only individual, but generational and communal (i.e., to generate opportunity for their children or other immigrants), holding them accountable to collective goals beyond their personal gain (Martinez, et al., 2021).

These connections provide insights and add complexity to how familismo—the cultural value emphasizing interconnectedness and family unity; reciprocity in familial relationships, obligations, responsibilities; and the well-being of family members (Cuevas, 2020)—functions in college access and completion within new Latinx destinations. Just as research has noted the various dimensions of familial capital (Rios-Aguilar & Kiyama, 2019), the types of family support that promoted college-going and completion varied among participants' families. While all participants described their family's unwavering value of education and unconditional support, they acknowledged their parents often lacked the financial and/or human resources to assist them. It often took culturally aware educators to recognize and strategically build off these familial strengths. In each case, however, participants described a collective process prioritizing family needs, even if it resulted in personal sacrifice (Hernández, 2015). Participants heavily weighed their family's advice, and their aspirations were grounded in their family's high value of education.

In the college access and completion process, families used dichos or Mexican sayings, which have extended metaphorical cultural significance and consejos to convey cultural wisdom and guidance about how to live and act. The study findings align with the literature on Latinx family's cultural communicative resources, which include pláticas, dichos, refranes, consejos, testimonios, and other cultural and linguistic resources (Durán et al., 2020). In addition, the cultural significance and meaning of these communicative resources often do not translate outside of the Spanish language. Thus, these communication channels cemented a linguistic tie to participants' home communities that connected to how they collectively made sense of their educational journey and how they would come to embrace and build upon their linguistic capital. Participants described a journey of linguistic resilience as they overcame many significant barriers as bilingual individuals. Despite multilingualism being seen as an asset in many areas of the world and the evidence of its cognitive benefits (Hakuta, 1983), participants (especially those for who English was a second language) had to combat negative connotations, which included both subtle messaging and overt discrimination that had real consequences on their lives and self-perceptions. Confirming similar findings on Latinx college students (Pérez, 2014), later in their development as young adults, participants drew on this linguistic capital to affirm their ethnic identity. This validation of their identity as bilingual individuals was critical to minimizing the harmful effects of microaggressions and negative messaging they received about their bilingualism. In an established accepting community, some of these support structures might have already been in place, but in the context of New Latinx Destinations, Latinx have to band together to share cultural wealth and provide a social safety net for each other (Martinez, et al., 2021).

Navigational, social, and resistance capital emerged in the participant narratives as forces that moved their educational trajectories forward and were categorized as driving forms of capital. Navigational capital in the form of high-stakes information allowing them to better access college-ready resources (i.e., honors courses, extracurricular activities, key enrichment programs) was critical to participants' long-range academic success (Liou et al., 2009). Reflecting on their experience, many noted that the information they were able to access was often incomplete or out of context, given their limited reference points as first-generation college students. Consequently, this knowledge was still inaccessible without mentors who could explain and walk them through the process. Thus, many realized the need to develop an essential navigational strategy in seeking mentors who could interpret and assist them in translating this information into action (Liou et al., 2016), along with social capital gained through support programs. Participants noted the programs' asset-based efforts in legitimizing their home experiences, which increased engagement in the learning process by building off students' cultural backgrounds (Gildersleeve, 2009). Additionally, they provided bilingual staff with migrant backgrounds who could personally relate to students' experiences of discrimination and cultural and linguistic marginalization, which is another vital aspect of migrant programs (Gibson & Hidalgo, 2009). Social capital was exemplified through activities that addressed translating services, assisting with basic needs, and sharing educational services among DACA student networks (Martinez, et al., 2021). These intentional cultural components are associated with the program's successful outcomes in increasing college awareness and enrollment (Gandara & Contreras, 2009; Nuñez, 2009)

Lastly, one of the most significant findings of this study relates to how resistance capital was demonstrated in participants' narratives. Aligned with Solórzano & Delgado Bernal's (2001) assertion that individuals enact resistance based on their recognition of the need for social justice, participants' motivations to uplift their communities were rooted in their community and family histories and legacies narratives of resistance within new Latinx destinations. This collective identity shaped their drive for social change and instilled a sense of reciprocity where they saw their success as a product of their family's and community's collective sacrifice, which held a responsibility to give back (Gonzales, 2012). Given their critical awareness of the severe lack of Latinx educators, professionals, and community leaders, participants sought to fill this gap by serving as community role models for future generations. They strived to increase visibility and confront and dismantle the negative stereotypes permeating social and educational systems within new Latinx destinations. Participants addressed the challenges they encountered such as dehumanization, systemic xenophobia, racism in policies, and negative assumption of their intentions in the United States (Martinez, et al., 2021). Throughout their academic and professional journeys, their work to impact representation shifted from individual efforts toward transformational resistance, which critiques systems of oppression to advance systemic level change (Revelo & Baber, 2018; Solórzano & Bernal, 2001).

Utilizing a critical lens, the findings demonstrated the unique funds of knowledge that Mexican American students possess and draw upon in pursuing their educational goals. Their success was achieved despite the challenges rooted in their unique racialized histories and contexts of new Latinx destinations. Their experiences with racism and systemic barriers spanned from implicit deficit assumptions to overt forms of discrimination. Yet, participants not only persevered but highlighted the powerful familial/community strengths that were drawn on to develop robust strategies to navigate educational systems that were not created for them. The participants' stories of their evolution into the next generation of educators and leaders demonstrate the significant impact that increasing representation and building capacity within communities can have for future generations.

Connections to the Field

This study has several implications for improving educational outcomes within new Latinx destinations. First, considering the large emphasis on family that emerged in the participant narratives, there are significant implications for family outreach and engagement. The ways in which family influences all stages of the Latinx college choice process—from developing attitudes toward attending college, to what institutions to consider, and finally to the school they decide to attend—is well documented in the literature (Acevedo-Gil, 2017). Research has shown that for Latinx students, college choice is not seen as an individual process but a collective one, where parents and students must have frank discussions about mitigating the costs and realizing the benefits of college attendance (Alvarez, 2015). Therefore, educators and counselors must do more to engage parents, siblings, and other relatives in the college-going process early on in K-12 by providing culturally relevant programming and linguistically appropriate resources (i.e., bilingual materials).

Confirming prior research (Carreón et al., 2005), many participants described educational settings and schools as overall unwelcoming for their parents and families, and minimal efforts were undertaken to engage them and provide culturally-specific college access information. Unfortunately, deficit viewpoints of Latinx family engagement prevail where parents are perceived as uninvolved and/or disconnected as they may not adhere to middle-class White norms (Fernández & Rodela, 2020). Parental involvement looks different depending on an individual's background, experiences, and culture (Carreón et al., 2005); therefore, it is short-sighted to assume that all must adhere to the traditional parental involvement expectations of participation in school committees, PTA, school events, buying educational materials for the home, and seeking tutoring for their children (De Carvalho, 2000).

While the role of the family has been well-documented in the academic success of Latinx students at the K-12 level and the college-choice process, less attention has been paid to the continuous support and role that parents, siblings, and other relatives play in college persistence and completion. Family engagement at the college level contributes to students' sense of belonging on campus, yet family involvement is often limited to orientation, graduation, and family weekends. Furthermore, higher education family programing is often not inclusive or strategically focused on engaging diverse families (Harper et al., 2018). Institutional policies and practices must be examined as colleges and universities continue to develop parent outreach programs and family-friendly initiatives on campus to be more inclusive overall (Kiyama & Harper, 2018) and ensure that they address the unique needs of Latinx families.

Part of the challenge in engaging Latinx families in new destination states is that educators are adjusting to the rapidly growing Latinx populations and the shifting demographics within schools. Study participants noted that the most helpful individuals were those who had experience with Mexican/Mexican American communities outside of educational settings and those who took the time and effort to get to know them and their families personally. Therefore, the first step toward professional development for educators and counselors unfamiliar with Latinx populations is to understand the community. Training should include the history of Latinx communities within their region to encourage a more intimate understanding and combat deficit stereotypes or views. Unfortunately, educators and counselors often fall back on deficit views that place blame on the students or their parents, focusing on so-called individual and cultural deficiencies rather than systemic influences that shape disparities in social and educational outcomes (Davis & Museus, 2019; Valencia, 2012). Thus, training culturally competent educators within new Latinx destinations requires an understanding of the communities they serve and must include a deeper inquiry into the larger historical and sociopolitical contexts that perpetuate educational inequities in these regions. To do this, community engagement is required to build trust and see Latinx families as partners who bring unique contributions to collaboratively identifying strategies that capitalize on cultural strengths by empowering families (Fernández & Rodela, 2020). This takes not only individual efforts, such as those noted by participants, but also institutional commitment to make this a priority and review and implement policies centered on culturally specific family involvement.

In addition to building capacity through professional development, a critical mass of diverse educators is necessary. Representation tremendously impacted participants and motivated many of them to seek educational careers. Research shows that while there is a critical shortage of Latinx teachers and counselors, they are well-equipped to meet the needs of and impact Latinx student outcomes and are more likely to value students' cultural knowledge (Amos, 2018; Irizarry & Donaldson, 2012; Monzo & Rueda, 2001). Furthermore, because they are deeply connected Latinx communities and, like other teachers of color, they typically enter the profession with a heightened awareness of the sociopolitical contexts in which students of color are educated (Caldas, 2021; Quiocho & Rios, 2000). This grassroots level of expertise is far more valuable than any professional development could provide for teachers who are disconnected from their student populations. Considering the unique contexts of new Latinx destinations, it is imperative to champion more sustainable, funded teacher of color pipelines that recruit from and build capacity from within local Latinx communities is imperative. While there are many challenges in recruitment, preparation, and graduation of students in the Latinx teacher pipeline and the need for more robust efforts (Ocasio, 2019), the participants in this study are proof of the tremendous contributions and potential for growing your own from within the community.

The research findings have significant implications for how we understand the processes in which Latinx think about, pursue, and choose where to attend college. We know there are geographical differences that can impact the experiences across Latinx populations. Thus, Latinx educational trajectories vary depending on whether students are located within established Latinx settlement states versus new Latinx destinations. Even within new and emerging Latinx destinations, there are different sociohistorical economic and political factors at play. For example, students in new Latinx destinations continue to struggle to establish collective representation and equal access to education, which may be even more amplified in areas historically operating under a Black-White paradigm (Deguzmán, 2011), such as in the Nuevo South, which includes: Alabama, Arkansas, Georgia, Kentucky, North Carolina, South Carolina, Virginia, and West Virginia. Therefore, we need more representation across regions to gain a complete picture of Latinx educational experiences in the United States. Beyond simply ensuring the inclusion of various geographical areas in Latinx research, it is vital to explore the ways in which context matters and shapes experiences. Emerging research has begun to focus on the impact of new Latinx destination contextual factors (Camargo et al., 2022; Ramos et al., 2021). Thus, future research should take a multilayered approach to examine how Latinx students make sense of their experiences based on their positioning within specific geographic locations, historical contexts, and current political cultures.

REFERENCES

Abrego, L. J., & Gonzales, R. G. (2010). Blocked paths, uncertain futures: The postsecondary education and labor market prospects of undocumented Latinx youth. *Journal of Education for Students Placed at Risk*, 15(1-2), 144–157. DOI: 10.1080/10824661003635168

Acevedo-Gil, N. (2017). College-conocimiento: Toward an interdisciplinary college choice framework for Latinx students. *Race, Ethnicity and Education*, 20(6), 829–850. DOI: 10.1080/13613324.2017.1343294

Alvarez, C. (2015). A model for understanding the Latina/o student and parent college-going negotiation process. In Perez, P., & Ceja, M. (Eds.), *Higher education access and choice for Latino students: Critical findings and theoretical perspectives* (pp. 55–66).

Baum, S., & Flores, S. M. (2011). Higher education and children in immigrant families. *The Future of Children*, 21(1), 171–193. DOI: 10.1353/foc.2011.0000 PMID: 21465860

Bell, D. (1992). *Faces at the bottom of the well: The permanence of racism*. Basic Books.

Borjian, A., & Padilla, A. M. (2010). Voices from Mexico: How American teachers can meet the needs of Mexican immigrant students. *The Urban Review*, 42(4), 316–328. DOI: 10.1007/s11256-009-0135-0

Bransberger, P., Falkenstern, C., & Lane, P. (2020). *Knocking at the College Door. Projections of High School Graduates*. Western Interstate Commission for Higher Education.

Caldas, B. (2021). "I felt powerful": Imagining re-existence through an embodied fugitive pedagogy for Mexican American/Latinx teachers. *Equity & Excellence in Education*, 54(2), 136–151. DOI: 10.1080/10665684.2021.1951628

Carreón, G. P., Drake, C., & Barton, A. C. (2005). The importance of presence: Immigrant parents' school engagement experiences. *American Educational Research Journal*, 42(3), 465–498. DOI: 10.3102/00028312042003465

Carrillo, J. F. (2016a). I grew up straight 'hood: Unpacking the intelligences of working-class Latino male college students in North Carolina. *Equity & Excellence in Education*, 49(2), 157–169. DOI: 10.1080/10665684.2015.1086247

Carrillo, J. F. (2016b). Searching for "home" in Dixie: Identity and education in the new Latin@ South. *Educational Studies (Ames)*, 52(1), 20–37. DOI: 10.1080/00131946.2015.1120208

Ceja, M. (2004). Chicana college aspirations and the role of parents: Developing educational resiliency. *Journal of Hispanic Higher Education*, 3(4), 338–362. DOI: 10.1177/1538192704268428

Ceja, M. (2006). Understanding the role of parents and siblings as information sources in the college choice process of Chicana students. *Journal of College Student Development*, 47(1), 87–104. DOI: 10.1353/csd.2006.0003

Contreras, F. (2009). Sin papeles y rompiendo barreras: Latinx students and the challenges of persisting in college. *Harvard Educational Review*, 79(4), 610–632. DOI: 10.17763/haer.79.4.02671846902gl33w

Creswell, J. W. (2013). *Qualitative inquiry & research design: Choosing among five approaches* (3rd ed.). Sage Publications.

Cuevas, S. (2020). Ley de la vida: Latina/o immigrant parents experience of their children's transition to higher education. *The Journal of Higher Education*, 91(4), 565–587. DOI: 10.1080/00221546.2019.1647585

Davis, L. P., & Museus, S. D. (2019). What is deficit thinking? An analysis of conceptualizations of deficit thinking and implications for scholarly research. *Currents (Ann Arbor)*, 1(1), 117–130. DOI: 10.3998/currents.17387731.0001.110

De Carvalho, M. E. (2000). *Rethinking family-school relations: A critique of parental involvement in schooling*. Routledge. DOI: 10.4324/9781410600332

Dixson, A. D., & Rousseau, C. K. (2005). And we are still not saved: Critical Race Theory in education ten years later. *Race ethnicity and education*, 8(1), 7-27.Enriquez, L. (2011). "Because we feel the pressure and we also feel the support": Examining the educational success of undocumented immigrant Latina/o students. *Harvard Educational Review*, 81(3), 476–500.

Fernández, É., & Rodela, K. C. (2020). "Hay poder en numeros": Understanding the Development of a Collectivist Latinx Parent Identity and Conscientizacao Amid an Anti-Immigrant Climate. *Teachers College Record*, 122(8), 1–40. DOI: 10.1177/016146812012200804

Flores, A. (2017, September 18). *How the US Hispanic population is changing*. Pew Research Center. https://pewrsr.ch/2wBy0qS

Flores, S. M., & Horn, C. L. (2009). College persistence among undocumented students at a selective public university: A quantitative case study analysis. *Journal of College Student Retention*, 11(1), 57–76. DOI: 10.2190/CS.11.1.d

Frum, J. L. (2007). Postsecondary educational access for undocumented students: Opportunities and constraints. American Academic, 3(1), 81–108.Fry, R. (2011). The Hispanic diaspora and the public schools: Educating Hispanics. In Leal, D. L., & Trejo, S. J. (Eds.), *Latinos and the Economy: Integration And Impact In Schools Labor Markets And Beyond* (pp. 15–36). Springer New York.

Fuligni, A. J., Witkow, M., & Garcia, C. (2005). Ethnic identity and the academic adjustment of adolescents from Mexican, Chinese, and European backgrounds. *Developmental Psychology*, 41(5), 799–811. DOI: 10.1037/0012-1649.41.5.799 PMID: 16173876

Gallo, S. L., & Wortham, S. (2012). Sobresalir: Latino parent perspectives on new Latino diaspora schools. *International Journal of Multicultural Education*, 14(2). Advance online publication. DOI: 10.18251/ijme.v14i2.490

Gandara, P. C., & Contreras, F. (2009). *The Latino education crisis: The consequences of failed social policies*. Harvard University Press. DOI: 10.4159/9780674056367

Gay, G. (2014). Race and ethnicity in US education. In Race, R., & Lander, V. (Eds.), *Advancing race and ethnicity in education* (pp. 63–81). Palgrave Macmillan. DOI: 10.1057/9781137274762_5

Gibson, M., & Hidalgo, N. (2009). Bridges to success in high school for migrant youth. *Teachers College Record*, 111(3), 683–711. DOI: 10.1177/016146810911100301

Gildersleeve, R. E., Rumann, C., & Mondragón, R. (2010). Serving undocumented students: Current law and policy. *New Directions for Student Services*, 131(1), 5–18. DOI: 10.1002/ss.364

Gonzales, L. D. (2012). Stories of success: Latinas redefining cultural capital. *Journal of Latinos and Education*, 11(2), 124–138. DOI: 10.1080/15348431.2012.659566

Guarneros, N., Bendezu, C., P Pérez Huber, L., Velez, V., & Solórzano, D. (2009). Still dreaming: Legislation and legal decisions affecting undocumented AB 540 students. *CSRC Latinx Policy & Issues Brief, (23)*.

Hakuta, K. (1983). New methodologies for studying the relationship of bilingualism and cognitive flexibility. *TESOL Quarterly*, 17(4), 679–681. DOI: 10.2307/3586621

Hamann, E., Wortham, S., & Murillo, E. G.Jr., (Eds.). (2015). *Revisiting education in the new Latino diaspora*. IAP.

Harper, C. E., Kiyama, J. M., Ramos, D., & Aguayo, D. (2018). Examining the inclusivity of parent and family college orientations: A directed content analysis. *Journal of College Orientation, Transition, and Retention*, 25(1), 30–42.

Hatch, D. K., Mardock Uman, N., & Garcia, C. E. (2016). Variation within the "New Latino Diaspora" a decade of changes across the United States in the equitable participation of Latina/os in higher education. *Journal of Hispanic Higher Education*, *15*(4), 358-385.Hakuta, K. (1983). New methodologies for studying the relationship of bilingualism and cognitive flexibility. *TESOL Quarterly*, 17(4), 679–681.

Herrera, A., & Chen, A. (2010). Strategies to support undocumented students. *Transitions*, 5(2), 3–4.

Higher Education Coordinating Commission. (2021). *Higher Education and Training for Students in Oregon.*https://www.oregon.gov/highered/research/Documents/Equity/HE%20for%20Students%20By%20Race_Latino_Hispanic.pdf

Hurtado, S., & Carter, D. F. (1997). Effects of college transition and perceptions of the campus racial climate on Latinx college students' sense of belonging. *Sociology of Education*, 70(4), 324–345. DOI: 10.2307/2673270

Hussar, B., Zhang, J., Hein, S., Wang, K., Roberts, A., Cui, J., Smith, M., Mann, F. B., Barmer, A., & Dilig, R. (2020). *The Condition of Education 2020* (NCES 2020-144). US Department of Education. Washington, DC: National Center for Education Statistics. https://files.eric.ed.gov/fulltext/ED605216.pdf

Irizarry, J., & Donaldson, M. L. (2012). Teach for America: The Latinization of US schools and the critical shortage of Latina/o teachers. *American Educational Research Journal*, 49(1), 155–194. DOI: 10.3102/0002831211434764

Jones, S. R., Torres, V., & Arminio, J. L. (2014). *Negotiating the complexities of qualitative research in higher education: Fundamental elements and issues.*Routledge.

Kelly, A. P., Schneider, M., & Carey, K. (2010). *Rising to the Challenge: Hispanic College Graduation Rates as a National Priority.* American Enterprise Institute for Public Policy Research. https://files.eric.ed.gov/fulltext/ED508846.pdf

Kiyama, J. M., & Harper, C. E. (2018). Beyond hovering: A conceptual argument for an inclusive model of family engagement in higher education. *Review of Higher Education*, 41(3), 365–385. DOI: 10.1353/rhe.2018.0012

Kovats, A. G. (2010). *Invisible students and marginalized identities the articulation of identity among Mixteco youth in San Diego, California.* [Doctoral dissertation, San Diego State University]. ProQuest Dissertations Publishing.

Krogstad, J. M. (2016, July 28). *5 facts about Latinx and education*. Pew Research Center. https://www.pewresearch.org/fact-tank/2016/07/28/5-facts-about-Latinx-and-education/

Liou, D. D., Antrop-González, R., & Cooper, R. (2009). Unveiling the promise of Community Cultural Wealth to sustaining Latina/o students' college-going information networks. *Educational Studies (Ames)*, 45(6), 534–555. DOI: 10.1080/00131940903311347

Lowenhaupt, R., & Reeves, T. (2015). Toward a theory of school capacity in new immigrant destinations: Instructional and organizational considerations. *Leadership and Policy in Schools*, 14(3), 308–340. DOI: 10.1080/15700763.2015.1021052

Machado-Casas, M. (2009). The politics of organic phylogeny: The art of parenting and surviving as transnational multilingual Latinx indigenous immigrants in the US. *High School Journal*, 92(4), 82–99. DOI: 10.1353/hsj.0.0034

Martinez, M. A. (2013). (Re) considering the role familismo plays in Latina/o high school students' college choices. *High School Journal*, 97(1), 21–40. DOI: 10.1353/hsj.2013.0019

Martinez, R. R.Jr, Dye, L., Gonzalez, L. M., & Rivas, J. (2021). Striving to thrive: Community cultural wealth and legal immigration status. *Journal of Latina/o Psychology*, 9(4), 299–314. DOI: 10.1037/lat0000191

Merriam, S. B. (2009). *Qualitative research: A guide to design and implementation*. Jossey-Bass.

Moll, L. C., Amanti, C., Neff, D., & González, N. (1992). Funds of knowledge for teaching: Using a qualitative approach to connect homes and classrooms. *Theory into Practice*, 31(2), 132–141. DOI: 10.1080/00405849209543534

Montiel, G. I. (2017). "Hacerle la lucha": Examining the value of hard work as a source of funds of knowledge of undocumented, Mexican Ivy League students. In Kiyama, J. M., & Rios-Aguilar, C. (Eds.), *Funds of knowledge in higher education: Honoring students' cultural experiences and resources as strengths* (pp. 125–142). Routledge. DOI: 10.4324/9781315447322-8

Monzo, L. D., & Rueda, R. S. (2001). Professional roles, caring, and scaffolds: Latino teachers' and paraeducators' interactions with Latino students. *American Journal of Education*, 109(4), 438–471. DOI: 10.1086/444335

Moslimani, M., & Noe-Bustamante, L. (2023, Aug.). *Facts on Latinos in the US*. Pew Research Center. https://www.pewresearch.org/race-and-ethnicity/fact-sheet/latinos-in-the-us-fact-sheet/

Murillo, E. G., Wortham, S. E. F., & Hamann, E. T. (2002). *Education in the new Latino diaspora: Policy and the politics of identity* (Vol. 2). Greenwood Publishing Group.

Núñez, A. M. (2017). What can Latina/o migrant students tell us about college outreach and access? In M. E. Zarate, P. Perez *Facilitating educational success for migrant farmworker students in the US* (pp. 82-93). Routledge.

Ocasio, K. M. (2019). A Review of Literature Surrounding the Latino Teacher Pipeline. In E. G Murillo Jr (Ed.), *Critical Readings on Latinos and Education* (62-79). Routledge.

Parker, K., Morin, R., Horowitz, J. M., Lopez, M. H., & Rohal, M. (2015, June 11). *Multiracial in America: Proud, diverse and growing in numbers.* Pew Research Center. https://www.pewresearch.org/social-trends/2015/06/11/multiracial-in-america/

Patton, M. Q. (2014). *Qualitative research & evaluation methods: Integrating theory and practice.* Sage publications.

Perez, W. (2009). *We are Americans: Undocumented students pursuing the American dream.* Sterling, VA: Stylus Publishing.

Perez, W. (2011). *Americans by heart: Undocumented Latinx students and the promise of higher education.* Teachers College Press.

Perez, W., Cortes, R., Ramos, K., & Coronado, H. (2010). Cursed and blessed: Examining the socioemotional and academic experiences of undocumented Latinx/a college students. *New Directions for Student Services*, 2010(131), 35–51. DOI: 10.1002/ss.366

Perez, W., Espinoza, R., Ramos, K., Coronado, H. M., & Cortes, R. (2009). Academic resilience among undocumented Latinx students. *Hispanic Journal of Behavioral Sciences*, 31(2), 149–181. DOI: 10.1177/0739986309333020

Pérez Huber, L. (2010). Using Latina/o Critical Race Theory (LatCrit) and racist nativism to explore intersectionality in the educational experiences of undocumented Chicana college students. *Educational Foundations*, 24, 77–96.

Perreira, K. M., Fuligni, A., & Potochnick, S. (2010). Fitting in: The roles of social acceptance and discrimination in shaping the academic motivations of Latinx youth in the US Southeast. *The Journal of Social Issues*, 66(1), 131–153. DOI: 10.1111/j.1540-4560.2009.01637.x PMID: 22611286

Quiocho, A., & Rios, F. (2000). The power of their presence: Minority group teachers and schooling. *Review of Educational Research*, 70(4), 485–528. DOI: 10.3102/00346543070004485

Revelo, R. A., & Baber, L. D. (2018). Engineering resistors: Engineering Latina/o students and emerging resistant capital. *Journal of Hispanic Higher Education*, 17(3), 249–269. DOI: 10.1177/1538192717719132

Rios-Aguilar, C., & Kiyama, J. M. (2019). Funds of Knowledge: An Approach to Studying Latina(o) Students' Transition to College. In E. G Murillo Jr (Ed.), *Critical Readings on Latinos and Education* (pp. 26–43). Routledge.

Sánchez, P., & Machado-Casas, M. (2009). At the intersection of transnationalism, Latina/o immigrants, and education. *High School Journal*, 92(4), 3–15. DOI: 10.1353/hsj.0.0027

Solórzano, D. G., & Bernal, D. D. (2001). Examining transformational resistance through a critical race and LatCrit theory framework: Chicana and Chicano students in an urban context. *Urban Education*, 36(3), 308–342. DOI: 10.1177/0042085901363002

Solórzano, D. G., Villalpando, O., & Oseguera, L. (2005). Educational inequities and Latina/o undergraduate students in the United States: A critical race analysis of their educational progress. *Journal of Hispanic Higher Education*, 4(3), 272–294. DOI: 10.1177/1538192705276550

Stepler, R., & Lopez, M. H. (2016, September 8). *U.S. Latino population growth and dispersion has slowed since onset of the Great Recession*. Pew Research Center. https://www.pewresearch.org/hispanic/2016/09/08/latino-population-growth-and-dispersion-has-slowed-since-the-onset-of-the-great-recession/

Suárez-Orozco, C., Suárez-Orozco, M., & Todorova, I. (2008). *Learning a new land. Immigrant students in American society*. Harvard University Press. DOI: 10.4159/9780674044111

Suárez-Orozco, C., & Todorova, I. L. (2003). The social worlds of immigrant youth. *New Directions for Youth Development*, 2003(100), 15–24. DOI: 10.1002/yd.60 PMID: 14750266

US Census Bureau. (2000). *Population and Housing Unit Estimates*. Retrieved from www.census.gov/popest/

US Census Bureau. (2010). *Population and Housing Unit Estimates*. Retrieved from www.census.gov/popest/

Valencia, R. R. (2012). *The evolution of deficit thinking: Educational thought and practice*. Routledge. DOI: 10.4324/9780203046586

Valencia, R. R., & Black, M. S. (2002). "Mexican Americans don't value education!"—On the basis of myth, mythmaking, and debunking. *Journal of Latinos and Education*, 1(2), 81–103. DOI: 10.1207/S1532771XJLE0102_2

Wortham, S., Clonan-Roy, K., Link, H., & Martinez, C. (2013). The new Latino Diaspora: The surging Hispanic and Latino population across the country has brought new education challenges and opportunities to rural and small town America. *Phi Delta Kappan*, 94(6), 14. DOI: 10.1177/003172171309400604

Wortham, S., Hamann, E. T., & Murillo, E. G.Jr., (Eds.). (2002). *Education in the New Latino Diaspora: Policy and the politics of identity*. Ablex Publishing.

Yosso, T., Smith, W., Ceja, M., & Solórzano, D. (2009). Critical Race Theory, racial microaggressions, and campus racial climate for Latina/o undergraduates. *Harvard Educational Review, 79*(4), 659-691. Yosso, T. J., & Solórzano, D. G. (2006). Leaks in the Chicana and Chicano Educational Pipeline. *CSRC Latinx Policy & Issues Brief, (13)*.

Yosso, T. J. (2005). Whose culture has capital? A critical race theory discussion of community cultural wealth. *Race, Ethnicity and Education*, 8(1), 69–9. DOI: 10.1080/1361332052000341006

Zabin, C., Kearney, M., Garcia, A., Runsten, D., & Nagengast, C. (1993). *A new cycle of poverty: Mixtec migrants in California agriculture*. California Institute for Rural Studies.

Zúñiga, V., & Hernández-León, R. (Eds.). (2005). *New destinations: Mexican immigration in the United States*. Russell Sage Foundation.

Chapter 7
Breaking Down Barriers:
Nurturing Our Resistance, Reclaiming Our Space, and Calling for Shared Responsibility

Françoise Thenoux
Independent Researcher, Chile

ABSTRACT

This chapter examines the systemic inequities faced by Latinx teachers in the predominantly white U.S. education system. It explores the evolving concept of self-care, originally coined by Audre Lorde, which has become commodified and stripped of its radical roots. For Latinx educators, self-care transcends wellness trends; it is a survival strategy against anti-immigrant policies, tokenism, accentism, and the devaluation of their assets. My experience as an immigrant teacher highlights the burnout from visa renewals and institutional bias. The emotional and economic strain underscores the abusive conditions Latinx teachers often endure. Dismantling these oppressive systems requires shared responsibility from school leaders and administrators in reforming hiring practices and policies. By sharing our stories this chapter reveals collective experiences shaping our identities and the need for transformation. True self-care is rooted in resistance, community building, and advocacy, empowering Latinx educators to reclaim their narratives and become advocates for change.

INTRODUCTION

"Caring for myself is not self-indulgence, it is self-preservation, and that is an act of political warfare." — Audre Lorde, A Burst of Light: Essays (1988)

DOI: 10.4018/979-8-3373-1340-5.ch007

Copyright © 2025, IGI Global Scientific Publishing. Copying or distributing in print or electronic forms without written permission of IGI Global Scientific Publishing is prohibited.

Before I begin my story, I want to acknowledge that this narrative is deeply personal, rooted in my journey of decolonization, identity, and core values. Because this story is authentically mine and woven into the fabric of who I am, I will switch into Spanish—my mother tongue—throughout. Language is identity, and Spanish holds pieces of me that cannot always be translated. This fluid use of language reflects my intention to reclaim my space, honoring my multiplicity and defying a world that often demands I fragment myself to fit in.

Language—like identity labels—is complex. Throughout this chapter, I use the term Latinx despite its imperfections. While umbrella terms can flatten the rich diversity of our cultures, Latinx aligns with my values, offering a space that includes my non-binary and gender non-conforming siblings. By contrast, "Hispanic" remains tethered to the colonial legacy of the Spanish Empire, whose wounds still scar our communities. Divesting from that legacy is an act of liberation, one I will explore further in these pages. Additionally, the term "Hispanic" often excludes Brazilians, Haitians, and others whose struggles with systemic oppression mirror our own in the U.S.

Our diasporas—shaped by colonization, migration, and resistance—are as diverse as the lands, languages, and histories we carry. This is why I wrestle with umbrella terms; they risk homogenizing the distinct geolects, cultures, and ethnicities that define us. There is space for everyone in our diaspora, but it is reductive and dangerous to assume our lived experiences are identical. Debates over who qualifies as "authentically Latinx" often divide us, a legacy of colonialism and imperialism. As Paulo Freire noted, "The oppressed, having internalized the image of the oppressor and adopted his guidelines, are fearful of freedom" (Freire & Mellado, 1970). Within our diaspora, some fight for liberation, while others operate from internalized oppression, mimicking the systems that harm us. Recognizing this complexity humanizes us and sharpens our collective fight for justice. Liberation must be intersectional, leaving no one behind.

What kind of educational leader would I be without recognizing how power, privilege, and marginalization shape the experiences of our diaspora? Anti-Blackness and colorism persist within our own communities and across the U.S., making it especially difficult for Black and Indigenous educators (Crenshaw, 1989; Ladson-Billings, 1998). Homophobia and transphobia further compound the challenges many endure, while ableism is often overlooked in conversations about inclusion (Simmons, 2019).

The most marginalized among us—like Dreamers and undocumented community members—bear the burden of an arbitrary and racist immigration system (Abrego & Menjívar, 2011). While storytelling and sharing *vivencias* connect us, we must also examine our own positionality within the wheel of privilege. As Audre Lorde (1984) said, "There is no such thing as a single-issue struggle because we do not live single-issue lives." Our liberation is tied together. It has never been achieved through individualism—it must be a collective endeavor.

When we step into these spaces, we honor our differences and celebrate them. Liberation means fighting for me, for you, and for us—together.

Story Time

Our stories hold the power to heal and transcend time. They carry the seeds of our ancestors and the wounds of colonization, flowing through us like an underground river, nourishing even the most barren landscapes. As Eduardo Galeano eloquently said at the Feria del Libro de Buenos Aires, *"Los científicos dicen que estamos hechos de átomos, pero a mí un pajarito me contó que estamos hechos de historias"* (2012). Stories—born of days, resistance, and people—shape who we are and who we can become.

This is my story: a journey of resistance, reclaiming space, and asserting my identity as a Latina woman in the U.S. It is uniquely mine yet shared in spirit because, in community, we thrive. I carry the multitude of women who never had the chance to tell their stories or resist. I carry their strength—their stories etched into my veins. My Indigenous ancestras, the curanderas, the ones who endured violence in silence, and those who raised their voices for change—they guide me with unwavering strength.

As Maya Angelou said, "Each time a woman stands up for herself, without knowing it possibly, without claiming it, she stands up for all women." My story is mine, yes, but it is also a collective story, one offered with the hope that its ripple effect will inspire others to reclaim their spaces, rewrite their narratives, and resist systems that seek to diminish us. Sharing our stories not only heals—it creates the world we deserve.

The year was 2016, a time when the U.S. prepared to bid farewell to the Obama era and faced a surreal presidential election. The country stood at a crossroads: elect the first woman president or a pseudo-businessman, con artist, and reality star whose campaign relied on inflammatory rhetoric, racism, and discriminatory propaganda. After 11 years living in the U.S.as a racialized immigrant, I wasn't shocked someone like him had risen this far. I had spent all those years immersing myself in the history that shaped the nation's reality.

My first five years in Atlanta revealed both the possibilities and oppressive undercurrents of the South. I witnessed the historic election of the first Black president while working at an extraordinary African American school in College Park, where Black brilliance thrived. At the same time, I encountered Southern racism—blatant, pervasive, and unyielding—in both adults and children at an independent school where I taught later on. Toxic masculinity, overt racism, and casual conversations about guns were everyday realities, normalized alongside the horror of active shooter drills. Yet, nothing prepared me for the insidious racism of the so-called liberal North when I moved to Philadelphia to teach at an independent school.

In Philadelphia, racism wore a different mask—subtle, insidious, and steeped in denial. It was wrapped in progressive rhetoric, where white feminism flourished, performative activism abounded, and conversations about dismantling power structures were rare or highly performative. The spaces that celebrated inclusion perpetuated exclusion through denial and deflection. It was in these spaces where I learned that racism and biases don't always shout; sometimes, they whisper behind smiles and claims of solidarity.

It would be unfair to paint my entire U.S. experience with a single brushstroke. I built meaningful relationships and experienced plenty of moments of fulfillment and joy during my 18 years there. No place is perfect! I carry my fair share of criticisms of my home country, Chile, as well. Growing up under a U.S.-backed fascist dictatorship left its mark, but the restoration of democracy and the civic education I received inspired my commitment to justice—a drive that has been with me since birth and sharpened through age and experience.

One of the most impactful opportunities I had was earning my master's degree in Early Childhood and Elementary Education at Kennesaw State University. It was a rigorous program led by international scholars, and at its helm was a remarkable educator—a woman whose leadership spanned roles as Chair of the Department and Director of the Minority Future Teacher-Scholars Program. Her influence, along with the academic challenges I encountered, helped me develop my voice as a social justice leader in education. Those college years in Chile and my studies in the U.S. shaped the leader I would become.

Throughout my time in the U.S., one silver lining was the continuous presence of Black women in my life. They either saw my potential and mentored me or stood with me in solidarity within predominantly white spaces. Many became not just friends but cheerleaders, encouraging me to share my knowledge and rally others in my liberatory journey toward becoming a decolonial scholar and ABAR (Anti-Bias, Anti-Racist) educator. Alongside them were Latina women with whom I shared not just trauma but, perhaps even more significantly, joy. Our common experiences created bonds that sustained me—and those connections will play a significant role later in this chapter.

Now, coming back to that pivotal day in 2016, when the U.S. presidential election was unfolding. As I sat at that polished dinner table, surrounded by "friends"— mostly well-meaning liberal white people—the atmosphere was thick with disbelief as the results trickled in. Their nervous laughter and dramatic comments about the consequences felt surreal, as if they were performing their disappointment rather than reckoning with what it truly meant. And then it hit: Donald Trump was declared the winner.

My heart sank. I was the immigrant at the table—the one who would feel the most direct repercussions—but my concerns were brushed aside with the chorus of "We're all in this together." I knew in my gut that we weren't. Their privilege was swinging at me like a red flag. These people, raised in the U.S., could easily separate themselves from Trump voters even though these voters were either family members, neighbors, friends or clients. They couldn't see the profound betrayal that someone like me felt, someone whose permanence in the country was now under threat by this decision.

As the wine flowed, their privilege began to feel suffocating. I listened to them distance themselves from the people responsible for this outcome, never fully grasping that their indifference had also played a role. Tomorrow, they could return to their daily lives, navigating liberal spaces where white supremacy was disguised with tolerance and inclusion. But for me and others from the global majority, the stakes were higher, and the consequences were already unfolding.

The next day, I had to go to work. At my school, a lot of us wore black in silent mourning. In the hallways, the knowing glances exchanged between the few of us from marginalized communities said everything—we understood that this was more than a mistake. It was a disaster, one in which liberals were complicit, whether through action or inaction. The costs would be borne by us. After November 2016, the group of friends who sat with me at that table slowly began to vanish. In a predominantly white school environment, where the few pillars of support I had were women of the global majority, I often felt isolated. This independent, liberal institution like many others in the country, failed to recognize the unique challenges faced by educators like me.

Despite my numerous accomplishments, I felt like an outsider, particularly when I had to implore for sponsorship for my green card. I was continuously undermined by a white administrator who seemed threatened by my commitment to social justice. Complaints from a few white caregivers about my advocacy fell on attentive ears as he sided with them instead of recognizing my humanity and the importance of ABAR work, especially in the current sociopolitical context. His actions were a manifestation of the systemic issues that devalue women of the global majority, especially those who dare to speak up.

Our Silences Will Not Protect Us

"Calladita te ves más bonita"—a phrase echoed across Latinx households, teaching silence as a virtue and submission as beauty. If I had a penny for every time I was scolded for not staying *calladita*, I'd be a millionaire. But silence was never

my language. Not as a child. Not as a woman. And never as an educator navigating spaces that sought to diminish me. I've learned through experience—and through Audre Lorde's resonant words—that silence only serves the oppressor. "Your silence will not protect you," Lorde reminds us, and her truth has become my mantra.

Lorde's wisdom underscores the suffocating reality of unspoken grievances: they do not disappear; they settle within us, corroding until they demand acknowledgment. Speaking out invites risk—rejection, harm, or even ostracization—but it also holds transformative power. I have raised my voice against machismo and patriarchal familismo, refusing to perpetuate silence. Later in this chapter, I will delve deeper into how marianismo and societal expectations shape Latinas' identities, often at the expense of their mental health.

Much like Lorde, I have found solidarity in shared struggles. "For every real word spoken," she wrote, "we made contact with other women while bridging our differences." This resonates with my own journey. After the 2016 election, I began sharing my experiences as an immigrant educator on my personal social media platform. What started as political expression quickly evolved into a community-building space, connecting me with other educators—especially women of the global majority—whose values aligned with mine.

In 2018, The Woke Spanish Teacher was born. What began as an Instagram account blossomed into a sanctuary of joy, resistance, and collective empowerment. Within this virtual community, I found solidarity, rediscovered my voice, and redefined boundaries. Latina women often struggle with setting boundaries, as societal expectations teach us to prioritize others at our own expense. Through therapy and decolonial healing, I learned to guard my energy while continuing to nurture this vital space of connection.

The irony, however, was glaring. Outside my school walls, I thrived. Caregivers, colleagues, and professional organizations sought my expertise, praising my vision and leadership. Inside, I was belittled by my supervisor, whose performative liberalism masked deep-seated bias. His hostility became overt when I confronted him, stating, "You cannot treat women of color this way." His indignant response—"Nobody has ever accused me of racism before!"—exposed the fragility of his so-called allyship.

I confided in a "friend" from the 2016 election dinner table, venting about the harassment I endured. Her flippant suggestion, "Why don't you just quit?" revealed her profound detachment from my reality. As an immigrant dependent on a visa, leaving wasn't an option. Her ignorance stung, but it was a bitter reminder that not everyone understands the stakes of survival.

The harassment intensified. Meetings turned into ambushes, filled with fabricated accusations and baseless criticisms. I was thriving everywhere but here, yet I had no choice but to endure. How was it possible that I was thriving in every space outside this environment, yet enduring so much harm inside it? The school held the sponsorship for my visa, so there were times when I had to swallow my words and silence my anger. And that silence took its toll. The weight of suppression, frustration, and contained rage began to manifest physically. Insomnia crept in, anxiety followed, and I found myself unraveling.

The harassment I endured came in waves,that was his style so 2019 offered a brief break. A year earlier, in 2018, I reported him to my principal, only to find I wasn't the only woman who had raised concerns. Yet, nothing changed. Warned but emboldened, he turned to weaponizing white women in the workplace, who carried out his bids. On top of their harassment, I grappled with what I suspected were symptoms of endometriosis—a pain I had to mask to keep going. Yet, under this inequitable scrutiny, I thrived as a teacher. My students were excelling, their Spanish proficiency nearing immersion levels.

Still, his most absurd claim was that my students were learning too much social justice and not enough Spanish. This lie gained traction with a small group of white parents who viewed my ABAR (Anti-Bias, Anti-Racist) curriculum as a threat. All this unfolded in a self-proclaimed "progressive" school—a space that proudly flaunted its DEI statement while failing to live up to its promises. Complaints about toxic leadership abounded, but fear paralyzed most from taking action. Advocacy from supposed allies turned out to be *de los dientes pa' fuera*—all talk, no substance.

Then, in 2019, a significant shift occurred: we got a DEI director, a Black woman who encouraged me to present at my first conference. That experience was transformative. I attended two PoCC (People of Color Conference) events, finding solace and solidarity among educators navigating similar struggles. These spaces, particularly the Latinx affinity groups, became sanctuaries of healing and empowerment. It was at the 2019 PoCC that I first heard Kimberlé Crenshaw discuss intersectionality and discovered Dr. Tone Rawlings, whose work deepened my commitment to decolonial education.

As Gloria Anzaldúa so beautifully described, I had begun using my "wild tongue." Social media became my outlet for everything I couldn't say at school. My online presence grew, and invitations to podcasts and articles followed. Sharing my personal narrative allowed me to heal and connect with others on similar journeys. This marked the beginning of my *conocimiento*, a transformative process Anzaldúa described as relational and intuitive—a gathering of wisdom from lived realities and dreams that leads to action and social change. It became my compass as I committed to decolonizing every system I encountered, inspiring others to join me in this liberatory work.

At the same time, my homeland, Chile, erupted in protests. What began as outrage over a subway fare hike grew into a mass movement demanding systemic change. Millions defied curfews and military repression, their resistance echoing the courage of my ancestors. From afar, my heart sang *El pueblo unido jamás será vencido.* I channeled that fire into my classroom, teaching my students Victor Jara's songs of protest and freedom while exploring the movement's significance, weaving it into our curriculum.

Decolonization became more than an academic pursuit—it was a personal and professional revolution. My curriculum embraced non-binary Spanish, shifting away from language oppression to create spaces of belonging and affirmation. Self-care through *conocimiento* became my political warfare. Flourishing despite toxic leadership was my way of reclaiming my identity and space unapologetically. I unpacked every layer of my life—family history, colonial trauma, personal experiences—to write a new, empowering narrative for myself. I seized the opportunity to rebuild. The protests in Chile reignited my resolve for decolonization, not just in my classroom but in every facet of my life. My wild tongue was unstoppable, carrying me toward a future where healing, resistance, and joy could coexist.

The Coyolxauhqui Imperative

The Coyolxauhqui Imperative, as coined by Gloria E. Anzaldúa, describes the ongoing process of healing and reconstruction after trauma—confronting the wounds that fragment us and piecing ourselves back together in pursuit of wholeness. This concept resonated profoundly with me back in 2020, a year of relentless upheaval. The social awakening sparked by George Floyd's murder and the global Black Lives Matter movement collided with my own battles: immigration uncertainties, bureaucratic delays, and the devastating loss of my abuela, who passed away while I remained isolated, unable to say goodbye.

As protests erupted, I felt like the submerged iceberg of racial injustice was finally brought to the surface. But what was most jarring was witnessing the urgency of well-meaning white people scrambling to "solve" a problem that Black and Brown communities had been shouting about for generations. Their sudden activism, though perhaps well-intentioned, exposed a fundamental disconnect—one that revealed the privilege of approaching racism as if it were new, a crisis to be resolved quickly rather than a centuries-old wound demanding deep, sustained reckoning.

These forces fragmented me—spiritually, emotionally, and psychologically. Yet, even amid this mental health crisis, I felt an imperative stirring within: the need to understand my fragmentation and begin the cyclical, imperfect, and deeply political work of reconstruction. As 2020 dismantled familiar norms, forcing us into survival mode, the cracks in my life became impossible to ignore.

The pandemic's collective trauma was compounded for me by the weight of systemic inequities. Teachers like me were expected to reinvent ourselves while receiving hollow reassurances from administrators about unity: "We're all in this together." At school these words rang especially false. Caregivers were treated as clients, and teachers as expendable labor. This chaos coincided with the expiration of my work visa and the agonizing start of my green card process. For three years, this process dragged on, worsened by an incompetent lawyer recommended by someone on the school board. Every interaction with their office exacerbated my anxiety—a stark reminder that my life in the U.S., built over 16 years, could crumble at any moment.

The intersectionality of my experiences—immigration battles, systemic discrimination, and an isolating school environment—made my struggles invisible to most. The pandemic exposed systemic inequities, but my reality as an immigrant remained alien to many in my community, especially well-meaning white friends who drifted away, their privilege allowing them to disengage. While COVID-19 was a collective trauma, I faced the added burden of legal uncertainty and relentless fear of deportation, with little support.

In the midst of this isolation, the few lifelines I had were the warmth of Zoom calls with my family and the unwavering support of my Mexican friends. Social media became another unexpected source of solace, connecting me with like-minded people who were also navigating personal and collective awakenings. The weight of these awakenings was heavy, but they also gave me a sense of purpose, guiding my teaching as I incorporated decolonization, protest songs, and discussions of resistance into my classroom.

The summer of 2020, my school demanded we return to in-person teaching without a sufficient health plan, exposing teachers to unnecessary risks. We resisted, uniting in solidarity, but the administration pushed forward, forcing us into classrooms with minimal preparation. Meanwhile, my immigration struggles persisted. Harsh, unhelpful responses from my lawyer left me desperate. Only after seeking second opinions and finding a new lawyer—recommended by a trusted colleague—did hope begin to glimmer. But the cumulative toll of these experiences had already set the Coyolxauhqui imperative in motion, preparing me for another cycle of breaking and rebuilding, one that would extend far beyond 2020.

As 2020 ended, 2021 brought its own set of challenges. In January, I endured one of the most profound losses of my life—the passing of my 96-year-old abuela, my second mother and role model. Although her peaceful departure brought some comfort, the inability to travel to Chile for a proper farewell was a wound that COVID restrictions only deepened. Even my mother couldn't attend her service, leaving our mourning unfinished. At the same time, my school clung to the pretense of normalcy, ignoring our personal and professional struggles while gaslighting teachers into compliance with unrealistic demands.

Despite my grief, I forced myself to meet the professional commitments I had made, inspired by my abuela's strength and intellectual brilliance. She would not have wanted me to give up. In her honor, I completed articles, presented at conferences, and finished a book chapter. Yet, the pressure was relentless. My school, which was sponsoring my green card process, made it impossible to speak up about their unrealistic expectations without jeopardizing my immigration status. Paying for the process myself was illegal, trapping me in an exhausting, delicate balancing act. At one point, I even rallied my social media community and colleagues to write letters to representatives on my behalf—a story I'll revisit later. But through it all, self-care became more than survival; it became an act of political warfare. Moments of joy, rest, and care were small, deliberate acts of rebellion in a world that demanded more than I could give. Speaking up within the spaces I carved was a radical act of resistance, especially in the face of overwhelming grief, professional strain, and systemic failures.

Even with these acts of resistance, my health steadily declined. The pain from my endometriosis worsened, incapacitating me at times. Inequitable work conditions compounded the stress. Although I no longer had a classroom—it had been reassigned to create social distancing—administrators demanded I pack up my belongings during spring break, with no help or compensation. When I advocated for basic accommodations like bathroom breaks to manage my symptoms, I was met with harshness and dismissal. I kept moving forward, bolstered by the knowledge that my new lawyer had successfully extended my visa and that my social media campaign was gaining traction. Yet, the weight of being a Latina eldest daughter loomed large. Conditioned to be strong and self-sufficient, I internalized the need to endure, much like Luisa from *Encanto*. Even as I sensed myself unraveling, I continued, driven by the path I had paved—one my ancestors could only dream of.

Amidst the chaos, questions began to surface. Was enduring an immigration process that stripped me of my dignity worth it? Was sacrificing my health for a job rooted in colonial expectations and white supremacy justifiable? These questions gnawed at me, forcing me to confront the relentless demands of a system designed to dehumanize. Yet, I moved forward—caught between survival and resistance, knowing the weight of my journey was too heavy to set down but too significant to abandon.

The latter half of 2021 offered a fleeting sense of relief. After years of medical neglect, I finally advocated for myself and switched to an all-women's clinic that validated my pain. A proper diagnosis—endometriosis and fibroids—gave me clarity, and I turned to the ancestral wisdom of the herbalists in my family. Plant medicine became a crucial part of my healing, allowing me a semblance of normalcy. Though the chronic insomnia and anxiety from years of immigration uncertainty eased slightly, they never fully disappeared. In pursuit of healing, I rekindled my yoga practice at a welcoming studio and leaned on the warmth of my Mexican and international friends. Inspired by Adrienne Maree Brown's *Pleasure Activism: The Politics of Feeling Good*, I embraced the philosophy that joy and self-care are acts of political resistance. As Brown writes, *"We need to learn how to practice love such that care—for ourselves and others—is understood as political resistance and cultivating resilience."*

This ethos became my lifeline. Every act of self-care—whether cooking a comforting meal or laughing with friends—was an intentional act of defiance against a world that demanded too much. Yet, the weight of systemic barriers and workplace suppression reminded me that personal joy, while vital, was not enough.

At work, the silence from leadership and their suppression of my voice weighed heavily on me, amplifying the frustration of navigating a system I could never fully belong to. These challenges were compounded by the precariousness of my immigration status—a reality those with citizenship privilege could never fully understand. Securing a green card wasn't just a bureaucratic hurdle; it was an existential necessity.

But to achieve it, I had to suppress core parts of myself. The outspoken, socially conscious Latina in me—the one with a "wild tongue" unapologetically advocating for justice—had to keep silent sometimes.

Life Goes On –

2021 was a year of profound grief, transformative realizations, and relentless immigration struggles. It felt like an emotional roller coaster—each high and low leaving me gasping for breath. At every turn, I asked myself: Is it worth it? Is it worth enduring a dehumanizing immigration process that reduces your humanity to forms, fees, and approvals, just to belong somewhere you might never fully belong? Is it worth sacrificing your well-being for a job steeped in colonial ideals—complicit in harm, no matter how much good you try to bring?

Grief forces clarity. It demands we confront dreams we once clung to, exposing their fragility. For Latinx educators, particularly women, the weight of societal expectations often makes choosing ourselves seem impossible. The cultural narrative of *marianismo* teaches us to serve others at the expense of our own joy, yet 2021 was the year I began to break that cycle. When one of my closest friends invited me to a BTS concert in December, the timing was perfect—like the universe had conspired to guide me toward healing. And yet, I hesitated. Could I take the personal days? Could I prioritize myself without fear of retaliation—of being fired, denied sponsorship, or reprimanded? But eventually, I said yes, and for that, I am eternally grateful.

The concert was more than music; it was catharsis. It became a pivotal moment where I shed guilt, reclaimed joy, and began to leave fear behind. BTS's *Magic Shop* became my refuge—a sanctuary that helped me endure one of the most turbulent periods of my life. It filled me with lightness and courage, reminding me that I, too, deserve joy. Joy doesn't have to conform to expectations—it is deeply personal. Allowing myself to feel it was revolutionary, especially as a Latina raised in a culture that often glorifies sacrifice over self-fulfillment. The concert embodied a promise: to embrace joy and practice the self-love that BTS champions so wholeheartedly.

Outside of school, my professional achievements flourished. I received recognition for my work, proving that I was worthy of dignity and success—not just survival. That moment marked a shift. I committed to living authentically, no longer confined by fear or guilt.

The *BE* album, which a new friend gifted me at the concert, became a guidepost—its songs illuminating my path and prompting deep reflection on the past and the future ahead. I asked myself: What does it mean to live authentically? This section's title comes from BTS's song *Life Goes On*, and it perfectly encapsulates my journey. The combination of these transformative experiences and my specialization in trauma-informed education not only helped me understand my own childhood wounds and the trauma carried by many in the Latinx community but also reshaped my teaching practice. When I returned to the classroom, my students' mental health became a top priority. I now embrace the idea that healing is not linear, and joy—no matter how it looks—belongs to me. Moving forward, I honor my path, my joy, and the promise to live fully and authentically.

As I shared the story of the concert on my Instagram account, I was deeply moved by the outpouring of responses from fellow Latinx educators. Many DM'd me or commented, sharing their own stories of honoring themselves and nurturing their inner child. So many of us, having been forced into the role of parent at a young age, finally recognized the importance of caring for ourselves as adults. The emotional connection was profound, reminding me that when we choose joy, we empower each other to do the same.

The personal transformations I underwent—decolonization, mental health work, reckoning, breaking, and rebuilding—profoundly shaped my teaching practice. Between 2020 and 2021, I honed my skills as an ABAR educator, seeking trauma-informed training that aligned with the realities of COVID and the social awakening sparked by the Black Lives Matter movement. Freeing my practice from systemic oppression allowed me to create a classroom community rooted in equity and care. Together, my students and I practiced affirmations, conducted emotional check-ins, discussed topics like body positivity, colonization, activism, and explored identity—including the use of nonbinary Spanish. Many units centered on their identities and those of marginalized communities.

This approach to mental health mirrored Audre Lorde's philosophy: self-care as both resistance and a necessary act of survival. Recognizing systemic oppression underscored that nurturing ourselves is essential in dismantling these systems. Through this lens, our classroom became a space where care and learning intertwined—a decolonized culture that fostered both growth and healing.

A Moment of Clarity

In December 2021, just after attending the BTS concert, I found myself in the midst of the final ambush. What began as a meeting about curriculum soon spiraled into a personal attack. My supervisor, after rehashing old baseless accusations, finally had found an excuse in which to anchor his decision—a Latino student, whom I had helped reconnect with his heritage language, had allegedly felt uncomfortable learning about Hanukkah and Jewish traditions in Spanish-speaking countries. The discomfort, I suspected, was influenced by the mother's views—views rooted in a longstanding history of antisemitism that persists in some parts of the Latinx community, especially among those with ties to Spain. This cultural prejudice was subtly perpetuated by the family's discomfort with a curriculum that embraced diversity and cultural responsiveness. This was shocking news, especially after receiving that thank-you email from the same family only weeks earlier. Despite my explanations, the supervisor grew increasingly aggressive. He informed me that my contract would not be renewed and subtly threatened my immigration status, implying that he had the power to force my departure at any moment if I complain or speak to anybody. At that moment, I stood up and calmly said, "This conversation is not being fruitful anymore," and left. I later learned that neither my principal nor the DEI coordinator had been informed of this decision, which the supervisor made unilaterally. The school, lacking an HR department, had no oversight on the matter, leaving me vulnerable and unsupported.

My students—many of whom were Jewish—thrived in our classroom discussions about the connections between the Jewish community in the U.S. and Spanish-speaking Jewish communities. They were thrilled to see mirrors of them and their community in my curriculum. This situation was not only painful to see but a reminder that biases against marginalized communities are carried through generations and that our students might bring these inherited biases into our educational spaces.

In January, the irony reached its peak. The school marketing team interviewed me for their magazine, completely unaware that my contract had already been terminated. They featured me both online and in print as an exemplary educator embodying the ABAR principles the school professed to champion. The disconnect between their public praise and their private actions was astounding. How could such blatant cynicism be hidden behind the veneer of progressiveness?

In March, I sought guidance from a therapist friend on how to break the news to my students. After 13 years at the school, saying goodbye was deeply emotional—many students had started with me in pre-K and stayed until fourth grade. Together, we built something truly special. I gave them stationery and pencils to write what was in their hearts, and their letters became the most touching reference I could have asked for. They wrote about how our class felt like a family, where everyone was accepted and represented. They reflected on not just language, but culture and social justice. I received heartfelt messages from LGBTQ+ students, neurodivergent learners, and students from the global majority, all expressing gratitude for our time together. Caregivers also reached out, sharing their disbelief and appreciation. Those final months, free from micromanagement, allowed me to focus on joyful learning and meaningful farewells.

During the last week, my colleagues organized a farewell circle, and almost everyone spoke—this was rare. The two supervisors, who had been central in the ambush meetings, feigned kindness, but their faces spoke volumes as they witnessed the tears, hugs, and words of gratitude that disproved their lies. I only wish I had recorded it! The farewell was bittersweet. While the circle brought closure, the administration gave me only three days to pack and clean my classroom—rushing a process that deserved more time and care.

In those final days, my support network—both online and offline—became pivotal. I had hoped my family would be more of a pillar, but their passive reassurances—"*todo va a estar bien*"—fell short. As the eldest daughter, I've always carried the weight of doing it all, but there was no room to openly discuss mental health in my family, where it's often denied. I knew this chapter had to close, though the ending was abrupt. The burnout I had fought to prevent was already taking its toll. I wondered how much worse it could have gotten if I had continued suppressing myself, waiting for my green card process to progress. Despite my hopes, it had remained stuck in the labor department, nowhere near immigration. The fleeting moments of well-being I felt were impossible to sustain as long as the white supremacy culture persisted within the organization, upheld by the usual suspects.

No Visa. No Sponsorship.

I'm paraphrasing a sentence that stuck with me from one of the many job listings I scoured during my job search: "No visa. No sponsorship." The process was strenuous, but I was ready. I had a stellar resume, national recognition from my work with ACTFL, articles, and podcasts I'd contributed to. Or so I thought. Reality hit hard. I interviewed with multiple schools, bringing the sharp insight of a burnout veteran—asking the right questions about bathroom breaks, substitute coverage, and benefits. What I found was disheartening. One school didn't even have a cafeteria, and on my visit, the roof was leaking. The Spanish department was wonderful, but the DEI director dodged my questions. I refused to settle for such conditions, determined not to replicate the toxic environment I had just escaped.

Many NYC schools known for their DEI initiatives had anti-immigrant policies, offering no visa sponsorship. They essentially wanted only U.S.-born Spanish teachers. One Brooklyn school, despite not offering a competitive salary or a dedicated classroom, charmed me. Their supervisor was eager to hire me, promising support, solidarity, and freedom to implement my ABAR curriculum. The demo lesson went amazingly well. The students were lively and engaged, and the retiring Spanish teacher endorsed me wholeheartedly. The principal, an Afro-Latina woman even shared her own immigration story during our interview. That evening, they extended a job offer—only to retract it the next day after realizing I needed visa sponsorship. The departing Spanish teacher kept in touch with me throughout this process, infuriated when the offer fell through. She vented about the unpreparedness of the other candidates. She and the Lower School director worked tirelessly to convince the principal to reverse the decision, but it was all in vain. Later, the director sent me an apology. This was not just personal disappointment; it was an illustration of how the education system, often championing diversity, can still operate under policies that exclude immigrants and uphold colonial structures. It was a painful reminder that marginalized people's contributions are often seen as expendable unless they align with the dominant culture's interests. The principal, whose activism in social justice spaces made the hypocrisy even more apparent made me wonder, how could someone who claimed to champion these causes also participate in such exclusion? It left me with a bitter sense of disbelief, a painful realization that the very systems we fight to dismantle are the ones that still hold power over us.

Amid this chaos, I made a decision that I had long avoided: for the first time in my career, I would step away from the classroom. I chose to return to Chile for a few months, to rest, heal, and figure out who I was outside of the educator role I had held so tightly. It was a decision filled with fear and uncertainty—would I be able to return? Would freelancing sustain me? Was it all worth it? But I had learned something vital in the past year: I was not here to simply survive. I was here to live fully, to be respected, and to find joy in what I do.

This section is just one of the many lessons learned throughout this journey—a reminder that in a world where the systems we challenge are vast and entrenched, we must keep moving forward, advocating for ourselves, and pushing back against oppression wherever we can. This journey is not over, and the best truly is yet to come.

Community and Storytelling

A mixed-method study by Gomez et al. (2024), titled *Self- and Collective Care as Radical Acts: A Mixed-Method Study on Racism-Based Traumatic Stress Among Emerging Adults*, found that "a significant proportion of participants, ranging from 19% to 42%, reported experiencing racism-based traumatic stress and racism-based stress in the recent past, indicating the pervasiveness of these experiences" (p. 7). The study also highlights how participants engaged in "cultural, ancestral, spiritual, and religious practices as a means of healing," framing self- and collective care as both wellness and activism (Gomez et al., 2024, p. 15). This is especially important in the Latinx community, where healing is often intertwined with cultural, collective practices that connect us to our roots and empower us against systemic oppression.

Two concepts from the study that deeply resonate with my personal and professional journey are *Radical Hope*—a profound belief in a better future that sustains resilience in the face of oppression—and *Radical Healing*, which emphasizes collective liberation, cultural affirmation, and dismantling oppressive systems. Affinity spaces, both online and in person, embody these ideas. These are spaces where Latinx educators, like myself, connect to heal, share, and resist. My Instagram, *The Woke Spanish Teacher*, serves as one such space, where followers contribute their stories via DMs or comments, fostering a community of care and solidarity.

Through storytelling—whether written or spoken—we reclaim an ancestral practice rooted in indigenous traditions, where listening and sharing create a healing circle of care. In these brave spaces, I discovered that many of the barriers I faced—such as accentism—were shared experiences. Accentism, a form of racism that infantilizes individuals based on their accents, even when their speech is fully understood, excludes us from leadership roles and devalues our expertise. Often, those who reinforce these dynamics are monolingual individuals who, despite being less qualified, benefit from systems of privilege that marginalize us further.

In many ways, these shared experiences mirror the fear of "*revolver el gallinero*" (stirring the pot) within our communities. Rooted in parentification—the phenomenon of children assuming adult responsibilities at a young age—many of us refrain from speaking up. The fear of breaking this silence is compounded by the cultural pressures that women in Latinx communities face, such as marianismo, the idea that women should be submissive, sacrificing their well-being for others.

Another persistent issue is the mispronunciation of our names, which reflects a systemic disregard for our identities. Mispronouncing Spanish names is treated as acceptable, while pronouncing names like "Tchaikovsky" is considered perfectly fine. This everyday erasure speaks volumes about the culture of disrespect that thrives in many spaces, including our schools. The irony lies in how these spaces claim to celebrate Hispanic Heritage Month while assigning white, monolingual individuals to lead Spanish departments, telling us how to teach our own language and culture. This is not an isolated issue but a pervasive problem across U.S. education, particularly in language instruction.

As Schwartz (2020) notes in *Spanish So White: Conversations on the Inconvenient Racism of a 'Foreign' Language Education*, many curricula overlook critical conversations on language variation and bilingualism, treating Spanish classrooms as "white public spaces" (p. 35). These classrooms prioritize immersion abroad while ignoring the cultural histories of U.S. Latinx communities, reinforcing colonial ideologies that marginalize the diverse voices and experiences of Latinx students and educators (Schwartz, 2020, p. 42).

In this context, mental health remains a significant challenge. In Latinx communities, mental health is often stigmatized, leading to shame and reluctance to seek help (National Alliance on Mental Illness [NAMI], 2021). The historical trauma passed down through generations, combined with systemic oppression, creates additional barriers to open communication (American Psychiatric Association, 2020). While there is growing recognition of the need for culturally responsive care, language barriers and a lack of accessible services make it difficult for many to find the support they need.

Nonetheless, resilience is embedded within our communities. We draw strength from cultural practices and collective care. In our affinity spaces—whether online or in person—we engage in collective healing. We share our stories, dance, laugh, validate each other's experiences, and uplift our feelings, which are often dismissed in the spaces where we work and even by our families. These spaces become havens for rejecting silence and embracing the strength in speaking out. As Audre Lorde said, *"Your silence will not protect you."* Our silences serve only the oppressor, while our voices give us power.

Reclaiming our voices is part of the healing journey. In these spaces, we also shed patterns ingrained by colonial legacies—such as patriarchy, heteronormativity, and religious dogma. By reconnecting with our indigenous roots and practices, we reaffirm our identities and affirm our right to be fully ourselves. This process is not just about personal healing; it is about collective liberation.

Ultimately, embracing our identities—our bilingualism, multiculturalism, and multifaceted selves—becomes revolutionary. Our students thrive when we show up as our whole, healed selves. Our work is to serve our students, guide them toward radical hope and collective liberation, and challenge the systems that seek to diminish us.

Healing, of course, has social, historical, and cultural components—it is not just a cause-and-effect process but an intricate and beautiful one (Saad, 2020). Decolonizing self-care means recognizing that healing extends beyond the body; it encompasses mind, spirit, and community. Our cultural pride becomes a protective factor: studies show that identifying with the traditions and accomplishments of one's ethnic group lowers depression rates and improves well-being (APA, 2020). Incorporating this revitalization of identity into our pedagogical praxis is essential. Freire's concept of *praxis*—a continuous cycle of action and reflection to transform the world—guides us in merging theory and lived experience within our classrooms (Freire, 1970). Education becomes a revolutionary act when we move away from traditional "banking models" of teaching and instead co-create spaces that foster healing and care. We cannot undertake this journey alone; our students are integral to this transformation.

As Layla F. Saad (2020) beautifully states, "The primary force that drives my work is a passionate desire to become a good ancestor." Becoming good ancestors means dismantling oppressive systems within education. The classroom, therefore, is a site of immense possibility—a place where we begin to unravel the structures of white supremacy and colonialism. This work is not only pedagogical but political; we are called to create brave, affirming spaces where differences are celebrated, and marginalized voices are elevated. Healing is not an individual endeavor but a communal responsibility. It is our duty to cultivate sustainable, trauma-informed spaces where students, teachers, and caregivers work in solidarity toward collective liberation. This shared responsibility underscores the importance of acting as "good ancestors"—fostering a culture of care within our communities, supporting one another as we navigate these necessary transformations.

Shared Responsibility

Throughout my journey, and through the stories shared in affinity spaces, one undeniable theme arises: burnout in our communities is often exacerbated by performative activism, weak leadership, and superficial DEI (Diversity, Equity, and Inclusion) efforts. Our needs are overlooked, and every election cycle brings more harmful rhetoric, further harming the most vulnerable members of our diaspora. These forces create unnecessary strain on those already living on the margins.

One key issue is the wage gap, particularly for Latina women, who make up the majority of bilingual and Spanish teachers. Data from the National Women's Law Center (2023) reveals that Latina women earn just 58 cents for every dollar paid to white, non-Hispanic men. This gap doesn't just affect our wallets—it impacts our sense of worth, often pushing us to perform unpaid labor, such as translating and mediating, without compensation. This often goes unnoticed and becomes a normal part of the job, reinforcing the idea that our labor is undervalued.

This pay disparity shapes my mentoring approach, where I teach Latina educators to advocate for themselves, negotiate salaries, and ask the right questions to reveal a school's true values. I encourage them to avoid institutions that compromise their mental and physical health. I also emphasize that leadership and ABAR initiatives should go beyond superficial efforts—change must be systemic. I've seen pockets of real transformation, but true progress requires more than silence from privileged colleagues—it requires leaders to confront their own biases and actively dismantle harmful systems.

Despite the growing demand for Spanish and Bilingual teachers, many schools are not addressing the root causes of the shortage—poor working conditions, low pay, and exclusionary hiring practices. This must be recognized as a shared responsibility. Latinx educators bring a wealth of cultural knowledge, multilingual skills, and unique experiences to the classroom. We are not tokens to be molded into mono-cultural systems; we bring nuance, love, and color to organizations, and institutions must understand that retaining us means valuing our full identities. Speaking up for ourselves is not "spicy" or out of line—it is an act of survival and transformation.

While we, as Latinx educators, are part of the solution, the burden of change should never rest solely on the oppressed. Real change can only come when those in power—leaders, colleagues, and institutions—take shared responsibility. They must hold themselves accountable for creating spaces of equity and inclusivity, not only for marginalized teachers but for all students who benefit from this work. It is through collective action that we will make our schools safer, more inclusive, and more just.

As we move forward, let us recognize that the work we do in classrooms is not just about delivering content—it is about healing, liberation, and building a future that honors our identities and the stories we carry. The responsibility to transform education lies not only with us, but with everyone in the community—students, colleagues, leaders, and systems alike.

Our journey toward healing, justice, and liberation in education is neither linear nor solitary—it is a collective endeavor grounded in love, courage, and intentionality. Every action we take in dismantling oppressive systems is not only a resistance but also a commitment to the future we envision—a future where all educators, students, and communities can thrive unapologetically.

Creating affirming spaces is an act of profound care, where we not only honor those who came before us but also uplift those walking beside us. It is a promise to future generations to co-create educational spaces where identity, difference, and belonging are celebrated as strengths. These spaces act as both sanctuaries and battlegrounds, confronting systems of oppression while nurturing hope, joy, and healing.

The classroom holds transformative potential—it is a place where colonial narratives are unlearned, where power structures are interrogated, and where the richness of multilingual and multicultural identities is embraced. This work is both political and personal, communal and revolutionary. It demands not only that we resist but that we reimagine education as a space of liberation. In these shared spaces, we fight against tokenism, wage disparities, and performative activism, while lifting each other through mutual care and solidarity. We become good ancestors by fostering trauma-informed practices and sustainable well-being—ensuring that the burdens of change are not borne by marginalized teachers alone but shared through equitable leadership.

The path forward demands that we nurture ourselves, each other, and the students in our care, not just for survival but for joy and fulfillment. It invites us to resist assimilation and reclaim our stories, voices, and identities with boldness. This is a call to build classrooms not merely as sites of academic rigor but as homes for connection, purpose, and transformation.

We fight not just for ourselves but for those who come after us. This is how we honor the past, embrace the present, and shape the future. Together, we reclaim education as a space of possibility—a place where no one is left behind. With fierce commitment, shared responsibility, and radical love, we continue the work toward collective liberation.

This is how we fight—
For me. For you. For all of us.

REFERENCES

American Psychiatric Association. (2020). *Mental health disparities: Latinx/Hispanic Americans.*

Anzaldúa, G. E. (2015). *Light in the dark/Luz en lo oscuro: Rewriting identity, spirituality, reality* (Keating, A., Ed.). Duke University Press.

Bishop, R. S. (1990). *Mirrors, windows, and sliding glass doors.* Perspectives. *Choosing and Using Books for the Classroom*, 6(3), ix–xi.

Brown, A. M. (2019). *Pleasure activism: The Politics of Feeling Good.*

Crenshaw, K. (1989). Demarginalizing the intersection of race and sex: A Black feminist critique of antidiscrimination doctrine, feminist theory, and antiracist politics. *University of Chicago Legal Forum*, 1989(1), 139–167.

Feria del Libro. (2012, April 28). *Eduardo Galeano (parte 1 de 4) en la Feria del Libro de Buenos Aires* [Video]. YouTube. https://www.youtube.com/watch?v=zVtBcxyj3t8

Freire, P., & Mellado, J. (1970). *Pedagogia del oprimido* (Spanish Edition). Siglo XXI Editores.

Georgia Dow. (2022, January 18). *The Psychology of Encanto: Luisa's surface pressure — therapist reacts!* [Video]. YouTube. https://www.youtube.com/watch?v=ZoA_aL54yEY

Gomez, R., Martinez, L., & Rivera, J. (2024). Self- and collective care as radical acts: A mixed-method study on racism-based traumatic stress among emerging adults. *The American Journal of Orthopsychiatry*, 15(3), 7–15. DOI: 10.1037/ort0000705 PMID: 37768607

Lorde, A. (1984). *Sister Outsider: Essays and Speeches*. Crossing Press.

Lorde, A. (2017). *A burst of light: And Other Essays*. Courier Dover Publications.

National Alliance on Mental Illness. (2021). *Latinx/Hispanic community and mental health.*

Saad, L. F. (2020). *Me and white supremacy: Combat racism, change the world, and become a good ancestor*. Sourcebooks.

Schwartz, A. I. (2020). *Spanish so white: Conversations on the inconvenient racism of a 'foreign' language education*. Multilingual Matters.

Self-Care & Marianismo: Tending to Mental Health in Latino/x Cultures. (n.d.). Inclusive Therapists.https://www.inclusivetherapists.com/blog/self-care-marianismo -tending-to-mental-health-in-latino-x-cultures

Chapter 8
Leveraging Identity and Positional Power in Service of Latinx Youth:
The Journey of Two Latina Doctoras in Pursuit of Community Advancement

Fabiola Bagula
https://orcid.org/0009-0004-6387-8141
University of San Diego, USA

Haydee Zavala
https://orcid.org/0009-0000-6777-2652
University of California, San Diego, USA

ABSTRACT

This paper explores the intersection of Latina leadership and the development of equitable educational systems that foster Latinx student success. It examines initiatives within a large Southern California school district to create more diverse leadership, particularly by elevating Latina voices, building transnational partnerships, and developing student-centered strategies. These include the Latinx Student Success Plan and efforts to designate the district as a Hispanic-Serving School District (HSSD). The paper highlights the unique challenges faced by first-generation Latinx students and leaders, while also celebrating the transformative power of representation, community, and identity in education. This paper will be written by two Latina doctoras in new leadership spaces in a very large urban school district in the United States. Our district educates close to 100,000 students and

DOI: 10.4018/979-8-3373-1340-5.ch008

Copyright © 2025, IGI Global Scientific Publishing. Copying or distributing in print or electronic forms without written permission of IGI Global Scientific Publishing is prohibited.

is situated very close to the large international border with Mexico. Almost half of our student population is Latinx.

INTRODUCTION

Our school district is responsible for the education of close to 100,000 students, nearly half of whom identify as Latinx, a reflection of our proximity to the U.S.-Mexico border. This presents both unique opportunities and complexities. Historically, the academic performance of our Latinx students aligns closely with national trends, with 83% graduating from high school, according to the most recent 2021–2022 data from the National Center for Education Statistics (2024). While this is graduation data, overall achievement levels exacerbate the achievement gap that long plagues American education systems. A persistent issue is the frequent conflation of Latinx students with English Learners (ELs), a narrative that oversimplifies their experiences and imposes a deficit lens on one of our largest student populations. Nationally, 10.6% of students were classified as English learners in 2021, a figure that rises to 18.9% in California (NCES, 2024), but it is crucial to note that not all ELs are Latinx. Our district has a rich linguistic diversity, with some schools hosting as many as 30 different spoken languages.

Representation matters, and our educators do not yet reflect the diversity of our student body (Ijoma et al., 2022). As two Latina leaders in this district, we, Dr. Bagula and Dr. Zavala, recognize the immense responsibility we carry to transform the system for our community. This is the first time our district has seen a Latina in the highest position of leadership, and it coincides with the development of a high-functioning equity department led by a Black queer woman, in partnership with another Latina doctor.

We recognize and celebrate that Latinx identity is represented across racial categories, cultural traditions, and languages. We know one term cannot capture all the beauty within the culture, however, for the purpose this chapter, we use the term Latinx when referring to any individual who self-identities as Latino/a/e/x.

As we navigate this work together, we are committed to telling the story of our journey—one marked by different roles yet united in purpose. This chapter will reflect on how we leverage our identities and positional authority to improve conditions for Latinx youth, leading systemic change rooted in equity consciousness.

Together, we will reflect on how our shared identity has shaped our leadership and the strategies we have employed to create liberating structures for Latinx youth in public education, including the role and challenges of being the first Latina superintendent and the impact this has had on the dynamics within our departments, and experiences as a Latina equity leader and how they have informed specific initiatives aimed at supporting Latinx scholars in our district.

This work is grounded not only in our personal narratives but also in research that underscores the importance of representation in educational leadership (Gonzales, 2021; Gist, Bianco, & Lynn, 2019). As Latina leaders, we face the challenge of navigating educational systems that have often excluded voices like ours, but we are committed to fostering environments where all students, particularly Latinx youth, can thrive. By elevating student voices, diversifying leadership, and forming transnational partnerships, we seek to challenge entrenched educational norms and cultivate a system that is inclusive and equitable for all.

LATINA LEADERSHIP REFLECTIONS

Representation

Representation in educational leadership is essential for fostering equitable learning environments, particularly in districts with a majority Latinx student population. Research demonstrates that diverse leadership leads to more inclusive decision-making, as leaders are better equipped to understand and address the specific cultural and societal needs of their communities (Gist, Bianco, & Lynn, 2019). In our district, Latina leaders play a pivotal role in shaping policies that directly impact Latinx students. This connection between leaders and their communities creates a powerful dynamic where students see themselves reflected in those who hold positions of authority.

Latina leadership is essential in advocating for students who may otherwise feel marginalized. As Méndez-Morse, Murakami, Byrne-Jiménez, and Hernández (2015) highlight, Latina leaders often face the challenge of underrepresentation, even in districts where Latinx students form the majority. By elevating Latina voices, we challenge the status quo and provide role models for students, showing them that their cultural identities are not obstacles but assets in navigating the educational landscape.

One such cultural identity is that of a multilanguage learner. Being a multilanguage learner and speaker is not always viewed as an asset. Throughout my own K-12 experience, I always served as the interpreter between my mother and teachers during conferences, yet I was expected to speak only in English throughout the school day. The excuse given that by speaking only English it would help myself and other become fluent, though I was just as fluent in English as I was in Spanish. I often switched between English and Spanish at a young age when I wasn't yet fluent in either language, or lacked vocab for certain words, which some refer to as "Spanglish."

Directly related, I rarely saw myself or my culture reflected in the curriculum throughout my K-12 experience. It was not until I reached high school and took Advanced Placement (AP) coursework that I was exposed to the beauty of Spanish literature and began to fully appreciate my cultural heritage. However, even in that advanced setting, I was often one of the only Latinx students in the classroom. The lack of representation in both my peers and the course content was isolating and did little to foster a healthy sense of identity. For too long, students like me have been denied access to culturally affirming education until later in their academic careers, and even then, those opportunities are often limited to elite academic tracks that are not accessible to all students (Delgado Bernal, 2002).

Las Primeras / The First

The term "first-generation" can carry various meanings, but for this Latina, that concept was a real-life experience that my sisters and I navigated as the first generation in our family to be born in the United States, and the first generation of our family to navigate the K-12 public school system in this country. Though I am the youngest of my sibling groups, I am the first to graduate from college. Had they received the education they deserved, I know my sisters would have walked across the stage to receive their higher education degree before me. I do not say I am the first in my family to graduate from college with pride, nor do I say it with shame. Rather, it is a formative experience I share to highlight my public-school experience as a first-gen Latina, an experience that has shaped my positionality around vocalizing challenges and barriers our Latinx and first-gen youth still encounter today. Just the same, elevating the brilliance and strength that comes from being Latinx and first-gen is equally important. The joy, community, and love from our culture should always be front and center. While I am the first to graduate from college, my sisters were the first to teach me how to read. My parents took me to the library every weekend before I even entered kindergarten, and my sisters would sit and read book written in English with me. My sisters volunteered as chaperones on my field trips, helped me secure office jobs when I started college, and now pour that same love into my nieces and nephew, who have or about to graduate from college. The hope is that all our Latinx youth can all graduate from college if they choose that path, regardless of generational status. To do this, we need to both empower students by celebrating their identities, and shift from the deficit lens of seeing students' backgrounds as barriers and obstacles, to acknowledging and removing the barriers that exist within our systems.

While no first-generation, nor Latinx, experience is the same, many of the barriers, biases, and obstacles that first-generation and Latinx students meet in their own educational journeys overlap. After more than fifteen years working in public education, I still see many of the same obstacles and barriers I faced plague other students from similar backgrounds, hindering not only first-generation students but predominantly students of color. This continues to fuel my passion to advocate for students, particularly those who have been historically overlooked and underestimated. These barriers are often exacerbated by educational inequities and implicit biases (Valencia, 2010; Ladson-Billings, 2006), disproportionately affecting marginalized communities. Research consistently shows that systemic inequities, such as lower funding for schools serving high populations of students of color, lack of culturally relevant curricula, and implicit biases among educators, continue to create educational disparities (Gándara & Contreras, 2009; U.S. Department of Education, 2016). These disparities impact Latinx students' academic outcomes, making it harder for them to succeed and thrive in a system that was not designed with their needs in mind. As a Latina educator and leader, I am deeply committed to dismantling these barriers and fostering an educational environment where all students, especially those who have been historically marginalized, can succeed.

Knowing who I am and where I come from has been the driving force behind my advocacy for systemic change, which I believe is essential for creating lasting improvements for all students. My work is deeply rooted in my identity as a Latina, and I carry my loved one's stories in my heart. I aspire to help create a future where the next generation of Latinx students will have an easier, more equitable, and joyful educational experience. Yet I do not see myself as a savior or even warrior in this work; rather it is a blessing to be able to advocate for my community. My community has always seen me beyond titles and roles and embraced my authentic self. If I can serve in this role by helping make the path lighter for the next generation, then I view it as both a privilege and a responsibility. By leveraging my lived experience and cultural identity, I am working to ensure that all students, particularly those who face systemic challenges, have access to the opportunities they deserve (Gutiérrez, 2017; Nieto, 2000).

In a system where representation matters (Gonzales, 2021), it is vital that educators of color, particularly Latinas, serve as both role models and advocates, pushing for the systemic transformation that will lead to equitable outcomes for all students.

Recently, I was publicly introduced as the "first" Latina to hold this leadership position, a milestone that garnered significant media attention. Many outlets were curious about what this achievement meant for me personally. However, the question I found myself asking was not what this meant for me, but rather: what does this mean for the broader education system? A system that is supposed to be educating all students equitably yet has consistently allowed Latinx students to underperform and underachieve. The real question should be: why is my promotion viewed as such an anomaly within a system that has historically failed to adequately support and elevate Latinx individuals? Shouldn't my appointment be a natural outcome of a system that claims to serve its diverse student population?

While I felt a sense of personal pride in reaching this milestone, it also highlighted the dissonance between a system that educates Latinx students and a system that seldom hires or promotes Latinx leaders. This disparity points to a broader issue of underrepresentation and systemic inequities that extend beyond the classroom and into leadership structures. Research has shown that when students see themselves reflected in their educators and leaders, it has a significant positive impact on their academic success and sense of belonging (Gándara & Contreras, 2009; Villegas & Irvine, 2010). Yet, despite Latinx students constituting nearly half of our district's population, leadership positions have not reflected this demographic. The under-representation of Latinx educators and leaders is a systemic issue that the media and public discourse should focus on, rather than merely celebrating an individual milestone.

This reality is a stark reminder that for true educational equity to be achieved, systems must not only serve Latinx students academically but also empower them through representation in leadership. As scholars like Ladson-Billings (2006) and Yosso (2005) have argued, systemic change requires dismantling deficit perspectives that perpetuate the marginalization of communities of color. Instead of focusing solely on the novelty of "the first," we should interrogate the conditions that made it possible for Latinx students and educators to be historically excluded from these roles in the first place.

The media attention should shift from individual accomplishments to the insti-tutional and structural barriers that need to be addressed. Only then can we ensure that future generations of Latinx students see themselves reflected not only in their peers but also in the leadership guiding their educational journey. By reframing this narrative, we can begin to ask the right questions—those that push for system-ic change and a more inclusive, representative future for all students (Santamaría, 2020; Nieto, 2000).

Embracing Joy as Liberation

One of the most critical aspects of our work as Latina leaders is embracing joy and positive representation in education. In too many educational settings, the nar-rative around Latinx students is framed primarily through the lens of challenges—achievement gaps, language barriers, and systemic inequities. While these are genuine issues that require attention, this focus often overshadows the pride, culture, and joy that are intrinsic to Latinx identities. Our work is personal because we want our own children, as well as the children in our communities, to walk into schools that celebrate who they are, where they come from, and the cultural heritage that shapes their lives. Education and learning should be filled with joy, curiosity, and wonder, and our efforts are focused on ensuring that our students and their families experience this joy throughout their educational journey.

For Latinx students, having role models who reflect their cultural identities can make a profound difference in their educational experience. It reinforces the message that their culture is not something to hide or assimilate away from, but something to celebrate and take pride in. As Latina leaders, we are committed to uplifting our students by ensuring that they experience the joy that comes from embracing their heritage.

As Latina leaders, we are deeply invested in ensuring that joy and positive representation are at the center of our educational work. We know that when our children and community members walk into a school that celebrates who they are, they are more likely to thrive both academically and personally. By creating opportunities for students to express their cultural pride, incorporating diverse Latinx voices into the curriculum, and leveraging the identities of Latinx educators, we are building a school system that uplifts, celebrates, and affirms all students. We celebrate all that we are- recognizing that there are multiple variations of what a Latinx identity means to an individual. To center joy is center the humanity of our Latinx students and community at large. Joy is not an add-on—it is a vital component of a healthy, thriving educational community.

Latinx educators play a pivotal role in this cultural celebration and are essential to creating an educational environment where students can thrive. For us, leveraging our identities as Latina leaders means focusing not just on the obstacles we overcome, but also on the joy and pride that come from our heritage and origin stories. This duality liberates us to fully acknowledge the reality of our identities- there are systemic challenges placed in front of us because of who we are, AND we experience unique joys and cultures heritage because of who we are. We believe joy is at the center of our struggles and triumphs. Too often the focus has been on equipping Latinx youth with grit or resiliency through social emotional programs. We leverage joy and welcoming school communities as social emotional learning tools. We believe that being first-generation, or a multilanguage learner, or the first Latina superintendent builds more than enough grit on its own. We shift our focus on systemic change to create the liberating structures and education systems that our Latinx youth and communities deserve to succeed.

SYSTEMIC CHALLENGES LATINX STUDENTS FACE

As has been mentioned, almost half of our student population is Latinx, yet analysis of achievement data consistently reveals significant disparities between Latinx students and the general student population, particularly in areas such as math, literacy, A-G completion rates, graduation rates, and chronic absenteeism. While we have made considerable progress in closing these gaps—outperforming national averages in some areas—the work is far from complete (National Center for Education Statistics, 2024). Rather than focusing specifically on academic "shortfalls" about Latinx youth, we address systemic barriers that have been plaguing our diverse Latinx community. We believe these barriers are root causes of academic disparities and opportunity gaps, and addressing these will lead to improved academic outcomes for all students, including Latinx youth.

Under/Misrepresentation of Latinidad

Latinx Educators

Historically, San Diego County has been home to a large and growing Latinx student population—currently comprising over 47% of the K-12 student demographic (San Diego County Office of Education, 2023). Yet, despite this significant student representation, there has been a stark underrepresentation of Latinx individuals in both teaching and administrative roles. Recent data shows that while 60% of students in California public schools are students of color, only 20% of teachers and less than 10% of school administrators share similar backgrounds (California Department of Education, 2023). This gap is even more pronounced in leadership roles, where Latinx administrators remain in the minority despite the overwhelming presence of Latinx students in San Diego schools.

Research suggests that Latinx students who have teachers that share their cultural background experience greater academic success and a stronger sense of belonging in school (Murillo, 2017). Additionally, studies have shown that when educators of color share their cultural backgrounds with students, it can foster a sense of connection and motivation, as students see someone who shares their experiences succeeding in a leadership role (Nieto, 2010).

Yet when Latinx educators go into administrative and leadership roles, they often find themselves in the unique position of supervising staff who represent the "majority" while they themselves are the "minority," even though they may represent the student population (Méndez-Morse, 2004). This dynamic can create significant challenges, including microaggressions, implicit bias, and the pressure to conform to dominant cultural expectations. For Latina leaders, this dynamic can be even harder to navigate, often facing double discrimination from gender and ethnicity (Crenshaw, 1991).

Being a Latina leader in means facing microaggressions and challenges that arise from leading predominantly white staff while representing a predominantly Latinx student body. This dichotomy is difficult to navigate, as it requires Latina leaders to act as cultural mediators while also advocating for systemic changes that benefit Latinx students. Latina leaders are often tasked with shouldering the weight of improving outcomes for students who share their cultural background while simultaneously facing resistance from colleagues who may not fully understand or appreciate the need for culturally responsive leadership (Santamaría & Jean-Marie, 2014).

Additionally, many Latina leaders experience what is known as "cultural taxation," wherein they are expected to take on extra responsibilities related to diversity and inclusion efforts simply because of their ethnic background (Padilla, 1994). These expectations can lead to burnout, as Latina leaders often find themselves stretched thin between their formal administrative duties and the informal role of cultural advocate.

First-Generation Students

First-generation students face unique challenges as their families navigate not only the school system, but also broader societal structures in a new country. Many Latinx families may not be familiar with the U.S. education system, and language barriers can further complicate their involvement (Gándara & Contreras, 2009). Current research highlights that when schools foster strong relationships with families, particularly through culturally relevant and linguistically appropriate practices, student achievement and engagement significantly improve (Ishimaru & Lott, 2015). For Latinx students, whose families often bring rich cultural knowledge and strong values around education, it is essential that schools work to bridge any gaps in communication and involvement, ensuring families feel empowered to participate fully in their children's academic journeys.

One of the key insights we hope to impart to educators is the critical role that many first-generation American students play as the "English voice" for their families. These students often serve as interpreters in high-stakes situations, including medical appointments and legal or financial discussions, navigating complex language demands far beyond the typical expectations placed on them within the school system. However, the educational experiences we offer do not always align with the level of linguistic and cognitive rigor these students are already managing in their daily lives (Hernandez, 2012).

For students from first generation immigrant or low-income families, who often lack the familial knowledge and resources to navigate the higher education system independently, the process of applying for college, securing financial aid, and balancing academic demands can be daunting. (Cortez & Johnson, 2019).

Finally, deficit thinking and assumptions associated with first-generation economic status contribute to the savior mentality that some educators and schools have for serving "at-risk" and "underprivileged" students and limits the understanding of how first-generation families do have the academic cultural capital to help their students succeed (Sánchez-Connally, 2018). To create educational communities in which first-generation students feel like they belong, teachers should be known as responsive educators who advocate for their immigrant, refugee, and undocumented student populations as generators of knowledge (DeNicolo et al., 2017).

Transnational Youth

Transnational students, particularly those of Mexican descent, often live in "binational households," where family members work and reside across the U.S.-Mexico border. According to the Migration Policy Institute, over 500,000 U.S.-born children live in Mexico as part of transnational families (Zong & Batalova, 2019). Many of these students move between both countries multiple times throughout their lives, disrupting their education and making it difficult for them to achieve academic continuity. Language barriers pose significant challenges, as many U.S.-born students struggle to integrate into the Mexican education system if they are not proficient in Spanish, and similarly, Mexican-born students may struggle in the U.S. school system if they lack English proficiency (Valdés, 2019).

This situation is particularly prevalent in border regions like Baja California, where students and families frequently cross the U.S.-Mexico border for work, family, or schooling purposes. A growing number of students in our district are *transnational youth*, crossing international borders between the United States and Mexico throughout their academic journeys. These students face unique challenges as they move between two countries with different educational systems, languages, and cultural expectations. Data from the Mexican Ministry of Public Education (SEP) indicates that, in Baja California alone, approximately 60% of the student population in certain areas have familial ties to the United States (SEP, 2022). However, as my conversation with the Deputy Secretary of Education revealed, a significant number of U.S.-citizen students are not attending school in Mexico because they lack the necessary Spanish language skills. This group of students—estimated to be around 40,000 in Baja California—represents a vulnerable population that is at risk of falling further behind in their education due to language barriers and the transitory nature of their lives.

The educational challenges faced by transnational youth are multifaceted. These students often experience fragmented schooling, moving between countries during critical stages of their academic development, which affects their ability to keep up with peers in either system. According to research by Hamann, Zúñiga, and Sánchez García (2010), transnational students frequently struggle with adapting to different academic standards, school structures, and curricular expectations, resulting in academic underperformance and disengagement. Language acquisition is a particularly significant barrier, as many U.S.-born students who relocate to Mexico do not speak Spanish fluently, making it difficult for them to fully participate in the Mexican education system. Likewise, students who return to the U.S. after living in Mexico may face challenges in their English language proficiency, further compounding their academic struggles.

For these students, the lack of consistent support in both countries can lead to significant educational gaps. In addition to language barriers, they often deal with issues such as cultural adjustment, social isolation, and economic instability, which can further impede their academic success (Valdés, 2019). Without targeted interventions, transnational students are at a higher risk of dropping out of school or underperforming academically compared to their peers.

One of the most concerning issues we are currently exploring is the plight of American citizen students who reside in Mexico but do not attend school because they do not speak Spanish. During an informal meeting with the Deputy Secretary of Education for the Mexican state of Baja California, it was revealed that there are close to 40,000 American citizen students in her region alone who have moved back to Mexico with their families and are not attending school due to language barriers. This startling statistic highlights a critical gap in educational services for these transnational students, who frequently travel back and forth between Mexico and the United States. Their academic progress is often stunted by the lack of continuity in their education, language proficiency challenges, and the difficulty of adapting to two distinct school systems.

Academic Disparities

Multilanguage Learners

Teacher beliefs directly impact student outcomes, and multilingualism is often framed as a barrier rather than an asset. One study showed teachers across three districts who worked directly in dual-language programs showed deficit thinking towards their multilanguage students and their families, regardless of teaching experience or education level of teachers themselves (Hernandez, 2022), blaming failures on students and families rather than on inequities within the school system.

Dual-language programs are a critical component of California's education system, and depending on the quality of the program, academic success of multilanguage learners can vary (Alfaro & Hernandez, 2016). The hope is students in dual-language programs become proficient in both languages of the program, yet it's been shown that during Spanish instruction, 68% of the time student conversations were held in English and only 32% in Spanish (Potowski, 2004).

For students who do not have the option of a dual language program, deficit thinking around multilanguage learners usually results in students being placed in remedial courses, often resulting in a delay of their academic progress and prevent them from accessing more advanced coursework (García & Wei, 2014). Even in math classes, where it is often thought that students can be successful regardless of language due to the use of numerical operations, it was found that deficit thinking around multilanguage learners impacted their learning outcomes (Araujo et al., 2018). Teacher preparation challenges have made it more difficult for teachers to engage in critical conversations with each other and administrators around creating responsive environments to meet the needs of all their learners, as well as engaging in mentorship and long-term support (Samuels et al., 2020).

Curriculum

Research shows that students are more likely to engage and succeed academically when they see themselves reflected in the curriculum (Gándara & Contreras, 2009). Too often, however, students encounter the same limited representation in their textbooks, learning only about historical figures like César Chávez or cultural practices like making tamales, while the breadth and depth of Latinx contributions to society are overlooked.

Unfortunately, many Latinx students have reported feeling marginalized by the narrow scope of representation in their textbooks. During recent student interviews, participants expressed frustration that their stories are often reduced to stereotypes—such as migrant laborers or making tamales as mentioned above—rather than celebrating their cultural strengths and contributions to society. As one student remarked, "We want to learn about more than just making tamales. We want to see ourselves in history, in science, in art—as inventors, leaders, and change-makers."

As of 2023, the Cooperative Children's Book Center (CCBC) reports that out of the 3,491 children and young adult books they received, only 11.7% were written by Latinx authors, and 11.4% of books written about Latinx peoples. Latinx identity is tragically underrepresented and misrepresented throughout traditional curriculum and commercial books.

Joy, Belonging, and Student Agency

Research has shown that positive cultural representation in schools not only improves academic outcomes but also fosters a stronger sense of belonging and identity for students (Gándara, 2015). When students see themselves reflected in the curriculum and the broader school culture, they are more likely to engage and thrive both socially and academically.

Research has shown that when students experience joy, curiosity, and excitement in their learning environments, they are more likely to be engaged, motivated, and academically successful (Immordino-Yang & Damasio, 2007). It is important to recognize that joy in education is not just a feel-good addition to the curriculum; it is a critical component of student success. Joy creates an emotional connection to learning, fostering deeper engagement and a love for learning that can last a lifetime. For Latinx students, who often face systemic barriers and negative stereotypes, joy is a radical act of resistance—it is a way of claiming space and celebrating their identities in a system that has historically marginalized them.

Research has shown that teachers have the biggest impact on student sense of belonging- teachers are the biggest determinant to whether a student experiences a sense of belonging or exclusion. Further, students who feel excluded or a lower sense of belonging often act out in schools in anger and defiance (Riley, 2022).

Latinx students face higher suspension levels than their white peers, and when displaying the same "misbehaviors" are three times more likely to be suspended or expelled than their white peers. Latinx boys represented 13% of overall students in the United States public school system in 2016, yet represented 15% of students who were suspended and 16% of students who were expelled (Dolan et al., 2018). Research shows that barriers such as fear of ridicule, teacher bias, and adultification are some of the obstacles that hinder Black and Latinx girls seeing themselves as leaders (Jacobs, 2020). This same report highlighted that teachers perceive lack of confidence to be an issue for Black and Latinx girls, but in fact, Black and Latinx girls have the highest rates of self-reported confidence, yet sadly face higher discipline rates than their white peers.

When students do not feel like they belong or welcome in school systems, their feelings of alienation have a direct impact on their academic and emotional needs (Young & Easton-Brooks, 2022). We believe that by addressing these systemic barriers that Latinx face, welcoming and belonging school communities will lead to improved social, academic, and emotional outcomes for Latinx youth.

A MORE LIBERATING SYSTEM: FRAMEWORK AND INITIATIVES

The Latinx Student Success Plan

In response to these systemic disparities, we have developed the Latinx Student Success Plan, a comprehensive strategy aimed at addressing the unique challenges put in front of our Latinx students by implementing asset-based strategies and programs. More than a plan, it is a framework for embedding the cultural wealth of our Latinx community throughout academic and social outcomes. We envision that implementing this plan will lead to a more liberating, equitable, and rigorous educational experience for our Latinx youth, with data reflecting improved academic and social-emotional outcomes for our Latinx students. This plan is the first of its kind for our district, and it represents a culmination of existing resources, new community partnerships, and a commitment to an asset-based approach to student identity. Central to the plan is the recognition that the cultural and linguistic diversity of our Latinx students is not a deficit, but rather a strength that must be celebrated and nurtured (Yosso, 2005).

Before launching the plan, we received feedback from students, staff, families, and community members. A draft of the plan was shared with members of each group mentioned, and the valuable feedback provided was then implemented into the official Latinx Student Success Plan. The Latinx Student Success Plan has been vetted and supported by the community, making it much more likely to bring about the lasting and fundamental shifts needed.

The Latinx Student Success Plan is a critical step toward achieving equity for Latinx students in our district. By promoting multilingualism as an asset, offering targeted professional development for educators, and fostering systemic change through community partnerships, the plan aims to close achievement gaps and create an inclusive learning environment. This work is essential not only for the success of Latinx students but for the overall health and equity of our educational system. As we move forward, it is our hope that the Latinx Student Success Plan will serve as a model for other districts looking to implement similar equity-driven initiatives.

Through this plan, which is explained in more detail throughout this section, we reaffirm our commitment to seeing, hearing, and valuing every Latinx student, ensuring that their cultural and linguistic identities are recognized as vital components of their academic success. By building on the strengths of our Latinx community, we strive to create a future where all students—regardless of race, ethnicity, or language—can thrive in our schools.

Becoming a Hispanic-Serving School District (HSSD)

In line with our district's commitment to supporting our Latinx student population, we are proudly pioneering efforts to become the nation's first federally recognized Hispanic-Serving School District (HSSD). While the federal government does not currently provide an official designation for K-12 institutions, we are intentionally aligning our efforts with the goals and frameworks of Hispanic-Serving Institutions (HSIs) in higher education. This designation, typically reserved for colleges and universities where at least 25% of the student population is Hispanic, is critical to increasing educational access and success for Latinx students across the country (Hispanic Association of Colleges and Universities [HACU], 2023). By achieving this milestone, we are setting a precedent in K-12 education that underscores the importance of centering the needs and strengths of Latinx students from the earliest stages of their educational journeys.

Hispanic-Serving Institutions (HSIs) play a crucial role in higher education by fostering environments that support the academic and professional success of Latinx students. According to the U.S. Department of Education, HSIs enroll over two-thirds of all Latinx undergraduates, making these institutions vital pathways for Latinx students to achieve college degrees and pursue successful careers (Excelencia in Education, 2022). HSIs also contribute significantly to improving graduation rates and providing essential resources such as financial aid, mentorship, and culturally relevant programming. These institutions are especially important for first-generation and low-income students, who often face additional barriers to navigating the complexities of higher education (Cortez & Johnson, 2019).

By positioning our district as a Hispanic-Serving School District, we are expanding the HSI model to K-12 education, ensuring that Latinx students have the preparation, support, and resources necessary to seamlessly transition into higher education. Given that nearly half of our student population identifies as Latinx, this initiative is both timely and essential to fostering educational equity in our schools.

Representation- Shifting the Narrative

Support Systems for First-Generation Students

To address these challenges of navigating college, our district has implemented support systems tailored to the unique needs of first-generation students. These include specialized clubs, mentorship programs, and workshops focused on financial literacy, college applications, and scholarship opportunities. Research demonstrates that targeted interventions, such as these, are effective in increasing college access and success for first-generation students. We have embedded these supports withing our Latinx Student Success Plan, but also within our broader framework of our Hispanic Serving School District (HSSD) pathway.

As part of our HSSD initiative, we will be hosting our district's first-ever HSI College Fair in January, in collaboration with the Mexican Consulate. This event illustrates a significant opportunity to strengthen our family and community engagement efforts while also reinforcing our HSSD status. By bringing together local Hispanic-Serving Institutions, including universities and community colleges, we can provide students and their families with information about academic programs, scholarships, and pathways to college success at this bilingual college fair. Services are offered in English in Spanish, including workshops, tabling, and access to college counselors. Workshops are led by community partners, including representatives from the California Student Aid Commission, who provide critical information around financial aid, updates on the California Dream Act, and other vital information for students and families. This is especially important who first-generation students, who may have undocumented family members. This event is open to students and families from across San Diego County, as well as those travelling from Tijuana, Mexico. Buses are provided for free for our students and families and serve as shuttles throughout the day to and from the event at specific school sites throughout the city. Through this, we hope to alleviate any transportation barriers that may prevent families from attending.

The event will serve as more than just a college fair; it will be a celebration of the cultural wealth and potential of our Latinx students. Through this collaboration with the Mexican Consulate, we aim to create a welcoming space where families can feel confident in supporting their children's academic futures. Research shows that family engagement is a critical factor in Latinx student success, particularly for first-generation students, who often rely heavily on their families for emotional and logistical support in navigating higher education (Gándara & Contreras, 2009). By hosting events like the HSI College Fair, we hope to provide families with the tools and resources they need to become active partners in their children's academic journeys.

Additionally, we have formed partnerships with community groups that serve as student clubs and mentors, with one such club focusing on first generation scholars. The club is open to any first-generation students and serves as a catalyst to help these students secure full scholarships to colleges of their choice. Students can join this club chapter at their high school starting their junior year, and begin learning about the college application process, financial aid, and other important information on their road to becoming a first-generation college graduate.

The journey toward becoming a Hispanic-Serving School District is both exciting and transformative. As the first TK-12 district to pursue this as a federal designation, we are breaking new ground in educational equity and setting the stage for future generations of Latinx students to thrive. This initiative positions us as leaders in rethinking how public schools can better serve diverse populations and create equitable educational systems. Our collaborations with Hispanic-Serving Institutions in higher education, coupled with initiatives like the HSI College Fair and expanded support systems for first-generation students, are key to legitimizing and strengthening our HSSD label We hope to be a leading force in the efforts to make HSSD a federal designation.

Fostering Transnational Partnerships: Supporting Transnational Youth

To support our transnational youth, we have initiated partnerships with educational leaders in Mexico, particularly in the states of Sonora and Baja California, where a significant portion of these students reside.

Our partnership with Mexican educational leaders in Sonora and Baja California aims to address the challenges transnational students face by developing strategies that provide consistent support for transnational students, regardless of where they are in their educational journey. One of our primary goals is to create binational agreements that allow for more seamless transitions between the two school systems, ensuring that students do not lose academic credits or face unnecessary delays in their education when they move between countries. Additionally, we are exploring the possibility of offering bilingual or dual-language educational programs that would allow students to strengthen both their English and Spanish skills, thereby facilitating their academic success in both the U.S. and Mexican systems.

In the short term, we are also looking into ways to provide direct support to the 40,000 American citizen students in Baja California who are not currently attending school due to language barriers. This may include offering remote or hybrid learning opportunities in partnership with Mexican schools, creating language immersion programs to help these students gain proficiency in Spanish, or providing access to online educational resources in English. While we are still in the exploratory stages of these initiatives, we recognize that addressing this issue is not only a moral imperative but also a shared responsibility between the U.S. and Mexico. Transnational students represent a unique population that contributes to both countries, and as such, it is essential that we find ways to support their academic success.

Navigating Legal and Policy Barriers

One of the complexities of supporting transnational students is the legal and policy framework that governs the sharing of student information and resources between the U.S. and Mexico. Education is largely regulated at the national and state levels in both countries, and there are significant differences in how student records, academic standards, and certifications are managed. However, we believe that through strong partnerships and collaboration, we can navigate these challenges and create solutions that benefit transnational students on both sides of the border. Our goal is to establish frameworks that allow for the sharing of best practices, the recognition of academic credentials, and the provision of language and academic support services that cater to the unique needs of transnational youth.

The educational success of transnational students is a shared responsibility that transcends national borders. Through our transnational partnerships with educational leaders in Mexico, we are working to develop strategies that ensure students who move between the U.S. and Mexico receive the support they need to succeed academically. By addressing language barriers, creating binational educational programs, and fostering collaboration between U.S. and Mexican schools, we are taking important steps to bridge the gap for transnational youth. While we are still in the early stages of this work, we remain committed to exploring innovative solutions that meet the needs of these students and provide them with the opportunities they deserve.

Elevating Latina Leadership: Collective Action and Support

A central component of our district's ongoing commitment to equity and representation is the elevation of Latina leadership. To amplify and sustain the voices of Latina educational leaders, we have co-founded the San Diego Chapter of the California Association of Latino Superintendents and Administrators (CALSA). CALSA, a statewide organization dedicated to advancing equity in educational leadership for Latinx students and administrators, plays a critical role in addressing the underrepresentation of Latino leaders in California schools.

Given this demographic reality of low Latinx administrators in education, San Diego should have established a CALSA chapter long ago. The absence of a local chapter meant that Latina and Latino leaders in the region lacked a formal network to advocate for the systemic changes necessary to improve educational outcomes for Latinx students. Now, with the establishment of this chapter, we aim to rectify this oversight and provide a platform where Latinx leaders can collaborate, share strategies, and celebrate their successes. The San Diego Chapter of CALSA, which began as a small gathering of five Latina leaders, has now grown into a robust network of over 60 educational leaders. Together, we are advancing a shared vision of educational equity, rooted in both cultural affirmation and academic excellence.

One of our chapter's notable achievements in the past year was raising $50,000 for Latinx student scholarships, providing critical financial support to ensure that more students can access higher education. This scholarship fund directly addresses the economic barriers that disproportionately affect Latinx students, many of whom come from low-income families and are the first in their families to pursue a college education (Excelencia in Education, 2022). The way this fundraising was done is also notable– educational companies paid Latino administrators and super-intendents to provide them feedback on their product. We wanted to elevate Latino voice in the efforts of many companies that espouse supporting our students. Our chapter's commitment to building pathways to higher education for Latinx students aligns with CALSA's broader goals of fostering Latinx student achievement and increasing Latinx representation in educational leadership. In San Diego, we are not only focused on creating opportunities for our students but also on celebrating the achievements of our Latinx leaders—leaders who have a proven track record of improving outcomes for Latinx students but whose contributions are often over-looked. This recognition and celebration of Latinx leadership is vital as it helps to disrupt the narrative of invisibility that too often surrounds educators of color in majority-white spaces (Gándara, 2015).

Creating Safe Spaces for Latina Leaders: The Latina Leadership Affinity Group

In addition to formal organizations like CALSA, we have recognized the need for affinity spaces within our district where Latina leaders can gather for professional and personal support. To meet this need, we established an informal *Latina Leadership Affinity Group*, providing a safe and empowering space for Latina administrators to navigate the complexities of leading in predominantly non-Latinx environments. Affinity spaces, like the one we have created, are essential for Latina leaders to re-flect, recharge, and strategize on how to navigate these challenges effectively. The *Latina Leadership Affinity Group* provides a space to discuss and navigate the joys and tensions of being a Latinx leader, while offering both emotional support and practical strategies for overcoming the barriers Latina leaders face. This network is not only crucial for the retention of Latina leaders but also for ensuring that our leadership practices remain aligned with the needs and experiences of our Latinx students.

Research underscores the importance of affinity groups in supporting the professional development and retention of underrepresented leaders, particularly women of color in leadership roles. These spaces foster a sense of community and belonging, which is often lacking in environments where leaders of color are in the minority (Acevedo, 2021). Affinity groups provide an opportunity for leaders to share their experiences of navigating institutional racism, sexism, and cultural isolation, while also celebrating their cultural identities and leadership practices.

For Latina leaders, who often face the added burden of leading in systems that do not reflect their cultural experiences, these spaces are invaluable.

The establishment of the San Diego Chapter of CALSA and the *Latina Leadership Affinity Group* marks a significant step forward in our district's efforts to elevate and support Latina leadership. These initiatives recognize the unique challenges faced by Latina leaders and provide the structures needed to foster their professional growth and resilience. Through collective action and the creation of supportive affinity spaces, we are ensuring that Latina leaders are not only visible but celebrated for the vital role they play in improving educational outcomes for Latinx students. By building these networks of support, we aim to create a future where Latina leadership is both normalized and valued, reflective of the communities we serve.

Academic Initiatives

Multilingualism as an Asset

A key initiative within our district's Latinx Student Success Plan has been the renaming of the Office of Language Acquisition to the *Multilingual Education Department*. This change reflects an intentional shift from a deficit-based model, which often views English learners through the lens of remediation, to a positive paradigm that celebrates linguistic diversity as an asset. This rebranding is not merely symbolic; it signals a broader systemic transformation. By reframing the narrative around language acquisition, we aim to create an educational environment where students' multilingual abilities are viewed as strengths rather than obstacles. This approach aligns with research demonstrating the cognitive and social benefits of bilingualism and multilingualism (Bialystok, 2011; García & Wei, 2014).

In addition to renaming the department, we have launched Newcomer Centers across the district. These centers serve as vital hubs of support for families who are newly arrived in the U.S. and navigating both the challenges of acclimating to a new culture and a new school system. The centers offer a comprehensive range of services, including English language acquisition for students and parents, and access to essential resources such as food and clothing pantries. These supports are critical for ensuring that families are not only integrated into the school community but also receive the socio-emotional and practical assistance they need to thrive (Calderón, Slavin, & Sánchez, 2011).

At the high school level, we are also rethinking the traditional approach to language learning. In doing so, we have forged a partnership with a local university to develop a *Translation Pathway*. This program enables students who are proficient in multiple languages to earn a certification in translation by the time they graduate. Instead of offering remedial English coursework, the Translation Pathway leverages students' linguistic strengths and provides them with a marketable skill that can lead to employment opportunities after high school. This innovative approach not only recognizes students' multilingual capabilities but also aligns with our district's broader goal of preparing students for real-world success (Flores, 2017).

We are extending this work into our middle schools by redesigning elective coursework to serve the dual purpose of language acquisition and elective fulfillment. Rather than relegating English learners to remedial language classes that often displace electives, we are creating electives that incorporate language learning into the curriculum. This change disrupts traditional practices that have served as barriers to student engagement and academic progression, particularly for Latinx students who have historically been marginalized by these systems (Gándara & Hopkins, 2010). These innovations are still viewed as progressive within the broader educational landscape, but they are necessary steps toward creating a more equitable and inclusive school system.

Our Latinx students who are learning English as a second, or even third language, may not be fluent in their primary language yet either, just as "native" English speakers may also struggle with a lack of terminology at certain times. By leveraging their real-world language tasks and translating them into academic and professional opportunities, we aim to strengthen students' voices both within and beyond the classroom. Further, we challenge deficit perspectives, assumptions, and stereotypes that have traditionally been associated with being a multilanguage learner. We want to lift the notion that all students are language learners; some are just learning multiple languages at once.

The Latinx Student Success Plan not only aims to address academic disparities but also seeks to reframe how we view the cultural and linguistic assets that our students bring to the table. By rethinking traditional practices, such as remedial coursework, and introducing innovative pathways that value multilingualism, we are disrupting systemic inequities and creating a more inclusive educational landscape. These efforts underscore our commitment to ensuring that all students, particularly Latinx students, are seen, heard, and valued in ways that reflect their unique identities and contributions.

Diversifying Curriculum: Reflecting Cultural Strength and Contribution

Another key initiative within the *Latinx Student Success Plan* is the diversification of curriculum and instructional materials that reflect the rich cultural heritage and contributions of Latinx communities, moving beyond stereotypes and tokenism. We are working to ensure that our curriculum includes diverse Latinx voices, highlighting inventors, scientists, artists, and leaders from a range of Latin American countries. This type of curriculum not only enriches the learning experience but also allows Latinx students to see themselves in roles of influence and innovation, helping to dismantle harmful stereotypes and broaden the scope of representation (Valenzuela, 1999).

We are committed to diversifying our syllabi and ensuring that instructional materials portray Latinx communities in ways that celebrate their contributions to history, culture, and society. The goal is to provide a curriculum where students see themselves reflected as history-makers, innovators, and contributors to the American fabric. Our students are required to take at least one ethnic studies course as a graduation requirement, a requirement that began in the last five years. We have created identity modules available to all educators and students that explore the concept of "Latinx" and diversity of the culture. Additionally, educators have access to a culturally responsive text online "hub" with lesson plans accompanying each title listed. By expanding the range of voices and perspectives represented in our books and lessons, we can foster a stronger sense of identity and pride among Latinx students, ultimately leading to greater engagement and academic success (Paris & Alim, 2017).

By incorporating a wider range of Latinx cultural narratives and contributions into the curriculum, we can create a more inclusive educational experience for all students. It is critical that we move beyond tokenism and provide substantive, diverse content that reflects the strength, resilience, and accomplishments of Latinx communities. This is essential not only for fostering a sense of belonging but also for ensuring that students develop a strong, positive identity that they can carry with them beyond the classroom (Yosso, 2005).

These efforts are not merely progressive but necessary steps toward building a more inclusive and equitable educational system. By recognizing the unique strengths of our Latinx students and creating an environment that celebrates their cultural and linguistic identities, we can help them achieve their full potential and contribute meaningfully to the world beyond the classroom.

Professional Development for Educators: Elevating Capacity for Equity and Inclusion

A large component of our work focuses on creating opportunities for our Latinx students to be seen, heard, and valued. This involves preparing educators to meet this call to action and foster a learning environment where the cultural identities are recognized as assets. To address this need, ongoing professional development (PD) designed to equip educators, particularly school site administrators and teachers, with the skills and knowledge to effectively support Latinx students is interweaved throughout the *Latinx Student Success Plan.* Addressing the systemic inequities that persist in education requires more than just awareness; it demands actionable strategies rooted in culturally responsive pedagogy and anti-racist, anti-biased educational practices (Ladson-Billings, 2006). If we are to shift persistent deficit based thinking around first-generation students and multilanguage learners, these approaches are essential to disrupting the entrenched disparities in achievement and access that disproportionately impact students of color, particularly Latinx youth.

The PD series within the *Latinx Student Success Plan* provides educators with the tools necessary to engage in difficult conversations about race, equity, and inclusion. To begin, participants are guided towards self-reflection, naming and considering their own identities and positionalities, before moving into interrogating systems and pedagogies. These sessions also build the practical skills required to identify and dismantle culturally unresponsive instructional practices. For example, participants are trained to recognize and challenge deficit perspectives, engaging in implicit bias and microaggressions throughout various sessions, including how to counter microaggressions in classroom setting and audit curriculum for biases. The professional development sessions are designed as a year series that takes educators through the journey of critical self-reflection through critical consciousness, critical self-awareness, and praxis. Meaning, educators start by examining their own identities and positionality before we move into interrogating the education system. A gradual build in the series introduces participants to concepts such as equality, intersectionality, the 4 i's of oppression, restorative justice practices, and anti-racist pedagogy. Through equipping educators with skills, strategies, and the lens to know themselves, the system, and then pedagogy rooted in liberatory outcomes, the PD series seeks to create classroom environments where Latinx students feel seen, valued, and supported.

Data collected from the first cohort of educators taking part in the PD program reveals significant growth in their confidence and ability to address issues of inequity and racism. The percentage of participants who felt comfortable guiding others through conversations about inequality and racism increased from 51.3% to 75%. Additionally, 80% of participants reported feeling confident delivering constructive feedback to colleagues about culturally unresponsive instructional practices, up from 56.4%. Finally, the percentage of educators who believed they could effectively advocate for equity in racially charged situations rose from 53.9% to 77.5%. These results underscore the importance of ongoing, structured PD that builds educators capacity to lead equity work, therefore cultivating a school culture that prioritizes equity and inclusion (Chism, 2022). Further, this approach builds sustainability, in that site equity teams feel equipped and empowered to address issues of inequity when they arise, having built their capacity individually and collectively to lead this work.

In alignment with these efforts, last year we offered a micro-credential learning series focused on best practices for supporting Black students, which was well-received by educators. Building on that success, we plan to offer a similar series specifically tailored to the needs of Latinx students. This new series will draw on research-based practices that emphasize the strengths of both language acquisition and culturally responsive teaching strategies, ensuring that Latinx students' unique learning styles are recognized and supported (Nieto, 2010). By teaching educators about evidence-based practices for supporting Latinx students, we aim to create a learning environment where all students can thrive.

Belonging and Agency

Joy in Action: Student-Led Initiatives and Cultural Representation

In our district, we are working to shift the narrative around Latinx students by intentionally celebrating their cultural heritage, contributions, and experiences. Instead of focusing solely on overcoming obstacles, we want to highlight the beauty, strength, and resilience that come with being Latinx.

One example of this shift is our student-led flag-raising ceremonies and conferences for Latinx Heritage Month. These ceremonies allow students to express pride in their identity through speeches, songs, and art. Students emcee the entire event- from welcoming the community and media who attend the public event, to the flag raising that signifies the end of the ceremony. This flag, which represents all Latinx countries, was a powerful symbol of unity and pride. Student clubs and groups, such as MEChA, Chavistas, and first-generation scholar organizations, were active participants in the planning and execution of the event, ensuring that student voices were at the forefront of this celebration. Students write and share personal speeches, poems, and dances that celebrate their identities with a larger community that is there to celebrate their cultural heritage along with them.

Our student conference is an opportunity embedded into the school day for our students to soak in the collective wisdom of the local Latinx community. Community partners and local Latinx leaders share their resources, stories, and knowledge with our students. In these moments, students see themselves not just as individuals overcoming adversity but as leaders, artists, and creators contributing meaningfully to society. These events foster a deep sense of belonging, ensuring that students and their families feel seen, heard, and celebrated. Latinx students, through these acts of cultural affirmation, can find joy in being who they are—multilingual, first-generation, and proud of their heritage (Gutiérrez, 2017).

We have seen firsthand the impact that student-led cultural initiatives can have on fostering joy and pride in identity. One student speaker shared, " The Latinx Flag Raising held a really special place in my heart, I had so much fun interacting with other students and embracing my culture along with it. When I spoke at the event, I truly was overwhelmed with feelings, particularly nervousness, but also pride…I feel like I was able to find common ground with the speakers and also the audience."

Finally, we cannot mention celebrating Latinx culture without mentioning the community. Our community is such an active presence, and key piece of our Latinx Student Success Plan is strengthening our community relationships. This includes partnering with local groups that offer resources for parents and families, and other local groups that offer mentoring to our Latinx students. This community partnership enables students to see themselves represented in positive, relevant, and everyday interactions.

In addition to events like these, we are also expanding programs that highlight the rich cultural traditions of our Latinx community. One example is the growth of mariachi programs in our music departments across our schools. These programs not only provide students with an opportunity to engage with their cultural heritage through music but also serve as a source of pride for the entire school community. Mariachi, like other forms of Latinx art and culture, is a powerful tool for building joy and connection, both for the students who participate and for the broader school community that celebrates with them.

These initiatives are just a few examples of how we are working to center the stories of our Latinx students, ensuring that they see their culture and heritage represented in a positive light. By creating spaces for students to share their stories, thoughts, and joy, we are building a liberative school community where all students can thrive.

Restorative Justice Tools

Restorative Justice is an existing framework within our district we are utilizing to support our Latinx Student Success Plan and HSSD. Many of the practices and beliefs that exist withing the pedagogy of restorative justice practices, such as the focus on relationships, community building, and inherent worth of all individuals (Vaandering, 2013) are in alignment with the transformative changes we are working towards in our system. We work with our restorative justice department and collaborative on equity team professional development opportunities for teachers, curriculum development, and structured supports for addressing harm. These efforts in conjunction with the districts adoption of the Restorative Discipline Policy a few years prior have led to a decrease in the suspension rate of our Latinx youth. According to the California Department of Education Dashboard, suspension rates for Latinx youth were 4.2% and 4.5% in 2018 and 2019, respectively, and have decreased to

3.2% and 3.1% in 2023 and 2024. While the percentage might seem small, about half the student population is Latinx. For comparison, suspension rates for White students currently stands at 1.5%. We hope to see a decrease in suspension rates for our Latinx student population.

Strengthening Family Engagement: A Critical Component for Latinx Student Success

A vital aspect of the *Latinx Student Success Plan* is the recognition of the vital role families play in the educational success of Latinx students, particularly those who are first-generation. While we have made strides in cultivating strong partnerships with community groups like our Latino Advisory Committee—composed of educational leaders across the city—there is still much work to be done in fully integrating family engagement into our strategy. Research consistently demonstrates that family involvement is one of the most significant predictors of student success, particularly for students navigating new cultural and educational systems (Jeynes, 2016). In California, where Latinx students make up more than half of the K-12 public school population (California Department of Education, 2023), and in San Diego specifically, where over 47% of students are Latinx (San Diego County Office of Education, 2023), engaging families is critical to ensuring equitable outcomes for these students.

As part of our commitment to strengthening family engagement, we are in the process of expanding initiatives that provide families with the resources they need to support their children's success. This includes offering parent workshops through our Newcomer Centers that focus on understanding the school system, acquiring English, and accessing community resources such as food and clothing pantries. These efforts are aimed at ensuring that families feel welcomed, supported, and capable of navigating the educational system alongside their children. Moving forward, we plan to launch additional family engagement programs that build on the strong foundation established by our Latino Advisory Committee, ensuring that families are seen as partners in their children's education.

The Latinx Student Success Plan not only focuses on student achievement but also aims to build long-term capacity for systemic change. By fostering community partnerships and promoting family engagement, the plan ensures that Latinx students receive support from all angles—within and beyond the classroom.

The Power of Joy in Belonging

Our commitment to designing for joy is also a commitment to designing welcoming school environments. When students experience joy in their educational journey, they are more likely to feel that school is a place where they belong, where they are valued for who they are, and where their future is bright. By ensuring that Latinx students and families experience joy in our schools, we are not only improving academic outcomes but also contributing to the creation of more just and inclusive educational environments.

SUMMARY: LEVERAGING IDENTITY AND ORGANIZATIONAL POWER FOR SYSTEMIC CHANGE

As two Latina leaders navigating the complexities of educational leadership, our work is both deeply personal and professionally driven. The initiatives outlined in this paper reflect our commitment to leveraging our identities and positional authority to create transformative, equity-driven change for our Latinx students. In a district where nearly half of the student population identifies as Latinx, it is not enough to merely acknowledge the systemic barriers that have historically hindered their success; we must actively work to dismantle them. Our leadership is rooted in the recognition that our cultural identities are powerful assets, not only for our own professional journeys but for the students and communities we serve.

Through the development of the *Latinx Student Success Plan*, our efforts to achieve designation as a *Hispanic-Serving School District*, and the creation of culturally affirming spaces like *Newcomer Centers*, we are setting a new standard for what educational equity should look like in a district as diverse as ours. These initiatives are not only designed to address academic disparities but also to celebrate and uplift the cultural and linguistic strengths of our Latinx students. By shifting from a deficit-based approach to an asset-based model, we are fostering an environment where student identities are not received as barriers but embraced as sources of pride and power. This shift is particularly important for first-generation students, who often bear the dual burden of navigating both school systems and family responsibilities in ways that are rarely acknowledged by traditional educational frameworks.

Our work also highlights the importance of representation in educational leadership. As Latina leaders in positions of significant influence, we understand firsthand the critical role that visibility plays in shaping the aspirations of our students. When Latinx students see themselves reflected in the leadership of their schools, it sends a powerful message: that their voices, experiences, and contributions matter. This is why initiatives like the *San Diego Chapter of CALSA* and our *Latina Leadership*

Affinity Group are so vital. These spaces not only provide support and mentorship for current and aspiring Latina leaders but also ensure that the next generation of Latinx educators and students can see pathways to success that are rooted in their cultural identities.

Moreover, our transnational partnerships with educational leaders in Mexico underscore the global nature of our work. The challenges faced by transnational students—many of whom move between the U.S. and Mexico during their academic journeys—demand solutions that transcend borders. We are committed to building binational agreements and bilingual educational programs that support these students in both countries, ensuring they do not fall through the cracks of two distinct educational systems. Our leadership in this area is guided by a simple but powerful belief: that the success of transnational students is a shared responsibility that both the U.S. and Mexico must uphold.

At the heart of all these efforts is the concept of joy—a radical, transformative force in education that has too often been denied to marginalized students. We firmly believe that joy and positive cultural representation are essential to the academic and personal success of our Latinx students. Joy is not a luxury; it is a necessity. It fosters engagement, belonging, and motivation, creating a foundation for lifelong learning and success. As Latina leaders, we are committed to designing educational experiences that center joy and representation, ensuring that our students not only thrive academically but also take pride in who they are and where they come from.

Our journey as Latina *doctoras* in leadership is about more than just breaking barriers—it is about transforming the system to ensure that future generations of Latinx students have access to the opportunities, support, and representation they deserve. Through our work, we aim to create an educational environment that is as rich and diverse as the students we serve, one where joy, equity, and cultural pride are woven into the fabric of every classroom and leadership decision. Together, we are building a future where Latinx students can not only succeed but excel, contributing to a society that values and celebrates their unique identities and potential.

By working collectively to address systemic inequities, we aim to create a district where all students can thrive academically, socially, and emotionally.

REFERENCES

Acevedo, M. (2021). The role of affinity groups in supporting underrepresented leaders in education. *Journal of Educational Leadership*, 15(2), 123–138.

Acevedo, N. (2021). The power of affinity groups for women of color in leadership. *Journal of Educational Leadership*, 45(3), 201–215.

Alfaro, C., & Hernández, A. M. (2016). Dual language equity lens: A conceptual framework for educators. Multilingual Educator, 2016 California Association for Bilingual Education Conference Edition, 8-11. Retrieved from http://www.gocabe .org/wp-content/uploads/2016/03/ME2016.pdf

Anzaldúa, G. (1987). How to tame a wild tongue. In *Borderlands/La Frontera: The New Mestiza* (pp. 36-43). Aunt Lute Books.

Bialystok, E. (2011). Reshaping the mind: The benefits of bilingualism. *Canadian Journal of Experimental Psychology*, 65(4), 229–235. DOI: 10.1037/a0025406 PMID: 21910523

Calderón, M., Slavin, R., & Sánchez, M. (2011). Effective instruction for English learners. *The Future of Children*, 21(1), 103–127. DOI: 10.1353/foc.2011.0007 PMID: 21465857

California Association of Latino Superintendents and Administrators. (2023). *Latinx leadership and student success: The CALSA San Diego chapter impact report*. CALSA Press.

California Department of Education. (2023). Data and statistics. Retrieved from https://www.cde.ca.gov/ds/

California Department of Education. (2023). Teacher and administrator demographics. Retrieved from https://www.cde.ca.gov/demographics

Chism, D. (2022). Leading Your School Toward Equity. ASCD. Cooperative Children's Book Center (CCBC), School of Education, University of Wisconsin–Madison. "Publishing Statistics on Children's/YA Books about People of Color and First/Native Nations and by People of Color and First/Native Nations Authors and Illustrators." Children's Books by and about People of Color, ccbc.education .wisc .edu/books/pcstats.asp.

Cortez, A., & Johnson, R. (2019). Supporting first-generation Latinx college students: The importance of financial literacy and mentorship. *Journal of College Student Development*, 60(3), 324–328.

Cortez, A., & Johnson, R. L. (2019). Latino education and leadership: Challenges and opportunities. *Educational Leadership Review*, 20(1), 11–25.

Crenshaw, K. (1991). Mapping the margins: Intersectionality, identity politics, and violence against women of color. *Stanford Law Review*, 43(6), 1241–1300. DOI: 10.2307/1229039

de Araujo, Z., Roberts, S. A., Willey, C., & Zahner, W. (2018). English Learners in K-12 Mathematics Education: A Review of the Literature. *Review of Educational Research*, 88(6), 879–919. https://www.jstor.org/stable/45277268. DOI: 10.3102/0034654318798093

Delgado Bernal, D. (2002). Critical race theory, Latino critical theory, and critical raced-gendered epistemologies: Recognizing students of color as holders and creators of knowledge. *Qualitative Inquiry*, 8(1), 105–126. DOI: 10.1177/107780040200800107

DeNicolo, C. P., Yu, M., Crowley, C. B., & Gabel, S. L. (2017). Reimagining Critical Care and Problematizing Sense of School Belonging as a Response to Inequality for Immigrants and Children of Immigrants. *Review of Research in Education*, 41(1), 500–530. https://www.jstor.org/stable/44668705. DOI: 10.3102/0091732X17690498

Dolan, K., Slaughter-Johnson, E., Sampson, M., Jones, K., & Miles, B. (2018). WHO DOES THE SCHOOL TO PRISON PIPELINE AFFECT? In *STUDENTS UNDER SIEGE: How the school-to-prison pipeline, poverty, and racism endanger our school children* (pp. 8–18). Institute for Policy Studies. https://www.jstor.org/stable/resrep27070.5

Excelencia in Education. (2022). *Latino college completion: United States 2022*. Retrieved from https://www.edexcelencia.org

Flores, N. (2017). The complex intersection of language and education: Bilingualism as an asset. *Journal of Multilingual and Multicultural Development*, 38(5), 407–414.

Gándara, P. (2015). *Fulfilling America's future: Latinas in the U.S., 2015*. The White House Initiative on Educational Excellence for Hispanics. Retrieved from https://sites.ed.gov/hispanic-initiative

Gándara, P., & Contreras, F. (2009). *The Latino education crisis: The consequences of failed social policies*. Harvard University Press. DOI: 10.4159/9780674056367

Gándara, P., & Hopkins, M. (2010). *Forbidden language: English learners and restrictive language policies*. Teachers College Press.

García, O., & Wei, L. (2014). *Translanguaging: Language, bilingualism, and education*. Palgrave Macmillan. DOI: 10.1057/9781137385765

Gist, C. D., Bianco, M., & Lynn, M. (2019). Examining grow your own programs across the teacher development continuum: Mining research on teachers of color and nontraditional educator pipelines. *Journal of Teacher Education*, 70(1), 13–25. DOI: 10.1177/0022487118787504

Gonzales, M. L. (2021). Breaking barriers: The rise of Latina leaders in education. *Journal of Latinos and Education*, 20(2), 130–143.

Gutiérrez, K. D. (2017). Designing resilient ecologies: Social design experiments and a new social imagination. *Educational Researcher*, 46(3), 187–195.

Hamann, E. T., Zúñiga, V., & Sánchez García, J. (2010). Transnational students: Between worlds, between times. *Journal of Latinos and Education*, 9(3), 202–219.

Hernandez, A. E. (2012). Bilingualism and cognitive development: A neuropsychological perspective. *Developmental Science*, 15(4), 465–481.

Hernandez, D. J. (2012). Young children in Black immigrant families from Africa and the Caribbean. In Capps, R., & Fix, M. (Eds.), *Young children of Black immigrants in America: Changing flows, changing faces* (pp. 75–117). Migration Policy Institute.

Hispanic Association of Colleges and Universities (HACU). (2023). *What is a Hispanic-Serving Institution (HSI)?* Retrieved from https://www.hacu.net

Immordino-Yang, M. H., & Damasio, A. (2007). We feel, therefore we learn: The relevance of affective and social neuroscience to education. *Mind, Brain and Education : the Official Journal of the International Mind, Brain, and Education Society*, 1(1), 3–10. DOI: 10.1111/j.1751-228X.2007.00004.x

Ishimaru, A. M., & Lott, J. (2015). Families in the driver's seat: Cultivating family leadership for educational change. *Journal of Educational Change*, 16(2), 117–144.

Jacobs, C. E. (2020). READY TO LEAD Report by Charlotte E. Jacobs, Ph.D. Research Directed by Simone Marean + Rachel Simmons Leadership Supports and Barriers for Black and Latinx Girls [Review of READY TO LEAD Report by Charlotte E. Jacobs, Ph.D. Research Directed by Simone Marean + Rachel Simmons Leadership Supports and Barriers for Black and Latinx Girls]. In girlsleadership.org (pp. 1–49). Girls Leadership. https://readytolead.girlsleadership.org/

Jeynes, W. H. (2016). A meta-analysis: The relationship between parental involvement and Latinx student academic achievement. *Education and Urban Society*, 49(1), 4–28. DOI: 10.1177/0013124516630596

Ladson-Billings, G. (2006). Yes, but how do we do it? Practicing culturally relevant pedagogy. In Landsman, J., & Lewis, C. W. (Eds.), *White teachers / diverse classrooms* (pp. 29–41). Stylus Publishing.

Méndez-Morse, S. (2004). Constructing mentors: Latina educational leaders' role models and mentors. *Educational Administration Quarterly*, 40(4), 561–590. DOI: 10.1177/0013161X04267112

Méndez-Morse, S., Murakami, E. T., Byrne-Jiménez, M., & Hernández, F. (2015). Latina/o educational leadership across borders: Learning, growing, and leading together. *The International Journal of Educational Leadership Preparation*, 10(1), 1–13.

Mexican Ministry of Public Education (SEP). (2022). *Educational statistics in Baja California.* Retrieved from https://www.sep.gob.mx

Murillo, E. G. (2017). Critical race theory in education: Review of past literature and a look to the future. *Urban Education*, 52(5), 563–598.

National Center for Education Statistics. (2024). *Achievement gaps and Latinx students in U.S. public schools.* U.S. Department of Education, Institute of Education Sciences.

National Center for Education Statistics. (2024). *English learners in public schools. Condition of education.* U.S. Department of Education, Institute of Education Sciences.

Nieto, S. (2010). *Language, culture, and teaching: Critical perspectives.* Routledge.

Padilla, A. M. (1994). Ethnic minority scholars, research, and mentoring: Current and future issues. *Educational Researcher*, 23(4), 24–27. DOI: 10.2307/1176259

Paris, D., & Alim, H. S. (2017). *Culturally sustaining pedagogies: Teaching and learning for justice in a changing world.* Teachers College Press.

Potowski, K. (2004). Student Spanish Use and Investment in a Dual Immersion Classroom: Implications for Second Language Acquisition and Heritage Language Maintenance. *Modern Language Journal*, 88(1), 75–101. https://www.jstor.org/stable/3588719. DOI: 10.1111/j.0026-7902.2004.00219.x

Riley, K. (2022). Schools where belonging works. In *Compassionate Leadership for School Belonging* (pp. 61–72). UCL Press., DOI: 10.2307/j.ctv20rsk8p.13

Samuels, S., Wilkerson, A., Chapman, D., & Watkins, W. (2020). Toward a Conceptualization: Considering Microaffirmations as a Form of Culturally Relevant Pedagogy and Academic Growth for K-12 Underserved Student Populations. *The Journal of Negro Education*, 89(3), 298–311. https://www.jstor.org/stable/10.7709/jnegroeducation.89.3.0298

San Diego County Office of Education. (2023). *Student demographics.* Retrieved from https://www.sdcoe.net

Sánchez-Connally, P. (2018). Latinx First Generation College Students: Negotiating Race, Gender, Class, and Belonging. *Race, Gender & Class (Towson, Md.)*, 25(3/4), 234–251. https://www.jstor.org/stable/26802896

Santamaría, L. J. (2020). Culturally responsive educational leadership and advocacy: A transformative agenda. *Educational Policy*, 34(1), 7–29.

Santamaría, L. J., & Jean-Marie, G. (2014). Cross-cultural leadership in school settings: Critical perspectives on race, ethnicity, and gender. *Multicultural Education Review*, 6(1), 39–54.

Vaandering, D. (2013). Implementing restorative justice practice in schools: What pedagogy reveals. *Journal of Peace Education*, 11(1), 64–80. DOI: 10.1080/17400201.2013.794335

Valdés, G. (2019). *Transnational students and schools: The borderlands of education.* Teachers College Press.

Valenzuela, A. (1999). *Subtractive schooling: U.S.-Mexican youth and the politics of caring.* State University of New York Press.

Villalpando, O., & Bernal, D. D. (2018). Latino/a students in higher education: Understanding their transitional experiences. *Journal of Hispanic Higher Education*, 17(3), 223–236.

Yosso, T. J. (2005). Whose culture has capital? A critical race theory discussion of community cultural wealth. *Race, Ethnicity and Education*, 8(1), 69–91. DOI: 10.1080/1361332052000341006

Young, J. L., & Easton-Brooks, D. (2022). The Impact of Teachers of Color on School Belonging: A Conceptual Framework. In Gist, C. D., & Bristol, T. J. (Eds.), *Handbook of Research on Teachers of Color and Indigenous Teachers* (pp. 637–644). American Educational Research Association., DOI: 10.2307/j.ctv2xqngb9.52

Zong, J., & Batalova, J. (2019). Mexican immigrants in the United States. *Migration Policy Institute.* Retrieved from https://www.migrationpolicy.org

Chapter 9
The Critical Work of the Blue–Collar Scholar:
Latinx Educators Working Towards the Heteroglossic and Liberated English Language Development Class

David De La Cruz Rosales
California State University, Fullerton, USA

ABSTRACT

This chapter explores the essential role of Latinx educators in nurturing critical linguistic and literacy awareness among English Learners, referred to as Emergent Bilinguals. Specifically, the focus will be on the impact of Latinx educators in the English Language Development (ELD) classroom. This chapter asserts that the work of a Latinx ELD educator is based on a critical understanding of the oppressive systemic structures of assimilation policies, linguistic dominance, and constructed academic challenges and labels imposed on Emergent Bilinguals due to historical marginalization and oppressive systems, often exacerbated by political agendas and anti-immigrant sentiments. Despite the challenges posed by the monoglossic and hegemonic nature of ELD policies, Latinx educators can employ culturally relevant practices to amplify the voices of their students and communities within the framework of the ELD classroom.

DOI: 10.4018/979-8-3373-1340-5.ch009

Copyright © 2025, IGI Global Scientific Publishing. Copying or distributing in print or electronic forms without written permission of IGI Global Scientific Publishing is prohibited.

INTRODUCTION

While working within the ELD structure may appear to be constraining and overly focused on assimilation, embracing their identity in connection to the Latinx Emergent Bilinguals they work with and promoting critical community awareness allows Latinx educators to empower and affirm the rich cultural identities of their students through caring pedagogical activism (hooks, 1994, Valenzuela, 1999).

Culturally and linguistically Sustaining practices as *bienestar*

The Merriam-Webster dictionary defines wellness as the "quality or state of being in good health, especially as an actively sought-after goal." Based on this definition, wellness can be construed as something we are responsible for acquiring through self-edification and drive. This definition is in tune with the tradition of meritocracy and productivity in the United States. However, seeing wellness as an individual endeavor one actively seeks to acquire ignores the conditions that may disrupt or prevent one from being well. Challenging living conditions, stressful experiences, oppressive systems, and limited wellness educational resources are factors that can impact an individual's wellness. This definition also ignores the collective effort it takes for one person to be well. There exists an interconnectedness of wellness found in an "everything is going to be all right" from a loved one that soothes a young student's anxiety the night before their first day of school, a counselor's guided breathing practices to calm a student's ire, and the safety of a mother's "Dios te bendiga" as a young scholar leaves to school first thing in the morning.

This definition of wellness is over-simplistic; instead, I propose two definitions that see wellness beyond something one seeks to obtain actively. The first definition is the Spanish definition of wellness, which is *bienestar*. According to the Real Academia de Español, *bienestar* is *conjuntos de las cosas necesarias para vivir bien,* which translates into a set of things necessary to live well. The definition of *bienestar* acknowledges that different things contribute to the ability to live. It is, in fact, in conversation with the second definition of wellness provided by the APA Dictionary of Psychology, which states wellness is "a dynamic state of physical, mental, and social well-being. It is considered to be a result of factors such as biology, environment, lifestyle, and healthcare management." This definition also acknowledges that interconnected factors contribute to one's ability to be well. In the context of wellness in the educational setting, I would like to postulate that the definition of *bienestar*, aligned with the APA's dictionary definition, is more relevant to the discussion of wellness in the English Language Development Classroom. Language development and wellness are highly social interactions interconnected and interdependent with multiple factors outside oneself. The search for wellness and language development are intertwined processes that one does not undergo alone. They require support, motivation, and emotional connections from others. Our language development and wellness paths do not all look the same, for we come from different histories and carry different testimonies that inform our attitudes and dispositions toward learning. Therefore, culturally and linguistically sustaining practices must be at the forefront of educators working with English Learners. The goal of developing academic language through assimilative linguistic practices and English-only expectations must not take precedence over the *bienestar* and the conditions educators can co-create to develop healthy social-emotional educational environments for students.

There is a rich tradition of studies that cement the importance of centering English Learners wellness in their language development journey, such as recognizing the emotional factors that can impact language development in an individual (Krashen, 1982), adopting an empowering framework with culturally relevant practices to an EL's background (Cummins, 2000), or reimagining the role of minority students first language in the English Language Development classroom (Lucas, Kratz, 1994). These liberating linguistic and pedagogical practices combat prevalent hegemonic and monolingual ideologies in English language development education. Scholars from numerous fields, including bilingual education, sociolinguistics, and anthropology, have moved the conversation forward by critiquing the negative impacts of subtractive and assimilative practices on English learners' academic identity, intrinsic motivation, and social-emotional wellness. The quest for a linguistically liberated ELD classroom outside of the white gaze of education is a quest for social justice and student wellness (Delpit, 1995). Educators must be invested in disrupting, unlearning, and learning anew alongside their students to develop a counternarrative that challenges assumptions and biases often arising from a white-centric perspective in the ELD classroom spaces.

In California, Latinx educators play a crucial role in raising critical linguistic and literacy consciousness among English Learners, who will be referred to as Emergent Bilinguals for the remainder of this chapter (See terminology section). This chapter posits that a Latinx ELD educator's intellectual work must be rooted in a critical awareness of the oppressive systemic structures of assimilation policies, linguistic dominance, and fabricated academic challenges and labels imposed on Emergent Bilinguals. These systems espouse anti-bilingual and anti-immigrant sentiments. The Latinx educator working with Latinx Emergent Bilinguals, the most significant population of Emergent bilinguals in California, must proceed with the understanding that the designated English Language Development classroom is a space that must be humanized by the connections they make with their students and the jointed linguistic and cultural co-liberation they enact alongside their students and communities.

The Collective Struggle of Latinx Educators and Emergent Bilinguals in the City of Angels

Latinx students constitute the largest group of Emergent Bilinguals in California; however, Latinx educators are significantly outnumbered by their white counterparts. According to the California Department of Education, during the 2018-2019 school year, there were only 64,904 Latinx educators compared to 188,229 white educators. This trend extends beyond California and reflects a broader national concern. The National Center for Educational Statistics reported that in 2021, 5.3 million students in the United States were classified as English Learners (ELs), with a striking 77.9 percent—approximately 4 million students—identified as Hispanic. In stark contrast, only 9 percent of teachers nationwide were Hispanic or Latinx, while an overwhelming 80 percent were white. Across various states, integrated and designated English Language Development (ELD) programs are designed to provide vital support for Latinx ELD educators. However, the social and political contexts within each school greatly influence the roles and responsibilities that these educators must navigate. The underrepresentation of Latinx educators in comparison to the number of Latinx English learners is a pressing issue that has been thoroughly examined in scholarly research (Lichon, Moreno; Villamizar, Arana, 2022; Barajas-Gonzalez, Linares, Torres, Urcuyo, Salamanca, Santos, & Pagán 20224). This chapter is firmly rooted in my experiences and positionality as an educator working in the Koreatown community of Los Angeles, California. The 2000 U.S. Census indicates that Koreatown boasts a population of 115,070 residents within a 2.7-square-mile area, making it the most densely populated community in Los Angeles, with an average of 42,611 people per square mile. This dynamic neighborhood, alongside its adjacent area of Westlake MacArthur Park, is home to a significant population of immigrant Latinx communities. Consequently, this chapter is distinctly situated within that social and demographic context.

In the context of the English Language Development classroom, the work of the few Latinx ELD educators must go beyond language development and acquisition. Latinx educators can employ culturally relevant practices to amplify the voices of their students and communities within the structure of the ELD classroom. In taking proactive, cultural roles in the language development process of emergent bilinguals, Latinx educators promote wellness and invite Emergent Bilinguals to take active roles in the ELD classroom. Working within the ELD framework may seem restrictive and hyper-focused on assimilation. Still, Latinx educators can empower and affirm their students' rich cultural identities through caring pedagogical activism by embracing their identity connected to the Latinx Emergent Bilinguals they work with and promoting critical community awareness (hooks, 1994, Valenzuela, 1999). Emergent Bilingual students benefit from relationships they may develop with educators who look and speak like them and enact a similar culture. Yet, there is more to simply diversifying the ELD classroom and giving brown students brown educators (Pour-Khorshid, 2018). Latinx educators stepping into the ELD classroom must develop anti-oppressive and critical lenses that are unapologetic and radical enough to disrupt a system of monolingualism and cultural hegemony that is deeply rooted in the history of systemic marginalization and racialization of the Latinx community in California's political and educational policymaking. (Dover, Rodriguez-Valls, 2022). They must recognize that an educator's labor is a labor of love and action highly relational to the students and communities they serve, which can often be limited or in negotiation with the standardized language policies developed in local, state, and national educational institutions.

The phrase *maestro de pueblo para el pueblo* encompasses the understanding of the disruptive force a social justice-oriented educator can have and the commitment that the ELD classroom demands from the Latinx educator. Latinx educators, similarly to other ethnic background educators, may experience cultural dissonance (Ladson-billings, 1995) from the Latinx student communities they serve. After all, educators who have undergone the higher education system have learned the academic language associated with their field of study. This language may be disconnected from their languages from home. Furthermore, Many Latinx language educators may see their role in the designated ELD classroom as solely an academic language development support and miss the opportunity to foster culturally linguistic practices that ensure student wellness. Therefore, it is pivotal to establish that Latinx educators in the classroom are not individual stories of success but stories of collaborative effort, communal aspirations, and dreams. There is a connecting thread that weaves the narrative of Latinx educators with the narratives of the Latinx students they teach. In the K-12 educational experience, many Latinx Emergent Bilinguals experience dissociation from home and school. Often, Emergent bilinguals are tasked with explaining reclassification criteria, grading systems, and school policies to parents who may have limited schooling experience or perceptions of schooling institutions informed by their own experiences; in some cases, experiences that saw their cultural practices and values disregarded or denigrated (Ishimaru,2020). Additionally, they have to negotiate interactions with adults and schooling institutions that may diminish their abilities based on preconceived perceptions of their language abilities.

The challenges for Emergent Bilinguals navigating the white-dominant California educational system continue even after they graduate high school. Similarly, to Latinx educators who went through the higher education system, Emergent Bilinguals who enroll in higher education institutions undergo challenges in navigating the higher education structures, being first generation, encountering the imposter syndrome, and figuring out resources and programs related to financial aid. Furthermore, Emergent Bilinguals who do not reclassify during their K-12 education are more than likely to take remedial courses, have less accessibility to AP courses during their High School years, and may face more financial constraints than their American-born counterparts. The growing population of Latinx students in the United States, specifically in California, does not reflect the higher education graduation rates. As postulated by Gandara and Contreras (2000), "Never before have we been faced with a population group on the verge of becoming the majority in significant portions of the country that is also the lowest performing academically. Furthermore, never before has the economic structure been less forgiving to the undereducated." Educational policies rooted in whiteness across California prevail regardless of the changing fabric of our country's population. Latinx educators in the ELD classroom have the positionality to advocate for collective progress and liberation from historically inherited deculturizing spaces that jeopardize the wellness and educational experience of Emergent Bilinguals. This chapter analyzes the role of Latinx educators in implementing liberatory pedagogical and community-oriented practices that focus on fostering critical consciousness and dialogue to create collaborative and co-liberated language development spaces (Freire, 1999), authentically caring for the diverse Latinx Emergent Bilingual population and their unique characteristics (Valenzuela, 1999), and centering community capital as the source and not a point of reference to white dominant culture (Yosso, 2009) in the ELD classroom.

Terminology Rooted in Resistance

The power of language is twofold: it is a tool of oppression, but it can also be a tool of resistance. The words or language tokens we choose significantly impact how we perceive the subjects we discuss. Our ability to comprehend the abstract and the concrete, and how we negotiate understanding, hinges on the language we use to describe and make sense of them. Therefore, Ofelia Garcia's thought-provoking question, "What is in a name?" prompts one to consider the profound implications of language choice when referring to our Latinx students. Her work with TESOL students provides a valuable opportunity for educators working with Latinx Emergent Bilinguals to ground themselves in the culturally and linguistically just work Latinx educators embark on when working with Emergent Bilinguals. It forces one to question whether we confine ourselves to language development education's "academic" and non-academic" dichotomies or whether we can envision alternate *spaces*. Furthermore, it urges us to reflect on whether the term "Emergent Bilingual" and its underlying ideology truly resonate with one's identity as a designated ELD educator. Are such terms and ideologies simply jargon adopted as part of professional development at a school site, district, or state level, or are they principles aligned to our role in the classroom? The Latinx educator working with Emergent bilinguals has to develop a conviction that defies deficit labels and terminology that reproduce oppressive ideologies and educational policy.

The term **Emergent Bilingual** is an intentional disruption of monolingual norms and labels that perceive bilingualism through an asset rather than a deficit lens (Garcia, 2009). Instead of using labels like Limited English Proficiency or English Language Learner (ELL) that may contribute to the internalization of deficit in Latinx students, Emergent Bilingual highlights the potential for growth in two languages. It acknowledges the importance of both languages in students' identities (Garcia, 2009). It is a direct response to additive ideologies that continue to compartmentalize the linguistic identities of English learners. The term recognizes that languages do not exist in isolation or boxes but are in constant conversation with one another. Therefore, if languaging exists in unison in the everyday lives of our Latinx emergent bilinguals, the effort to draw distinctions between the language of home, community, and academics is counterproductive to language development. This term is both disrupting and unifying.

In the context of this chapter, the term **Latinx** is used to encompass the various identities and experiences that educators, communities, and students bring to the classroom. The term is part of an effort to create gender-neutral language for linguistic inclusivity in languages that have masculine and feminine pronouns and nouns. Although the term is not fully embraced by the Latino/a community, mainly because of its origin and reproduction in mainstream U.S culture seen as "anglicism" of the Spanish language, it is popular amongst younger generations, higher education spaces, and Latinx who lean toward Democratic ideologies (Noe-Bustamante, 2020).

The polarized sentiments about the term are yet another example of the impacts of language and identity in the United States. In this case, English is the language that provides an inclusive and liberating space for members of the Latinx community who do not feel represented in the Spanish language dichotomies of masculinity and femininity. This unifying term also speaks to a certain pan ethnicity that these communities share. There are common values and sources of solidarity within the countless narratives of migration, assimilation, resistance, and perseverance in the United States, regardless of one's gender identity. In many cases, the Latinx identity's plasticity allows for transcending nationalities and socially constructed borders and invites a shared identity that holds steadfast in spaces like education, where Latinidad may be frowned upon or marginalized. (Suarez-Orozco 2009). This term is also used to emphasize the disruption of heterosexual and heteronormative spaces the identity of Latinx educators may have and model in the classroom. The common phrase "we teach who we are" must be embraced by the Latinx educator whose presence in the Californian-designated- ELD classroom is a testament to the history of struggle and liberation that pertains to Latinx educators living in California.

A **heteroglossic ideology** directly opposes the history of the **monoglossic** ideological schooling systems in the United States. It demands educators and anyone working with students to see language as a dynamic and fluid enactment rather than a static and prescriptive limited set of language rules (Dover, Rodriguez-Valls, 2022). Adopting a heteroglossic ideology disrupts defacto notions that establish white middle-class English as academic. These monoglossic ideologies also label any divergence from white middle-class English or the inclusion of languages other than English in educational settings as nonacademic. For far too long, the language of Latinx students has been chastised and reprimanded based on the perceptions of not meeting the monolinguistic molds that have been developed hand in hand with anti-immigrant and anti-bilingual social policies. The political agendas of policymakers and leaders of California and the greater United States have often seen the Latinx immigrant population as oppositional to the fabric of this country. Yet, in a growing population of Latinx communities across California, monolingualism and the definition of American safeguarded by folks who want to maintain a cultural hegemonic status quo, ignore the fact that the 21st-century Latinx student is not confined to one language or one modality of communication, but instead communicate in Englishes and modes that reflect their multiple identities (Garcia, Torres-Guevarra, 2009). Latinx educators and students use thief full linguistic repertoires to interact, navigate, negotiate, and survive in a country that prides itself on being a cultural melting pot and paying lip service to multiculturalism, yet continues a tradition of educational policies that work towards the rejection of Latinx Emergent Bilinguals full cultural and linguistic repertoires in the educational setting.

Grounding Theoretical Concepts

Emergent Bilinguals have endured the impact of subtractive schooling (Valenzuela, 1999) throughout the history of California educational policymaking (Moreno, 2008). Considering that 81.9% (CDE, 2022) of the Emergent Bilingual population in California is Spanish-speaking, it is pivotal that students feel that their identities are affirmed and invited into the learning space. Latinx educators have the responsibility to help students in the ELD class fulfill the reclassification requirements mandated by the state, but not at the expense of their student's linguistic identities and rich social capital. As educators who can advocate for their students and foster meaningful relationships based on trust and cultural connection to their community, Latinx educators are uniquely positioned to use their understanding of educational systems and policies in ELD classes to empower their students. By embracing their histories of aspirational and navigational capital (Yosso, 2009) that brought them into the classroom, Latinx educators can build authentic relationships of caring and relatability to create collaborative and co-liberated cultural and linguistic spaces alongside their students and communities. Critical awareness of Latinx communities' cultural dispositions and belief systems related to education can help dismantle borders that systemic monoglossic and assimilative practices have edified between the Latinx working-class community and academic institutions.

Critical Consciousness

Critical consciousness is a concept often associated with social justice and transformative education. While this idea primarily refers to interactions between students and educators in academic settings, it is rooted in Freire's observation of social systems of oppression and how they unravel in various spaces in society. As he explains, "It is rooted in concrete situations and describes the reactions of workers (peasant or urban) and middle-class people whom I have observed directly or indirectly during the course of my [his] educational work" (Freire, 1968, p. 37). Freire emphasized the importance of recognizing and understanding oppressive systems in society, reflecting on them, and acting in response to them (Freire, 1968). Through a critically conscious stance, Latinx educators who embrace their identity and positionality are committed to the transformative power of co-creating with their students while dismantling different forms of oppressive systems that take presence in the ELD classroom. Latinx educators grounded in a critical conscious stance are empowered to combat a history of English language development education entrenched in a banking model ideology that posits Emerging bilinguals as empty vessels to be filled with assimilative and academic language. The assumption that students in the designated ELD classroom lack the necessary skills to engage in academic conversations ignores the rich daily languaging skills students engage in. The Latinx educator can invite critical dialogue that posits students as active participants who can challenge and question social, economic, and linguistic conditions through a problem-based education. For students to partake in dialogue fostering critical consciousness, they must do so in the languages that reflect their identities inside and outside the classroom without the constant language policing that standardization expects.

In the spirit of connection to the labor of the Latinx working class, I offer the term blue-collar scholar to describe the intellectual work Latinx educators must invite to foster meaningful relationships that promote social change in the communities they serve. Latinx educators must be aware that dismantling linguistic systems of oppression goes beyond a well-developed multilingual lesson or the ecology of a classroom they co-create with their students; it also involves political and social activism. Educational unions have played a pivotal role in enacting social change in California. Unions are a space to learn about the educational and political decisions that impact our student population. More importantly, they are a space to garner support from like-minded community activists, educators, and educational policymakers to advocate for motions and policies that center on the wellness of emergent bilinguals and Latinx communities. In the words of a prominent American Federation of Teachers union member currently spearheading the English Language Learners task Force and developer of Colorin Colorado, "We live our history, and our union principles, in our daily actions. And that's why I'm proud to say, and why our union has said, supporting Latino children and families is union work." (Fortino, 2017) Latinx educators must intentionally raise awareness of the intersectionalities of our Emergent bilingual population. The work of the Latinx educator is concerned with developing linguistically and culturally inviting spaces for Emergent Bilinguals and labor justice for the working-class parents in the community. As members of the Latinx communities, one can situate the curriculum with the lived experiences, whether through dismantling a standardized monoglossic curriculum in the ELD space or taking action in labor union work that disrupts educational and political policies that further suppress Emergent bilingual identities. The work of the Latinx educator must not be disconnected from the everyday stories of resilience and resistance our students undergo in their communities.

Politics of Caring

Angela Valenzuela's work in politics of caring challenges the definition of a "caring" adult in the educational space. In her study with Latinx students, both Emergent bilinguals and U.S.-born, from Seguin High School, Valenzuela found that students gravitated to teachers and curricula centered on "connectedness" to their persons, experiences, and communities. Her findings around authentic caring practices demonstrate the importance of establishing meaningful and affirming connections with students from a nondominant background. It also illuminates the peril of disconnect that comes with the lack of cultural and linguistic awareness of the student population one works with. Many educators in her study perceived Latinx youth and Emergent Bilinguals as uninvested because their dispositions did not abide by their ideologies of academic behavior, language, and prowess. Most Latinx educators working with Latinx communities have the advantage of being familiar with core values, such as the role of "hard work" that many Latinx parents instill in their student's academic identities (Lopez, 2001). For Latinx educators that are familiar with the Spanish language, the famous dicho *"ponte las pilas"* or the *educacion* from home that parents equate to good upbringing and their student's comportment in society, are clear indicators of cultural competence (Taggart, 2022) that a non-Latinx educator cannot perceive as well as someone who possesses this competence through their lived experiences. For community-estranged Latinx educators and non-Latinx educators who are unwilling to perceive this cultural competence because of their cultural dissonance or monolinguistic, monocultural dispositions, this is a missed opportunity to establish a meaningful connection between the lived experiences of students and the content they impart. When Latinx students are perceived as disengaged from the content in an ELD classroom, it is easier to imprint labels such as "unprepared," "below grade level," or "unacademic" than to be self-critical and self-reflective (Ordoñez-Jasis et al., 2016) of classroom practices that may not foster or reflect the identities of our students or their communities.

Valenzuela's work also explores the ideas of subtractive schooling and how it impacts Latinx students and immigrant youth by placing assimilation practices before students' cultural identities and suppressing languages from home in pursuit of academic language and linguistic hegemony. Latinx educators working with emergent bilinguals must foster relationships that acknowledge the "students' cultural world and structural positions" to engage in discourse that is relevant and inviting to students (Valenzuela, 1999). Emergent Bilinguals from urban settings come to school with different needs and challenges in life, as well as multiple interconnected forms of oppression that may impact their perceptions in the classroom. These forms of oppression can be reproduced by educators or confronted through anti-oppressive practices that humanize the classroom space. (Kumashiro, 2000) To engage students commonly labeled as "not caring," the ELD Latinx educator must know the needs and challenges that one's students may have outside of the classroom. A Latinx educator's awareness of competing factors that impact the language development and academic dispositions of Emergent Bilinguals is essential in dismantling pervasive stereotypes and generalizations of a group of students that has to be treated with caring and understanding rather than judgment and alienation.

Community Cultural Wealth

The concept of community cultural wealth challenges the notion that communities of color lack the capital necessary for social mobility and success, typically associated with the white middle class, placing them at a disadvantage and unable to move from impoverished cultural capital. (Bourdieu & Passeron, 1977). Yosso posits that Bourdieu focuses on the white middle-class accumulation of assets and resources as the standard, causing all other forms and expressions of culture to be judged compared to this norm. To this day, the measures of social capital and social mobility in the United States are designed to accommodate the characteristics and conditions of the white middle class. The Critical Race Theory lens that informs Yosso's writing acknowledges the history of racialization and obstruction that communities of color have encountered in the United States. Various oppressive systemic practices have marginalized and inhibited the financial, educational, and social development of communities of color. Nevertheless, communities of color continue to survive and resist oppressive systems of racialization and inequality through unique forms of capital that inspire and motivate them in education and society (Yosso, 2009). Yosso proposes that there are alternate forms of capital that students of color bring to the classroom that are often unacknowledged and underutilized. In acknowledging community cultural wealth, such as familial, aspirational, and resistant capital, educators are disrupting oppressive systems that empower students and affirm their commitment to social justice education (Delgado-Gaitan, 2001).

Being an ELD Latinx educator requires challenging the "deficit view" of communities of color as culturally impoverished and disadvantaged (Yosso, p. 69, 2009) and developing a vulnerable ear recognizing the linguistic capital that Emergent Bilinguals apport to the ELD classroom. Through this lens, one finds the narratives of resilience, resistance, and aspirations that abound in our communities. By actively giving precedence to Latinx forms of social wealth, Latinx educators combat linguistic and literacy fabricated deficits often associated with the working-class Latinx communities. Latinx educators who foster Emergent bilingual linguistic and community wealth in the classroom are directly challenging a pervasive dominant ideology of linguistics purity that has marginalized the Latinx Emergent Bilingual population (Delgado Bernal, 1998). By acknowledging and affirming the full linguistic repertoire Emergent bilinguals bring to the classroom, one honors their social capital and the conditions that factor into their linguistic identities. Rather than constantly monitoring the appropriateness of Emergent bilingual language, there needs to be a listening disposition keen on the stories gifted in the creative expression, the accents, and the enactment of languaging in the ELD classroom. By seeing the cultural capital that Emergent bilingual students bring to the table and situating it to their lived experiences and community realities, one moves away from Bourdieu's measurement of what is socially desired in relation to white middle-class social capital and instead perceives what are the forms of capital that have sustained and ensured the survival of historically disadvantaged communities. Countless testimonies of resilience are embedded in the linguistic capital of a *dicho* or *a consejo* passed down from one generation of Latinx family members to the next (Carrion & Torres, 2023).

The Monoglossic Fabric of the ELD Classroom

Each academic year, ELD educators across California create curricula, craft lessons, and attend Professional Developments to support the reclassification journey of Emergent Bilinguals. Local Learning Educational Agencies (LEA) use approved reclassification processes that must adhere to the criteria mandated by the state (California Department of Education, 2022) to assess student English proficiency. ELD classes are designated spaces created to develop English language skills necessary for academic content learning in English. They are also a space where students are expected to transition from EL status to Fluent English Proficiency (RFEP).

While these spaces are meant to support the language development of Newcomers and long-term Emergent bilinguals (Olsen, 2010), by original design, the fabric of the ELD classroom is prone to reproducing monolingual and hegemonic linguistic ideologies that make academic language synonymous with white, middle-class English while making nondominant languages and registers "non-standard" (Rosa & Flores, 2017). The perception that Emergent Bilinguals in an ELD classroom's language are lacking or nonacademic is a result of a history of anti-immigrant and anti-bilingual sentiments that have shaped the educational policy of California. It is, therefore, a social issue that is not rooted in objective ways to measure language proficiency but rather in the racialization and stigmatization of minority modes of existence that stem from colonial ideologies and are sustained by systemic assimilative and imperialistic practices embedded in the United States society and educational systems (García, Flores, et al., 2021).

Throughout the 1700s, California's educational systems served as vehicles for the subjugation and assimilation of indigenous populations. Through the conversion and coercion of Spanish rule, many Indigenous people of California were forcefully indoctrinated and imprinted with the Spanish language. During the Spanish rule, race, class, and language were weaponized to eradicate the identity and language of the indigenous people. The mission system served as a way to progress the noble savage narrative that sought to assimilate indigenous peoples to Spanish racial order and hierarchy. The catholic church played an important role in establishing and maintaining the colonial order throughout this period. Through the mission system and private and public-school systems, many of the cultural and linguistic features of assimilation remained in place (Moreno, 1999). Mexican Americans could communicate and create systems promoting the Spanish heritage language; this would gradually change.

In the mid-1800s, after the Treaty of Hidalgo, Anglo settlers and the decrease of legislative representation of Mexican Americans and Spanish leadership led to anti-bilingual sentiments and the denial of citizenship often associated with attacks on Mexican American Spanish language and culture. The culture that once reigned supreme and had subjugated the original Indigenous nations of California was replaced by a far more pervasive dominant culture that associated citizenship and rights with whiteness. Through protestant belief systems, the belief in manifest destiny, and the eradication of the Spanish Catholic church from the 1860s to the early 1890s, Anglo settlers were able to pass policies that prescribed English as the medium of instruction in schools and penalized the use of Spanish in California schools. These policies laid the foundation and often reflected social policies that criminalized and discriminated against the weakened Mexican American population that tried to keep their language (Moreno, 1999). As stated by San Miguel (1999), "their goal was to transform public schooling into an essentially American institution before they could successfully embark on the transformation of ethnic identities of those perceived to be different" (p. 40). As is often the case, the shift in Americanization of the curriculum in California was a mirror to the societal destitution that the Mexican American population would further undergo in the United States. These sentiments and linguistic and racial hierarchy established in California and the new southwest would lay the foundation for contemporary language policies that have impacted the framework and development of bilingual education in recent years.

Throughout the early 19th hundreds up until the civil rights movement, there were countless forms of systemic oppression to suppress bilingualism and Spanish education in California. There were also forms of inequality that "predicated that a separate but equal" educational system for primary Mexican American students was necessary. In this trying time, the fight for bilingual education and equity moved many advocates who used the legal system to challenge anti-immigrant educational policies. Among some of the victories in California's fight for equitable bilingual education were *Alvarez v. The Board of Trustees of the Lemon Grove School District (1931), Mendez v. Westminster (1946),* and *Lau v. Nichols (1974).* These cases were essential to California but were also part of broader education and social justice advocacy trends for civil rights sweeping the rest of the country (Flores, Murillo, 2001). Many cases in California directly impacted the national-level rulings regarding bilingual education and equity. Others were challenges or direct responses to federal-level educational policies that would counter the narrative of English-only education. Through a collective struggle and the mobilization and organizing of bilingual and equitable education activists, there would be gains in the education of Emergent Bilinguals.

Kenzo Sung posits that the National Bilingual Education Act of 1968 was derived as a response to the post-war political climate in the United States and the agreement between Latinx activists and institutional policymakers. He uses the term hegemonic interest's convergence, from Derrick Bell's critical race theory of interest convergence (1980), to describe the economic motifs that impulse Latinx activists and policymakers to converge on a bilingual education policy. The development of the Bilingual Education Act in Date County during a time of anti-immigrant rhetoric and depictions of immigrant populations reflected a sentiment felt throughout the nation. Although the immigration levels to this country were not the highest then, the view of immigrants taking resources from American citizens was still as pervasive as today. In this paradigm, the Bilingual Education program served as a way to push the agenda of the war on poverty and gain supporters for politicians who needed to tap into the Latinx vote and for labor and educational activists, it was a promise of economic betterment for communities of color (Kung, 2017).

However, while the Bilingual Education Act addressed the educational needs of the Latinx community, it reproduced the narrative of linguistically and culturally handicapped populations. The fervor that came with the activism being done by different factions of advocates for Bilingual education had to compromise with the narrative of a political bipartisan agenda that saw Bilingual education as a force that would promote social and economic development in "impoverished" migrant communities while affirming the need to assimilate and be productive English-speaking members of the American society. Bilingual education in 1968 brought financial support for Emergent Bilinguals, the development of different English language development programs, and the recognition of a growing linguistically and culturally diverse population that called the United States home. However, the step forward for Bilingual education had to be compromised with the underlying truth that the ultimate goal continued to be the vision of a hegemonic culture with an official national language, a message that would surface and resurface in the bilingual education conversation.

Proposition 227 (1998) and Proposition 58 (2016) California depict the pendulum of English language development programs in California in response to the political perceptions of immigrants and languages other than English. In 1998, the passage of Proposition 227 led to the reduction of bilingual education programs and opportunities and the demand for English-only immersion practices in schools that required educators of Emergent Bilinguls to teach "overwhelmingly" in English unless parents signed a waiver that opted for bilingual instruction. (Quezada, 2016) Proposition 227 aligned to the English-only and linguistic hegemony ideals voiced by political, economic, and mainstream forces that disregarded the wellness and cultural linguistic support Emergent Bilinguals received through bilingual education systems. The few languages developmental and morale wins of the Bilingual Education Act of 1968 were replaced by years of sink-or-swim immersion practices impacting the students and educators who felt the needs of ELs were being ignored and did not have the tools or training to cater to their needs. Under Proposition 227, California cemented English Language Development courses as spaces of erasure and assimilation where Bilingual Education was perceived as un-American. According to Ovando, the popularity of Proposition 227 was rooted in nationalistic and anti-immigrant sentiments (2003). Spanish symbolized a threat often associated with illegal immigration and the economic and resource burden that impoverished immigrant communities that did not want to assimilate were on the development of the country's prosperity. Governor Wilson's remark supporting the passing of Proposition 227 encompasses the nativist racialinguistic hierarchy that this proposition sought to affirm openly. "In California's schools, English should not be a foreign language, and yet it remains one for too many limited English proficient students because of the failure of bilingual programs" (Ingram, 1998).

In 2016, nearly two decades after Proposition 227 passed, sentiments over English Language Development and Bilingual Education classes shifted again. Proposition 58 attempted to repeal the English-only mandates that restricted bilingual education in California's English language development programs and the harm it had caused to a generation of English learners (Matas, Rodriguez, 2014). Surprisingly, proposition 58 passed under the Trump presidency, a time when Anti-immigrant and America first nativist rhetoric peaked. The same people who voted for Trump voted for the passage of Proposition 58. Critical scholars are analytical about the "heteroglossic seeds" that may derive from the adoption of multilingual and translingual opportunities for English language development through the enforcement of Proposition 58 or whether the promotion of cultural pluralism and language diversity is limited illusions promoted by Neoliberal agendas that will continue to keep the English only status quo in language development programs in the United States (Muñoz-Muñoz et al., 2023). Such scholars attribute the passage of this proposition to the wording that commodifies linguistic diversity as a component of globalization and economic development.

Nevertheless, Proposition 58, like the Bilingual Act of 1968, resulted from collective struggle and pushback from activists, parents, teachers, students, and stakeholders who saw the disservice and the failure of Proposition 227. Through Proposition 58, parents had more autonomy and choice in deciding the language development programs their children could partake in. Section 2 of the proposition, in particular, countered the notion that bilingual education wastes state resources and that English-only practices are the most beneficial in language development (Taylor & Udang, 2016). The passage of Proposition 58 also provided autonomy to the local educational agencies to adopt English language development programs that met the local needs of their district and regional population. Since then, many districts have developed English Language Development programs that encourage multilingual spaces as long as the goal is acquiring and assimilating Emergent Bilinguals into the mainstream American vision of globalization and economic development.

In today's classroom context, listening to the narrative about diversity and multilingual language development in the ELD classroom is pivotal. Educators are tasked with nurturing culturally relevant and affirming practices that see our student's linguistic repertoire as more than just a commodity or another item in the Neoliberal agenda. There is a continuous search for authentic and genuine heteroglossic practices that should not be co-opted by any politician's promise of capital revenue at the expense of our student's hopes and dreams. Educators designated for English Language Development (ELD) may inadvertently contribute to the alienation and deficit view of students' linguistic practices, which have historically been marginalized, misrepresented, and mislabeled. Still, they can also be implicit reproducers of the narrative that sees multilingual students and multiculturalism as parts of a broader neo-colonizing strategy that leverages and occupies the bilingual education and multicultural ticket when politicians and exterior social factors outside educational spheres deem it necessary.

The fact of the matter is that the ELD classroom is a micro-reflection of the hurdles and the tumultuous history of language development programs in California. Statewide English proficiency assessments that explicitly penalize responses in languages other than English, locally adopted basic skills English proficiency assessments that are subject to change at the discretion of local districts, and subjective ELA and ELD teacher evaluations are part of the standardization crusade. Emergent Bilinguals endure. Students who need the most social, emotional, and authentic academic support are the most tested across California. Caring educators can humanize the classroom space and create safe and culturally affirming learning ecologies that foster joy and meaningful connections amidst the anxieties of testing and political climates that, in the words of Nikki Giovanni, "are not poetic times." (Hendrix-Soto & LeeKeenan) (Giovanni,1996) Latinx ELD educators can enact anti-oppressive practices affirming the linguistic, familial, and aspirational capitals that Latinx emergent Bilingual students bring to the classroom while being conscientious that they are working to undo systems of oppression that are rooted in the very fabric of our country's systems of expansion and colonization.

I. Shifting Toward a Genuine Heteroglossic, Liberated ELD Classroom

On July 31, 2005, the NCTE issued a position statement supporting self-reflexive practices in research and teaching to combat inequalities through language and literacy empowerment in humane classrooms. (2005) Twenty years later, the vision to support culturally and linguistically diverse learners continues to expand—alongside the practices promoting language and literacy in the changing demographics of the American classroom. One simply cannot disregard a student's linguistic and cultural repertoire on the path to academic English; therefore, classroom spaces must affirm and center a student's full linguistic and cultural repertoires. (Paris, 2012) To create co-liberated spaces in the ELD classroom, Latinx ELD educators must ignite critical conversations about the racialization of language with their students. Latinx educators should be aware of the gatekeeping effect of reclassification, the emphasis on academic English, and the standardization of our students' language. Having open and age-appropriate conversations with our students about these topics is essential to ensure they fully understand them and are prepared to be resistant and resilient throughout their language development journey. This practice does not encourage abandoning all the requirements of an ELD classroom and closing our eyes to the reality that monolingual expectations remain the status quo in Emergent Bilingual's language development programs and expectations. However, decentering linguistic assimilation practices is required in our curriculum. In the classroom, one can leverage meaningful content affirming cultural and linguistic identity and still complete test preparation materials to prepare them for local and state proficiency assessments.

In order to shift from a monolingual ELD classroom to a liberated heteroglossic classroom, educators and educator preparation programs must look to prepare Latinx educators to reflect on our positionality and the impact of our *testimonios* in our journey as learners first and educators second. Testimonios go beyond personal accounts or narratives and include "political, social, historical, and cultural histories that accompany one's life experiences as a means to bring about change through consciousness-raising. In bridging individuals with collective histories of oppression, a story of marginalization is re-centered to elicit social change. (Delgado Bernal, et al, 2012)" The lived experiences of Latinx educators who intentionally work with an emergent bilingual population are part of the social and labor consciousness fostered in educational activism. Each interaction an educator has as a student in the K-12 system or later in the higher education system, including teacher preparation programs, contributes to their teaching philosophy and what they present to Latinx student populations they work with. Understanding that the more vulnerable we are with ourselves and our students in sharing our testimonios is a pedagogical revolutionizing moment described by Dr. Rodriguez Valls as a journey onto a prophetic vocation that allowed him to explore his immigrant student's identities and social realities while simultaneously engaging in self-reflexive pedagogical practices that augmented the meaning of his practice (Rodriguez Valls, 2016).

The work of the blue-collar scholar goes beyond district mandates and is interconnected to the identification and dismantling of oppressive systems one lesson, one student at a time. The blue-collar scholar recognizes that the current political climate and the open attacks on immigrant communities that ran a rampage during the 2016 presidential election will uptake in the following months. It is time to defend the emotional, societal, and educational bienestar of our Emergent Bilinguals. Our stories of collective activism to move the conversation of linguistically and culturally inclusive English language Development education continue to bring the conversation forward. Although interest convergence may be a small step in the path of educational social justice, these compromises pave the way to enact change. We must expect politicians to refrain from passing language development education bills that shift away from the structures of power. However, we can begin a bottom-up grassroot movement in our communities and classrooms that resists and navigates the restrictions of standardization and reclassification requirements.

Amongst some of the culturally and linguistically relevant practices that Latinx educators can incorporate into their curriculum and daily practice are:

- Auto ethnographical assignments that share your journey as a Latinx educator and affirm the journey of your students and families; this takes vulnerability and requires us to listen attentively to the cultural intuition (Delgado Bernal, 2002) developed through our shared experiences. Students see themselves mirrored in our stories, and if we listen closely enough, their stories pull at the memory chords of our experiences as members of the Latinx community. Finding places in the classroom where we can connect with the day-to-day experiences of our students allows us to humanize our content. It encourages students to participate in ELD test preparation material that is not necessarily the most culturally affirming or engaging. Because the ELD classroom is a space of standardized testing and test preparation, Latinx ELD educators must maximize the opportunities to discuss our educational journeys openly.

- Diversify literary choices with texts that promote multilingualism and multiculturalism themes and topics. Incorporate work that reflects the stories of our demographic in meaningful and celebratory ways and defy the stereotypes or generalizations that exist towards the Latinx community. Recognize that our panethicity is rich. Some commonalities unite us as people who have immigrated to the United States, but some experiences pertain to only specific Latinx communities and should be honored as such. An example of a text that speaks not only to the diversity of our people is The Poet X by Elizabeth Acevedo. Her poetry explores the intersectionality of being a woman of Afro-Latina descent growing up in the United States. Another example of literature that explores the multicultural and multilingual identity is the poem Bilingual/Bilingue by Rina P. Espaillat. In the poem, the speaker explores the duality of her language and identity about her father and his culture.

- Leverage assessments where students can display their (trans)languaging practices; what Ofelia Garcia has coined as *la corriente* (Garcia, 2022) happens whether we encourage it or not. Students' full linguistic repertoires must be reflected in the classroom and viewed from an asset-based rather than a subtractive perspective (Valenzuela, 1999). In California, assessments that penalize students writing and speaking practices continue to see their language as "somewhat developed" or "not meeting standard." These assessments reject the reality that our student's languaging is a testament to their existence. Our Newcomers, speak a language that sits foreign to their tongue. It is unnatural to assess them in a manner that makes them feel further alienated from the country they are trying to acclimate to. Assessments for them should focus on their transition to the country. What is their *bienestar* like in a place where they were brought under various circumstances? Our interest in Newcomer assessments should be based on articulating the emotions of being a Newcomer in whatever language they speak.

- Make test preparation practices relevant to community-related topics, landmarks, events, or people; this can be accomplished while assessing the mastery of a particular ELD standard(s). There are ways to assess the same standards and expectations of a test, such as the English Language Performance Assessment California (ELPAC). This test consists of writing, listening, speaking, and reading tasks aligned to a learning target/standard. Although test preparation is not a joyful experience for students who have been tracked and over tested throughout their educational system, it can be relevant to their community and familiar topics. In the task "write about an experience," for example, students can be centered on describing familiar places and experiences that they have lived through. The content is something they can write about because they lived it; the skill is what we have to focus on developing. We work with our student's grammar, sentence structure, cohesion, and style so they can articulate what they know in an "academic" way during these tests.
- Create spaces for students to share *testimonies* celebrating their families and communities. Many schools implementing Project-Based Learning overlook our Emerging Bilinguals because it may be "too difficult" for them. Yet, Emerging Bilinguals can develop creative projects that showcase their content skills inclusively. Students can showcase their comprehension by incorporating their entire linguistic repertoire in multiple ways.

It is also essential to understand that Latinx educators are not liberators by virtue of their last name, which in some school sites automatically qualifies them to teach Emergent Bilinguals. Nor are they liberators by extolling Latinx heritage. Latinx educators become liberators when they commit to the communities that sustain them in their educational journey. When we recognize the aspirational, navigational, resistant, linguistic, and familial capitals (Yosso, 2009) that have shaped our positionality, we can recognize the same capitals in the lives of the students we serve. When we embrace our positionality as Latinx ELD educators, we gravitate towards people with a similar mission and can build a caring community. Administrators, counselors, parents, and community members are part of the village that can help transform the fabric of the ELD classroom. As long as a Latinx educator sees the cultural richness in everyday working-class literacy, the rich sermons of the congregation, the witty enactment of language in our *convivios* (Jasis, Ordonez-Jasis, 2004), and the aspirations that Latinx parents have for their children, we can become critical community advocates and co-liberators with our students and communities. Amongst some of the critical community awareness practices Latinx ELD educators can engage in are:

- Identify community literacies that occur in the communities; for example, library events, ESL classes for parents, and church congregations our students and parents partake in. Community systems in place have contributed to literacy and learning support far longer than the school year students have with their teachers. Becoming acquainted with institutions where our students practice literacy, such as their local congregations, libraries, or extracurricular programs, can help educators make meaningful connections that can further translate the learning in the classroom into the community. There are also after-school literacy programs that many parents partake in. Identifying such spaces allows educators to foster the importance of literacy in familial spaces for students and parents.

- Inviting parents to participate in the curriculum is also a meaningful way to honor the languages, cultures, traditions, and experiences of Emerging Bilinguals. Whether inviting parents to read with their children as part of an ongoing reading assignment or having students interview their parents to write memoirs or stories of resilience and perseverance, our parents and students need to know that we value and are interested in their knowledge. It is pivotal to approach this through a lens of humility where parents can be vulnerable, and students can feel comfortable providing authentic stories that center their experiences and position the educator as an active listener rather than the imparter of knowledge. Once more, for students to open up about their experiences and their parents' experiences, they must see our vulnerability and samples that show how writing can be a form of honoring, celebration, and remembrance in our communities.

- Organizing events that celebrate the linguistic and cultural richness of the Latinx community is essential in fostering pride and a firm understanding of identity in our Latinx students. Aside from the typical celebrated days and commonly celebrated heroes, we need to look for diverse opportunities that celebrate the different forms of Latinidad we are a part of. The demographics of Latinx Emergent Bilinguals vary. Therefore, one has to be conscious of the events and cultural celebrations that are to take place in our school sites. Often, cultural events in California are limited to Hispanic Heritage Month remembrance of heroes on mainstream Mexican celebrations. However, the cultural diversity in California is rich and goes beyond these celebrations.

- Review English proficiency assessments and expectations with students' parents in ways in which they understand and can develop a collaborative plan to support their students at home through recurring community town hall meetings or workshops.

REFERENCES

Barajas-Gonzalez, R. G., Linares Torres, H., Urcuyo, A., Salamanca, E., Santos, M., & Pagán, O. (2024). "You're Part of Some Hope and Then You Fall into Despair": Exploring the Impact of a Restrictive Immigration Climate on Educators in Latinx Immigrant Communities. *Journal of Latinos and Education*, 23(2), 492–513. DOI: 10.1080/15348431.2022.2153846

Bell, D. A.Board of Education and the Interest-Convergence Dilemma. (1980). Brown v. Board of Education and the interest-convergence dilemma. *Harvard Law Review*, 93(3), 518–533. DOI: 10.2307/1340546

Bourdieu, P., & Passeron, J. (1977). *Reproduction in education, society and culture*. Sage.

Carrión, A. E., & Torres, M. (2023). Leaning on family: Examining college-going and help-seeking behaviors of Latino male high school students through dichos, consejos, and community cultural wealth. *International Journal of Educational Research, 122*, 102256-. DOI: 10.1016/j.ijer.2023.102256

Cummins, J. (2000). *Language, power and pedagogy: Bilingual children in the crossfire*. Multilingual Matters. DOI: 10.21832/9781853596773

Delgado Bernal, D. (1998). Using a Chicana feminist epistemology in educational research. *Harvard Educational Review*, 68(4), 555–582. DOI: 10.17763/haer.68.4.5wv1034973g22q48

Delgado Bernal, D. (2002). Critical Race Theory, Latinx Critical Theory, and Critical Raced Gendered Epistemologies: Recognizing Students of Color as Holders and Creators of Knowledge. *Qualitative Inquiry*, 18(1), 105–126. DOI: 10.1177/107780040200800107

Delgado-Gaitan, C. (2001). *The power of community: mobilizing for family and schooling*. Rowman and Littlefield Publishers.

Delpit, L. (1995). *Other people's children: cultural conflict in the classroom*. New Press.

Designated and integrated English language development. Designated and Integrated ELD - Letters (CA Dept of Education). (2022) https://www.cde.ca.gov/nr/el/le/yr22ltr0111.asp

Dover, A. G., & Rodríguez-Valls, F. (2022). *Radically inclusive teaching with newcomer and emergent plurilingual students: braving up*. Teachers College Press.

Flores, S. Y., & Murillo, E. G. Jr. (2001). Power, Language, and Ideology: Historical and Contemporary Notes on the Dismantling of Bilingual Education. *The Urban Review*, 33(3), 183–206. DOI: 10.1023/A:1010361803811

Fortino, C. R. (2017, Spring). The professional educator: why supporting Latino Children and families is union work. *American Educator, 41*(1), 14+. https://link -gale-com.lib-proxy.fullerton.edu/apps/doc/A488510167/OVIC?u=csuf_main&sid =bookmark-OVIC&xid=0962636f

Freire, P. (2018). *Pedagogy of the oppressed* (M. B. Ramos, Trans.; 50th-anniversary edition.). Bloomsbury Academic.

Gandara, P., & Contreras, F. (2010). *The latino education crisis: the consequences of failed social policies*. Harvard University Press. DOI: 10.2307/j.ctv13qftm4

Garcia, O. (2009). Emergent Bilinguals and TESOL: What's in a Name? *TESOL Quarterly*, 43(2), 322–326. DOI: 10.1002/j.1545-7249.2009.tb00172.x

García, O., Flores, N., Seltzer, K., Wei, L., Otheguy, R., & Rosa, J. (2021). Rejecting abyssal thinking in the language and education of racialized bilinguals: A manifesto. *Critical Inquiry in Language Studies*, 18(3), 203–228. DOI: 10.1080/15427587.2021.1935957

Garcia, O., Johnson, S. I., & Seltzer, K. (2022). *The translanguaging classroom: Leveraging student bilingualism for learning*. Caslon.

Garcia, O., & Torres Guevara, R. (2009). Monoglossic ideologies and language policies of education of U.S Latina/os. In E. Muñoz, J. S., Machado-Casas, M., Murillo, J. E. G., & Martínez, C. (Eds.). *Handbook of latinos and education: Theory, research, and practice*. Taylor & Francis Group. (pp 182- 193). Routledge.

Giovanni, N. (1996). *The Selected Poems of Nikki Giovanni*. William Morrow and Company, Inc. hooks, bell. (1994). *Teaching to transgress : education as the practice of freedom*. Routledge.

Hendrix-Soto, A., & LeeKeenan, K. (2023). Humanizing Learning Spaces in Dehumanizing Times: The Role of Joy and Meaningful Connection. *Multicultural Perspectives*, 25(3), 152–159. DOI: 10.1080/15210960.2023.2257224

Ingram, C. (1998). "Wilson backs ballot measure to ban bilingual education." Los Angeles Times, May 19, 1998.

Ishimaru, A. M. (2020). *Just schools: Building equitable collaborations with families and communities*. Teachers College Press.

Kinloch, V., Bucholtz, M., Casillas, D. I., Lee, J.-S., Lee, T. S., McCarty, T. L., Irizarry, J. G., San Pedro, T., Wong, C., Peña, C., Ladson-Billings, G., Haupt, A., Rosa, J., Flores, N., Lee, S. J., González, N., Gutiérrez, K. D., Johnson, P. M., & Lee, C. D. (2017). *Culturally sustaining pedagogies: teaching and learning for justice in a changing world* (D. Paris & H. S. Alim, Eds.). Teachers College Press.

Krashen, S. D. (1982). Principles and Practice in Second Language Acquisition

Kumashiro, K. K. (2000). Toward a Theory of Anti-Oppressive Education. *Review of Educational Research*, 70(1), 25–53. DOI: 10.3102/00346543070001025

Ladson-Billings, G.LADSONBILLINGS. (1995). Toward a theory of culturally relevant pedagogy. *American Educational Research Journal*, 32(3), 465–491. DOI: 10.3102/00028312032003465

Lichon, K., Moreno, I., Villamizar, A. M., & Arana, K. (2022). Fortalecer Raíces y Formar Alas: Empowerment, Advancement, and Retention of Latinx Educators and Leaders in Catholic Schools. *Journal of Catholic Education, 25*(2), 44-. https://doi.org/DOI: 10.15365/joce.2502032022

Lopez, G. R. (2001). The Value of Hard Work: Lessons on parent involvement from an (im)migrant household. *Harvard Educational Review*, 71(3), 416–437. DOI: 10.17763/haer.71.3.43x7k542x023767u

Lucas, T., & Katz, A. (1994). Reframing the debate: The roles of native languages in English-only programs for language minority students. *TESOL Quarterly*, 28(3), 537–562. DOI: 10.2307/3587307

Matas, A., & Rodríguez, J. L. (2014). The education of English learners in California following the passage of proposition 227: A case study of an urban school district. *Penn GSE Perspectives on Urban Education*, 11(2), 44–56.

Moreno, J. F. (1999). The elusive quest for equality: 150 years of Chicano/Chicana education. *Harvard Educational Review*.

Muñoz-Muñoz, E. R., Poza, L. E., & Briceño, A. (2023). Critical Translingual Perspectives on California Multilingual Education Policy. *Educational Policy*, 37(6), 1791–1817. https://doi-org.lib-proxy.fullerton.edu/10.1177/08959048221130342. DOI: 10.1177/08959048221130342

National Center for Education Statistics. (2020). *Characteristics of public school teachers*. U.S. Department of Education. https://nces.ed.gov/pubs2020/2020103/index.asp

NCTE. (2021, August 31). *Supporting linguistically and culturally diverse learners in English education*. National Council of Teachers of English. https://ncte.org/statement/diverselearnersinee/

Noe-Bustamante, L. (2020, August 11). *About one-in-four U.S. hispanics have heard of Latinx, but just 3% use it*. Pew Research Center. https://www.pewresearch.org/race-and-ethnicity/2020/08/11/about-one-in-four-u-s-hispanics-have-heard-of-latinx-but-just-3-use-it/

Olsen, L. (2014). *Reparable Harm: Fulfilling the unkept promise of educational opportunity for California's long-term English learners*. California Together.

Ordoñez-Jasis, R., Dunsmore, K., Herrera, G., Ochoa, C., Diaz, L., & Zuniga-Rios, E. (2016). Communities of Caring: Developing Curriculum That Engages Latino/a Students' Diverse Literacy Practices. *Journal of Latinos and Education*, 15(4), 333–343. DOI: 10.1080/15348431.2015.1134538

Ovando, C. J. (2003). Bilingual Education in the United States: Historical Development and Current Issues. *Bilingual Research Journal*, 27(1), 1–24. DOI: 10.1080/15235882.2003.10162589

Paris, D., & Alim, H. S. (Eds.). (2017). *Culturally sustaining pedagogies: Teaching and learning for justice in a changing world*. Teachers College Press.

Pour-Khorshid, F. (2018). H.E.L.L.A: A bay area critical racial affinity group committed to healing, empowerment, love, liberation, and action (Order No. 10935583). Available from Ethnic NewsWatch; ProQuest Dissertations & Theses Global: The Humanities and Social Sciences Collection. (2128055672). Retrieved from https://www.proquest.com/dissertations-theses/h-e-l-bay-area-critical-racial-affinity-group/docview/2128055672/se-2

Quezada, M. S. (2016). Proposition 227 and the Loss of Educational Rights: A Personal Perspective and Quest for Equitable Educational Programs for English Learners. In *Latino Civil Rights in Education* (1st ed., pp. 158–169). Routledge. https://doi.org/DOI: 10.4324/9781315672526-15

San Miguel, G. (1999). The schooling of Mexicanos in the Southwest, 1848–1891. In Moreno, J. F. (Ed.), *The Elusive Quest for Equality: 150 Years of Chicano/Chicana Education, Harvard Educational Review:31–52*.

Sung, K. K. (2017). "Accentuate the Positive; Eliminate the Negative": Hegemonic Interest Convergence, Racialization of Latino Poverty, and the 1968 Bilingual Education Act. *Peabody Journal of Education*, 92(3), 302–321. DOI: 10.1080/0161956X.2017.1324657

Taggart, A. (2022). The Influence of Educación on Latinx Students' Academic Expectations and Achievement. *Journal of Latinos and Education*, 22(4), 1728–1743. https://doi-org.lib-proxy.fullerton.edu/10.1080/15348431.2022.2043864. DOI: 10.1080/15348431.2022.2043864

Taylor, J., & Udang, L. (2016). "Proposition 58: English Proficiency. Multilingual Education. "California Education for a Global Economy Initiative," California Initiative Review (CIR): Vol. 2016, Article 9. Available at: https://scholarlycommons .pacific.edu/california-initiative-review/vol2016/iss1/

U.S. Census Bureau. (2000). *Census 2000, demographic profile data for California.* https://www2.census.gov/library/publications/2003/dec/phc-2-6.pdf Retrieved from https://www.census.gov/data/"

Valenzuela, A. (1999). Subtractive schooling: U.S.-Mexican youth and the politics of caring. State University of New York Press. Chapter 3 The politics of caring

Yosso, T. J. (2005). Whose culture has capital? A critical race theory discussion of community cultural wealth. *Race, Ethnicity and Education*, 8(1), 69–91. DOI: 10.1080/1361332052000341006

Chapter 10
Understanding Dyslexia in Multilingual Environments

Concepción Moncada Cummings
https://orcid.org/0009-0003-3804-0710
University of Florida, USA

Norma Gómez-Fuentes
https://orcid.org/0009-0003-3804-0710
Independent Researcher, USA

Vivian Gonsalves
University of Florida, USA

ABSTRACT

Given its prevalence, most teachers across the U.S. are likely to have students with dyslexia in their classrooms, and many of them may come from homes where English is not the primary language of communication. This chapter aims to provide insights, methods, and strategies for addressing dyslexia within multilingual environments, which often complicates identification and intervention. The chapter has three main sections. First, it begins with multilingual students' unique challenges, including language dominance, cross-linguistic transfer, and distinguishing between language differences and disorders. Then, it provides an overview of implications for literacy instruction for multilingual students with dyslexia, like the importance of culturally responsive teaching practices and evidence-based instructional strategies, such as including the Science of Reading, tailored to support the literacy development of multilingual students with dyslexia. The final section summarizes the recommended strategies across the literature discussed throughout the chapter.

DOI: 10.4018/979-8-3373-1340-5.ch010

Copyright © 2025, IGI Global Scientific Publishing. Copying or distributing in print or electronic forms without written permission of IGI Global Scientific Publishing is prohibited.

UNDERSTANDING DYSLEXIA IN MULTILINGUAL ENVIRONMENTS

The area of learning disabilities is constantly growing and changing, and it is one of the most active areas of special education research and scholarship. Thirty-two percent of all children and youth receiving special education services in the United States (U.S.) are diagnosed with specific learning disabilities (National Center for Education Statistics, 2024). In 2020, the Office of Special Education Programs estimated that 35% of students receiving special education services under the specific learning disability category identified as Hispanic (U.S. Department of Education, 2021).

Dyslexia is the most prevalent type of specific learning disability. The International Dyslexia Association estimates that, on average, as many as 15% to 20% of the population may experience symptoms of dyslexia, which may include but is not limited to, inaccurate or laborious reading, poor spelling, and writing (International Dyslexia Association, 2002). One of the most common myths about dyslexia is that it only affects people who speak English, but in reality, dyslexia occurs in all written languages (Pugh & Verhoeven, 2018). Understanding how dyslexia presents in multilingual students is an area of research that is still evolving. For example, we know that for students with dyslexia who are learning English, their primary deficit may appear with difficulty decoding or reading words. However, for students learning more transparent orthographies, such as Spanish, the more significant difficulties appear to be in developing reading automaticity or fluency (Ziegler & Goswami, 2005).

Given its prevalence, most teachers across the U.S. are likely to have students with dyslexia in their classrooms, and many of them may come from multilingual environments. The three authors contributing to this chapter are Hispanic/Latina women who also happen to work as education professionals serving students with dyslexia and their teachers. In our work, we have observed that many students with dyslexia do not have access to teachers, tutors, and other practitioners who are well-equipped, despite their best efforts, to implement evidence-based practices for multilingual struggling readers. Therefore, this chapter aims to provide insight, methods, and strategies for addressing dyslexia within multilingual environments from our perspective, based on our experience and research working with this population of students and their teachers.

In an effort to clarify which "multilingual environments" we are focusing on in this chapter, we would like to offer a quick description of important terms. Students whose heritage language is not English are often identified in policy, the literature and common discourse as English Learners (ELLs) (National Center for Education Statistics, 2024). In our practice we have observed that this term is often associated with a lack of English ability. Dr. Ofelia García, researcher and scholar, popularized the term "emergent bilingual" in 2008 in an attempt to emphasize a more asset-based mindset when identifying or discussing these students. The term "emergent bilingual" considers the plethora of language and literacy knowledge the students have in their heritage language and are now acquiring their second language, English (Piñón et al., 2022). Other common terms are "multilingual student" or "multilingual learner." Multilingual students can be speakers of a variety of heritage languages who are in the process of learning the dominant language (Cenoz, 2013). In this chapter we have decided to emphasize the term "multilingual student" to refer to students who may know one or more languages and are acquiring English as their additional language, which is the dominant language in the U.S. The term "multilingual" honors the knowledge that the students bring, celebrates their assets, and acknowledges the new language acquisition process, rather than highlighting it. Because the bulk of our experiences and expertise relates to students whose heritage language is Spanish and are situated in the U.S., most of our examples will focus on Spanish as a primary language and English as the additional language. Our chapter will also more specifically focus on multilingual students with reading difficulties, such as dyslexia, and therefore we will begin with a discussion of the characteristics of dyslexia and implications for identification and instruction for multilingual students.

Characteristics of Dyslexia

Dyslexia is a specific learning disability of neurobiological origin, primarily affecting a person's ability to accurately and fluently recognize words and causing difficulties with spelling and decoding (International Dyslexia Association, 2002). These challenges typically arise from a deficit in the language domain, which can seem unexpected given the individual's cognitive abilities and quality of classroom instruction. One of the most common misconceptions about dyslexia is that it is linked to visual perception of symbols, like letters of objects. Contrary to common belief, these difficulties are not visual in nature and are not related to seeing letters or words backward. Dyslexia is typically the result of a deficit in processing the phonological elements of language (phonological processing). Students with dyslexia will often have difficulty identifying and manipulating the phonemes (or sounds) in the language. For example, a child may struggle to identify the word "mug" as having three phonemes: /m//u//g/. Furthermore, students with dyslexia will also have difficulty with making connections between the phonemes and the letters (or graphemes) that represent them. That same student may have difficulty connecting the phonemes to the graphemes m, u, g in the word "mug" and therefore may not be able to read and write this word with automaticity. These difficulties in fluent or automatic word reading will likely have broader impacts for the student. As a result, individuals with dyslexia may also struggle with reading comprehension, leading to reduced reading experiences that can impede vocabulary growth and the accumulation of background knowledge (International Dyslexia Association, 2002). Dyslexia is not indicative of the level of intelligence and is not the result of poor motivation or poor effort. Dyslexia is not indicative of the level of intelligence and is not the result of poor motivation or poor effort. Students with dyslexia often experience heightened fatigue, in addition to their academic difficulties, due to the increased effort required to keep up academically with their peers. Research shows that these students may need to exert much more effort than their classmates, often with limited success in achieving comparable grades (Peer & Reid, 2014). This exhaustion can manifest in various ways, such as falling asleep in class, appearing distracted, avoiding tasks, or showing signs of anxiety when faced with assignments or tests.

Identification and Manifestations of Dyslexia for Multilingual Students

Misidentification and lack of identification of a dyslexia diagnosis for multilingual students raise concerns about equity for these historically marginalized students. Multilingual students often do not get the necessary support and may be over- or under-diagnosed in special education (Burr et al., 2015; Sullivan, 2011). There is often an assumption that multilingual students who are struggling are doing so because of a language difference rather than a potential learning disability. One important tool to prevent the misdiagnosis of multilingual students with disabilities is to ensure that all classroom teachers have a strong foundation in teaching bilingual and multilingual students so that they can more accurately and quickly identify who needs to be referred for special education testing. This is even more imperative in the early grades, which are the most pivotal years for diagnoses, identification, and intervention.

Identifying dyslexia in monolingual students often involves a straightforward process using measures of print knowledge (i.e. letter and sounds), phonemic decoding (i.e. reading words and nonwords), oral reading fluency, and rapid naming speed (Moats & Foorman, 2003). However, multilingual students with dyslexia experience unique challenges that differ from those encountered with monolingual learners. While the core characteristics of dyslexia—such as difficulties with word recognition, decoding, and spelling—remain the same, the influence of multiple languages on literacy acquisition adds layers of complexity to assessment and intervention. Dyslexia identification for multilingual students follows a similar process as for monolingual students, but it is important to recognize the unique factors that may affect multilingual learners (Bedore et al., 2020). Although the general definitions provided by organizations like the International Dyslexia Association often do not explicitly address multilingualism, differences in language development and exposure can influence how dyslexia manifests. Variations such as cross-linguistic transfer, language dominance, and differing literacy skills across languages (Francis et al., 2019; Adlof, 2020) must be considered to ensure accurate identification and appropriate support (Miciak et al., 2022). It is important to distinguish between the normal process of acquiring a second language and the specific learning deficits associated with dyslexia so that multilingual students receive appropriate support tailored to their needs.

Cross-Linguistic Transfer. The concept of cross-linguistic transfer refers to the situation where a multilingual learner utilizes their knowledge of their heritage language to aid in acquiring a new language (Yang et al., 2017; Nsengiyumva et al., 2021). For instance, a student with Spanish as their heritage language and learning English may use their phonological understanding of Spanish to support their acquisition of English phonology (Nsengiyumva et al., 2021; Ijalba et al., 2020). Research has shown that their phonological abilities can predict their reading proficiency in both languages (Francis et al., 2019; Ferreira et al., 2016; Álvarez-Cañizo et al., 2023). If possible, it is important to assess their skills in their heritage language because, having been exposed to it since birth, they are likely to have a stronger command of it than their second language (Álvarez-Cañizo et al., 2023). The assessment results can aid in ensuring accurate identification and appropriate support.

Language dominance. It is critical to take into account language dominance when identifying multilingual students with dyslexia. Language dominance means that the multilingual student is better at one of their languages than the other (Canas et al., 2020). In the US, where English is the primary language of assessment, evaluating a multilingual student's language dominance is necessary to determine their preferred language (Ferreira et al., 2016). Their dominant language may shift over a multilingual student's lifetime due to exposure through social, academic, and environmental factors (Canas et al., 2020; Ferreira et al., 2016). Assessing language dominance can help distinguish between a language difference and a literacy difficulty or disability, similar to the role of cross-linguistic transfer.

It is important to carefully consider the literacy skills of multilingual students in all of their known languages. Literacy skills should be assessed in each of the students' known languages to determine if a student is more proficient in one language over another or if they have a disability. This allows for the appropriate support to be provided and minimizes the achievement gap for multilingual students. Early literacy skills in different languages are strong predictors of future academic success (Francis et al., 2019).

Language Difference or Language Disorder?

Language is an important tool in communication, expression of ideas, and interpersonal relations. However, language comprehension is different for everyone due to variability in cultural background, cognitive ability, and linguistic environment. In the context of education, it is critical to understand the differences between language differences and language-based disorders like dyslexia. Understanding the difference between these concepts is imperative to have reasonable and adequate expectations of our multilingual children and better understand their academic and linguistic needs.

Language Differences

It can be helpful to think of this example, a bilingual student whose first language is Spanish and who is learning English at school, as an illustration of the difference between language differences and language-based disorders. While sharing a personal anecdote, the student says: "this is very [es]pecial to me!". The student pronouncing the word "special" with /es/ at the beginning is one example that illustrates what a language difference is. A language difference is the natural variations in a language due to an individual's cultural, regional, or social context. It can be dialects, accents, discourse, and vocabulary variation—all uniquely affected by the environments and experiences of the one who speaks (Roseberry-McKibbin, 2002). Furthermore, it could be helpful for educators to know that in Spanish, words rarely start with an "s" and are followed by another consonant (consonant clusters), so in this case, the student compensated by adding an es at the beginning of the word to approximate it to a more recognized phonetic representation of the word in Spanish (especial).

A language difference can occur when a child communicates in a language different from the language of instruction and the predominant language spoken in the surrounding community (Roseberry-McKibbin, 2002). Having a language difference does not mean the child has a language disorder. Language differences can even occur among speakers of the same language. For example, when a child speaks African American English, they are using a language difference influenced by his environment and culture, not related to a disability or disorder. Equally, when a student from the Southern U.S. uses regional expressions and pronunciation like 'y'all' instead of you all, these differences are part of regional dialects and cultural identity, reflecting linguistic diversity or variability.

Language differences not only occur at the phonetic level (sounds) but can also be evident in semantics (meaning) and pragmatics (language use). For example, a child from a Spanish-speaking family uses the Spanish idiom and expression "No hay mal que por bien no venga," literally translated to English as: "There is no evil that does not come for good" illustrates a difference in language use. The child is trying to convey the exact meaning of the colloquialism: "every cloud has a silver lining," but instead is using a literal translation of the phrase he knows in Spanish. These variations in languages do not represent linguistic or cognitive deficits and are, in fact, different linguistic practices that new language users implement as they learn to communicate. Educators should recognize these attempts as evidence of problem-solving and enriching communication. Therefore, recognizing and valuing language differences can build up total literacy and learning potential in our emergent bilingual students. Valuing language differences can be enhanced in our classrooms by integrating students' linguistic heritage into the curriculum and respect for diverse linguistic backgrounds, hence turning the differences into an asset for students.

Language Disorders

In contrast, a language-based disorder can be defined as "an inability to understand and process language, whether in expressive or receptive forms" (Tompkins, 2002, p. 6). This difficulty happens at the structure (grammar), meaning (semantics), or functional use (pragmatics) levels of the language, often causing challenges in expressing or understanding any language. Difficulties can occur in all four domains of language: speaking, listening, reading, writing, or any other language comprehension medium. The flow from the origin of the difficulty, challenges, and the four domains affected are represented by Figure 1 below.

Figure 1. Language-based disorders

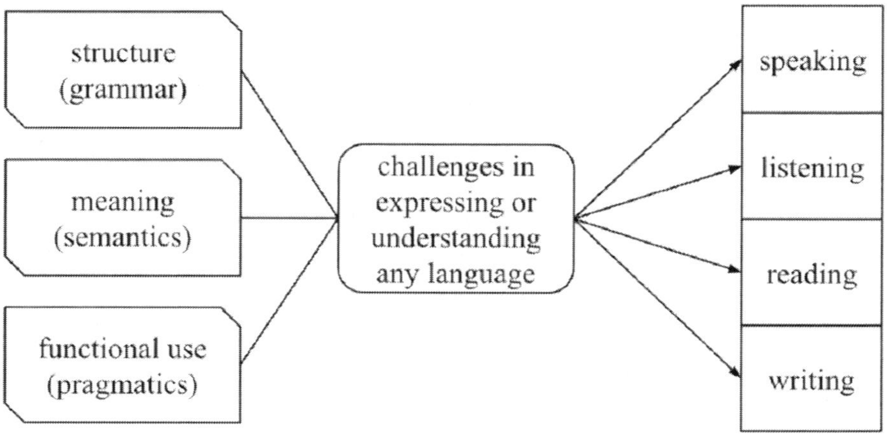

Note. A language-based disorder can affect structure (grammar), meaning (semantics), or functional use (pragmatics), impacting both understanding and expression, which can occur across speaking, listening, reading, writing, or other language comprehension mediums.

More importantly, since language disorders influence core language processes, they are likely to impact children in all the languages they speak (Tompkins, 2002). For bilingual children, a language disorder would not only affect their primary language, but difficulties may arise in communication in both languages. An accurate diagnosis of language disorders must be based on comparing the child's language behaviors with those of the same cultural peers who speak the same dialect and have similar language exposure and usage (Farnsworth, 2018). If a child demonstrates language difficulties that are unexpected for their linguistic community, then a complete evaluation to diagnose or discard a language disorder may be appropriate.

Dyslexia is a language-based disorder that affects an individual's reading, writing, and decoding of language, regardless of their linguistic background. As we established earlier, the International Dyslexia Association (International Dyslexia Association, 2002) defines dyslexia as typically characterized by difficulties in accurate and/or fluent word recognition, poor spelling, and difficulties with decoding—irrespective of the language in question. Despite these challenges, individuals with dyslexia often can understand spoken language but cannot generalize these skills to reading and writing tasks. Dyslexia is a learning disorder that also affects language processing, which impacts the efficiency of responding quickly to visual (print) or verbal information.

Distinguishing Language Differences from Disorders

The line between language differences and language-based disorders can be hard to distinguish, particularly in multicultural classrooms where one can find many children from different linguistic backgrounds. To evaluate whether an issue is due to a language difference or a language disorder, a variety of factors must be considered (Farnsworth, 2018). According to Gillespie (2015), language difference is "the result of the normal process of second language acquisition and its impact on the development of the second language." Although the process of acquiring a second language may look like a delay in the new language, children who have a language difference possess language skills in the native language that are similar to those possessed by typically developing kids. For instance, a child's mother tongue and second language may develop simultaneously or successively, and such development may well take place at various rates or in different patterns, depending on their linguistic environment and exposure. Research shows that emergent bilinguals with strong heritage language and literacy skills should reach second language fluency between 5-7 years (Roseberry-McKibbin & Brice, 2000). On the other hand, it may take longer for those learning a second language to acquire fluency if they have yet to develop these skills in their mother tongue.

Research has shown that "children with weak language skills are at a high risk of experiencing reading problems, but language difficulties are often hidden from view" (Adlof, 2020). Poor language development has been found to put children at a far greater risk of reading failure. This relationship underscores the critical role that strong foundational language abilities play in the development of reading proficiency. When children have difficulties with language, they struggle with word decoding, reading comprehension, and engaging in discussions about texts, all the skills necessary for proficient reading in the classroom.

Whereas some learning disabilities are often associated with noticeable symptoms, the signs indicative of a language problem may be extremely subtle and easily overlooked by educators, parents, and the children themselves. The invisibility of the disorder often makes its detection and intervention somewhat late, and this allows reading problems to mature and set over time. Moreover, children who possess weak language skills may often use strategies to compensate for the same, such as memorization of texts or overreliance on contextual clues that mask their difficulties. They, therefore, may appear as achieving at grade level in reading even with deficient comprehension and decoding skills. Understanding how language develops and influences reading can help professionals and caretakers advocate for early instruction and intervention. It is important to note that each emergent bilingual has a unique language, cultural, and educational background, which will influence their English acquisition process.

Farnsworth (2018) notes that some emergent bilingual children will have limited skills in English, and concerns may be raised around their ability to properly engage in tasks that require them to use English in the classroom. It is crucial to note that many children have appropriate language systems in their heritage language and are able to transfer them while learning English as a second language. These emergent bilinguals are progressing through the stages of second language acquisition (Krashen, 2000). During this stage, children are acquiring the components of a new language, including phonetics, vocabulary, grammar, writing, and conventions, "with varying time spent in each stage depending on factors related to aptitude, native language proficiency, personality, motivation, previous exposure to content in the native language, and quality of instruction" (Fillmore, 1979, 1991). Multilingual students may have significant and noticeable language differences; however, their cognitive abilities may not be affected, and these should not be mistaken for a lack of linguistic ability. Some common traits of multilingual students with learning differences include speaking English with different accents, understanding and applying nonverbal communication conventions of their native language, communicating effectively with others who share their first language and cultural background, effectively learning and applying grammatical rules, and struggling to meet academic expectations (Artiles & Ortiz, 2002).

On the other hand, a language disorder is characterized by "deficits in language comprehension and/or production in both the native language and the second language" (Gillespie, 2015). Children with a language disorder are unable to communicate effectively in either their first or second language. Historically, several terms have been used to refer to dyslexia, including "specific reading disability, "but the general agreement, confirmed by more recent studies, is that dyslexia is fundamentally a language-based disorder that has its basic origins in the phonological domain" (Adlof & Hogan, 2018). Phonological deficits are at the core of dyslexia and affect the child's ability to store, retrieve, and manipulate the sounds within words and to map them onto their corresponding letters so that words may be read (Catts, 1989). In contrast, children with language differences, especially those with dyslexia, show difficulties in generating or comprehending language, interpreting and using nonverbal cues, interacting with people from one's own cultural background, constructing well-structured, grammatically correct sentences, and with their academic achievement.

It is important to understand that if multilingual students with dyslexia are struggling readers in one language, they might struggle in all the languages they are immersed in. Also, the manifestations of dyslexia in Spanish may not mirror those of English because of the characteristics of the two languages. Spanish is considered a more "transparent" or "shallow" language because letters represent a constant sound, making words easier to decode. In contrast, English is an "opaque" language wherein spelling-to-sound correspondence is much less constant, and decoding is often far more difficult. For example, in Spanish, the letter 'a' always corresponds to the same sound, /ă/, regardless of the part of the word where it is being used. On the other hand, "ough" in English can be pronounced in several ways, for example, in the words "though" (/T Hō/), "rough" (/rəf/), and "cough" (/kôf/). That means that the impact of dyslexia will be more prominent in the case of the English language— where the linguistically complex orthography might further exacerbate reading problems in dyslexic multilinguals. Farnsworth (2018) outlines and explains the steps to determine and distinguish if a student has a specific learning disability or is just showing characteristics of language acquisition, as depicted in Figure 2 below. The Farnsworth (2018) steps are provided to determine and distinguish students' abilities against typical or atypical characteristics of language acquisition, such as understanding the forms and function of language, understanding specific learning disabilities, utilizing authentic assessments, observing in social contexts, advocacy and ethical practices, and ongoing education and data collection.

Figure 2. Learning disability or language acquisition

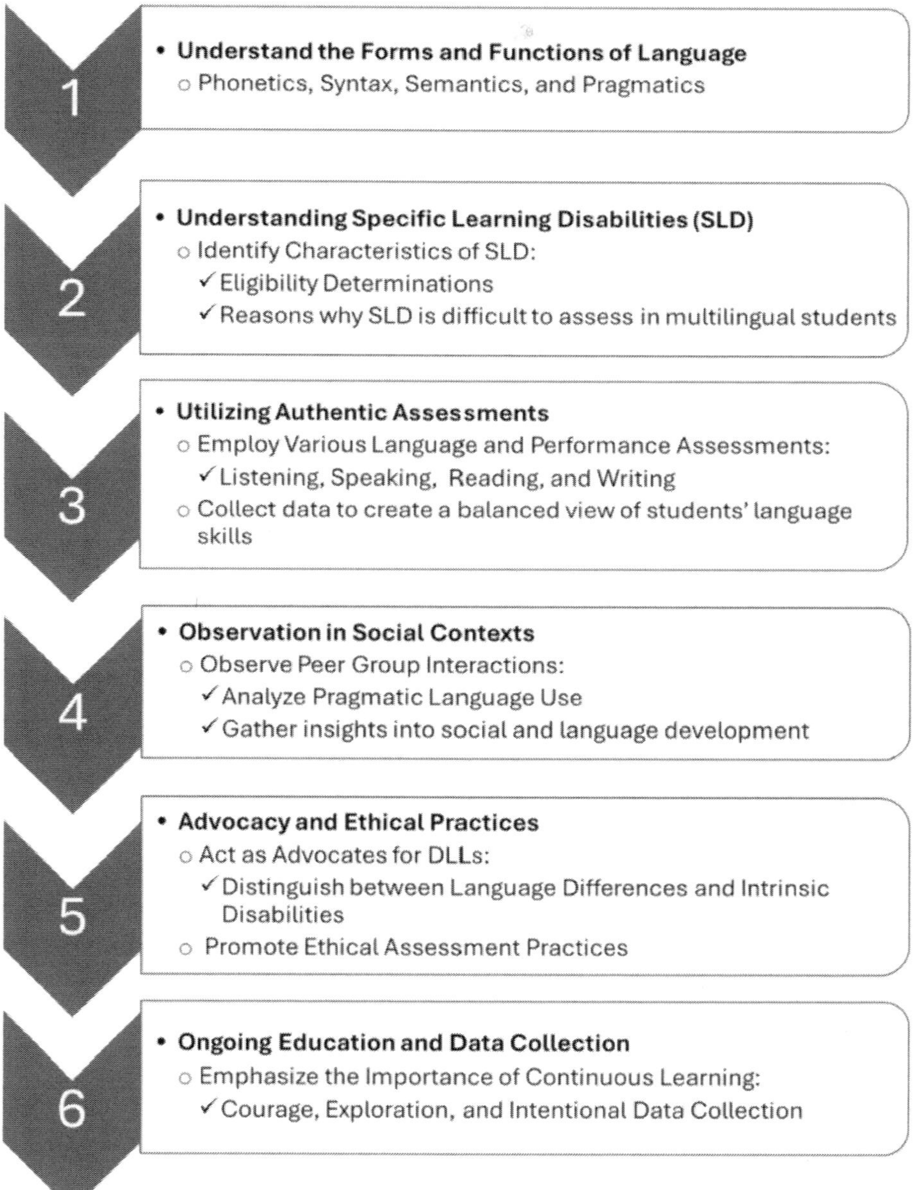

1
- **Understand the Forms and Functions of Language**
  - Phonetics, Syntax, Semantics, and Pragmatics

2
- **Understanding Specific Learning Disabilities (SLD)**
  - Identify Characteristics of SLD:
    - ✓ Eligibility Determinations
    - ✓ Reasons why SLD is difficult to assess in multilingual students

3
- **Utilizing Authentic Assessments**
  - Employ Various Language and Performance Assessments:
    - ✓ Listening, Speaking, Reading, and Writing
  - Collect data to create a balanced view of students' language skills

4
- **Observation in Social Contexts**
  - Observe Peer Group Interactions:
    - ✓ Analyze Pragmatic Language Use
    - ✓ Gather insights into social and language development

5
- **Advocacy and Ethical Practices**
  - Act as Advocates for DLLs:
    - ✓ Distinguish between Language Differences and Intrinsic Disabilities
  - Promote Ethical Assessment Practices

6
- **Ongoing Education and Data Collection**
  - Emphasize the Importance of Continuous Learning:
    - ✓ Courage, Exploration, and Intentional Data Collection

Note. The steps that Farnsworth (2018) provides to determine and distinguish if a student has a specific learning disability or is showing typical characteristics of language acquisition.

This flowchart format helps outline the multi-step process clearly and logically, making it easier for practitioners to follow and understand the necessary steps to assess language development in multilingual students. It is imperative for practitioners to take into consideration multilingual students' behaviors due to their cultural differences to better interpret evaluation and screening results. When the cultural aspect of language is not considered, students may be mistakenly identified as at risk of significant deficits (Baca & Almanza, 1991). When evaluating results following the steps in the flowchart, the outcomes can offer valuable insights to educators on how students learn most effectively, regardless of whether they have a learning disability (Farnsworth, 2018). However, language barriers can also make the evaluation process more complicated, as misinterpretations of students' abilities may arise from difficulties in communication rather than actual learning deficits.

For multilingual students, it is imperative that we distinguish language differences from literacy difficulties and disabilities. The International Dyslexia Association (n.d.) points out the importance of correctly identifying multilingual students with dyslexia, which can often be misunderstood as difficulties in acquiring their new language. It's very important to provide targeted support and interventions that address multilingual students' language learning needs and any potential literacy challenges that they may face. This can involve specialized instructional strategies and assessments tailored to their specific linguistic and literacy profiles.

Language Barriers for Multilingual Learners

Language barriers, language differences, and language-based disorders are interconnected concepts, but it is important to trace the differences between them. Let us distinguish language differences from language barriers. A language barrier typically refers to difficulties in communication that result from a lack of proficiency in the language being used, often experienced by non-native speakers (Wright, 2019). Therefore, students with a language barrier will often need help understanding the language of instruction and difficulties expressing themselves clearly in the academic setting. For example, a multilingual learner who has recently moved to the U.S. may struggle to follow lectures and communicate with peers because of a lack of proficiency in English. This child may not be able to participate in class discussions or cannot complete assignments. However, when assessed in their first language, the student is able to perform at grade level. This student's difficulties are due to limited English proficiency, not from cognitive or developmental issues. Unlike language differences and language-based disorders, language barriers generally reflect situational challenges rather than underlying cognitive issues.

Language Barriers for Multilingual Students with Dyslexia

One of the most dangerous beliefs regarding dyslexia and multilingualism is that it is caused or aggravated by learning several languages. The article "What Research Can Tell Us About the Interaction Between Dyslexia and Bilingualism: An Integrative Review" by do Amaral and de Acevedo (2021) explores the complex relationship between dyslexia and bilingualism. The common assumption is that learning two languages might exacerbate the difficulties that dyslexic individuals might face in literacy acquisition. The authors concluded that bilingualism does not universally aggravate dyslexia. Although bilingual children with dyslexia face challenges, they do not necessarily struggle more than their monolingual dyslexic peers. The difficulty level may vary depending on the linguistic characteristics between the two languages being learned and the language skills they possess. Skills learned in one language, such as phonological awareness, can sometimes transfer to another language, helping to mitigate some of the difficulties faced by dyslexic bilinguals. For example, it will be easier for students to learn languages with similar structures and alphabets, like Spanish and English, where they can make cross-linguistic transfers. It is important to stress that bilingualism should not be viewed as an added complicating factor for the dyslexic learner; rather, the interaction between dyslexia and bilingualism would depend upon factors such as language proficiency and the quality of educational support provided. For multilingual children, language transfer and influence are typical of language development and are not indicators of a disorder. If a child has dyslexia in their heritage language and is not diagnosed, it will cause problems in all other languages learned. Some families are advised to give up multilingualism and to focus on one language. Following this advice will often do more harm than good for children, depriving them of the many advantages multilingualism can bring.

Implications for Literacy Instruction for Multilingual Students with Dyslexia

Teaching students with dyslexia requires considerable expertise. Sadly, research has exposed that, despite their best efforts, teachers often lack the knowledge and skills necessary to meet the needs of students with dyslexia (Wadlington & Wadlington, 2005; Washburn et al., 2011; Washburn et al., 2014). Less is known about teacher expertise in teaching *multilingual* students with language differences, like dyslexia. Such students need specially designed, evidence-based reading interventions that are individualized to meet their unique learning profiles. The question that often arises in education is what language literacy instruction should start for a young child diagnosed with dyslexia. While there is no single answer that would apply to each individual case, it might be helpful for multilingual families to know that starting literacy skills in a more transparent or regular language—the one where correspondence is more predictable between spelling and sounds—is most helpful. For example, in more transparent phonetic languages—like Spanish, where there is little variability in the pronunciation of words based on letter or letter combinations—struggling learners can get a quicker grasp of sound-letter relationships. Quicker knowledge acquisition could be very encouraging and motivating for children with dyslexia. However, this may not be the case in English, a language with highly irregular and opaque orthography rules. The struggle for a dyslexic learner is much more complex. Thus, it can be much easier and more beneficial to start literacy instruction in a more regular and transparent language that may help make the child's learning smoother and more accessible.

Academic success highly depends on a good command of the language used in school. Therefore, it is important that English language and literacy knowledge acquisition also be prioritized. English provides a basis for understanding, expression, and participation. Experts do, however, agree that one must not discourage the dyslexic child from attempting to obtain literacy skills in their heritage language and additional languages. On the other hand, with proper support and applicable strategies, multilingual students with dyslexia can do well in literacy in both contexts, building on strengths gained in one language to support overall academic and personal development. Literacy instruction centered on multiculturalism creates a more engaging environment and an inclusive learning process.

What The Science of Reading tells us about teaching Multilingual Students

The Science of Reading (SOR) comprises a body of knowledge from a collective of fields that investigate the reading process and effective reading instruction (The Reading League, 2022). Several disciplines contribute to SOR, including communication sciences, cognitive and developmental psychology, special education, linguistics, and neuroscience amongst others. SOR researchers have repeatedly pointed to explicit phonics as a more effective instructional approach than whole language instruction and support findings from over three decades of research in this area. A bulk of the research coming out of the SOR movement is based on the findings of the National Reading Panel (National Reading Panel & National Institute of Child Health and Human Development, 2000), a panel of researchers convened by Congress in 1999, who reviewed the extensive research on key elements of reading to assess the effectiveness of different approaches used to teach children to read. The Panel's report in 2000 explained that the most effective reading instruction includes explicit instruction in phonemic awareness, systematic phonics instruction, fluency, vocabulary, and comprehension. One of the main criticisms of the NRP is the lack of consideration for research that specifically impacted multilingual learners. A later publication through the National Literacy Panel on Language Minority Children and Youth (August et al., 2006) concurred with the findings of the NRP as it relates to second language learners but added additional considerations that pertain to multilingual learners in particular, including

- linguistic variability,
- cognitive demands,
- socio-cultural influences,
- the role of home language,
- the uniqueness of the dual language brain,
- the importance of background knowledge, and
- scaffolds to support oral language

The current science of reading movement reminds us of the bodies of knowledge mentioned above. It covers research across all age groups, from various districts, cities, states, and countries, and includes work with both monolingual and multilingual students.

Explicit and Systematic Instruction. Explicit and systematic instruction is a fundamental principle of the science of reading, emphasizing the direct, explicit teaching of foundational literacy skills for multilingual students with dyslexia. This type of instruction can involve teaching phonemic awareness, phonics, fluency, vocabulary, and comprehension in a direct and systematic manner (International Dyslexia Association, n.d.). Multilingual students with dyslexia should receive targeted instruction in these reading components as they are crucial for word recognition. These skills are essential for all learners but particularly significant for multilingual students struggling with dyslexia. Accurately and fluently decoding written words to comprehend text is a key focus and a fundamental aspect of the science of reading (Grosjean, 2019). Explicit and systematic instruction is often not as commonly used in mainstream multilingual classrooms; it is more often utilized in dyslexia therapy or intervention sessions. However, the principles of the science of reading should be shared and implemented widely to benefit the majority of students.

Emphasis should be placed on the unique linguistic backgrounds of multilingual students, and their instruction should be tailored to accommodate this diversity. When teaching literacy, it is important to consider students' language diversity and address their specific needs (International Dyslexia Association, n.d.). This approach helps create an inclusive learning environment where all students can thrive.

Comprehensive Literacy Instruction

Most recently, The Reading League (2023) and the National Committee for Effective Literacy joined forces to echo the findings from both previously mentioned panels and heavily emphasized "the importance of not focusing exclusively on foundational skills; nurturing the profound interconnections among knowledge, language, and literacy must be considered." (The Reading League, 2023, p.1) The Reading League members and the National Committee for Effective Literacy convened for the very first in-person bilingual/multilingual summit in 2023, where they discussed the early literacy needs of multilingual students (The Reading League, 2023). Out of the summit grew a joint statement that provides valuable insights into the intersection of dyslexia and multilingual students, particularly by emphasizing a comprehensive, research-based approach to literacy instruction. Several important recommendations can be drawn from the statement on instruction for students with dyslexia who are also multilingual which we have summarized in the paragraphs below.

The first recommendation is that effective literacy instruction must be comprehensive (The Reading League, 2023). For multilingual students with dyslexia, this means literacy programs need to support their development in their target and heritage languages, as multilingualism can enhance cognitive skills, including reading. Although students with dyslexia often benefit from targeted interventions with a heavy focus on areas like phonemic awareness and decoding, multilingual students with dyslexia also need support in vocabulary, comprehension, and oral language development. The Reading League and National Committee for Effective Literacy's joint statement emphasizes the need for interventions to address the full spectrum of literacy development and not limited to foundational skills (The Reading League, 2023). This is crucial for multilingual students with dyslexia, who, along with struggling with dyslexia, may also struggle with language comprehension and expression.

Next, the joint statement highlights that both multilingual and monolingual students with dyslexia benefit from explicit, systematic instruction in phonics and decoding, as well as strategies that map oral language to written language. This recommendation is critical for classroom teachers who may have both types of students and serves as a reminder that multilingual students with dyslexia may also face unique challenges in processing multiple languages. Instruction should explicitly address both their language learning needs and their specific challenges with dyslexia (The Reading League, 2023).

Third, the statement highlights the importance of culturally and linguistically responsive instruction. For multilingual students with dyslexia, it is essential to use materials that value their heritage language and cultural background, making literacy instruction more meaningful and supportive of their cognitive development. This includes dual language programs, when possible, or strategies that leverage their heritage language to support their target language's literacy development (The Reading League, 2023). This recommendation converges with the guidance from the International Dyslexia Association, which establishes that emphasis should be placed on the unique linguistic backgrounds of multilingual students, and their instruction should be tailored to accommodate this diversity (International Dyslexia Association, n.d.). This approach helps create an inclusive learning environment where all students can thrive. Assessments should be also linguistically and culturally appropriate, ensuring that progress in their heritage and target languages is monitored (The Reading League, 2023). The data from these assessments should inform instruction and intervention strategies, particularly for multilingual students whose literacy development may differ from that of their monolingual peers.

Finally, the statement also highlighted emerging research that suggests that bilingualism can enhance cognitive control and executive functioning, which may be beneficial for students with dyslexia (The Reading League, 2023). Cognitive control is the capability of an individual to regulate attention to attend to task-relevant stimuli while inhibiting the processing of task-irrelevant stimuli; shifting attention from one task to another or from one stimulus to the other efficiently is included in cognitive control (Bialystok & Craik, 2010; The Reading League, 2023). The other related set of processes, referred to as executive functioning, includes working memory and problem-solving activities (Diamond, 2013; The Reading League, 2023). When students are learning a new language, their heritage language can facilitate introduction and a link between familiar language patterns with a new language. Therefore, instruction for multilingual students with dyslexia should not aim to suppress their heritage language but instead use it as a scaffold for learning in both their heritage and targeted languages, helping them leverage their full linguistic repertoire. In addition, keeping and developing heritage language may strengthen cultural as well as linguistic self-identification, motivation, and interest, which are indispensable preconditions for language learning. By applying specific instructional methods and structural tools that promote the bilingual development of children with dyslexia, first- language, and targeted language, students can learn how to achieve literacy in multilingual schools as opposed to mainstream monolinguistic education and feel and become empowered.

Educators need professional development that integrates the science of reading and effective strategies for teaching multilingual students with dyslexia. The joint statement calls for educator training programs to focus on equipping teachers with the knowledge to address the intersection of language and literacy development, specifically for students who face dual challenges with dyslexia and learning their targeted language (The Reading League, 2023).

Conceptual Models to Guide Instruction for Multilingual Learners

The Reading Rope Model is a conceptual model that accurately depicts the principles of the SOR movement. Educators supporting students with linguistic differences, such as multilingual learners, can rely on such models to help guide instruction and to understand which skills learners must master in order to learn to read (The Reading League, 2022). The Reading Rope (Scarborough, 2001) is a reading process model that summarizes the patterns of reading skills of all readers (see Figure 3). In this model, two sets of skills (represented by rope strands), word recognition and language comprehension, work together to produce skilled reading.

The reading rope, created by Dr. Hollis Scarborough in 2001, is a model that illustrates the complexities of skilled reading. It consists of two main strands. The first strand is word recognition, which includes phonological awareness, decoding, and sight recognition. The second strand is language comprehension, which includes background knowledge, vocabulary, and verbal reasoning. Dr. Scarborough described these components as interwoven strands, with each becoming more tightly woven as students advance in reading. The integration of these elements supports fluent, skilled reading, emphasizing the essential role of both decoding and comprehension in literacy development (Scarborough, 2001).

For multilingual students, the reading rope helps us understand the intricate nature of reading development, particularly how language comprehension and word recognition are interconnected. This highlights the critical components of both oral language skills and decoding abilities. It is important to consider the needs of multilingual students in the context of the reading rope. Some multilingual students may develop language comprehension at a rate equivalent to their peers but struggle with word recognition. In contrast, others may develop word recognition skills but struggle with language comprehension due to limited exposure to their target language. This underscores the importance of addressing both sides of Scarborough's Reading Rope for multilingual students and not prioritizing one over the other (International Dyslexia Association, n.d.).

Scarborough's Rope underlines the necessity of paying close attention to phonological awareness, decoding, and sight recognition acquisition of multilingual students. While also building the background knowledge, vocabulary, language structures, verbal reasoning, and literacy knowledge within comprehensive language instruction that considers their heritage language and their progress in their target language. To effectively utilize Scarborough's Reading Rope for multilingual students, educators should equally teach language comprehension and word reading skills in their heritage and target languages. Adapting Scarborough's model for multilingual students may require providing more explicit vocabulary instruction, scaffolding content to support comprehension, and ensuring that students have opportunities to engage with rich oral language activities in both their heritage and target languages equally (International Dyslexia Association, n.d.).

As teachers focus on strengthening the various strands of Scarborough's Reading Rope, depicted in Figure 3, multilingual students can become proficient readers. The Rope aligns with the broader understanding of the science of reading, recognizing that both monolingual and multilingual students benefit from explicit and systematic instruction tailored to their unique linguistic backgrounds. Monolingual and multilingual students with dyslexia benefit greatly from this alignment of Scarborough's Reading Rope and the science of reading, especially when taught in whole groups, small groups, and interventions. When alignment occurs across all instructional tiers, the only adjustments needed are intensity and repetition.

Figure 3. Scarborough's reading rope

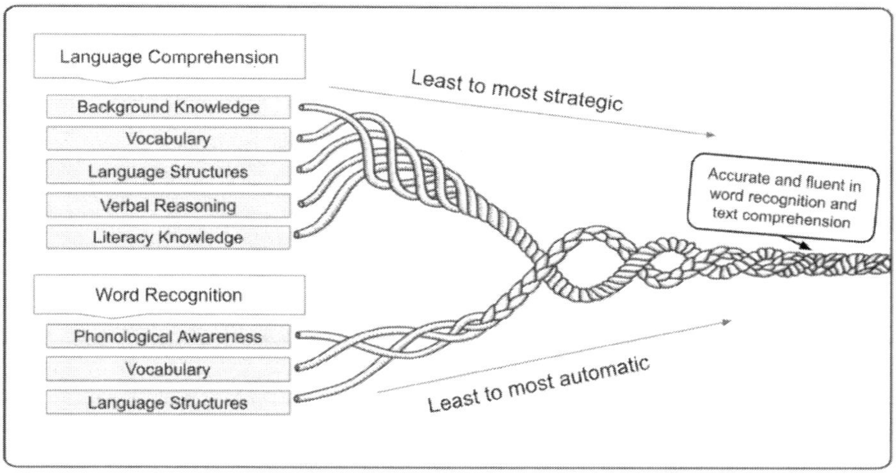

Note. A model adapted from Dr. Hollis Scarborough's research illustrates the complexities of skilled reading. There are two main strands: 1. Word recognition- includes phonological awareness, decoding, and sight recognition. 2. Language comprehension- includes background knowledge, vocabulary, and verbal reasoning. The interwoven strands become more tightly woven as students advance in reading (Scarborough, 2001).

Bilingualism and Literacy Implications

Research indicates that bilingualism significantly influences literacy development in children, particularly those with dyslexia, in comparison to their monolingual peers learning a second language (Kovelman et al., 2016). Bilingual learners often exhibit the ability to transfer literacy skills between their languages, which can enhance their reading proficiency, especially in languages with more transparent phonological systems, such as Spanish. Neuroimaging studies suggest that bilingualism positively impacts brain regions associated with reading (Kovelman et al., 2016).

Furthermore, bilingual children with dyslexia can develop language-specific reading strategies based on the phonological transparency of each language. For instance, students learning English, which has an opaque orthography, may adopt different strategies compared to those learning Afrikaans, a language with a more transparent structure (Kovelman et al., 2016). Early literacy intervention remains beneficial for bilingual children with dyslexia, even when conducted in a single language (Kovelman et al., 2016).

The significance of phonological awareness is highlighted across both alphabetic and character-based languages, such as Chinese, where bilingual children with dyslexia may exhibit unique deficits. Phonological and morphological awareness are essential components in addressing their literacy challenges (Kovelman et al., 2016). When provided with appropriate interventions, bilingualism can offer cognitive advantages for reading, including for those with dyslexia (Kovelman et al., 2016).

Moreover, it is recommended that parents focus on providing reading instruction in their child's most proficient language, fostering literacy foundations that are transferable to a second language. Despite the challenges associated with learning a second language, children with dyslexia can still thrive in literacy acquisition and may even find the process enjoyable (Kovelman et al., 2016).

Recommended Strategies for Working with Multilingual Learners

To effectively support multilingual students with dyslexia, it's crucial to combine various strategies that address their linguistic and cognitive needs. Early intervention is crucial in preventing severe reading difficulties. Interventions should be structured, systematic, and explicit, starting as early as possible and focusing on foundational and advanced skills to reduce the risk of further exacerbating reading difficulties (Jiménez et al., 2021). The following section will summarize key recommendations for instruction outlined in the literature.

Systematic and Explicit Instruction for Foundational Reading

Across the studies, a common characteristic for fostering reading growth for multilingual students is the delivery of explicit and systematic instruction (Richards-Tutor et al., 2016). Explicit and systematic instruction cannot only have a direct impact on skill growth, but can also play a critical role in enhancing retention and comprehension. For multilingual learners, interventions that focus on explicit and systematic instruction of foundational skills, such as phonemic awareness, can provide a better and more consistent effect than other intervention outcomes, such as vocabulary (Richards-Tutor et al., 2016). Furthermore, Phonological awareness activities, such as phoneme segmentation in students' heritage languages, can significantly strengthen literacy skills in both their heritage and target languages (Gonzales & Tejero Hughes, 2018; Ijalba & Bustos, 2017). These activities can be effectively applied across various instructional settings, including whole groups, small groups, intensive intervention groups, and one-on-one sessions. Using lowercase letters to model sounds for the students and selecting target words from their connected text to make the learning of sound and symbol connections explicit and meaningful to the students (Pullen & Lane, 2013; 2016). Incorporating manipulative letters as a form of multisensory instruction within a comprehensive reading program is particularly beneficial for students with dyslexia, as it supports their ability to understand the steps involved in reading letters and words, leading to better text comprehension. Providing systematic and explicit phonological awareness instruction and sound-symbol connections is essential for all students, especially those not yet reading at grade level. For bilingual students, in particular, reinforcing reading comprehension through their heritage language and reinforcing that foundation in their target language is an especially effective method for building literacy using explicit and systematic methods.

Monitoring Progress

Keeping detailed records of each student's progress and the specific interventions they receive is critical for assessing the effectiveness of a given strategy or program. This data allows us to spot trends and make well-informed decisions about which interventions are working best for different students. It also helps ensure that our approach remains flexible and responsive to individual needs. Regularly communicating with parents or guardians about their child's progress is just as important, as their involvement is key to reinforcing the support we provide through supplemental reading interventions. Together, these practices form a strong foundation for driving meaningful improvement in reading outcomes.

Continuous feedback loops between the teacher and the students when monitoring, assessing, and communicating help identify areas where students are struggling and where instruction might need adjustment. These feedback loops are processes where teachers collect data through monitoring and assessment, and with the help of their knowledge through professional development, they adjust their instruction based on the gathered information (Hattie & Timperley, 2007), creating a cycle of improvement for the student and a cycle of responsiveness for the teacher. One example of this is when a teacher has flexible small groups. These groups are malleable and based on the assessments or monitoring done by the teacher. For instance, when a student is in a small group who is practicing their letter sounds, and the student masters this skill, they will be moved to a group focusing on decoding CVC words. This system ensures that students receive instruction that meets their current needs, leading to more personalized and targeted learning experiences. Over time, feedback loops improve both teacher effectiveness and student outcomes by fostering a responsive teaching environment.

Language-focused Instruction for Cultural Relevance

Combining grammar and vocabulary instruction with engaging, interactive activities has shown promise in improving grammatical skills and literacy in the student's multiple languages. Activities that reinforce grammar rules and storytelling in both languages are beneficial, as improvements in one language often transfer to the other (Bedore et al., 2020). Supporting literacy development in the dominant and less dominant languages is essential. This approach not only enhances language proficiency but also promotes cultural understanding and appreciation. It's important to create an inclusive learning environment that values and supports linguistic diversity. Incorporating culturally significant elements can enhance engagement by reflecting students' heritage cultures and bilingual skills (Ferreira et al., 2016).

Creating programs that connect personally with students through meaningful texts and activities is essential. Personal relevance increases motivation and engagement. Strategies like having students create personal books and texts that reflect their interests and identities can significantly enhance their literacy development and involvement in learning (Bernhard et al., 2006). This combination of targeted, culturally relevant, and engaging strategies ensures a more effective and supportive learning environment for multilingual students with dyslexia. For example, in my bilingual kindergarten classroom, we would engage in a small group activity where students were asked to create a story and become their own authors. Despite having varying ability levels, all students were encouraged to use as much of their literacy skills as possible to create the book and even act as their own illustrators. For those students who struggled to put words down on the page, the teacher would write the story based on their narration. Personal relevance increases student engagement, and their motivation to participate in literacy is greatly enhanced.

Structured Literacy for Multilingual Students

There is minimal, but promising, research on the implementation of structured literacy to develop English skills for multilingual students, with only a few studies in the past 20 years (see, e.g., Richards-Tutor et al., 2016; Vaughn et al., 2006). The term "structured literacy" (SL) was more recently coined by the International

Dyslexia Association (2023) as an explicitly teaching systematic word identification and decoding strategies through these six elements: phonology, sound-symbol association, syllables, morphology, syntax, and semantics. In SL These elements are taught through three principles: systematic, cumulative, explicit, and diagnostic.

Multilingual students whose heritage language is Spanish and who are at risk for reading difficulties can make significant growth in their English language acquisition when they receive supplemental instruction that includes phonemic awareness, letter knowledge, alphabetic decoding, decodable text practice, and comprehension strategies (Vaughn et al., 2006). In addition, multilingual students who receive instruction to develop their Spanish literacy and decoding skills can also make improvements in English reading skills, suggesting a cross-linguistic transfer of skills and suggesting that learning to decode in the student's heritage language transfers to decoding in English (Baker et al., 2021). However, the same effects cannot be necessarily expected for growth in the heritage language (Spanish), as SL techniques and sequence can not be executed exactly in the same manner as for English literacy instruction and have to be adjusted for the variances in language (Mathes et al., 2007). For multilingual students, reading instruction in only one language or the other will not be sufficient, so they need daily instructional time explicitly devoted to academic language development in both their heritage language and English (Baker et al., 2016; Branum-Martin et al., 2012).

CONCLUSION

The multilingual population in the US is vast, which requires addressing dyslexia with a comprehensive understanding of the interplay between language acquisition and learning disabilities in multilingual students. As this chapter has illustrated, dyslexia is not confined to any single language; instead, it manifests across various linguistic backgrounds, introducing unique challenges that educators must navigate. Misidentification and inadequate support for multilingual learners with dyslexia often arise from assumptions that their reading difficulties stem solely from language differences rather than from the inherent complexities of dyslexia itself.

Recognizing the distinction between language differences and language-based disorders is critical for providing equitable educational opportunities. Educators must be equipped with knowledge and strategies to discern these differences, ensuring that multilingual students receive the appropriate interventions tailored to their needs. Emphasizing the importance of culturally responsive teaching practices and evidence-based instructional approaches can foster a supportive environment where all students can thrive.

Furthermore, the evidence suggests that bilingualism can enhance cognitive skills and facilitate reading development when proper support is in place. By leveraging students' heritage languages and implementing systematic, explicit literacy instruction, educators can help multilingual learners with dyslexia achieve proficiency across languages. Ultimately, creating inclusive classrooms that celebrate linguistic diversity and prioritize evidence-based practices will empower multilingual students to overcome their reading challenges and succeed academically.

REFERENCES

Adlof, S. M. (2020). Promoting reading achievement in children with developmental language disorders: What can we learn from research on specific language impairment and dyslexia? *Journal of Speech, Language, and Hearing Research: JSLHR*, 63(10), 3277–3292. DOI: 10.1044/2020_JSLHR-20-00118 PMID: 33064604

Adlof, S. M., & Hogan, T. P. (2018). Understanding dyslexia in the context of developmental language disorders. *Language, Speech, and Hearing Services in Schools*, 49(4), 762–773. DOI: 10.1044/2018_LSHSS-DYSLC-18-0049 PMID: 30458538

Álvarez-Cañizo, M., Afonso, O., & Suárez-Coalla, P. (2023). Writing proficiency in English as L2 in Spanish children with dyslexia. *Annals of Dyslexia*, 73(1), 130–147. DOI: 10.1007/s11881-023-00278-4 PMID: 36705859

Artiles, A. J., & Ortiz, A. A. (2002). *English language learners with special education needs: Identification, assessment, and instruction*. Center for Applied Linguistics and Delta Systems Co., Inc.

August, D., Shanahan, T., & Escamilla, K. (2009). English language learners: Developing literacy in second-language learners—Report of the National Literacy Panel on Language-Minority Children and Youth. *Journal of Literacy Research*, 41(4), 432–452. DOI: 10.1080/10862960903340165

Baca, L. M., & Almanza, E. (1991). *Language Minority Students with Disabilities. Exceptional Children at Risk: CEC Mini-Library*. Council for Exceptional Children, 1920 Association Dr., Reston, VA 22091-1589 (Stock No. P357: $8.00).

Baker, D. L., Basaraba, D. L., & Polanco, P. (2016). Connecting the present to the past: Furthering the research on bilingual education and bilingualism. *Review of Research in Education*, 40(1), 821–883. DOI: 10.3102/0091732X16660691

Baker, D. L., Park, Y., & Andress, T. T. (2021). Longitudinal predictors of bilingual language proficiency, decoding, and oral reading fluency on reading comprehension in Spanish and in English. *School Psychology Review*, ●●●, 1–14. DOI: 10.1080/2372966X.2021.2021447

Bedore, L. M., Peña, E. D., Fiestas, C., & Lugo-Neris, M. J. (2020). Language and literacy together: Supporting grammatical development in dual language learners with risk for language and learning difficulties. *Language, Speech, and Hearing Services in Schools*, 51(2), 282–297. DOI: 10.1044/2020_LSHSS-19-00055 PMID: 32255748

Bernhard, J. K., Cummins, J., Campoy, F. I., Ada, A. F., Winsler, A., & Bleiker, C. (2006). Identity texts and literacy development among preschool English language learners: Enhancing learning opportunities for children at risk for learning disabilities. *Teachers College Record*, 108(11), 2380–2405. DOI: 10.1111/j.1467-9620.2006.00786.x

Bialystok, E., & Craik, F. I. (2010). Cognitive and linguistic processing in the bilingual mind. *Current Directions in Psychological Science*, 19(1), 19–23. DOI: 10.1177/0963721409358571

Branum-Martin, L., Tao, S., Garnaat, S., Bunta, F., & Francis, D. J. (2012). Meta-analysis of bilingual phonological awareness: Language, age, and psycholinguistic grain size. *Journal of Educational Psychology*, 104(4), 932–944. DOI: 10.1037/a0027755

Burr, E., Haas, E., Ferriere, K., & West, E. (2015). Identifying and supporting English learner students with learning disabilities: Key issues in the literature and state practice. *Regional Educational Laboratory. WestEd.*

Canas, A., Bordes Edgar, V., & Neumann, J. (2020). Practical considerations in the neuropsychological assessment of bilingual (Spanish-English) children in the United States: Literature review and case series. *Developmental Neuropsychology*, 45(4), 211–231. DOI: 10.1080/87565641.2020.1746314 PMID: 32264704

Catts, H. W. (1989). Defining dyslexia as a developmental language disorder. *Annals of Dyslexia*, 39(1), 50–64. DOI: 10.1007/BF02656900 PMID: 24233471

Cenoz, J. (2013). Defining multilingualism. *Annual Review of Applied Linguistics*, 33, 3–18. DOI: 10.1017/S026719051300007X

Diamond, A. (2013). Executive functions. *Annual Review of Psychology*, 64(1), 135–168. DOI: 10.1146/annurev-psych-113011-143750 PMID: 23020641

do Amaral, J., & de Azevedo, B. (2021). What research can tell us about the interaction between dyslexia and bilingualism: An integrative review. *Letrônica*, 14(2), e38695–e38695. DOI: 10.15448/1984-4301.2021.2.38695

Farnsworth, M. (2018). Differentiating second language acquisition from specific learning disability: An observational tool assessing dual language learners' pragmatic competence. *Young Exceptional Children*, 21(2), 92–110. DOI: 10.1177/1096250615621356

Ferreira, A., Gottardo, A., Javier, C., Schwieter, J. W., & Jia, F. (2016). Reading comprehension: The role of acculturation, language dominance, and socioeconomic status in cross-linguistic relations. *Revista Española de Lingüística Aplicada/Spanish Journal of Applied Linguistics. Published under the auspices of the Spanish Association of Applied Linguistics, 29*(2), 613-639.

Fillmore, L. W. (1979). Individual differences in second language acquisition. In Fillmore, C. J., Kempler, D., & Wang, W. S.-Y. (Eds.), *Individual differences in language ability and language behavior* (pp. 203–228). Academic Press. DOI: 10.1016/B978-0-12-255950-1.50017-2

Fillmore, L. W. (1991). When learning a second language means losing the first. *Early Childhood Research Quarterly*, 6(3), 323–346. DOI: 10.1016/S0885-2006(05)80059-6

Francis, W. S., Strobach, E. N., Penalver, R. M., Martínez, M., Gurrola, B. V., & Soltero, A. (2019). Word–context associations in episodic memory are learned at the conceptual level: Word frequency, bilingual proficiency, and bilingual status effects on source memory. *Journal of Experimental Psychology. Learning, Memory, and Cognition*, 45(10), 1852–1871. DOI: 10.1037/xlm0000678 PMID: 30570325

Gillespie, T. (2015). Language differences versus language disorder. Retrieved December 10, 2015, from http://teresagillespie.wikispaces.dpsk12.org/Language+Difference+versus+Language+Disorder

Gonzales, W., & Tejero Hughes, M. (2018). Libros en mano: Phonological awareness intervention in children's native languages. *Education Sciences*, 8(4), 175. DOI: 10.3390/educsci8040175

Grosjean, F. (2019, March 11). Dyslexia, bilingualism, and learning a second language. *Psychology Today*. https://www.psychologytoday.com/us/blog/life-bilingual/201903/dyslexia-bilingualism-and-learning-second-language

Hattie, J., & Timperley, H. (2007). The power of feedback. *Review of Educational Research*, 77(1), 81–112. DOI: 10.3102/003465430298487

Ijalba, E., & Bustos, A. (2017). Phonological deficits in developmental dyslexia in a second grade Spanish-English bilingual child. *Perspectives of the ASHA Special Interest Groups*, 2(1), 212–228. DOI: 10.1044/persp2.SIG1.212

Ijalba, E., Bustos, A., & Romero, S. (2020). Phonological–orthographic deficits in developmental dyslexia in three Spanish–English bilingual students. *American Journal of Speech-Language Pathology*, 29(3), 1133–1151. DOI: 10.1044/2020_AJSLP-19-00175 PMID: 32750285

International Dyslexia Association. (2002). *Definition of dyslexia*. https://dyslexiaida .org/definition-of-dyslexia/

International Dyslexia Association. (2023). *Structured literacy: An overview*. https:// dyslexiaida.org/structured-literacy/

International Dyslexia Association. (n.d.). *English learners and dyslexia*. https:// dyslexiaida.org/english-learners-and-dyslexia/

Jiménez, J. E., Gutiérrez, N., & de León, S. C. (2021). Analyzing the role of fidelity of RTI Tier 2 reading intervention in Spanish kindergarten and first grade students. *Annals of Dyslexia*, 71(1), 28–49. DOI: 10.1007/s11881-021-00221-5 PMID: 33713278

Kovelman, I., Bisconti, S., & Hoeft, F. (2016, April). *Literacy & dyslexia revealed through bilingual brain development*. International Dyslexia Association. https:// dyslexiaida.org/literacy-dyslexia-revealed-through-bilingual-brain-development/\

Krashen, S. (2000). Bilingual education, the acquisition of English, and the retention and loss of Spanish. *Research on Spanish in the US*, 432-444.

Mathes, P. G., Pollard-Durodola, S. D., Cárdenas-Hagan, E., Linan-Thompson, S., & Vaughn, S. (2007). Teaching struggling readers who are native Spanish speakers: What do we know?. https://doi.org/DOI: 10.1177/088840640402700

Miciak, J., Ahmed, Y., Capin, P., & Francis, D. J. (2022). The reading profiles of late elementary English learners with and without risk for dyslexia. *Annals of Dyslexia*, 72(2), 276–300. DOI: 10.1007/s11881-022-00254-4 PMID: 35608744

Moats, L. C., & Foorman, B. R. (2003). Measuring teachers' content knowledge of language and reading. *Annals of Dyslexia*, 53(1), 23–45. DOI: 10.1007/s11881-003-0003-7

National Center for Education Statistics. (2024). *English learners in public schools*. U.S. Department of Education. https://nces.ed.gov/programs/coe/indicator/cgf/ english-learners

National Reading Panel (US), & National Institute of Child Health and Human Development (US). (2000). *Report of the National Reading Panel: Teaching children to read: An evidence-based assessment of the scientific research literature on reading and its implications for reading instruction: Reports of the subgroups*. National Institute of Child Health and Human Development, National Institutes of Health.

Nsengiyumva, D. S., Oriikiriza, C., & Nakijoba, S. (2021). Cross-Linguistic Transfer and Language Proficiency in the Multilingual Education System of Burundi: What Has the Existing Literature so Far Discovered? *Indonesian Journal of English Language Teaching and Applied Linguistics*, 5(2), 387–399. DOI: 10.21093/ijeltal.v5i2.770

Peer, L., & Reid, G. (2014). *Multilingualism, literacy and dyslexia: A challenge for educators*. Routledge. DOI: 10.4324/9780203432372

Piñón, L., Carreón-Sánchez, S., & Bishop, S. (2022). *Emergent bilingual learner education – Literature review*. Intercultural Development Research Association. https://files.eric.ed.gov/fulltext/ED629281.pdf

Pugh, K., & Verhoeven, L. (2018). Introduction to this special issue: Dyslexia across languages and writing systems. *Scientific Studies of Reading*, 22(1), 1–6. DOI: 10.1080/10888438.2017.1390668 PMID: 30718941

Pullen, P. C., & Lane, H. B. (2013). Teacher-directed decoding practice with manipulative letters and word reading skill development of struggling first-grade students. *HEX, 22*(1).

Pullen, P. C., & Lane, H. B. (2016). Hands-on decoding: Guidelines for using manipulative letters. *Learning Disabilities (Pittsburgh, Pa.)*, 21(1), 27–37. DOI: 10.18666/LDMJ-2016-V21-I1-6797

Richards-Tutor, C., Baker, D. L., Gersten, R., Baker, S. K., & Smith, J. M. (2016). The effectiveness of reading interventions for English learners: A research synthesis. *Exceptional Children*, 82(2), 144–169. DOI: 10.1177/0014402915585483

Roseberry-McKibbin, C. (2002). *Multicultural students with special language needs: Practical strategies for assessment and intervention* (2nd ed.). Academic Communication Associates.

Roseberry-McKibbin, C., & Brice, A. (2000). Acquiring English as a second language. *ASHA Leader*, 5(12), 4–7.

Scarborough, H. S. (2001). Connecting early language and literacy to later reading (dis)abilities: Evidence, theory, and practice. In Neuman, S., & Dickinson, D. (Eds.), *Handbook for research in early literacy* (pp. 97–110). Guilford Press.

Sullivan, A. L., & Proctor, S. L. (2016, September). The shield or the sword? Revisiting the debate on racial disproportionality in special education and implications for school psychologists. *School Psychology Forum*, 10(3), ●●●.

The Reading League. (2022). *Science of reading: Defining guide*. https://www.thereadingleague.org/what-is-the-science-of-reading/

The Reading League. (2023). *Understanding the difference: The science of reading and implementation for English learners/emergent bilinguals (ELs/EBs)* [Joint statement]. The Reading League. https://www.thereadingleague.org/wp-content/uploads/2023/09/TRLC-ELEB-Understanding-the-Difference-The-Science-of-Reading-and-Implementation.pdf

Tompkins, M. (2002). Sign with your baby: Opening the doors to communication. *Infant Development Association of California News, 29*(1).

U.S. Department of Education. (2021). *EDFacts Data Warehouse (EDW): IDEA Part B Child Count and Educational Environments Collection, 2019-20. OSEP Fast Facts: Race and ethnicity of children with disabilities served under IDEA Part B.* U.S. Department of Education.

Vaughn, S., Mathes, P., Linan-Thompson, S., Cirino, P., Carlson, C., Pollard-Durodola, S., Cardenas-Hagan, E., & Francis, D. (2006). Effectiveness of an English intervention for first-grade English language learners at risk for reading problems. *The Elementary School Journal*, 107(2), 153–180. DOI: 10.1086/510653

Wadlington, E. M., & Wadlington, P. L. (2005). What educators really believe about dyslexia. *Reading Improvement*, 42(1), 16–33.

Washburn, E. K., Binks-Cantrell, E. S., & Joshi, R. M. (2014). What do preservice teachers from the USA and the UK know about dyslexia? *Dyslexia (Chichester, England)*, 20(1), 1–18. DOI: 10.1002/dys.1459 PMID: 23949838

Washburn, E. K., Joshi, R. M., & Binks-Cantrell, E. S. (2011). Teacher knowledge of basic language concepts and dyslexia. *Dyslexia (Chichester, England)*, 17(2), 165–183. DOI: 10.1002/dys.426 PMID: 21290479

Wright, W. E. (2019). *Foundations for teaching English language learners: Research, theory, policy, and practice* (3rd ed.). Caslon Publishing.

Yang, M., Cooc, N., & Sheng, L. (2017). An investigation of cross-linguistic transfer between Chinese and English: A meta-analysis. *Asian-Pacific Journal of Second and Foreign Language Education*, 2(1), 1–21. DOI: 10.1186/s40862-017-0036-9

Ziegler, J. C., & Goswami, U. (2005). Reading acquisition, developmental dyslexia, and skilled reading across languages: A psycholinguistic grain size theory. *Psychological Bulletin*, 131(1), 3–29. DOI: 10.1037/0033-2909.131.1.3 PMID: 15631549

KEY TERMS AND DEFINITIONS

Dyslexia: is a specific learning disability with a neurobiological origin, primarily affecting a person's ability to accurately and fluently recognize words and causing difficulties with spelling and decoding.

Emergent bilingual: term that considers the language and literacy knowledge a student has in their heritage language and is now acquiring their second language.

English Learners (ELLs): a term often used in the literature, policy, or common discourse to describe students whose heritage language is not English.

Heritage language: a language or languages other than the dominant language in a given social context. Often referred to as the "home language" or "primary language."

Language-based disorders: disorders that may affect an individual's ability to understand and process written and/or spoken language.

Multilingual students: users of a variety of heritage languages who are in the process of learning the dominant language.

Phonological processing: the process of identifying and manipulating the phonemes (or sounds) in the language. Phonological processing facilitates the ability to read and write words.

Chapter 11
Integrating Reproductive Justice in Social Work Education:
Empowering Hispanic Communities Through Holistic Practice

Caelin Elizabeth McCallum

https://orcid.org/0009-0001-8617-2414

Monmouth University, USA

Amanda Marie Goodwin

https://orcid.org/0009-0007-9252-2701

Monmouth University, USA

ABSTRACT

This chapter examines the integration of reproductive justice into social work education, focusing on its importance for empowering Hispanic communities. Rooted in a framework developed by women of color, reproductive justice addresses not only reproductive rights, but also the social, economic, and political conditions that influence autonomy. The chapter highlights how Hispanic populations face unique barriers, such as limited healthcare access, cultural stigmas, and legal challenges. It advocates for embedding reproductive justice in MSW-level curricula to prepare social workers for culturally competent practice and policy advocacy. Through interdisciplinary education and systemic reforms, social workers can help dismantle barriers and promote reproductive autonomy for marginalized groups.

DOI: 10.4018/979-8-3373-1340-5.ch011

Copyright © 2025, IGI Global Scientific Publishing. Copying or distributing in print or electronic forms without written permission of IGI Global is prohibited.

I. INTRODUCTION

A. Overview of Reproductive Justice

Reproductive justice is a framework that broadens the conversation around reproductive rights, emphasizing not only the right to choose whether to have children but also the social, economic, and political conditions necessary to make those choices freely and safely. It was developed by Black women, particularly through the work of SisterSong, a women of color collective formed in 1997, which developed the following three core principles:

1. The right to have a child - this principle affirms that every person should have the freedom to decide if and when to have children without interference from external forces, which may include laws, policies, or social pressure.
2. The right not to have a child - this principle addresses how individuals must have access to safe, affordable, and comprehensive reproductive healthcare, including abortion, contraception, and family planning services, to decide not to have children.
3. The right to parent children in safe and supportive environments - this principle addresses the broader conditions required to raise children in safe, healthy, and dignified environments, such as access to healthcare, education, housing, and protection from violence.

Reproductive justice goes beyond the legal right to access reproductive healthcare; it recognizes how race, class, gender, ability, sexual orientation, and other identities intersect to impact individuals' reproductive autonomy. It focuses on systemic inequality and structural barriers, advocating for the overall well-being of marginalized communities (Ross & Solinger, 2017).

I. The Relevance of Reproductive Justice to Social Work with Marginalized Communities

Reproductive justice is an important framework for social work practice, particularly when working with marginalized communities. For marginalized groups– such as people of color, low-income individuals, immigrants, and LGBTQ+ communities, among others– the intersection of these identities leads to compounded barriers to access of reproductive healthcare and reproductive autonomy. This makes the reproductive justice framework incredibly relevant to social work, which is committed to promoting social justice, equity, and empowerment for the most vulnerable populations (National Association of Social Workers, 2021).

Social work practice, in alignment with the reproductive justice framework, also emphasizes addressing broader social determinants of health (SDOH), that influence reproductive choices. The SDOH are factors within the environments individuals are born and live in that impact a broad range of health, functioning, and quality of life outcomes and risks (Office of Disease Prevention and Health Promotion, n.d.). Some examples of these factors include safe housing, job opportunities, polluted air and water, income, and language (Office of Disease Prevention and Health Promotion, n.d.). Social workers are in a prime position to advocate for marginalized communities through the promotion of culturally sensitive service provision and aid in navigating complex healthcare systems. Social workers can also advocate for systemic change, such as reforms that improve healthcare access, support immigrant health, and address economic disparities that impact reproductive autonomy and access to other services that support health and wellbeing. The incorporation of the reproductive justice framework into social work practice ultimately strengthens the profession's commitment to social justice and human rights. By focusing on systemic inequalities and advocating for equitable healthcare and policy reform, social workers can ensure that marginalized communities have the resources and support necessary to exercise their reproductive rights and autonomy.

B. The Importance of Focusing on Hispanic Communities

Hispanic communities in the United States face distinct and multifaceted challenges in achieving reproductive justice; these challenges are shaped by a combination of systemic barriers, cultural influences, and intersecting identities. One of the most pressing challenges is access to comprehensive reproductive healthcare, as many Hispanic individuals, particularly immigrants, encounter significant obstacles, including language barriers, lack of health insurance, and fear of legal consequences for undocumented individuals (Tyson & Hugo Lopez, 2023, October 30). Studies show that Hispanics have the highest uninsured rates of any racial or ethnic group in the U.S., which severely limits their ability to access essential healthcare services, such as contraception, prenatal care, and abortion (ASPE, 2021; Planned Parenthood Action Fund, n.d.). These barriers are exacerbated by restrictive state laws that further disproportionately affect low-income Hispanic women, who already face economic challenges in affording care (Planned Parenthood of Greater New York, 2024, October 3).

Cultural factors also significantly shape reproductive health experiences in Hispanic communities. Traditional gender roles, family expectations, and religious beliefs shape attitudes toward contraception, abortion, and family planning (Planned

Parenthood of Greater New York, 2024, October 3; Planned Parenthood Action Fund, n.d.). In many Hispanic cultures, there is a strong emphasis on family and motherhood, which can pressure women to prioritize childbearing over personal health, education, or career goals. These values can also contribute to stigmatization of contraceptive use or seeking abortion services, where individuals sometimes avoid reproductive healthcare due to fear of disapproval from their families or communities (Planned Parenthood of Greater New York, 2024, October 3; HealthStream, 2022, January 22).

The intersection of systemic racism and economic inequality further exacerbates the reproductive justice struggles of Hispanic communities. Discrimination within healthcare settings often contributes to substandard care, including higher rates of maternal mortality, inadequate prenatal care, and even coercive medical practices like forced sterilization (Tyson & Hugo Lopez, 2023, October 30; HealthStream, 2022, January 22). Hispanic women, especially those from low-income backgrounds, are often forced to make reproductive decisions in the context of financial instability, housing insecurity, and limited access to education– conditions that undermine their autonomy (Planned Parenthood Action Fund, n.d.; HealthStream, 2022, January 22).

In this landscape, the reproductive justice framework offers a critical lens to addressing the unique needs of Hispanic communities. It shifts the focus from individual reproductive choices to the broader societal conditions that shape those choices. Reproductive justice for Hispanic communities means dismantling systemic barriers, providing culturally responsive healthcare, and addressing the social and economic inequities that hinder their ability to make autonomous reproductive decisions (Planned Parenthood of Greater New York, 2024, October 3; HealthStream, 2022, January 22). Solutions lie not just in increasing healthcare access but also in creating supportive environments where economic stability is achievable and healthcare systems are equipped to provide culturally competent care. This holistic approach is essential for Hispanic communities to thrive and exercise full reproductive autonomy (Planned Parenthood Action Fund, n.d.; HealthStream, 2022, January 22).

II. THEORETICAL FRAMEWORK

A. Understanding Reproductive Justice in Social Work

Within the field of social work, incorporating reproductive justice allows for a more comprehensive approach to supporting clients, particularly when it comes to advocating for their reproductive rights and addressing systemic challenges. Social workers often encounter clients facing several obstacles related to their reproductive choices, such as healthcare access, economic limitations, and cultural constraints.

The application of a reproductive justice lens means addressing these barriers head-on. Advocating within healthcare systems and/or navigating legal challenges are just two examples of how social workers can proactively address these issues. This approach empowers clients to make fully informed reproductive decisions without facing undue influence of external biases of systemic obstacles (Gomez et al., 2021).

Reproductive justice in social work extends beyond individual practice to encompass community advocacy and policy reform. Social workers can amplify the voices of those who are often overlooked in policy discussions, ensuring that the intersections between reproductive rights and social determinants - such as housing, employment, and healthcare access - are addressed. By advocating for systemic changes, social workers contribute to creating environments where individuals have the resources needed to exercise reproductive autonomy (Beddoe, 2021).

Additionally, applying this approach in social work practice requires cultural sensitivity and an understanding of how various backgrounds influence reproductive decisions. Social workers must mitigate biases, both within themselves and within the systems they work in, a process that involves ongoing education and a commitment to understanding clients' unique cultural contexts (Beddoe, 2021; Gomez et al., 2021).

Key elements of reproductive justice in social work practice:

- Address systemic barriers such as limited healthcare access, economic inequities, and cultural restraints
- Advocate for clients within healthcare systems and navigate legal challenges to ensure equitable reproductive healthcare access.
- Amplify marginalized voices in policy discussions, particularly around social determinants like housing and employment.
- Commit to cultural sensitivity by recognizing and addressing biases in practice and systems.
- Foster environments that empower clients to make informed reproductive decisions free from systemic obstacles.

This layered approach highlights the multifaceted role of social workers in advancing reproductive justice and underscores the importance of both individual and systemic advocacy.

I. Intersectionality and Reproductive Justice

Intersectionality, a term created by civil rights advocate Kimberlé Crenshaw, is critical in the reproductive justice movement as it highlights how various forms of oppression – such as racism, sexism, classism, ableism, homophobia, and xenophobia – interact and shape the experiences of marginalized groups (Carbado, Crenshaw, Mays & Tomlinson, 2013). This concept reveals that focusing on a single point of identity, such as race or gender alone is insufficient to fully understand the experiences of marginalized individuals and groups.

With the development of the term 'intersectionality', the reproductive justice movement was founded because the mainstream reproductive rights movement did not fully address the unique challenges women of color experienced; thus, SisterSong was born (Ross & Solinger, 2017). They recognized that issues such as poverty, lack of healthcare access, and exposure to violence must be addressed alongside reproductive rights to achieve true justice (Ross & Solinger, 2017). For example, a low-income Black woman may experience barriers to healthcare access due to systemic racism in healthcare settings, economic constraints, and a lack of comprehensive services within her community. Additionally, a disabled person might face additional challenges related to the accessibility of services and cultural stigma around their reproductive autonomy. The reproductive justice framework consequently requires a holistic approach to understanding these overlapping identities and systemic barriers, highlighting the importance of the application and understanding of intersectionality.

At its core, reproductive justice goes beyond the right to access reproductive healthcare. It emphasizes the right to have children, the right to not have children, and the right to parent children in safe and supportive environments (Ross & Solinger, 2017). Intersectionality bolsters this framework by emphasizing how different individuals may face unique barriers to these rights based upon their overlapping identities. For example, the experiences of Black women seeking reproductive healthcare cannot be understood solely through the lens of gender or race, but through the combined effects of both, along with additional factors such as socioeconomic status. The identification and recognition of these intersections allows advocates and practitioners to develop more focused and comprehensive approaches to reproductive justice that address the full scope of oppression that individuals face.

In addition, intersectionality emphasizes the importance of addressing systemic structures of power that perpetuate inequality (Cho, Crenshaw & McCall, 2013). Reproductive justice cannot be achieved if these structures – such as racism, classism, sexism, and ableism – are not dismantled. For instance, policies that restrict access to contraception or abortion services disproportionately harm low-income women and women of color, who are already marginalized by economic inequality and racial discrimination. By utilizing an intersectional lens, reproductive justice advocates aim to challenge these systemic barriers and work toward a world where all individuals can access and exercise full control over their reproductive lives, free from discrimination and oppression.

B. Reproductive Justice and Hispanic Communities

Reproductive justice for Hispanic communities in the United States is shaped by a complex interplay of cultural, economic, and legal factors. These factors collectively create intersecting barriers that influence the reproductive autonomy and health outcomes of Hispanic individuals. Understanding these dynamics is essential for developing effective, culturally responsive solutions.

I. Cultural Context

Hispanic communities are often deeply influenced by values surrounding family, motherhood, and community (see Table 1). For example, *familismo*- the importance of family, loyalty, and support- can both empower and pressure individuals in their reproductive choices, which often prioritize familial expectations over personal desires or health needs (Kaelber, 2012). Traditional gender norms and religious beliefs shape attitudes towards contraception, abortion, and family planning, often leading to stigmatization and barriers to accessing reproductive health services (Batek, Leblanc, Alio, Stein, & McMahon, 2024). While these cultural factors remain resilient, younger generations are reinterpreting them, balancing traditional values with greater autonomy and modern reproductive practices. For instance, Mexican-American youth have reported integrating Catholic values with progressive views on contraception, reflecting this cultural evolution (Batek, et. al, 2024).

Table 1. Key cultural values and social work implications for reproductive justice by region

Country/ Region	Key Cultural Value	Impact on Reproductive Justice	Social Work Implications
Mexico	Familismo	Pressure to prioritize family needs	Engage family in reproductive discussions
Central America	Religious Conservatism	Limited access to contraception	Tailor advocacy to respect religious norms
Caribbean (e.g. Puerto Rico)	Legacy of Forced Sterilization	Distrust in healthcare systems	Build trust through community-based care

II. Economic Inequities

Hispanic communities have faced systemic inequalities that limit access to resources necessary for reproductive justice. Historical disparities in poverty, education, and employment continue to restrict access to comprehensive healthcare, including reproductive services (Sonubi, Flores, & Spalluto, 2022). Economic instability, often compounded by immigration status, further limits job opportunities and access to employer-based health insurance. For example, in rural areas of Guatemala, where economic resources are scarce, women report significant delays in accessing reproductive care due to lack of nearby facilities - a challenge mirrored in underserved Hispanic communities in the U.S. (Batek, et. al, 2024).

III. Legal Barriers

Hispanic individuals' reproductive rights have been historically shaped by exclusionary practices. Restrictive immigration laws in states like Texas and Florida limit access to healthcare for undocumented immigrants and curtail reproductive health services such as abortion. Specifically, Texas Senate Bill 8 (SB8), which effectively bans abortions as early as six weeks into pregnancy, has had a profound impact on Hispanic women, particularly those who are low-income or undocumented. Studies have shown that the fertility rate among Hispanic women increased significantly after the enactment of SB8, as these women face greater challenges in traveling out of state for abortion care or accessing other reproductive health services due to financial, transportation, and childcare barriers (Johnson, 2022, February 24; Klibanoff, 2024, January 26). Hispanic women between the ages of 25 and 44 experienced an 8% rise in fertility rates following the passage of SB8, reflecting the restricted access to abortion and contraception (Klibanoff, 2024, January 26).

Hispanic women, who already face systemic barriers such as language limitations, lack of insurance, and fear of deportation, now face greater difficulties accessing care under restrictive policies like SB8. (Klibanoff, 2024, January 26). These compounded barriers exacerbate the risk of unintended pregnancies and increase rates of maternal mortality, particularly among undocumented women (Bell, Stuart, & Gemmill, 2023). Additionally, there is a troubling legacy of coercive reproductive practices, such as forced sterilizations, disproportionately targeting low-income Hispanic women, particularly those who are non-English speaking (Batek, et. al, 2024). For example, in the 1970s, forced sterilizations were widely documented in Puerto Rico, where systemic racism and economic exploitation intersected to strip women of reproductive autonomy - a historical injustice with echoes in contemporary practices. Although legal advocacy and policy reforms have sought to address some of these injustices, many barriers remain, particularly in states with more restrictive laws (Sonubi, et. al, 2022).

IV. A Holistic Approach

Addressing these intersecting barriers requires a reproductive justice framework grounded in cultural, legal, and economic equity. This framework emphasizes not only the right to have children, not have children, and parent in safe environments, but also the dismantling of systemic inequities that restrict these rights. For Hispanic communities, this means ensuring access to affordable and culturally competent reproductive healthcare while addressing the broader SDOH. Advocacy must focus on expanding healthcare regardless of immigration status, protecting against coercive practices, and implementing culturally responsive educational campaigns tailored to diverse Hispanic subgroups.

Reproductive justice for Hispanic communities in the United States is an ongoing journey shaped by the evolving dynamics of culture, economy, and law. It requires a commitment to understanding and addressing the unique challenges faced by these communities, ensuring that all individuals can make informed and autonomous decisions about their reproductive lives (Sonubi, et. al, 2022).

III. INTEGRATION OF REPRODUCTIVE JUSTICE IN SOCIAL WORK EDUCATION

Given the complexities and systemic inequities faced by Hispanic communities in accessing reproductive justice, the integration of this framework into social work education and practice is both necessary and urgent. Social work, a discipline committed to social justice and the empowerment of marginalized populations, is uniquely positioned to advance reproductive justice through education, advocacy, and culturally competent practice (Gomez, et. al, 2020).

The integration of reproductive justice into social work education is essential for preparing future practitioners to address the multifaceted challenges faced by marginalized communities. By integrating reproductive justice into social work curriculum, students will be equipped with the knowledge and skills to advocate for the reproductive rights and well-being of Hispanic communities and other marginalized groups. By examining the intersections of race, class, gender, immigration status, and reproductive health, social work students can develop a deeper understanding of how systemic inequities shape reproductive outcomes and how they can intervene to promote justice (Gomez, et. al, 2020; Smith, 2017).

A. Current State of Social Work Education

Reproductive justice as an academic and educational framework has gained increasing visibility in social work, public health, and gender studies curricula across the United States since the overturning of Roe v. Wade in 2022. These curricula typically incorporate a range of interdisciplinary topics, including the historical and political development of reproductive rights, the intersection of race, class, and gender in reproductive health, and the advocacy efforts aimed at expanding access to reproductive healthcare (Gomez, et. al, 2020).

Existing curricula often cover key issues such as access to contraception, abortion, prenatal and maternal healthcare, and the right to raise children in safe and supportive environments, though many may not explicitly link these key issues to the overarching "reproductive justice" framework. Some programs may also integrate case studies and practical exercises that encourage students to consider how legal, healthcare, and policy systems shape reproductive experiences for different communities. Yet, critical attention must be given to how marginalized groups - especially Black and Indigenous women - have been disproportionately affected by reproductive injustices, including forced sterilizations, inadequate healthcare, and discriminatory legal practices (Smith, 2017). Many curricula also prioritize advocacy skills, which prepare students to engage in policy work and community-organizing to address inequities. Through experiential learning, such as internships and field placements, students gain practical insights into how reproductive justice is applied in real-world settings, working with organizations that advocate for the reproductive rights and needs of diverse populations (Smith, 2017).

While the existing curricula offer a solid foundation to issues related to reproductive justice, there are notable gaps in how they effectively inform and address the specific needs and experiences related to reproductive justice, especially for marginalized groups, like Hispanic communities.

One of the most significant gaps is the lack of culturally responsive content that reflects the unique barriers marginalized groups, like Hispanic individuals, face in accessing reproductive healthcare. Curricula often focus on reproductive rights as it pertains to low-income women, with less emphasis on the intersecting challenges that women of color, particularly Hispanic women encounter, such as immigration status, language barriers, and cultural stigmas surrounding reproductive health (Smith, 2017). For example, many curricula do not sufficiently cover how immigration policies impact access to reproductive healthcare for undocumented Hispanic individuals, who often face fear of deportation when seeking services. Additionally, the lack of Spanish-language materials and bilingual education within reproductive healthcare settings is rarely explored in depth, despite being a critical barrier for many Hispanic women (Wright, Bird, & Frost, 2015). These challenges are compounded by economic instability and legal restrictions that disproportion-ately affect low-income and immigrant Hispanic women, who may lack access to healthcare insurance or be subject to state-level abortion restrictions.

Cultural factors, such as the importance of familismo and the role of religion in shaping reproductive decisions, are often underrepresented in the curricula as well. While existing programs may touch on cultural influences in reproductive health, they do not always delve deeply into how these values intersect with reproductive autonomy for Hispanic women. For instance, the pressure to prioritize childbear-ing and family over personal reproductive choices is a significant issue that needs more exploration, as it directly influences decision-making around contraception, abortion, and maternal health (Garcia, 2015, May 24; Poehling, et. al, 2023). To better serve Hispanic communities, reproductive justice curricula should include content that addresses the specific cultural, legal, and economic barriers they face. This could include case studies focused on Hispanic populations, the inclusion of bilingual materials, and/or discussions on immigration policy's impact on reproduc-tive healthcare access (Garcia, 2015, May 24). Additionally, more attention should be given to the intersection of cultural and legal issues, such as how traditional gender roles and religious beliefs may shape attitudes toward reproductive health in hispanic communities.

Improving the inclusivity of reproductive justice curricula will better equip students to understand the complex realities of Hispanic communities and empower them to advocate effectively for policies and practices that promote equitable reproductive healthcare access for all (Poehling, et. al, 2023).

B. Strategies for Integration

Incorporating reproductive justice into core social work courses requires a de-liberate approach that integrates reproductive justice principles into the foundation of social work education.

I. Embedded theory into existing curricula

One method is to embed reproductive justice throughout the social work cur-riculum, rather than treating it as a standalone topic. For example, in courses like Human Behavior and the Social Environment, instructors can introduce reproduc-tive justice as a framework for understanding how reproductive health intersects with race, gender, class, and sexuality, influencing individuals' life trajectories and overall well-being (Smith, 2017). Educators can include case studies and reflective assignments to help students explore how systemic barriers and cultural factors influence reproductive outcomes, particularly within marginalized communities. This allows students to explore how social systems shape reproductive experiences.

Policy courses are another critical area where reproductive justice can be embedded. In these courses, students can analyze current reproductive health policies, including access to contraception, abortion, and maternity care, through a reproductive justice lens. Assignments might include researching the effects of state or federal reproductive health legislation on marginalized populations, such as Hispanic women or immigrants, and designing policy reform proposals aimed at addressing these disparities. For example, students could be tasked with creating policy briefs or advocacy plans to address disparities affecting Hispanic women, immigrants, and low-income families (Gomez, et. al, 2020; Younes, et. al, 2021). Additionally, students can be taught to assess how policies disproportionately affect specific groups, encouraging them to advocate for equity and justice (Younes, et. al, 2021).

Practice-based courses, such as those on clinical social work or social work with families, can incorporate reproductive justice by teaching students how to navigate the reproductive healthcare system on behalf of their clients. Role-playing exercises, simulations, and group activities can help students develop practical skills such as advocating for clients within healthcare systems, addressing legal and financial barriers, and providing culturally competent support. Students can engage in role-playing exercises or simulations to advocate for clients facing reproductive health barriers. For instance, students could participate in a simulation where they assist a client navigating language barriers in accessing reproductive healthcare or support a family navigating prenatal care amidst financial challenges. These exercises build both empathy and competence in addressing client needs with a reproductive justice framework (Garcia et. al, 2022). These exercises help students develop practical skills, such as providing culturally competent support, navigating complex healthcare systems, and addressing legal or financial barriers to access (UB School of Social Work, n.d.).

II. Practicum-based Learning

Practicum placements should also reflect reproductive justice priorities by offering student opportunities to work in organizations that advocate for reproductive rights, healthcare access, or social justice for women and marginalized groups. For example, placements at reproductive health clinics or immigrant advocacy organizations can allow students to apply classroom knowledge to real-world contexts. Students might assist in delivering educational workshops on reproductive health or engage in policy advocacy efforts aimed at expanding healthcare access for underserved populations. Integrating reproductive justice into these experiences allows students to apply theoretical knowledge to real-world scenarios, preparing them to address reproductive justice challenges with both competence and compassion (Smith, 2017).

III. Interdisciplinary Approaches

To enrich social work education on reproductive justice, it is essential to adopt interdisciplinary approaches and build partnerships with other fields. Social work is inherently interdisciplinary, and leveraging collaborations with disciplines like public health, law, sociology, and women's studies can deepen students' understanding of reproductive justice (Gomez, et. al, 2020).

Collaborations with public health programs could include joint courses or seminars that explore the intersection of SDOH and reproductive health outcomes. Public health professionals could offer guest lectures or workshops on strategies for addressing health disparities, providing students with insights that complement social work's focus on systemic advocacy (Fores, 2018). Partnering with public health programs, for example, would allow social work students to learn about the public health implications of reproductive justice. Courses or joint seminars could explore how SDOH, like access to healthcare, housing, and education, intersect with reproductive outcomes. Public health professionals could offer insights into strategies for addressing health disparities and improving access to reproductive services, complementing social work's focus on advocacy and systemic change (Beddoe, 2022). Additionally, students could participate in projects that map these intersections and propose interventions combining public health and social work principles.

Collaboration with legal studies programs could help students understand the legal landscape of reproductive justice, including reproductive rights litigation, immigration law, and healthcare access regulations. Joint coursework or guest lectures by legal experts could provide students with a deeper understanding of the legal barriers many communities face when seeking reproductive healthcare. Additionally, social work students can partner with law students in advocacy projects to enable them to learn how to work together to navigate and challenge systemic barriers through policy advocacy or direct services (Gomez, et. al, 2020). Sociology and gender studies programs can provide critical perspectives on the cultural and societal factors that shape reproductive justice.

Through interdisciplinary partnerships, students can gain a richer understanding of how social norms, cultural values, and institutionalized inequality influence reproductive choices and outcomes (Beddoe, 2022). Collaborative research projects could explore how reproductive injustice disproportionately affects communities of color, emphasizing actionable solutions informed by evidence-based research.

IV. Community-based Learning

Community partnerships are another vital method of enriching reproductive justice education. Social work programs can collaborate with community-based organizations that serve marginalized populations, such as reproductive health clinics, immigrant rights groups, or advocacy organizations for women of color. For example, students could work with community organizations to develop educational workshops tailored to the unique needs of Hispanic women or assist in grassroots advocacy campaigns aimed at expanding access to reproductive healthcare. These partnerships can provide students with real-world experiences and foster a deeper connection between academic learning and community needs (Beddoe, 2022). By working directly with these organizations, students can witness firsthand how reproductive justice issues manifest in different communities and learn how to advocate for systemic change that is informed by the voices and experiences of those affected.

Integrating reproductive justice into social work education through a holistic integration of interdisciplinary approaches, experiential learning, and community partnerships not only enhances students' learning experiences but also equips them with practical tools to address systemic inequalities. By understanding the broader social, legal, and health systems that influence reproductive outcomes, students will work toward creating a more just and equitable society (Smith, 2017; Wright, et. al, 2015). This comprehensive approach ensures that social workers graduate with the skills and perspectives necessary to advance reproductive justice in both direct practice and systemic advocacy.

IV. IMPACT ON SOCIAL WORK PRACTICE

The reproductive justice framework and social work profession are incredibly interconnected, as both fields are dedicated to advancing human rights and equity. Through the application of a reproductive justice framework in social work practice, practitioners can address the complex, overlapping factors that shape clients' reproductive health experiences, particularly for marginalized populations, like Hispanic communities. As illustrated in Table 2: Micro, Mezzo, and Macro Social Work Levels, this framework can be applied across different levels of practice to create meaningful change. Within the micro, mezzo, and macro-levels, social workers can work towards greater change at the individual, group, and community-based levels (University of Southern California, 2018). At the micro level, practitioners may focus on providing one-on-one counseling or advocacy for clients navigating healthcare systems. At the mezzo level, efforts can include facilitating group therapy or collaborating with community organizations to address collective barriers. Meanwhile, at the macro level, social workers can engage in systemic advocacy to reform policies that impact reproductive health. Social workers are called to advocate for the reproductive rights of their clients and communities, recognizing that barriers such as healthcare access, socioeconomic limitations, and cultural biases often intersect to impact reproductive autonomy (Gomez et al., 2021). This framework aligns with social work's greater mission of social justice, making it crucial to address the unique needs of vulnerable groups through all levels of social work practice.

Table 2. Micro, mezzo, and macro social work levels

Level	Focus	Examples	Goals
Micro	Individual clients or small groups (e.g., families)	One-to-one counseling, crisis intervention, case management	Address personal and immediate needs, enhance individual and well-being
Mezzo	Small to medium-sized groups, organizations, or communities	Group therapy, community support groups, organizational collaboration	Strengthen support systems and improve group or organizational outcomes
Macro	Large systems, such as policies, laws, and societal structures	Policy advocacy, legislative reform, systemic research	Create systemic change to address widespread social issues and inequities

A. Micro Level: Individual Practice

At the micro level of social work practice, social workers engage directly with clients to address the personal and systemic barriers they experience. Applying a reproductive justice framework to client interactions is essential for ensuring that marginalized individuals can make informed, autonomous decisions about their reproductive health and wellbeing. With the goal of empowering clients and assisting them to navigate systems that often marginalize them, social workers must provide culturally competent, trauma-informed care while advocating for policies and services that address the complex variety of barriers that clients experience.

The provision of culturally competent care is an integral component of micro-level social work, particularly when working with Hispanic communities, who often face language barriers, immigration concerns, and traditional gender norms that can stigmatize the utilization of reproductive healthcare services, such as contraception or abortion services (Beddoe, 2022). To provide effective client care, social workers must engage in culturally responsive practices that are respectful of clients' backgrounds, while also delivering necessary services, resources, and support. For example, integrating bilingual services, utilizing culturally appropriate educational materials, and collaborating with community health workers can help work to reduce fear and mistrust, which often accompany interactions with healthcare systems (Garcia et al., 2022). Additionally, a trauma-informed approach is equally important, as many Hispanic individuals may have experienced traumas in their lives stemming from discrimination, immigration challenges, or negative healthcare interactions. Mental health challenges such as anxiety, depression, and trauma often intersect with reproductive health experiences, creating additional barriers to care. Addressing these issues within a reproductive justice framework requires social workers to integrate mental health support into their practice. This may include recognizing and validating the emotional toll of navigating systemic barriers and providing psychoeducation on coping strategies to empower clients. A trauma-informed approach to healthcare or direct-service involves recognizing the presence and effects of trauma and understanding how it influences individuals across different environments, services, and groups (Substance Abuse and Mental Health Services Administration, 2014). Social workers can create an environment where clients feel safe discussing sensitive issues, free from judgment. This involves validating their experiences, respecting their decisions, and ensuring clients are fully informed of their rights to access healthcare, which includes reproductive care. (Substance Abuse and Mental Health Services Administration, 2014). Additionally, culturally sensitive trauma-informed strategies, such as incorporating mindfulness exercises tailored to a client's cultural background or leveraging community-based support networks, can reduce the stigma surrounding mental health while improving engagement with reproductive healthcare services. The utilization of trauma-informed and culturally responsive services allows social workers to create safe and supportive environments while providing effective client care.

Following the discussion of the importance of cultural competence and trauma-informed care, building trust between clients and social workers or other healthcare providers is essential. Many individuals experience distrust within the healthcare system, especially immigrant populations (Planned Parenthood of Greater New York, 2024, October 3). Social workers have the ability to work as facilitators, advocating for their clients during medical appointments and working to ensure that they receive respectful and non-biased care. This includes assisting clients to communicate their needs effectively, translating medical information when necessary, and ensuring that their reproductive choices are supported without external pressures (Garcia et al., 2022). Advocacy in this regard is not only about facilitating access to care, but it also focuses on upholding the client's dignity and autonomy throughout their entire healthcare experience.

Social workers can act as advocates, helping clients navigate these systems and connecting them with accessible healthcare services. Social workers can also aid clients in enrolling in Medicaid or other health insurance options if eligible, ensuring access to necessary reproductive healthcare and other services (Gomez et al., 2021). Equally as important as providing high-quality services to marginalized individuals is challenging and transforming the societal structures that contribute to their marginalization (National Association of Social Workers, 2015). The advocacy role of social workers also expands to advocating for culturally competent practices within healthcare institutions, such as ensuring the availability of interpreters and developing policies that address discrimination against Hispanic clients and communities. Social workers play a key role in both delivering direct services and driving systemic changes that promote equitable healthcare access for Hispanic populations.

Another important strategy within micro-level practice is providing education tailored to the unique needs of Hispanic clients and communities. Many individuals in this population may have limited access to comprehensive reproductive health education. Therefore, the educational efforts of social workers should include topics such as contraception, family planning, prenatal care, and reproductive rights, while considering the cultural and religious factors that shape clients' decision-making processes (Poehling et al., 2023). By presenting this information in a way that is both accessible and culturally relevant, social workers can empower Hispanic clients to make informed reproductive decisions that align with their personal and cultural values. Offering culturally responsive education helps bridge gaps in knowledge and supports clients in exercising their reproductive autonomy and rights (Beddoe, 2022).

Micro-level social work practice plays a crucial role in addressing the multifaceted barriers that Hispanic individuals face in accessing reproductive healthcare. By applying a reproductive justice framework, social workers not only provide direct services, but also empower their clients to make autonomous decisions about their reproductive health. Through culturally competent, trauma-informed care, they ensure that services are responsive to the unique cultural, linguistic, and experiential needs of their clients. Additionally, social workers act as advocates, both in healthcare settings and at the policy level, working to eliminate systemic barriers such as language obstacles, lack of insurance, and discriminatory practices. Integrating mental health support into reproductive justice practice strengthens the role of social workers in addressing the psychological and emotional impacts of systemic oppression, fostering both reproductive and overall well-being. This combination of direct support and systemic advocacy is essential for promoting equitable healthcare access and improving reproductive autonomy for marginalized populations.

B. Mezzo Level: Community and Organizational Practice

Social workers play a pivotal role in community-based initiatives, particularly in advocating for reproductive justice in Hispanic communities. Social workers are uniquely positioned to influence local organizations and policies that can transform how these communities access reproductive healthcare, education, and support services (Ayon, 2014). An example of how social workers can support Hispanic communities through a reproductive justice lens is provided as a case study in Table 3.

Table 3. Case study of Promotores de Salud

Background: Latina women in various U.S. communities often face significant barriers to accessing reproductive health services, including language obstacles, cultural stigmas, and limited healthcare availability. To bridge these gaps, Planned Parenthood affiliates implemented the *Promotores de Salud* program, modeled after Mexican and Central American peer education initiatives (Planned Parenthood, n.d.).
Intervention: The program trains local community leaders, known as *promotores*, to serve as health educators within their communities. Key components include:
   ● **Bilingual Education:***Promotores* provide reproductive health information in both Spanish and English, ensuring accessibility for non-English-speaking individuals.
   ● **Community Engagement:** Education sessions are conducted in familiar settings such as homes, churches, and community centers, fostering trust and open dialogue.
   ● **Cultural Relevance:** The program incorporates culturally sensitive materials and discussions that resonate with the values and experiences of the Latina community.
Outcomes: The *Promotores de Salud* program has led to:
   ● **Increased Knowledge:** Participants report a better understanding of reproductive health topics, including contraception and sexually transmitted infections.
   ● **Improved Access:** By building trust and reducing stigma, the program encourages women to seek necessary healthcare services.
   ● **Community Empowerment:** Training community members as educators fosters leadership and empowers individuals to advocate for their health rights.
Implications for Social Work Practice: This case study exemplifies how community-based, culturally tailored interventions can effectively address reproductive health disparities. Social workers can adopt similar models to engage marginalized communities, ensuring that interventions are both accessible and relevant to the populations served.

Social workers collaborate with Community Health Workers (CHWs) to address barriers that Hispanic communities face in accessing reproductive healthcare. These collaborations often focus on the delivery of culturally and linguistically appropriate reproductive health services. CHWs serve as trusted partners in the community and, with the support of social workers, they can advocate for reproductive justice by promoting access to contraception, prenatal care, and safe reproductive health services (Garcia, Sprager, Jimenez, 2022, December 5).

Social workers participate in community organizing to promote reproductive justice by working directly with community-based organizations that focus on reproductive health. With this participation, social workers help elevate the voices of Hispanic women and other marginalized groups in local policy making. These partnerships enable social workers to advocate for systemic changes that improve the availability of reproductive services, reduce healthcare disparities, and empower individuals to make informed reproductive choices (Garcia, et. al, 2022, December 5).

C. Macro Level: Policy and Advocacy

Reproductive justice has far-reaching implications for social policies, as it highlights the ways in which access to healthcare, economic stability, education, housing, and legal protections intersect to influence an individual's ability to make informed and autonomous reproductive choices. This concept challenges policymakers to address social determinants of health and equity, advocating for systemic changes that extend beyond healthcare access to tackle the broader inequalities disproportionately impacting marginalized communities (Gomez, et. al, 2020). As outlined in Table 4: Practical Advocacy Strategies, addressing these intersecting barriers requires targeted efforts such as advocating for Medicaid expansion to mitigate economic instability or ensuring language accessibility to overcome cultural and linguistic obstacles.

Social policies that address reproductive justice must ensure that all individuals have the right to have children, not have children, and raise their families in safe and supportive environments. Achieving this requires access to affordable healthcare - including contraception, abortion, and prenatal care - and policies that provide economic security, protect against discrimination, and create safe, stable communities. For example, paid family leave, affordable childcare, living wages, and housing protections are all essential components of a reproductive justice framework, as they directly impact individuals' capacity to raise children without facing undue financial or social strain (Smith, 2017; Starrs, et. al, 2018). Table 4 further illustrates how culturally sensitive education and tailored workshops can help combat the stigma surrounding reproductive health in Hispanic communities, ensuring interventions resonate with community values.

Table 4. Practical advocacy strategies

Barrier	Advocacy Strategy	Example Application
Language Barriers	Advocate for bilingual healthcare staff	Partner with clinics for translator training
Economic Instability	Push for Medicaid expansion	Lead community campaigns for state reforms
Cultural Stigma	Promote culturally sensitive education	Develop workshops tailored to community needs

In Hispanic communities, these challenges are compounded by systemic barriers such as language obstacles, precarious immigration statuses, and a lack of culturally competent healthcare services. Immigration policies often exacerbate these inequities, as undocumented individuals may avoid seeking healthcare due to fear of deportation, and those with temporary legal status frequently lack access to essential social services (Arguedas-Ramirez & Wenner, 2023). Moreover, restrictive abortion laws, insufficient healthcare infrastructure in low-income areas, and limited insurance coverage further entrench disparities, making reproductive justice inaccessible for many Hispanic individuals (Gomez, et. al, 2020). Figure 1: Policy Impacts on Reproductive Justice highlights these barriers to equitable access of reproductive services.

Social policies that prioritize reproductive justice must address these intersecting barriers to ensure that Hispanic communities can fully exercise their reproductive rights. Grounded in a commitment to social justice, social workers are uniquely equipped to tackle these systemic issues and advocate for comprehensive reforms tailored to the needs of vulnerable populations (Gomez, et. al, 2020; Smith, 2017). In the context of reproductive justice, social workers are pivotal in pushing for policies that address the root causes of health disparities and the economic and social inequalities that impact Hispanic communities. They can advocate for Medicaid expansion to guarantee access to reproductive health services for low-income Hispanic individuals, ensuring equitable healthcare regardless of economic constraints (Arguedas-Ramirez & Wenner, 2023). Additionally, social workers can lead efforts to reform immigration policies that deny healthcare access to undocumented individuals, working to eliminate immigration status as a barrier to care.

Furthermore, social workers are essential in addressing the cultural and systemic barriers within reproductive healthcare systems. By collaborating with Hispanic community leaders, healthcare providers, and policymakers, social workers can promote culturally responsive healthcare systems that respect and reflect the value of their clients (Gomez, et. al, 2020). This includes advocating for comprehensive sex education that is inclusive of Hispanic cultural values, as well as pushing for healthcare practices that actively address the discrimination and bias that often result in substandard care for Hispanic women. Social workers can also engage in policy advocacy by drafting legislation, testifying at hearings, and leading community-based campaigns that prioritize the needs and voices of those most affected by reproductive injustice (Reproductive Health, 2015). For Hispanic communities, this advocacy includes ensuring language accessibility in healthcare settings, expanding healthcare coverage regardless of immigration status, and tackling socioeconomic challenges such as affordable housing and fair wages.

Social workers' direct experiences working with marginalized populations, combined with their commitment to social justice, equips them to push for the systemic reforms necessary to ensure that all individuals- particularly those from Hispanic communities- can exercise their reproductive rights and live in environments that support their families and well-being (Smith, 2017; Arguedas-Ramirez & Wenner, 2023). By addressing broader SDOH and advocating for equitable policies, social workers play a central role in advancing reproductive justice and fostering a more just society.

V. CHALLENGES AND BARRIERS

In an effort to integrate the reproductive justice framework into social work education and practice, particularly with Hispanic communities, a multitude of challenges and barriers emerge. These obstacles not only limit access to reproductive healthcare, but also exacerbate existing inequalities in healthcare, education, and social services. These barriers are multifaceted, encompassing institutional and structural challenges as well as cultural and societal factors. Hispanic individuals often experience unique barriers due to systemic inequalities tied to immigration status, language proficiency, and economic disparities, which make accessing reproductive health services difficult (Gomez et al., 2021). To create a more equitable framework for reproductive justice that empowers Hispanic communities, social workers must recognize and address this variety of challenges. Through the implementation of culturally competent strategies and the advocacy of systemic change, social workers can overcome these barriers and work towards a holistic practice that ensures that Hispanic communities can exercise their reproductive rights fully and equitably.

A. Institutional and Structural Barriers

There are challenges rooted in the broader structures of higher education, healthcare, social services, and policy frameworks, all of which shape how reproductive justice is understood and applied in social work contexts. One of the primary challenges is the traditional focus of social work education on clinical practice and individual-level interventions. This focus can limit the scope of the application of the reproductive justice framework. Many social work curricula tend to prioritize direct practice skills, leaving limited space for in-depth exploration of macro-level issues like systemic inequalities, policy reform, or the social determinants of health that reproductive justice revolves around (Younes, Goldblatt Hyatt, Witt, & Franklin, 2021). As a result, students may not fully grasp the broader social justice implications of reproductive justice or be equipped with the tools needed to address them in their future practice. Another challenge lies in the lack of interdisciplinary collaboration within social work education. Reproductive justice intersects with many fields, including public health, law, sociology, and women's studies. However, social work programs often operate in silos, making it difficult to fully integrate the interdisciplinary nature of reproductive justice into the curriculum. Without these connections, students may not receive comprehensive training on how legal policies, healthcare disparities, or social determinants of health impact reproductive justice (Poehling, et. al, 2023). This limits their ability to address reproductive issues holistically in their practice.

Social work programs often face external pressures that make it difficult to incorporate a comprehensive reproductive justice curriculum. These pressures may include accreditation requirements, limited resources, and a focus on meeting specific competencies that are not directly aligned with reproductive justice principles (Younes, et. al, 2021). Programs may feel constrained by these requirements, leaving little room to incorporate newer frameworks or address topics that may be considered politically or culturally sensitive, such as abortion, contraception, and LGBTQ+ reproductive health. This reluctance can result in a lack of critical engagement with the full spectrum of reproductive justice issues (Younes, et. al, 2021). In practice, social workers also face systemic challenges that hinder the integration of reproductive justice. One of these systemic challenges is the underfunding and overburdening of social service agencies, which often struggle to meet the basic needs of their clients. With limited time and resources, social workers may find it difficult to address the broader reproductive justice issues their clients face, such as economic insecurity, housing instability, or immigration-related barriers to healthcare. The structural constraints of the systems that social workers operate within often limit their ability to address the root cause of reproductive injustice (Younes, et. al, 2021).

Furthermore, many social workers encounter institutional policies and healthcare systems that do not prioritize or even recognize reproductive justice as a key issue. Healthcare systems, for example, may not offer comprehensive reproductive healthcare, particularly for marginalized communities, leaving social workers to navigate fragmented services and policies that are not designed to support holistic reproductive health (Beddoe, 2022; Poehling, et. al, 2023). For Hispanic communities, this is especially problematic, as cultural and language barriers, restrictive immigration policies, and a lack of culturally competent healthcare services can prevent access to comprehensive reproductive healthcare (Beddoe, 2022). Social workers, bound by the limitations of these systems, often struggle to advocate effectively for their clients within such rigid structures (Poehling, et. al, 2023). Reproductive justice encompasses a wide range of issues, including abortion access, LGBTQ+ reproductive rights, and the right to parent in a safe and supportive environment-topics that are often politically divisive. In conservative or politically polarized environments, social workers and educators may face resistance when trying to address these topics, either from within their institutions or from the communities they serve. This resistance can create a climate in which social workers are hesitant to fully engage with reproductive justice, limiting the scope of their practice and advocacy (Younes, et. al, 2021; Beddoe, 2022).

Lastly, the lack of diverse representation in both social work education and leadership positions within the profession can be a barrier to fully integrating reproductive justice. The reproductive justice movement is rooted in the experiences of women of color, particularly Black and Indigenous women, who have historically been marginalized in healthcare and social services (Gomez, et. al, 2020; Beddoe, 2022). However, social work education and leadership remain disproportionately white and middle class, which can lead to gaps in understanding or prioritizing the needs of communities most impacted by reproductive injustice, such as Hispanic and immigrant populations (Poehling, et. al, 2023; Younes, et. al, 2021).

Overcoming these systemic challenges requires a concerted effort to reshape social work education and practice to more fully integrate reproductive justice. This includes expanding curricula to address the macro-level issues at the heart of reproductive justice, fostering interdisciplinary collaboration, advocating for policy changes that prioritize reproductive health and rights, and ensuring that the profession reflects the diversity of the communities it serves (Beddoe, 2022; Poehling, et. al, 2023). By addressing these barriers, social work can become a more powerful force for advancing reproductive justice in both education and practice (Younes, et. al, 2021).

B. Cultural and Societal Barriers

When exploring barriers and challenges that prevent Hispanic individuals and communities from accessing reproductive justice, it is imperative to thoroughly explore cultural and societal barriers. These types of barriers often stem from traditional cultural norms, gender roles, and religious beliefs that shape individuals' perceptions of reproductive health and autonomy. Within many Hispanic families, motherhood is viewed as a central role for women, and there is societal pressure to adhere to large family structures (Batek et al., 2024). This can lead to the stigmatization of contraception and abortion, as seeking such services may be perceived as deviating from traditional values (Garcia et al., 2022). As a result, many Hispanic women may experience internalized feelings of guilt, shame, or fear of judgment when seeking reproductive healthcare services, significantly limiting their ability to make autonomous reproductive health decisions (Beddoe, 2022).

Another significant cultural factor that is present within many Hispanic communities is religion, more specifically Catholicism, that plays a powerful role in shaping beliefs surrounding contraception and abortion access. Catholic doctrine generally discourages the utilization of contraception and abortion, creating a conflict between individuals' healthcare needs and their religious upbringing and belief systems (Arguedas-Ramirez & Wenner, 2023). This tension can prevent individuals from accessing the care that they need, as they may fear disapproval from family members, social supports, or their religious community. It is important for social workers to acknowledge this cultural complexity when working with Hispanic clients, helping them navigate these internal conflicts while providing non-judgmental support that honors both their healthcare needs and their cultural identities (Ross & Solinger, 2017).

Additionally, societal stigma surrounding reproductive health, particularly abortion services, can result in feelings of isolation or fear in Hispanic individuals seeking reproductive healthcare. This can often be amplified by confidentiality concerns, particularly for undocumented individuals who fear deportation or legal repercussions. Research studies indicate that these concerns create substantial barriers for Hispanic individuals, often leading them to avoid seeking reproductive healthcare entirely (Gomez et al., 2021). In addition, many Hispanic individuals live in low-income areas where healthcare infrastructure is lacking, making access to reproductive services even more challenging.

To address these cultural and societal barriers effectively, social workers must utilize culturally responsive approaches that respect the values and experiences of Hispanic clients. Through the engagement in open, non-judgmental, and trauma-informed conversations about reproductive health, clients can feel empowered to make informed decisions regarding their reproductive health and autonomy. Additionally, it is essential for social workers to advocate for culturally appropriate reproductive health services, including those delivered in the client's preferred language and sensitive to their cultural and religious background (National Association of Social Workers, 2021). By fostering trust and building strong community relationships, social workers can help overcome the societal pressures that hinder access to care, while empowering clients to navigate complex cultural landscapes in making their reproductive choices (Beddoe, 2022).

C. Strategies to Overcome Challenges

After identifying the key barriers that prevent Hispanic communities from accessing reproductive justice - such as limited healthcare access, cultural stigma, language barriers, and restrictive immigration policies - it's crucial to explore effective strategies and solutions to address these challenges. Social workers, in collaboration with community leaders and policymakers, play a pivotal role in implementing initiatives that promote equity, reproductive autonomy, and justice in healthcare access.

One of the most significant steps towards achieving reproductive justice for Hispanic communities is expanding access to affordable and comprehensive healthcare. Advocating for Medicaid expansion to include underserved and undocumented populations is critical. This policy change would directly improve access to contraception, abortion, and prenatal care for low-income and Hispanic women, particularly in states that have not yet adopted Medicaid expansion (Robert Wood Johnson Foundation, 2024, June 1). Social workers can lead state and local advocacy campaigns, engaging stakeholders to highlight the disparities caused by restricted Medicaid access.

Expanding and supporting community health centers is another key strategy. These centers should provide bilingual reproductive healthcare services tailored to the specific needs of Hispanic communities, including culturally competent family planning and prenatal care. Providing culturally competent care is essential to overcoming cultural stigma and language barriers. Social workers can advocate for mandatory, ongoing training for healthcare providers to understand the unique cultural and religious dynamics shaping reproductive decisions in Hispanic communities. Additionally, healthcare systems must ensure that bilingual healthcare providers and translators are readily available to bridge language gaps, making healthcare services more inclusive and accessible. Community-based organizations, often supported by social workers, are instrumental in bridging the gap between healthcare systems and Hispanic communities. For example, such organizations can host reproductive health workshops in Spanish, tailored to the cultural values of the community, to educate individuals about their reproductive rights. These workshops can demystify stigmatized topics like contraception and abortion in ways that are respectful and engaging.

By focusing on these strategies, social workers and community advocates can significantly reduce the barriers Hispanic communities face in accessing reproductive justice. Ensuring culturally responsive care, expanding healthcare access, and pushing policy reforms are essential steps to empowering Hispanic communities and advancing reproductive equity. Through these efforts, social workers can foster trust and collaboration with Hispanic communities, enabling sustainable and meaningful progress in reproductive justice.

VI. OPPORTUNITIES AND FUTURE DIRECTIONS

As the integration of reproductive justice into social work education and practice continues to evolve, several key opportunities and future directions are emerging that will further enhance the profession's ability to address systemic inequalities and promote reproductive autonomy. These opportunities lie in the advancement of social work education, expanding practice frameworks, and strengthening advocacy and policy efforts. Together, these elements create a foundation for the future of social work to fully embrace reproductive justice, ensuring that social workers are equipped to address the multifaceted challenges experienced by marginalized communities, particularly Hispanic populations.

By embedding reproductive justice as a core component of social work curricula, students will be prepared to tackle the complex, intersectional barriers to reproductive health that disproportionality affects marginalized communities. Strengthening advocacy and policy initiatives will enable social workers to drive systemic reforms that ensure equitable access to healthcare with a focus on both legislative advocacy and community-based mobilization. These trends represent a transformative future for social work where reproductive justice is central to the profession's mission of advancing human rights and social equity (Poehling et al., 2023; Gomez et al., 2020).

A. Advancing Social Work Education

The future of integrating reproductive justice into social work education is poised to evolve through several key trends and innovations that will enhance the profession's capacity to address the intersectional and systemic challenges that individuals face regarding reproductive autonomy and health. As the field continues to embrace social justice frameworks, innovative approaches in education are likely to transform how social work students learn about and engage with reproductive justice (Gomez, et. al, 2020).

One major trend is the increasing use of technology to facilitate learning and expand access to reproductive justice education. Online courses, virtual simulations, and digital case studies are being developed to teach students about reproductive justice in real-world contexts, especially as social work programs move toward hybrid and online learning models. These technological tools allow for more dynamic and interactive learning experiences, enabling students to engage with complex issues like healthcare access, policy advocacy, and client-centered care in a flexible, accessible format. Virtual reality and artificial intelligence are emerging as potential tools that could simulate reproductive justice scenarios, such as navigating healthcare systems with limited resources, helping students better understand the systemic barriers faced by marginalized communities (Poehling, et. al, 2023).

Another emerging trend is the focus on interdisciplinary collaboration in social work education. As reproductive justice is inherently intersectional, it requires insights from multiple fields. Many social work programs are partnering with other academic departments to offer joint degrees or collaborative coursework, providing students with a broader, more comprehensive understanding of reproductive justice (Poehling, et. al, 2023). For example, programs may offer dual degrees in social work and public health, allowing students to gain expertise in both social work practice and the public health policies that directly impact reproductive health outcomes. This interdisciplinary approach not only broadens students' knowledge but also equips them to engage in more holistic advocacy and intervention strategies in their practice (Younes, et. al, 2021).

Experiential learning is also becoming a central component of how reproductive justice is integrated into social work education. Field placements and internships are evolving to include more opportunities for students to work with organizations that focus on reproductive health, rights, and justice. These placements can immerse students in reproductive justice work, exposing them to the challenges and opportunities of advocating for marginalized populations, including Hispanic and immigrant communities, who often face systemic barriers to reproductive healthcare (Poehling, et. al, 2023). This trend reflects a growing recognition that classroom learning must be accompanied by hands-on experience to prepare students for the complexities of reproductive justice work in real-world settings.

Another innovation involves the development of specialized curricula that center reproductive justice as a core component of social work education, rather than treating it as an elective or supplemental topic. Programs are beginning to embed reproductive justice principles into foundational courses, such as social policy, human behavior, and ethics, ensuring that students view reproductive justice not as a niche issue but as integral to social work practice. These curricula emphasize the systemic nature of reproductive injustice and equip students with the skills needed to advocate for policy changes that address these inequities (Poehling, et. al, 2023). By framing reproductive justice as central to social work education, schools can foster a generation of social workers who prioritize reproductive autonomy and social justice in their practice.

Culturally responsive education is another trend driving the integration of reproductive justice into social work programs. Given that reproductive justice is deeply rooted in the experiences of women of color and marginalized communities, there is increasing recognition of the need for education that addresses cultural competence and sensitivity. Future innovations in reproductive justice education will likely involve more curricula that center the voices and experiences of Black, Indigenous, Hispanic, and immigrant communities, reflecting the need to teach students how to provide culturally informed and equitable care. This could include collaborations with community-based organizations, guest speakers from diverse backgrounds, and case studies that explore the unique reproductive challenges faced by marginalized populations (Poehling, et. al, 2023).

Lastly, advocacy and policy engagement are becoming central to how reproductive justice is integrated into social work education. Social workers are often at the forefront of pushing for systemic change; therefore, programs are beginning to emphasize the importance of policy advocacy skills in advancing reproductive justice. Students are increasingly being trained in legislative advocacy, organizing, and policy analysis, ensuring they are equipped to advocate for reproductive justice at the local, state, and national levels. Innovations in this area include partnerships with advocacy organizations, opportunities to engage in grassroots activism, and coursework that focuses on the policy implications for reproductive justice, preparing students to be agents of change in both their direct practice and broader societal structures.

As social work education continues to evolve, these trends and innovations in integrating reproductive justice will shape a future where social workers are better prepared to address the complex, systemic challenges that influence reproductive autonomy and health. By embracing technology, interdisciplinary collaboration, experiential learning, culturally responsive education, and policy advocacy, social work programs can ensure that their graduates are equipped to advance reproductive justice for all communities (Poehling, et. al, 2023).

B. Expanding Practice Frameworks

The expansion of practice modalities in social work is an essential practice for integrating reproductive justice into client interactions and community-based services. As reproductive justice intersects with issues of race, class, gender, and immigration, traditional social work models must evolve to meet the diverse needs of marginalized populations. To effectively address these complex challenges, social workers must adopt interdisciplinary, culturally responsive, and trauma-informed approaches to their practice. Expanding practice frameworks means moving beyond direct service provision to incorporate strategies that address the systemic and institutional barriers to reproductive healthcare access, which disproportionately impact Hispanic individuals.

An important aspect of expanding these frameworks involves embracing interdisciplinary collaboration. Collaboration among social workers, public health professionals, and legal advocates is essential to addressing the multifaceted barriers to reproductive justice. Through these partnerships, social workers can holistically tackle the reproductive challenges experienced by Hispanic communities. For example, collaborating with healthcare providers can ensure that clients receive comprehensive reproductive healthcare that is culturally sensitive and accessible, while working with legal advocates can address issues related to immigration status and healthcare access. Additionally, joint initiatives with public health professionals may include developing community education programs on reproductive healthcare access or improving telehealth services to reach underserved populations, including those in rural or low-income areas.

Another integral component of expanding practice frameworks is using culturally responsive strategies. It is important that social workers are attuned to the unique cultural values and norms that influence and shape reproductive choices in Hispanic communities. This can include understanding the role of the family, religion, and community in shaping reproductive health decisions and developing interventions that respect these cultural factors. By incorporating culturally responsive and trauma-informed approaches, social workers can build trust with their clients and create an environment in which individuals feel safe to explore their reproductive options without fear of judgment or stigma (Substance Abuse and Mental Health Services Administration, 2014). For example, integrating bilingual telehealth platforms can bridge language and transportation barriers, enabling Hispanic clients to access reproductive healthcare in a more convenient and culturally sensitive manner.

Finally, expanding practice frameworks also involves addressing the SDOH that impacts reproductive justice. To achieve impactful outcomes, it is important that social workers integrate a broader understanding of how factors such as housing, employment, and education impact reproductive autonomy (Office of Disease Prevention and Health Promotion, n.d.). This may involve advocating more effectively on behalf of clients in areas beyond healthcare, including access to affordable housing, job opportunities, and education, which are all critical components of reproductive justice (Ross & Solinger, 2017). Through a holistic approach, social workers can ensure that their clients' reproductive health needs are addressed within the context of their broader social and economic conditions.

The expansion of practice frameworks in social work practice involves the utilization of interdisciplinary, culturally responsive, and holistic approaches that recognize the complexity of reproductive justice issues. By doing so, social workers can more effectively advocate for and empower marginalized communities, ensuring that clients can fully exercise their reproductive rights in safe and supportive environments.

C. Enhancing Advocacy and Policy Efforts

As social work moves toward a more comprehensive integration of reproductive justice, enhancing advocacy and policy efforts will be critical in addressing the systemic barriers that hinder reproductive autonomy. Reproductive justice, by nature, extends beyond individual healthcare access to the broader social, economic, and legal factors that shape reproductive choices. Strengthening advocacy and policy initiatives is key to dismantling these barriers and promoting equitable access to reproductive healthcare, especially for marginalized populations such as Hispanic, Black, and Indigenous communities (Poehling, et. al, 2023).

One effective strategy for enhancing advocacy efforts involves training social workers to engage in legislative advocacy. As frontline practitioners, social workers possess a unique perspective on how policies impact marginalized individuals. Legislative advocacy enables them to influence the development and reform of policies that directly affect reproductive health outcomes. For example, advocacy for expanding Medicaid coverage, which ensures affordable access to contraception, and protection of abortion rights are essential policy goals that can directly improve reproductive autonomy for vulnerable populations (Poehling, et. al, 2023). Social work programs must provide students with the tools to understand the policy-making process, draft policy proposals, and engage with lawmakers.

Collaborating with advocacy organizations is another crucial approach to enhancing reproductive justice efforts. Partnerships with established organizations, such as Planned Parenthood and the National Latina Institute for Reproductive Justice, provide social workers with access to critical resources and platforms to amplify their advocacy efforts. These collaborations enable social workers to engage in grassroots mobilization, community organizing, and policy campaigns that center the voices of marginalized communities (Poehling, et. al, 2023).

Another key aspect of advancing advocacy efforts is the inclusion of culturally responsive policy strategies. Given that reproductive justice is rooted in the experiences of women of color, advocacy efforts must reflect the cultural and socio-economic challenges faced by these communities. Policy reforms must address not only healthcare access but also the intersecting issues of immigration, language barriers, and cultural stigmatization. Advocating for comprehensive sex education that is inclusive of the values and needs of Hispanic and immigrant communities is one example of culturally responsive policy reform. Furthermore, social workers should be trained in policy analysis and evaluation, enabling them to assess the effectiveness of reproductive health policies. By analyzing how existing policies either support or undermine reproductive justice, social workers can advocate for data-driven reforms that promote greater equity. This requires an interdisciplinary approach that integrates public health, law, and social work to create policies that reflect the complex realities of reproductive health.

Enhancing advocacy and policy efforts within a reproductive justice framework is essential for creating systemic change. Social work must continue to prioritize legislative advocacy, interdisciplinary collaboration, and culturally responsive strategies to ensure that all individuals– regardless of race, gender, or socioeconomic status– have the ability to make autonomous reproductive decisions. By preparing social workers to engage in these efforts, the profession can contribute significantly to the advancement of reproductive justice for marginalized communities.

VII. CONCLUSION

A. Summary of Key Points

Integrating reproductive justice into social work education and practice is crucial for promoting equity and addressing the systemic barriers faced by marginalized communities, particularly Hispanic populations. Reproductive justice goes beyond individual reproductive rights to encompass the broader social, economic, and political conditions that shape a person's reproductive autonomy. This framework aligns with social work's core mission of advocating for social justice, human rights, and the well-being of vulnerable populations.

By incorporating reproductive justice into social work education, students gain a comprehensive understanding of the intersectional factors, such as race, class, immigration status, and gender, that disproportionately affect marginalized groups' access to healthcare. This prepares future social workers to address not only individual healthcare needs but also the systemic inequalities that hinder reproductive autonomy. In practice, social workers equipped with this framework can provide culturally competent, trauma-informed care, advocate for policy reforms, and ensure that marginalized communities receive equitable access to reproductive healthcare and social services. This integration strengthens the profession's commitment to social justice and empowers social workers to dismantle barriers that prevent reproductive freedom, making reproductive justice a vital component in promoting the well-being and autonomy of all individuals.

B. Final Thoughts on Empowering Hispanic Communities

Integrating reproductive justice into social work education and practice holds immense potential to significantly impact the well-being and empowerment of Hispanic communities. By addressing the unique social, economic, and cultural barriers that these communities face, reproductive justice can transform the ways in which Hispanic individuals and families access healthcare, exercise reproductive autonomy, and navigate systemic inequities (Poehling, et. al, 2023). The application of this framework equips social workers with the necessary tools to advocate for policies that not only ensure equitable healthcare access but also promote broader social conditions conducive to thriving communities.

The emphasis on policy advocacy and legislative reform is crucial in addressing the structural inequalities that disproportionately affect Hispanic communities. Social workers, as advocates, can push for policy changes that expand access to healthcare for undocumented individuals, ensure affordable contraception, and protect reproductive rights, regardless of immigration status (Poehling, et. al, 2023). These efforts not only improve healthcare outcomes but also empower Hispanic communities by reinforcing their reproductive rights and autonomy.

Integrating reproductive justice into social work practice has the power to uplift and empower Hispanic communities by promoting systemic changes that address their unique challenges. As social workers continue to advance this framework, the potential for improved health, autonomy, and well-being among Hispanic individuals becomes increasingly achievable.

C. Call to Action

Social workers have an incredibly integral role in advancing the reproductive justice movement, especially within Hispanic communities whom often face systemic barriers. These barriers limit their access to reproductive health services; however, social workers have the ability to model efforts to dismantle these barriers and other systemic challenges. The reproductive justice framework seeks to ensure that all individuals– regardless of race, socioeconomic status, or immigration status, among others– can fully exercise their reproductive rights and reproductive autonomy (Ross & Solinger, 2017). The reproductive justice framework aligns closely with social work's values of advocating for vulnerable populations and ensuring social equity and human rights.

An important area of focus for social workers, educators, advocates, and policymakers, among others, is the inequitable access to healthcare that many Hispanic communities experience. Social workers, in collaboration with other healthcare providers, can advocate and work to ensure that these services are accessible and culturally sensitive. This includes advocating for healthcare policies and practices that support access to reproductive services and working to dismantle systemic barriers preventing Hispanic communities from receiving equitable care (Gomez et al., 2021). Through advocacy, social workers can empower individuals to make informed decisions about their reproductive health without systemic constraints.

On a broader, more macro level, it is integral that social workers engage in policy reform and community advocacy that addresses underlying social factors that impact reproductive health and reproductive rights. A variety of issues such as housing, employment, and education, influence reproductive autonomy (Beddoe, 2021). Through advocacy for policy changes that address these issues, social workers, educators, and advocates contribute to creating environments that enable individuals to raise their families with dignity and safety. These policy changes and reforms are integral for advancing reproductive justice, especially within Hispanic communities where these systemic barriers are magnified.

A commitment to ongoing education and reflection is essential for social workers and other advocates. Reproductive justice is an inherently intersectional framework that requires understanding how race, class, and gender intersect to shape individual experiences (Ross & Solinger, 2017). Social workers, educators, policymakers, and advocates must actively confront their own biases and advocate for policies that promote inclusivity and equity. By engaging in this work, these individuals can play an important role in ensuring that reproductive rights and reproductive autonomy are maintained for all.

REFERENCES

Arguedas-Ramirez, G., & Wenner, D. M. (2023). Reproductive justice beyond borders: Global feminist solidarity in the post-*Roe* era. *The Journal of Law, Medicine & Ethics*, 51(3), 606–611. DOI: 10.1017/jme.2023.101 PMID: 38088629

ASPE. (2021). "Health Insurance Coverage and Access to Care Among Latinos: Recent Trends and Key Challenges". *Assistant Secretary for Planning and Evaluation, U.S. Department of Health and Human Services.* Retrieved from https://aspe.hhs.gov/sites/default/files/documents/68c78e2fb15209dd191cf9b0b1380fb8/ASPE_Latino_Health_Coverage_IB.pdf

Ayon, C. (2014). Service needs among Latino immigrant families: Implications for social work practice. *Social Work*, 59(1), 13–23. DOI: 10.1093/sw/swt031 PMID: 24640227

Batek, L. M., Leblanc, N. M., Alio, A. P., Stein, K. F., & McMahon, J. M. (2024). Facilitators and barriers to contraception access and use for Hispanic American adolescent women: An integrative literature review. *PLOS Global Public Health*, 47(4), 1–17. DOI: 10.1371/journal.pgph.0003169 PMID: 39052657

Beddoe, L. (2022). Reproductive justice, abortion rights, and social work. *Critical and Radical Social Work*, 10(1), 7–22. DOI: 10.1332/204986021X16355170868404

Bell, S. O., Stuart, E. A., & Gemmill, A. (2023). Texas' 2021 ban on abortion in early pregnancy and changes in live births. *Journal of the American Medical Association*, 330(3), 281–282. DOI: 10.1001/jama.2023.12034 PMID: 37382968

Carbado, D. W., Crenshaw, K. W., Mays, V. M., & Tomlinson, B. (2013). Intersectionality. *Du Bois Review*, 10(2), 303–312. DOI: 10.1017/S1742058X13000349 PMID: 25285150

Cho, S., Crenshaw, K. W., & McCall, L. (2013). Toward a Field of Intersectionality Studies: Theory, Applications, and Praxis. *Signs (Chicago, Ill.)*, 38(4), 785–810. DOI: 10.1086/669608

Garcia, M. L., Sprager, L., & Jimenez, E. B. (2022, December 5). "Latino Community Health Workers: Meeting their Community's Emotional Needs in Intuitively Culturally Appropriate Ways". *CHW Central.* Retrieved from https://chwcentral.org/resources/latino-community-health-workers-meeting-their-communitys-emotional-needs-in-intuitively-culturally-appropriate-ways/

Garcia, R. R. (2016, May 24). "How the Reproductive Justice Movement Benefits Latinas" *Scholars Strategy Network*. Retrieved from https://scholars.org/brief/how-reproductive-justice-movement-benefits-latinas

Gomez, A. M., Downey, M. M., Carpenter, E., Leedham, U., Begun, S., Craddock, J., & Ely, G. (2020). Advancing reproductive just to close the health gap: A call to action for social work. *Social Work*, 65(4), 358–367. DOI: 10.1093/sw/swaa034 PMID: 33020834

HealthStream. (2022, January 22). "Healthcare Disparities Among Hispanic Communities" *HealthStream*. Retrieved from https://www.healthstream.com/resource/articles/healthcare-disparities-among-hispanic-communities

Johnson, L. (2022, February 24). "The Disparate Impact of Texas' Abortion Ban on Low-Income and Rural Women" *Georgetown Journal Poverty Law & Policy*. Retrieved https://www.law.georgetown.edu/poverty-journal/blog/the-disparate-impact-of-texas-abortion-ban-on-low-income-and-rural-women/

Kaelbar, L. B. (2012). *Latinas and abortion: The role of acculturation, religion, reproductive history, and familism.* [Doctoral dissertation, University of Miami]. University of Miami Scholarship Repository. Retrieved from https://scholarship.miami.edu/esploro/outputs/doctoral/Latinas-and-Abortion-The-Role-of/991031447238602976

Klibanoff, E. (2024, January 26). "Hispanic and teen fertility rates increase after abortion restrictions" *The Texas Tribune*. Retrieved from https://www.texastribune.org/2024/01/26/texas-abortion-fertility-rate-increase/

National Association of Social Workers. (2015). *Standards and indicators for cultural competence in social work practice*. NASW. https://www.socialworkers.org/Practice/NASW-Practice-Standards-Guidelines/Standards-and-Indicators-for-Cultural-Competence-in-Social-Work-Practice

National Association of Social Workers. (2021). *Code of ethics of the National Association of Social Workers*. NASW Press. https://www.socialworkers.org/About/Ethics/Code-of-Ethics/Code-of-Ethics-English

Office of Disease Prevention and Health Promotion. (n.d.). *Social Determinants of Health*. Healthy People 2030. https://odphp.health.gov/healthypeople/priority-areas/social-determinants-health

Planned Parenthood Action Fund. (n.d.) "Health Equity Issues for the Latino Community". *Planned Parenthood Action Fund.* Retrieved from https://www.plannedparenthoodaction.org/communities/latinos-planned-parenthood/health-equity-issues-for-the-latino-community

Planned Parenthood of Greater New York. (2024, October 3). "The Importance of Reproductive Health for Latinx Communities". *Planned Parenthood of Greater New York*. Retrieved from https://www.plannedparenthood.org/planned-parenthood-greater-new-york/blog/the-importance-of-reproductive-health-for-latinx-communities

Poehling, C., Downey, M. M., Singh, M. I., & Beasley, C. C. (2023). From gaslighting to enlightening: Reproductive justice as an interdisciplinary solution to close the health gap. *Journal of Social Work Education*, 59(1), 36–47. DOI: 10.1080/10437797.2023.2203205 PMID: 38606421

Robert Wood Johnson Foundation. (2024, June 1). "Advancing Solutions for Reproductive Justice" *Robert Wood Johnson Foundation*. Retrieved from https://www.rwjf.org/en/insights/our-research/2024/06/advancing-solutions-for-reproductive-justice.html

Ross, L., & Solinger, R. (2017). *Reproductive Justice: An Introduction*. University of California Press.

Smith, B. D. (2017). Reproductive justice: A policy window for social work. *Social Work*, 62(3), 221–226. DOI: 10.1093/sw/swx015 PMID: 28444300

Sonubi, C., Flores, E., & Spalluto, L. (2022). How should US health care meet Latinx community health needs? *AMA Journal of Ethics*, 24(2), 261–266. PMID: 35405051

Starrs, A. M., Ezeh, A. C., Barker, G., Basu, A., Bertrand, J., Blum, R., Coll-Seck, A. M., Grover, A., Laski, L., Roa, M., Sathar, Z. A., Say, L., Serour, G. I., Singh, S., Stenberg, K., Temmerman, M., Biddlecom, A., Popinchalk, A., Summers, C., & Ashford, L. S. (2018). Accelerate progress - sexual and reproductive health and rights for all: Report of the Guttmacher-*Lancet* Commission. *Lancet*, 391(10140), 2642–2692. DOI: 10.1016/S0140-6736(18)30293-9 PMID: 29753597

Substance Abuse and Mental Health Services Administration. (2014). *Trauma-informed care in behavioral health services* (Treatment Improvement Protocol (TIP) Series 57). U.S. Department of Health and Human Services. https://store.samhsa.gov/sites/default/files/sma15-4420.pdf

Tyson, A., & Hugo Lopez, M. (2023, October 30). "5 facts about Hispanic Americans and health care". *Pew Research Center*. Retrieved from https://www.pewresearch.org/short-reads/2023/10/30/5-facts-about-hispanic-americans-and-health-care/

University at Buffalo. (n.d.). "SW 725 Reproductive Justice" Syllabus University of Southern California. (2018, February 27). *Do you know the difference between micro-, mezzo- and macro-level social work?* USC Suzanne Dworak-Peck School of Social Work. https://dworakpeck.usc.edu/news/do-you-know-the-difference-between -micro-mezzo-and-macro-level-social-work

Wright, R. L., Bird, M., & Frost, C. J. (2015). Reproductive health in the United States: A review of recent social work literature. *Social Work*, 60(4), 295–304. DOI: 10.1093/sw/swv028 PMID: 26489350

Younes, M., Goldblatt Hyatt, E., Witt, H., & Franklin, C. (2021). A call to action: Addressing ambivalence and promoting advocacy for reproductive rights in social work education. *Journal of Social Work Education*, 57(4), 625–635. DOI: 10.1080/10437797.2021.1895930

KEY TERMS AND DEFINITIONS

Culturally competent: refers to the ability of individuals and systems to effectively interact with people from diverse cultural backgrounds. It involves being aware of one's own cultural biases, understanding the cultural beliefs and practices of others, and adapting services or communication to meet the cultural needs of different populations. Culturally competent practice is essential for reducing disparities, promoting equity, and ensuring respectful, responsive care across diverse communities.

Familism or *Familismo***:** refers to the way Latinx individuals interact and associate with their families as well as extended family members.

Forced sterilization: A coercive medical practice in which individuals, often from marginalized communities, are sterilized without their consent, historically affecting women of color, including Hispanic women.

Intersectionality: refers to the way different aspects of a person's identity - like race, gender, class, and sexuality - combine to shape their experiences in society.

Reproductive justice: a framework that broadens the conversation around reproductive rights, emphasizing not only the right to choose whether or not to have children but also the social, economic, and political conditions necessary to make those choices freely and safely.

Social determinants of health (SDOH): the non-medical factors that influence health outcomes. These include the conditions in which people are born, grow, live, work, and age, such as access to education, economic stability, neighborhood environment, healthcare access, and social and community context. SDOH are shaped by the distribution of money, power, nad resources at global, national, and local levels, and they play a critical role in driving health disparities and inequities.

Systemic barriers: The societal and institutional structures, such as discriminatory policies or economic inequalities, that prevent individuals from accessing necessary services or exercising their rights.

Texas Senate Bill 8: A 2021 Texas law that effectively bans most abortions after six weeks of pregnancy, disproportionately impacting low-income and marginalized women who face additional barriers to seeking care out of state.

Compilation of References

Abrego, L. J., & Gonzales, R. G. (2010). Blocked paths, uncertain futures: The postsecondary education and labor market prospects of undocumented Latinx youth. *Journal of Education for Students Placed at Risk*, 15(1-2), 144–157. DOI: 10.1080/10824661003635168

Acevedo-Gil, N. (2017). College-conocimiento: Toward an interdisciplinary college choice framework for Latinx students. *Race, Ethnicity and Education*, 20(6), 829–850. DOI: 10.1080/13613324.2017.1343294

Acevedo, M. (2021). The role of affinity groups in supporting underrepresented leaders in education. *Journal of Educational Leadership*, 15(2), 123–138.

Acevedo, N. (2021). The power of affinity groups for women of color in leadership. *Journal of Educational Leadership*, 45(3), 201–215.

ACTFL Task Force on Decade of Standards Project. (2011, April). *A decade of foreign language standards: influence, impact, and future directions.* Survey results [Electronic report]. Retrieved February 24, 2024, from https://www.actfl.org/sites/ default/files/publications/standards/NationalStandards2011.pd

ACTFL. (2017a). *NCSSFL-ACTFL can-do-statements for intercultural communication.* Available from, https://www.actfl.org/publications/guidelines-and-manuals/ ncssfl-actfl-can-do-statements

ACTFL. (2017b). *Intercultural reflection tool.* Available from, https://www.actfl .org/publications/guidelines-and-manuals/ncssfl-actfl-can-do-statements

Adán, M. (2023). Sustaining the Empoderamiento of Spanish Heritage Learners at the Secondary Level through Critical Pedagogies. [Doctoral dissertation, Indiana University]. Thesis and Dissertations Collection, Indiana University Library. https:// hdl.handle.net/2022/29668

Adlof, S. M. (2020). Promoting reading achievement in children with developmental language disorders: What can we learn from research on specific language impairment and dyslexia? *Journal of Speech, Language, and Hearing Research: JSLHR*, 63(10), 3277–3292. DOI: 10.1044/2020_JSLHR-20-00118 PMID: 33064604

Adlof, S. M., & Hogan, T. P. (2018). Understanding dyslexia in the context of developmental language disorders. *Language, Speech, and Hearing Services in Schools*, 49(4), 762–773. DOI: 10.1044/2018_LSHSS-DYSLC-18-0049 PMID: 30458538

Alfaro, C., & Hernández, A. M. (2016). Dual language equity lens: A conceptual framework for educators. Multilingual Educator, 2016 California Association for Bilingual Education Conference Edition, 8-11. Retrieved from http://www.gocabe.org/wp-content/uploads/2016/03/ME2016.pdf

Alvarez, C. (2015). A model for understanding the Latina/o student and parent college-going negotiation process. In Perez, P., & Ceja, M. (Eds.), *Higher education access and choice for Latino students: Critical findings and theoretical perspectives* (pp. 55–66).

Álvarez-Cañizo, M., Afonso, O., & Suárez-Coalla, P. (2023). Writing proficiency in English as L2 in Spanish children with dyslexia. *Annals of Dyslexia*, 73(1), 130–147. DOI: 10.1007/s11881-023-00278-4 PMID: 36705859

American Psychiatric Association. (2020). *Mental health disparities: Latinx/Hispanic Americans.*

Anderson, M., & Jiang, J. (2023). *Digital divide trends among Latino youth*. Pew Research Center.

Andrews, D. H., Hull, T. D., & DeMeester, K. (2010). Storytelling as an instructional method: Research perspectives.

Anya, U. (2021). Critical race pedagogy for more effective and inclusive world language teaching. *Applied Linguistics*, 42(6), 1055–1069. DOI: 10.1093/applin/amab068

Anzaldúa, G. (1987). How to tame a wild tongue. In *Borderlands/La Frontera: The New Mestiza* (pp. 36-43). Aunt Lute Books.

Anzaldúa, G. (1987). *Borderlands/La frontera: The new mestiza*. Aunt Lute Books.

Anzaldúa, G. E. (2015). *Light in the dark/Luz en lo oscuro: Rewriting identity, spirituality, reality* (Keating, A., Ed.). Duke University Press.

Arguedas-Ramirez, G., & Wenner, D. M. (2023). Reproductive justice beyond borders: Global feminist solidarity in the post-*Roe* era. *The Journal of Law, Medicine & Ethics*, 51(3), 606–611. DOI: 10.1017/jme.2023.101 PMID: 38088629

Artiles, A. J., & Ortiz, A. A. (2002). *English language learners with special education needs: Identification, assessment, and instruction*. Center for Applied Linguistics and Delta Systems Co., Inc.

ASPE. (2021). "Health Insurance Coverage and Access to Care Among Latinos: Recent Trends and Key Challenges". *Assistant Secretary for Planning and Evaluation, U.S. Department of Health and Human Services.* Retrieved from https://aspe.hhs.gov/sites/default/files/documents/68c78e2fb15209dd191cf9b0b1380fb8/ASPE_Latino_Health_Coverage_IB.pdf

Atkins, K., Dougan, B. M., Dromgold-Sermen, M. S., Potter, H., Sathy, V., & Panter, A. T. (2020). "Looking at Myself in the Future": How mentoring shapes scientific identity for STEM students from underrepresented groups. *International Journal of STEM Education*, 7(1), 1–15. DOI: 10.1186/s40594-020-00242-3 PMID: 32850287

Atwater, M. M., Lance, J., Woodard, U., & Johnson, N. H. (2013). Race and ethnicity: Powerful cultural forecasters of science learning and performance. *Theory into Practice*, 52(1), 6–13. DOI: 10.1080/07351690.2013.743757

August, D., Shanahan, T., & Escamilla, K. (2009). English language learners: Developing literacy in second-language learners—Report of the National Literacy Panel on Language-Minority Children and Youth. *Journal of Literacy Research*, 41(4), 432–452. DOI: 10.1080/10862960903340165

Ayon, C. (2014). Service needs among Latino immigrant families: Implications for social work practice. *Social Work*, 59(1), 13–23. DOI: 10.1093/sw/swt031 PMID: 24640227

Baca, L. M., & Almanza, E. (1991). *Language Minority Students with Disabilities. Exceptional Children at Risk: CEC Mini-Library*. Council for Exceptional Children, 1920 Association Dr., Reston, VA 22091-1589 (Stock No. P357: $8.00).

Baker, D. L., Basaraba, D. L., & Polanco, P. (2016). Connecting the present to the past: Furthering the research on bilingual education and bilingualism. *Review of Research in Education*, 40(1), 821–883. DOI: 10.3102/0091732X16660691

Baker, D. L., Park, Y., & Andress, T. T. (2021). Longitudinal predictors of bilingual language proficiency, decoding, and oral reading fluency on reading comprehension in Spanish and in English. *School Psychology Review*, ●●●, 1–14. DOI: 10.1080/2372966X.2021.2021447

Baltes, P. B., & Baltes, M. M. (1990). Psychological perspectives on successful aging: The model of selective optimization with compensation. In Baltes, P. B., & Baltes, M. M. (Eds.), *Successful aging: Perspectives from the behavioral sciences* (pp. 1–34). Cambridge University Press. DOI: 10.1017/CBO9780511665684.003

Barajas-Gonzalez, R. G., Linares Torres, H., Urcuyo, A., Salamanca, E., Santos, M., & Pagán, O. (2024). "You're Part of Some Hope and Then You Fall into Despair": Exploring the Impact of a Restrictive Immigration Climate on Educators in Latinx Immigrant Communities. *Journal of Latinos and Education*, 23(2), 492–513. DOI: 10.1080/15348431.2022.2153846

Batek, L. M., Leblanc, N. M., Alio, A. P., Stein, K. F., & McMahon, J. M. (2024). Facilitators and barriers to contraception access and use for Hispanic American adolescent women: An integrative literature review. *PLOS Global Public Health*, 47(4), 1–17. DOI: 10.1371/journal.pgph.0003169 PMID: 39052657

Baum, S., & Flores, S. M. (2011). Higher education and children in immigrant families. *The Future of Children*, 21(1), 171–193. DOI: 10.1353/foc.2011.0000 PMID: 21465860

Beaudrie, S., & Wilson, D. V. (2022). Reimagining the Goals of HL Pedagogy through Critical Language Awareness. In S. Loza & S. Beaudrie (Eds.) (2022) Heritage Language Teaching: Critical Language Awareness Perspectives for Research and Pedagogy (pp. 63-79). New York, NY: Routledge

Beaudrie, S. M. (2020). Towards Growth for Spanish Heritage Programs in the United States: Key Markers of Success. *Foreign Language Annals*, 53(3), 416–437. DOI: 10.1111/flan.12476

Beaudrie, S. M., Amenzua, A., & Loza, S. (2021). Critical language awareness in the heritage language classroom: Design, implementation, and evaluation of a curricular intervention. *International Multilingual Research Journal*, 15(1), 61–81. DOI: 10.1080/19313152.2020.1753931

Beaudrie, S. M., Ducar, C., & Potowski, K. (2014). *Heritage language teaching: research and practice*. McGraw-Hill Education Create.

Beaudrie, S. M., & Loza, S. (2022). The Central Role of Critical Language Awareness in Spanish Heritage Language Education in the United States: An Introduction. In Loza, S., & Beaudrie, S. M. (Eds.), *Heritage Language Teaching: Critical Language Awareness Perspectives for Research and Pedagogy* (pp. 1–20). Routledge.

Beddoe, L. (2022). Reproductive justice, abortion rights, and social work. *Critical and Radical Social Work*, 10(1), 7–22. DOI: 10.1332/204986021X16355170868404

Bedore, L. M., Peña, E. D., Fiestas, C., & Lugo-Neris, M. J. (2020). Language and literacy together: Supporting grammatical development in dual language learners with risk for language and learning difficulties. *Language, Speech, and Hearing Services in Schools*, 51(2), 282–297. DOI: 10.1044/2020_LSHSS-19-00055 PMID: 32255748

Beers, K., & Probst, R. (2017). Disrupting thinking. Scholastic. https://scholastic.com/beersandprobst

Bell, L. (2016). Theoretical foundation social justice education. In M. Adam & L. Bell with D. Goodman & K. Joshi (Eds.), Teaching for diversity and social justice (3rd ed.) (pp. 3-26). New York: Routledge.

Bell, D. (1992). *Faces at the bottom of the well: The permanence of racism*. Basic Books.

Bell, D. A.Board of Education and the Interest-Convergence Dilemma. (1980). Brown v. Board of Education and the interest-convergence dilemma. *Harvard Law Review*, 93(3), 518–533. DOI: 10.2307/1340546

Bell, S. O., Stuart, E. A., & Gemmill, A. (2023). Texas' 2021 ban on abortion in early pregnancy and changes in live births. *Journal of the American Medical Association*, 330(3), 281–282. DOI: 10.1001/jama.2023.12034 PMID: 37382968

Benavides, R., & Medina-Jerez, W. (2017). No Puedo: "I don't get it"—Assisting Spanglish-speaking students in the science classroom. *Science Teacher (Normal, Ill.)*, 84(4), 30–35. DOI: 10.2505/4/tst17_084_04_30

Benegas, M., & Benjamin, N. (2024). *Language of Identity, Language of Access*. Corwin.

Bernhard, J. K., Cummins, J., Campoy, F. I., Ada, A. F., Winsler, A., & Bleiker, C. (2006). Identity texts and literacy development among preschool English language learners: Enhancing learning opportunities for children at risk for learning disabilities. *Teachers College Record*, 108(11), 2380–2405. DOI: 10.1111/j.1467-9620.2006.00786.x

Bialystok, E. (2011). Reshaping the mind: The benefits of bilingualism. *Canadian Journal of Experimental Psychology*, 65(4), 229–235. DOI: 10.1037/a0025406 PMID: 21910523

Bialystok, E., & Craik, F. I. (2010). Cognitive and linguistic processing in the bilingual mind. *Current Directions in Psychological Science*, 19(1), 19–23. DOI: 10.1177/0963721409358571

Bishop, R. S. (1990). *Mirrors, windows, and sliding glass doors.* Perspectives. *Choosing and Using Books for the Classroom*, 6(3), ix–xi.

Blazar, D. (2021, November 30). *Teachers of color, culturally responsive teaching, and student outcomes: Experimental evidence from the random assignment of teachers to classes. edworkingpaper no. 21-501.* Annenberg Institute for School Reform at Brown University. https://eric.ed.gov/?id=ED616770

Boris, V. (2023, January 9). *What makes storytelling so effective for learning?* Harvard Business Publishing. https://www.harvardbusiness.org/what-makes-storytelling -so-effective-for-learning/

Borjian, A., & Padilla, A. M. (2010). Voices from Mexico: How American teachers can meet the needs of Mexican immigrant students. *The Urban Review*, 42(4), 316–328. DOI: 10.1007/s11256-009-0135-0

Bourdieu, P., & Passeron, J. (1977). *Reproduction in education, society and culture.* Sage.

Bowles, M. A. (2011). Exploring the Role of Modality: L2-Heritage Learner Interactions in the Spanish Language Classroom. In Heritage Language Journal (Vol. 8, Issue 1).

Bowles, M. (2018). Outcomes of classroom Spanish heritage language instruction. In *The Routledge Handbook of Spanish as a Heritage Language*. Routledge Taylor & Francis Group. DOI: 10.4324/9781315735139-21

Bransberger, P., Falkenstern, C., & Lane, P. (2020). *Knocking at the College Door. Projections of High School Graduates.* Western Interstate Commission for Higher Education.

Branum-Martin, L., Tao, S., Garnaat, S., Bunta, F., & Francis, D. J. (2012). Metaanalysis of bilingual phonological awareness: Language, age, and psycholinguistic grain size. *Journal of Educational Psychology*, 104(4), 932–944. DOI: 10.1037/ a0027755

Bristol, T. J., & Martin-Fernandez, J. (2019). The added value of latinx and black teachers for latinx and black students: Implications for policy. *Policy Insights from the Behavioral and Brain Sciences*, 6(2), 147–153. DOI: 10.1177/2372732219862573

Bronfenbrenner, U. (1979). *The ecology of human development: Experiments by nature and design.* Harvard University Press. DOI: 10.4159/9780674028845

Brooms, D. R., Franklin, W., Clark, J. S., & Smith, M. (2018). 'It's more than just mentoring': Critical mentoring black and latino males from college to the community. *Race, Ethnicity and Education*, 24(2), 210–228. DOI: 10.1080/13613324.2018.1538125

Brown, A. M. (2019). *Pleasure activism: The Politics of Feeling Good.*

Brown, B. (2018). Dare to lead. Penguin Random House LLC. https://www.BreneBrown.com

Bucholtz, M., Casillas, D. I., & Lee, J. S. (2017). Language and Culture as Sustenance. In *Paris, D., & Alim, H. S. (2017). Culturally sustaining pedagogies : teaching and learning for justice in a changing world* (pp. 43–59). Teachers College Press.

Burciaga, R., & Kohli, R. (2018). Disrupting whitestream measures of quality teaching: The community cultural wealth of teachers of color. *Multicultural Perspectives*, 20(1), 5–12. DOI: 10.1080/15210960.2017.1400915

Burgo, C. (2017). *Culture and Instruction in the Spanish Heritage Language Classroom.* Philologica Canariensia., DOI: 10.20420/PhilCan.2017.145

Burr, E., Haas, E., Ferriere, K., & West, E. (2015). Identifying and supporting English learner students with learning disabilities: Key issues in the literature and state practice. *Regional Educational Laboratory. WestEd.*

Byram, M. (2008). *From foreign language education to education for intercultural citizenship: Essays and reflections.* Multilingual Matters. DOI: 10.21832/9781847690807

Byram, M. (2021). *Teaching and assessing intercultural communicative competence –Revisited.* Multilingual Matters. DOI: 10.21832/9781800410251

Caldas, B. (2021). "I felt powerful": Imagining re-existence through an embodied fugitive pedagogy for Mexican American/Latinx teachers. *Equity & Excellence in Education*, 54(2), 136–151. DOI: 10.1080/10665684.2021.1951628

Calderón, M., Slavin, R., & Sánchez, M. (2011). Effective instruction for English learners. *The Future of Children*, 21(1), 103–127. DOI: 10.1353/foc.2011.0007 PMID: 21465857

California Association of Latino Superintendents and Administrators. (2023). *Latinx leadership and student success: The CALSA San Diego chapter impact report.* CALSA Press.

California Department of Education. (2023). Data and statistics. Retrieved from https://www.cde.ca.gov/ds/

California Department of Education. (2023). Teacher and administrator demographics. Retrieved from https://www.cde.ca.gov/demographics

Callahan, R. M., & Gándara, P. C. (2014). *The bilingual advantage: Language, literacy and the US labor market.* Channel View Publications. DOI: 10.21832/9781783092437

Campesi, M. (2019). I am an english-language learner: The real and unique stories of immigrant children in america. LuLu Publishing. https://www.melissacampesi.com

Campesi, M. (2022). Imagine Song: A story about the kindred connection between a child, an instrument, and an imagination. ReadersMagnet. https://www.melissacampesi.com

Canas, A., Bordes Edgar, V., & Neumann, J. (2020). Practical considerations in the neuropsychological assessment of bilingual (Spanish-English) children in the United States: Literature review and case series. *Developmental Neuropsychology*, 45(4), 211–231. DOI: 10.1080/87565641.2020.1746314 PMID: 32264704

Carbado, D. W., Crenshaw, K. W., Mays, V. M., & Tomlinson, B. (2013). Intersectionality. *Du Bois Review*, 10(2), 303–312. DOI: 10.1017/S1742058X13000349 PMID: 25285150

Carreira, M., & Potowski, K. (2011). Commentary: Pedagogical Implications of Experimental SNS Research. In Heritage Language Journal (Vol. 8, Issue 1).

Carreira, M. (2018). *Strategies for Teaching Mixed Classes: Meeting the Needs of Heritage and Second Language Learners of Spanish.* In Webinar Series Center for Language Instruction and Coordination.

Carreira, M., & Chik, C. (2018). *Differentiated Teaching: A primer for heritage and mixed classes. The Routledge Handbook of Spanish as a Heritage Language.* Routledge Taylor & Francis Group. DOI: 10.4324/9781315735139-23

Carreón, G. P., Drake, C., & Barton, A. C. (2005). The importance of presence: Immigrant parents' school engagement experiences. *American Educational Research Journal*, 42(3), 465–498. DOI: 10.3102/00028312042003465

Carrillo, J. F. (2016a). I grew up straight 'hood: Unpacking the intelligences of working-class Latino male college students in North Carolina. *Equity & Excellence in Education*, 49(2), 157–169. DOI: 10.1080/10665684.2015.1086247

Carrillo, J. F. (2016b). Searching for "home" in Dixie: Identity and education in the new Latin@ South. *Educational Studies (Ames)*, 52(1), 20–37. DOI: 10.1080/00131946.2015.1120208

Carrión, A. E., & Torres, M. (2023). Leaning on family: Examining college-going and help-seeking behaviors of Latino male high school students through dichos, consejos, and community cultural wealth. *International Journal of Educational Research, 122*, 102256-. DOI: 10.1016/j.ijer.2023.102256

Carter Andrews, D. J., Castro, E., Cho, C. L., Petchauer, E., Richmond, G., & Floden, R. (2019). Changing the narrative on diversifying the teaching workforce: A look at historical and contemporary factors that inform recruitment and retention of teachers of color. *Journal of Teacher Education*, 70(1), 6–12. DOI: 10.1177/0022487118812418

Castro, A. S., & Calzada, E. J. (2021). Teaching Latinx students: Do teacher ethnicity and bilingualism matter? *Contemporary Educational Psychology*, 66, 101994. DOI: 10.1016/j.cedpsych.2021.101994 PMID: 34393328

Catts, H. W. (1989). Defining dyslexia as a developmental language disorder. *Annals of Dyslexia*, 39(1), 50–64. DOI: 10.1007/BF02656900 PMID: 24233471

Ceja, M. (2004). Chicana college aspirations and the role of parents: Developing educational resiliency. *Journal of Hispanic Higher Education*, 3(4), 338–362. DOI: 10.1177/1538192704268428

Ceja, M. (2006). Understanding the role of parents and siblings as information sources in the college choice process of Chicana students. *Journal of College Student Development*, 47(1), 87–104. DOI: 10.1353/csd.2006.0003

Cenoz, J. (2013). Defining multilingualism. *Annual Review of Applied Linguistics*, 33, 3–18. DOI: 10.1017/S026719051300007X

Chávez-Moreno, L. C., Villegas, A. M., & Cochran-Smith, M. (2022). The experiences and preparation of teacher candidates of color: A literature review. *Handbook of research on teachers of color and indigenous teachers, 165.*

Chen, S., Binning, K. R., Manke, K. J., Brady, S. T., McGreevy, E. M., Betancur, L., Limeri, L. B., & Kaufmann, N. (2021). Am I a science person? A strong science identity bolsters minority students' sense of belonging and performance in college. *Personality and Social Psychology Bulletin*, 47(4), 593–606. DOI: 10.1177/0146167220936480 PMID: 32659167

Chism, D. (2022). Leading Your School Toward Equity. ASCD. Cooperative Children's Book Center (CCBC), School of Education, University of Wisconsin–Madison. "Publishing Statistics on Children's/YA Books about People of Color and First/Native Nations and by People of Color and First/Native Nations Authors and Illustrators." Children's Books by and about People of Color, ccbc.education .wisc .edu/books/pcstats.asp.

Cholewa, B., Goodman, R. D., West-Olatunji, C., & Amatea, E. (2014). A qualitative examination of the impact of culturally responsive educational practices on the psychological well-being of students of color. *The Urban Review*, 46(4), 574–596. DOI: 10.1007/s11256-014-0272-y

Cho, S., Crenshaw, K. W., & McCall, L. (2013). Toward a Field of Intersectionality Studies: Theory, Applications, and Praxis. *Signs (Chicago, Ill.)*, 38(4), 785–810. DOI: 10.1086/669608

Chrousos, G. P., & Mentis, A.-F. A. (2020). Imposter syndrome threatens diversity. *Science*, 367(6479), 749–750. DOI: 10.1126/science.aba8039 PMID: 32054753

Clance, P. R. (1985). *The impostor phenomenon: Overcoming the fear that haunts your success*. Peachtree Pub Limited.

Cochran-Smith, M., & Lytle, S. (2009). Teacher research as stance. In Somekh, B., & Noffke, S. (Eds.), *The Sage handbook of educational action research* (pp. 39–49). Sage. DOI: 10.4135/9780857021021.n5

Coffey, H., Putman, S. M., Handler, L. K., & Leach, W. (2019). Growing them early: Recruiting and preparing future urban teachers through an early college collaboration between a college of education and an urban school district. *Teacher Education Quarterly*, 46(1), 35–54. https://www.jstor.org/stable/26558181

Conlon, D. (2024). Meeting the World-Readiness Standards for Learning Languages through Comprehensible Input Readers in Level 1 Spanish, A Comparative Analysis of Teachers' Perceptions [Doctoral dissertation, University of Connecticut]. Archives & Special Collections, University of Connecticut Library. https://ctdigitalarchive .org/node/3768402

Conlon, D., & Wagner, M. (2022). Enacting Social Justice in World Language Education through Intercultural Citizenship. In Wassell, B., & Glynn, C. (Eds.), *Transforming World Language Teaching and Teacher Education for Equity and Justice: Pushing Boundaries in US Contexts*. Multilingual Matters.

Connecticut State Department of Education. (n.d.). Naubuc School Report. Connecticut Report Cards. https://edsight.ct.gov/SASStoredProcess/guest?_district= Glastonbury+School+

Contreras, F. (2009). Sin papeles y rompiendo barreras: Latinx students and the challenges of persisting in college. *Harvard Educational Review*, 79(4), 610–632. DOI: 10.17763/haer.79.4.02671846902gl33w

Correa, M. (2011). Advocating for Critical Pedagogical Approaches to Teaching Spanish as a Heritage Language: Some Considerations. *Foreign Language Annals*, 44(2), 308–320. DOI: 10.1111/j.1944-9720.2011.01132.x

Cortez, A., & Johnson, R. (2019). Supporting first-generation Latinx college students: The importance of financial literacy and mentorship. *Journal of College Student Development*, 60(3), 324–328.

Cortez, A., & Johnson, R. L. (2019). Latino education and leadership: Challenges and opportunities. *Educational Leadership Review*, 20(1), 11–25.

Cortez, R. M., & Santiago, A. M. (2023). Digital mentoring strategies for Latino youth: Emerging practices and outcomes. *Journal of Technology Education*, 45(3), 278–295.

Crawford, J., & Krashen, S. D. (2015). *English learners in American classrooms: 101 questions, 101 answers*. DiversityLearningK12.

Crenshaw, K. (1989). Demarginalizing the intersection of race and sex: A Black feminist critique of antidiscrimination doctrine, feminist theory, and antiracist politics. *University of Chicago Legal Forum*, 1989(1), 139–167.

Crenshaw, K. (1991). Mapping the margins: Intersectionality, identity politics, and violence against women of color. *Stanford Law Review*, 43(6), 1241–1300. DOI: 10.2307/1229039

Creswell, J. W. (2013). *Qualitative inquiry & research design: Choosing among five approaches* (3rd ed.). Sage Publications.

Cuevas, S. (2020). Ley de la vida: Latina/o immigrant parents experience of their children's transition to higher education. *The Journal of Higher Education*, 91(4), 565–587. DOI: 10.1080/00221546.2019.1647585

Cummins, J. (2000). *Language, power and pedagogy: Bilingual children in the crossfire*. Multilingual Matters. DOI: 10.21832/9781853596773

Darhower, M. (2006). Where's the community? Bilingual Internet chat and the fifth C of the National Standards. *Hispania,* 89,1. 84-98

Davis, L. P., & Museus, S. D. (2019). What is deficit thinking? An analysis of conceptualizations of deficit thinking and implications for scholarly research. *Currents (Ann Arbor)*, 1(1), 117–130. DOI: 10.3998/currents.17387731.0001.110

de Araujo, Z., Roberts, S. A., Willey, C., & Zahner, W. (2018). English Learners in K-12 Mathematics Education: A Review of the Literature. *Review of Educational Research*, 88(6), 879–919. https://www.jstor.org/stable/45277268. DOI: 10.3102/0034654318798093

De Carvalho, M. E. (2000). *Rethinking family-school relations: A critique of parental involvement in schooling*. Routledge. DOI: 10.4324/9781410600332

Delgado Bernal, D. (1998). Using a Chicana feminist epistemology in educational research. *Harvard Educational Review*, 68(4), 555–582. DOI: 10.17763/haer.68.4.5wv1034973g22q48

Delgado Bernal, D. (2002). Critical race theory, Latino critical theory, and critical raced-gendered epistemologies: Recognizing students of color as holders and creators of knowledge. *Qualitative Inquiry*, 8(1), 105–126. DOI: 10.1177/107780040200800107

Delgado-Gaitan, C. (2001). *The power of community: mobilizing for family and schooling*. Rowman and Littlefield Publishers.

Delpit, L. (1995). *Other people's children: cultural conflict in the classroom*. New Press.

DeNicolo, C. P., Yu, M., Crowley, C. B., & Gabel, S. L. (2017). Reimagining Critical Care and Problematizing Sense of School Belonging as a Response to Inequality for Immigrants and Children of Immigrants. *Review of Research in Education*, 41(1), 500–530. https://www.jstor.org/stable/44668705. DOI: 10.3102/0091732X17690498

Designated and integrated English language development. Designated and Integrated ELD - Letters (CA Dept of Education). (2022) https://www.cde.ca.gov/nr/el/le/yr22ltr0111.asp

Diamond, A. (2013). Executive functions. *Annual Review of Psychology*, 64(1), 135–168. DOI: 10.1146/annurev-psych-113011-143750 PMID: 23020641

District&_school=Naubuc+School&_program=%2FCTDOE%2FEdSight%2FRelease%2FReporting%2FPublic%2FReports%2FStoredProcesses%2FConnecticutReportCard&_select=Submit

Dixson, A. D., & Rousseau, C. K. (2005). And we are still not saved: Critical Race Theory in education ten years later. *Race ethnicity and education*, 8(1), 7-27. Enriquez, L. (2011). "Because we feel the pressure and we also feel the support": Examining the educational success of undocumented immigrant Latina/o students. *Harvard Educational Review*, 81(3), 476–500.

do Amaral, J., & de Azevedo, B. (2021). What research can tell us about the interaction between dyslexia and bilingualism: An integrative review. *Letrônica*, 14(2), e38695–e38695. DOI: 10.15448/1984-4301.2021.2.38695

Dolan, K., Slaughter-Johnson, E., Sampson, M., Jones, K., & Miles, B. (2018). WHO DOES THE SCHOOL TO PRISON PIPELINE AFFECT? In *STUDENTS UNDER SIEGE: How the school-to-prison pipeline, poverty, and racism endanger our school children* (pp. 8–18). Institute for Policy Studies. https://www.jstor.org/stable/resrep27070.5

Dover, A. (2013). Teaching for social justice: From conceptual frameworks to classroom practices. *Multicultural Perspectives*, 15(1), 3–11. DOI: 10.1080/15210960.2013.754285

Dover, A. G., & Rodríguez-Valls, F. (2022). *Radically inclusive teaching with newcomer and emergent plurilingual students: braving up*. Teachers College Press.

Edenberg, H. J., & Foroud, T. (2013). Genetics and alcoholism. *Nature Reviews. Gastroenterology & Hepatology*, 10(8), 487–494. DOI: 10.1038/nrgastro.2013.86 PMID: 23712313

Excelencia in Education. (2022). *Latino college completion: United States 2022*. Retrieved from https://www.edexcelencia.org

Farnsworth, M. (2018). Differentiating second language acquisition from specific learning disability: An observational tool assessing dual language learners' pragmatic competence. *Young Exceptional Children*, 21(2), 92–110. DOI: 10.1177/1096250615621356

Fast, T. (2023). NESCO Story Circles in a TESOL Context. *International Forum of Teaching & Studies, 19*(1), 44–52.

Ferguson, R. (2019). The challenges of educating low-income students. *Educational Leadership*, 76(5), 30–35.

Feria del Libro. (2012, April 28). *Eduardo Galeano (parte 1 de 4) en la Feria del Libro de Buenos Aires* [Video]. YouTube. https://www.youtube.com/watch?v=zVtBcxyj3t8

Fernández, É., & Rodela, K. C. (2020). "Hay poder en numeros": Understanding the Development of a Collectivist Latinx Parent Identity and Conscientizacao Amid an Anti-Immigrant Climate. *Teachers College Record*, 122(8), 1–40. DOI: 10.1177/016146812012200804

Ferreira, A., Gottardo, A., Javier, C., Schwieter, J. W., & Jia, F. (2016). Reading comprehension: The role of acculturation, language dominance, and socioeconomic status in cross-linguistic relations. *Revista Española de Lingüística Aplicada/Spanish Journal of Applied Linguistics. Published under the auspices of the Spanish Association of Applied Linguistics, 29*(2), 613-639.

Fillmore, L. W. (1979). Individual differences in second language acquisition. In Fillmore, C. J., Kempler, D., & Wang, W. S.-Y. (Eds.), *Individual differences in language ability and language behavior* (pp. 203–228). Academic Press. DOI: 10.1016/B978-0-12-255950-1.50017-2

Fillmore, L. W. (1991). When learning a second language means losing the first. *Early Childhood Research Quarterly*, 6(3), 323–346. DOI: 10.1016/S0885-2006(05)80059-6

Flores, A. (2017, September 18). *How the US Hispanic population is changing.* Pew Research Center. https://pewrsr.ch/2wBy0qS

Flores, N. (2017). The complex intersection of language and education: Bilingualism as an asset. *Journal of Multilingual and Multicultural Development*, 38(5), 407–414.

Flores, N., & Rosa, J. (2015). Undoing appropriateness: Raciolinguistic ideologies and language diversity in education. *Harvard Educational Review*, 85(2), 149–171. DOI: 10.17763/0017-8055.85.2.149

Flores, S. M., & Horn, C. L. (2009). College persistence among undocumented students at a selective public university: A quantitative case study analysis. *Journal of College Student Retention*, 11(1), 57–76. DOI: 10.2190/CS.11.1.d

Flores, S. Y., & Murillo, E. G.Jr. (2001). Power, Language, and Ideology: Historical and Contemporary Notes on the Dismantling of Bilingual Education. *The Urban Review*, 33(3), 183–206. DOI: 10.1023/A:1010361803811

Fortino, C. R. (2017, Spring). The professional educator: why supporting Latino Children and families is union work. *American Educator, 41*(1), 14+. https://link-gale-com.lib-proxy.fullerton.edu/apps/doc/A488510167/OVIC?u=csuf_main&sid=bookmark-OVIC&xid=0962636f

Francis, W. S., Strobach, E. N., Penalver, R. M., Martínez, M., Gurrola, B. V., & Soltero, A. (2019). Word–context associations in episodic memory are learned at the conceptual level: Word frequency, bilingual proficiency, and bilingual status effects on source memory. *Journal of Experimental Psychology. Learning, Memory, and Cognition*, 45(10), 1852–1871. DOI: 10.1037/xlm0000678 PMID: 30570325

Freire, P. (2018). *Pedagogy of the oppressed* (M. B. Ramos, Trans.; 50th-anniversary edition.). Bloomsbury Academic.

Freire, P., & Mellado, J. (1970). *Pedagogia del oprimido* (Spanish Edition). Siglo XXI Editores.

Frost, R. (2017). Selected poems of Robert Frost. Fall Rivers Press. https://www.sterlingpublishing.com

Frum, J. L. (2007). Postsecondary educational access for undocumented students: Opportunities and constraints. American Academic, 3(1), 81–108.Fry, R. (2011). The Hispanic diaspora and the public schools: Educating Hispanics. In Leal, D. L., & Trejo, S. J. (Eds.), *Latinos and the Economy: Integration And Impact In Schools Labor Markets And Beyond* (pp. 15–36). Springer New York.

Fuligni, A. J., Witkow, M., & Garcia, C. (2005). Ethnic identity and the academic adjustment of adolescents from Mexican, Chinese, and European backgrounds. *Developmental Psychology*, 41(5), 799–811. DOI: 10.1037/0012-1649.41.5.799 PMID: 16173876

Furlong, D. (2022). Voices of newcomers: Experiences of multilingual learners. EduMatch Publishing. https://www.edumatch.org

Gallo, S. L., & Wortham, S. (2012). Sobresalir: Latino parent perspectives on new Latino diaspora schools. *International Journal of Multicultural Education*, 14(2). Advance online publication. DOI: 10.18251/ijme.v14i2.490

Gándara, P. (2015). *Fulfilling America's future: Latinas in the U.S., 2015*. The White House Initiative on Educational Excellence for Hispanics. Retrieved from https://sites.ed.gov/hispanic-initiative

Gándara, P., & Contreras, F. (2009). *The Latino education crisis: The consequences of failed social policies*. Harvard University Press. DOI: 10.4159/9780674056367

Gandara, P., & Contreras, F. (2010). *The latino education crisis: the consequences of failed social policies*. Harvard University Press. DOI: 10.2307/j.ctv13qftm4

Gándara, P., & Contreras, F. (2021). Latino educational opportunity in the post-pandemic era. *American Educational Research Journal*, 58(6), 1125–1159.

Gándara, P., & Hopkins, M. (2010). *Forbidden language: English learners and restrictive language policies*. Teachers College Press.

Gándara, P., & Mordechay, K. (2022). Post-pandemic educational recovery in Latino communities. *American Educational Research Journal*, 59(4), 1388–1422.

Garcia, M. L., Sprager, L., & Jimenez, E. B. (2022, December 5). "Latino Community Health Workers: Meeting their Community's Emotional Needs in Intuitively Culturally Appropriate Ways". *CHW Central*. Retrieved from https://chwcentral.org/resources/latino-community-health-workers-meeting-their-communitys-emotional-needs-in-intuitively-culturally-appropriate-ways/

Garcia, O., & Torres Guevara, R. (2009). Monoglossic ideologies and language policies of education of U.S Latina/os. In E. Muñoz, J. S., Machado-Casas, M., Murillo, J. E. G., & Martínez, C. (Eds.). *Handbook of latinos and education: Theory, research, and practice*. Taylor & Francis Group. (pp 182- 193). Routledge.

Garcia, R. R. (2016, May 24). "How the Reproductive Justice Movement Benefits Latinas" *Scholars Strategy Network*. Retrieved from https://scholars.org/brief/how-reproductive-justice-movement-benefits-latinas

Garcia, O. (2009). Emergent Bilinguals and TESOL: What's in a Name? *TESOL Quarterly*, 43(2), 322–326. DOI: 10.1002/j.1545-7249.2009.tb00172.x

García, O. (2009). *Multilingualism and Language Education*. The Routledge Companion to English Studies., DOI: 10.4324/9781315852515.ch6

García, O., Flores, N., Seltzer, K., Wei, L., Otheguy, R., & Rosa, J. (2021). Rejecting abyssal thinking in the language and education of racialized bilinguals: A manifesto. *Critical Inquiry in Language Studies*, 18(3), 203–228. DOI: 10.1080/15427587.2021.1935957

Garcia, O., Johnson, S. I., & Seltzer, K. (2022). *The translanguaging classroom: Leveraging student bilingualism for learning*. Caslon.

García, O., & Wei, L. (2014). *Translanguaging: Language, bilingualism and education*. Palgrave Macmillan. DOI: 10.1057/9781137385765

Garza, R. (2019). Paving the way for Latinx teachers: Recruitment and preparation to promote educator diversity. newamerica.org/education-policy/reports/paving-way-latinx.teachers/.

Gay, G. (2014). Race and ethnicity in US education. In Race, R., & Lander, V. (Eds.), *Advancing race and ethnicity in education* (pp. 63–81). Palgrave Macmillan. DOI: 10.1057/9781137274762_5

Georgia Dow. (2022, January 18). *The Psychology of Encanto: Luisa's surface pressure — therapist reacts!* [Video]. YouTube. https://www.youtube.com/watch?v=ZoA_aL54yEY

Gibson, M., & Hidalgo, N. (2009). Bridges to success in high school for migrant youth. *Teachers College Record*, 111(3), 683–711. DOI: 10.1177/016146810911100301

Gilchrist, G. (2018). *Practitioner Enquiry: Professional Development with Impact for Teachers, Schools and Systems*. Routledge. DOI: 10.4324/9781315232270

Gildersleeve, R. E., Rumann, C., & Mondragón, R. (2010). Serving undocumented students: Current law and policy. *New Directions for Student Services*, 131(1), 5–18. DOI: 10.1002/ss.364

Gillespie, T. (2015). Language differences versus language disorder. Retrieved December 10, 2015, from http://teresagillespie.wikispaces.dpsk12.org/Language+Difference+versus+Language+Disorder

Giovanni, N. (1996). *The Selected Poems of Nikki Giovanni*. William Morrow and Company, Inc. hooks, bell. (1994). *Teaching to transgress : education as the practice of freedom*. Routledge.

Gironzetti, E., & Belpoliti, F. (2021). The other side of heritage language education: Understanding Spanish heritage language teachers in the United States. *Foreign Language Annals*, 54(4), 1189–1213. DOI: 10.1111/flan.12591

Gist, C. D. (2019). For what purpose?: Making sense of the various projects driving grow your own program development. *Teacher Education Quarterly*, 46(1), 9–22. https://www.jstor.org/stable/26558179

Gist, C. D. (2019). Special issue: Grow your own programs and teachers of color: Taking inventory of an emerging field. *Teacher Education Quarterly*, 46(1), 5–8. https://www.jstor.org/stable/26558178

Gist, C. D., Bianco, M., & Lynn, M. (2019). Examining grow your own programs across the teacher development continuum: Mining research on teachers of color and nontraditional educator pipelines. *Journal of Teacher Education*, 70(1), 13–25. DOI: 10.1177/0022487118787504

Gloria, A. M., Castellanos, J., Lopez, A. G., & Rosales, R. (2005). An examination of academic nonpersistence decisions of Latino undergraduates. *Hispanic Journal of Behavioral Sciences*, 27(2), 202–223. DOI: 10.1177/0739986305275098

Glynn, C., & Spenader, A. (2020). Critical Content Based Instruction for the Transformation of World Language Classrooms. *Journal of Linguistics and Language Teaching*, 12(2). Advance online publication. DOI: 10.5070/L212246307

Goldhaber, D., Theobald, R., & Tien, C. (2015). The theoretical and empirical arguments for diversifying the teacher workforce: A review of the evidence. *The Center for Education Data & Research, University of Washington Bothell*, 202015-9.

Goldstein, B. A. (2022). *Bilingual Language Development & Disorders in Spanish–English Speakers* (3rd ed.). Brooks Publishing Co.

Gomez, A. M., Downey, M. M., Carpenter, E., Leedham, U., Begun, S., Craddock, J., & Ely, G. (2020). Advancing reproductive just to close the health gap: A call to action for social work. *Social Work*, 65(4), 358–367. DOI: 10.1093/sw/swaa034 PMID: 33020834

Gomez, R., Martinez, L., & Rivera, J. (2024). Self- and collective care as radical acts: A mixed-method study on racism-based traumatic stress among emerging adults. *The American Journal of Orthopsychiatry*, 15(3), 7–15. DOI: 10.1037/ort0000705 PMID: 37768607

Gonzales, L. D. (2012). Stories of success: Latinas redefining cultural capital. *Journal of Latinos and Education*, 11(2), 124–138. DOI: 10.1080/15348431.2012.659566

Gonzales, M. L. (2021). Breaking barriers: The rise of Latina leaders in education. *Journal of Latinos and Education*, 20(2), 130–143.

Gonzales, W., & Tejero Hughes, M. (2018). Libros en mano: Phonological awareness intervention in children's native languages. *Education Sciences*, 8(4), 175. DOI: 10.3390/educsci8040175

González, N., Moll, L. C., & Amanti, C. (2005). *Funds of knowledge: Theorizing practices in households, communities, and classrooms*. Lawrence Erlbaum Associates.

Gorski, P. C., & Dalton, K. (2020). Striving for critical reflection in multicultural and social justice teacher education: Introducing a typology of reflection approaches. *Journal of Teacher Education*, 71(3), 357–368. DOI: 10.1177/0022487119883545

Greenleaf, R. (2002). *Servant leadership: A journey into the nature of legitimate power & greatness*. Paulist Press.

Griffin, A. (2018). *Our stories, our struggles, our strengths: Perspectives and reflections from Latino Teachers*. Education Trust.

Grosjean, F. (2019, March 11). Dyslexia, bilingualism, and learning a second language. *Psychology Today*. https://www.psychologytoday.com/us/blog/life-bilingual/201903/dyslexia-bilingualism-and-learning-second-language

Guarneros, N., Bendezu, C., P Pérez Huber, L., Velez, V., & Solórzano, D. (2009). Still dreaming: Legislation and legal decisions affecting undocumented AB 540 students. *CSRC Latinx Policy & Issues Brief, (23).*

Gutiérrez, K. D. (2017). Designing resilient ecologies: Social design experiments and a new social imagination. *Educational Researcher*, 46(3), 187–195.

Hakuta, K. (1983). New methodologies for studying the relationship of bilingualism and cognitive flexibility. *TESOL Quarterly*, 17(4), 679–681. DOI: 10.2307/3586621

Hamann, E. T., Zúñiga, V., & Sánchez García, J. (2010). Transnational students: Between worlds, between times. *Journal of Latinos and Education*, 9(3), 202–219.

Hamann, E., Wortham, S., & Murillo, E. G.Jr., (Eds.). (2015). *Revisiting education in the new Latino diaspora.* IAP.

Hammond, Z. (2015). Culturally responsive teaching & the brain. Corwin a Sage Company. https://www.corwin.com

Han, I., & Onchwari, A. J. (2018). Development and implementation of a culturally responsive mentoring program for faculty and staff of color. *Interdisciplinary Journal of Partnership Studies*, 5(2), 3. Advance online publication. DOI: 10.24926/ijps.v5i2.1006

Hanson, S. L. (2018). *Building Understanding Among Students of Many Cultures: Story and Cultural Competence* [Master's thesis, Bethel University]. Spark Repository. https://spark.bethel.edu/etd/268

Harper, C. E., Kiyama, J. M., Ramos, D., & Aguayo, D. (2018). Examining the inclusivity of parent and family college orientations: A directed content analysis. *Journal of College Orientation, Transition, and Retention*, 25(1), 30–42.

Harris, C. (1993). Whiteness as property. *Harvard Law Review*, 106(8), 1709–1791. DOI: 10.2307/1341787

Hatch, D. K., Mardock Uman, N., & Garcia, C. E. (2016). Variation within the "New Latino Diaspora" a decade of changes across the United States in the equitable participation of Latina/os in higher education. *Journal of Hispanic Higher Education, 15*(4), 358-385.Hakuta, K. (1983). New methodologies for studying the relationship of bilingualism and cognitive flexibility. *TESOL Quarterly*, 17(4), 679–681.

Hattie, J., & Timperley, H. (2007). The power of feedback. *Review of Educational Research*, 77(1), 81–112. DOI: 10.3102/003465430298487

HealthStream. (2022, January 22). "Healthcare Disparities Among Hispanic Communities" *HealthStream*. Retrieved from https://www.healthstream.com/resource/articles/healthcare-disparities-among-hispanic-communities

Hendrix-Soto, A., & LeeKeenan, K. (2023). Humanizing Learning Spaces in Dehumanizing Times: The Role of Joy and Meaningful Connection. *Multicultural Perspectives*, 25(3), 152–159. DOI: 10.1080/15210960.2023.2257224

Henshaw, F. G. (2015). Learning Outcomes of L2–Heritage Learner Interaction: The Proof Is In the Posttests. *Heritage Language Journal*, 12(3), 245–270. DOI: 10.46538/hlj.12.3.2

Hernandez, M. (2024). Storytelling with purpose. ISTE. https://iste.org

Hernandez, A. E. (2012). Bilingualism and cognitive development: A neuropsychological perspective. *Developmental Science*, 15(4), 465–481.

Hernandez, D. J. (2012). Young children in Black immigrant families from Africa and the Caribbean. In Capps, R., & Fix, M. (Eds.), *Young children of Black immigrants in America: Changing flows, changing faces* (pp. 75–117). Migration Policy Institute.

Hernandez, D. J., & Napierala, J. S. (2023). Children of immigrants: Demographic patterns and educational attainment. *The Future of Children*, 33(1), 7–39.

Herrera, A., & Chen, A. (2010). Strategies to support undocumented students. *Transitions*, 5(2), 3–4.

Higher Education Coordinating Commission. (2021). *Higher Education and Training for Students in Oregon.* https://www.oregon.gov/highered/research/Documents/Equity/HE%20for%20Students%20By%20Race_Latino_Hispanic.pdf'

Hines-Gaither, K., & Accilien, C. (2023). *The Antiracist World language classroom.* Routledge.

Hispanic Association of Colleges and Universities (HACU). (2023). *What is a Hispanic-Serving Institution (HSI)?* Retrieved from https://www.hacu.net

Holguín Mendoza, C. (2018). Critical Language Awareness (CLA) for Spanish Heritage Language Programs: Implementing a Complete Curriculum. *International Multilingual Research Journal*, 12(2), 65–79. DOI: 10.1080/19313152.2017.1401445

Horton, K. E., Bayerl, P. S., & Jacobs, G. (2014). Identity conflicts at work: An integrative framework. *Journal of Organizational Behavior*, 35(S1), S6–S22. https://www.jstor.org/stable/26610872. DOI: 10.1002/job.1893

Hudson, P. (2013). Mentoring as professional development: 'Growth for both mentor and mentee'. *Professional Development in Education*, 39(5), 771–783. DOI: 10.1080/19415257.2012.749415

Hurtado, S., & Carter, D. F. (1997). Effects of college transition and perceptions of the campus racial climate on Latinx college students' sense of belonging. *Sociology of Education*, 70(4), 324–345. DOI: 10.2307/2673270

Hussar, B., Zhang, J., Hein, S., Wang, K., Roberts, A., Cui, J., Smith, M., Mann, F. B., Barmer, A., & Dilig, R. (2020). *The Condition of Education 2020* (NCES 2020-144). US Department of Education. Washington, DC: National Center for Education Statistics. https://files.eric.ed.gov/fulltext/ED605216.pdf

Ijalba, E., & Bustos, A. (2017). Phonological deficits in developmental dyslexia in a second grade Spanish-English bilingual child. *Perspectives of the ASHA Special Interest Groups*, 2(1), 212–228. DOI: 10.1044/persp2.SIG1.212

Ijalba, E., Bustos, A., & Romero, S. (2020). Phonological–orthographic deficits in developmental dyslexia in three Spanish–English bilingual students. *American Journal of Speech-Language Pathology*, 29(3), 1133–1151. DOI: 10.1044/2020_AJSLP-19-00175 PMID: 32750285

Immordino-Yang, M. H., & Damasio, A. (2007). We feel, therefore we learn: The relevance of affective and social neuroscience to education. *Mind, Brain and Education : the Official Journal of the International Mind, Brain, and Education Society*, 1(1), 3–10. DOI: 10.1111/j.1751-228X.2007.00004.x

Ingram, C. (1998). "Wilson backs ballot measure to ban bilingual education." Los Angeles Times, May 19, 1998.

International Dyslexia Association. (2002). *Definition of dyslexia*. https://dyslexiaida.org/definition-of-dyslexia/

International Dyslexia Association. (2023). *Structured literacy: An overview*. https://dyslexiaida.org/structured-literacy/

International Dyslexia Association. (n.d.). *English learners and dyslexia*. https://dyslexiaida.org/english-learners-and-dyslexia/

Irizarry, J., & Donaldson, M. L. (2012). Teach for America: The Latinization of US schools and the critical shortage of Latina/o teachers. *American Educational Research Journal*, 49(1), 155–194. DOI: 10.3102/0002831211434764

Ishimaru, A. M. (2020). *Just schools: Building equitable collaborations with families and communities*. Teachers College Press.

Ishimaru, A. M., & Lott, J. (2015). Families in the driver's seat: Cultivating family leadership for educational change. *Journal of Educational Change*, 16(2), 117–144.

Jacobs, C. E. (2020). READY TO LEAD Report by Charlotte E. Jacobs, Ph.D. Research Directed by Simone Marean + Rachel Simmons Leadership Supports and Barriers for Black and Latinx Girls [Review of READY TO LEAD Report by Charlotte E. Jacobs, Ph.D. Research Directed by Simone Marean + Rachel Simmons Leadership Supports and Barriers for Black and Latinx Girls]. In girlsleadership.org (pp. 1–49). Girls Leadership. https://readytolead.girlsleadership.org/

Jeynes, W. H. (2016). A meta-analysis: The relationship between parental involvement and Latinx student academic achievement. *Education and Urban Society*, 49(1), 4–28. DOI: 10.1177/0013124516630596

Jiménez, J. E., Gutiérrez, N., & de León, S. C. (2021). Analyzing the role of fidelity of RTI Tier 2 reading intervention in Spanish kindergarten and first grade students. *Annals of Dyslexia*, 71(1), 28–49. DOI: 10.1007/s11881-021-00221-5 PMID: 33713278

Johnson, L. (2022, February 24). "The Disparate Impact of Texas' Abortion Ban on Low-Income and Rural Women" *Georgetown Journal Poverty Law & Policy*. Retrieved https://www.law.georgetown.edu/poverty-journal/blog/the-disparate -impact-of-texas-abortion-ban-on-low-income-and-rural-women/

Jones, R., Holton, W., & Joseph, M. (2019). Call me MiSTER: Black male grow your own program. *Teacher Education Quarterly*, 46(1), 55–68. https://www.jstor .org/stable/26558182

Jones, S. R., Torres, V., & Arminio, J. L. (2014). *Negotiating the complexities of qualitative research in higher education: Fundamental elements and issues*. Routledge.

Kaelbar, L. B. (2012). *Latinas and abortion: The role of acculturation, religion, reproductive history, and familism*. [Doctoral dissertation, University of Miami]. University of Miami Scholarship Repository. Retrieved from https://scholarship.miami.edu/ esploro/outputs/doctoral/Latinas-and-Abortion-The-Role-of/991031447238602976

Kelly, A. P., Schneider, M., & Carey, K. (2010). *Rising to the Challenge: Hispanic College Graduation Rates as a National Priority*. American Enterprise Institute for Public Policy Research. https://files.eric.ed.gov/fulltext/ED508846.pdf

Kim, D., Kim, S. L., & Barnett, M. (2021). "That makes sense now!": Bicultural middle school students' learning in a culturally relevant science classroom. *International Journal of Multicultural Education*, 23(2), 145–172. DOI: 10.18251/ijme. v23i2.2595

Kinloch, V., Bucholtz, M., Casillas, D. I., Lee, J.-S., Lee, T. S., McCarty, T. L., Irizarry, J. G., San Pedro, T., Wong, C., Peña, C., Ladson-Billings, G., Haupt, A., Rosa, J., Flores, N., Lee, S. J., González, N., Gutiérrez, K. D., Johnson, P. M., & Lee, C. D. (2017). *Culturally sustaining pedagogies: teaching and learning for justice in a changing world* (D. Paris & H. S. Alim, Eds.). Teachers College Press.

Kirmaci, M. (2022). Examining Latinx teacher resistance: From margins to empowerment. *Journal of Latinos and Education*, 22(5), 2102–2115. DOI: 10.1080/15348431.2022.2092108

Kiyama, J. M., & Harper, C. E. (2018). Beyond hovering: A conceptual argument for an inclusive model of family engagement in higher education. *Review of Higher Education*, 41(3), 365–385. DOI: 10.1353/rhe.2018.0012

Klibanoff, E. (2024, January 26). "Hispanic and teen fertility rates increase after abortion restrictions" *The Texas Tribune*. Retrieved from https://www.texastribune .org/2024/01/26/texas-abortion-fertility-rate-increase/

Kovats, A. G. (2010). *Invisible students and marginalized identities the articulation of identity among Mixteco youth in San Diego, California.* [Doctoral dissertation, San Diego State University]. ProQuest Dissertations Publishing.

Kovelman, I., Bisconti, S., & Hoeft, F. (2016, April). *Literacy & dyslexia revealed through bilingual brain development*. International Dyslexia Association. https:// dyslexiaida.org/literacy-dyslexia-revealed-through-bilingual-brain-development/\

Krashen, S. (2000). Bilingual education, the acquisition of English, and the retention and loss of Spanish. *Research on Spanish in the US*, 432-444.

Krashen, S. D. (1982). Principles and Practice in Second Language Acquisition

Krashen, S. D., & Terrell, T. D. (1983). *The natural approach (Language acquisition in the classroom).* Alemany Press. https://www.sdkrashen.com

Krogstad, J. M. (2016, July 28). *5 facts about Latinx and education.* Pew Research Center. https://www.pewresearch.org/fact-tank/2016/07/28/5-facts-about-Latinx -and-education/

Kumashiro, K. K. (2000). Toward a Theory of Anti-Oppressive Education. *Review of Educational Research*, 70(1), 25–53. DOI: 10.3102/00346543070001025

Laden, B. V. (2000). The Puente Project: Socializing and mentoring Latino community college students. *Academic Exchange Quarterly*, 4(2), 90–99.

Ladson-Billings, G. (1995). Toward a theory of culturally relevant pedagogy. *American Educational Research Journal*, 32(3), 465–491. DOI: 10.3102/00028312032003465

Ladson-Billings, G. (1995, Summer). But That's Just Good Teaching! The Case for Culturally Relevant Pedagogy. *Theory into Practice*, 34(3), 159–165. DOI: 10.1080/00405849509543675

Ladson-Billings, G. (2006). Yes, but how do we do it? Practicing culturally relevant pedagogy. In Landsman, J., & Lewis, C. W. (Eds.), *White teachers / diverse classrooms* (pp. 29–41). Stylus Publishing.

Leeman, J. (2005). Engaging critical pedagogy: Spanish for native speakers. *Foreign Language Annals*, 38(1), 35–45. DOI: 10.1111/j.1944-9720.2005.tb02451.x

Leeman, J. (2018). Critical language awareness in SHL: Challenging the linguistic subordination of US Latinxs. In Potowski, K. (Ed.), *Handbook of Spanish as a Minority/Heritage Language* (pp. 345–358). Routledge. DOI: 10.4324/9781315735139-22

Leeman, J., Rabin, L., & Román-Mendoza, E. (2011). Identity and Activism in Heritage Language Education. *Modern Language Journal*, 95(4), 481–495. DOI: 10.1111/j.1540-4781.2011.01237.x

Leeman, J., & Serafini, E. J. (2016). Sociolinguistics for Heritage Language Educators and Students: A Model for Critical Translingual Competence. In Fairclough, M., & Beaudrie, S. M. (Eds.), *Innovative Strategies for Heritage Language Teaching: A Practical Guide for the Classroom* (pp. 56–79). Georgetown University Press.

Lichon, K., Moreno, I., Villamizar, A. M., & Arana, K. (2022). Fortalecer Raíces y Formar Alas: Empowerment, Advancement, and Retention of Latinx Educators and Leaders in Catholic Schools. *Journal of Catholic Education, 25*(2), 44-. https://doi.org/DOI: 10.15365/joce.2502032022

Liou, D. D., Antrop-González, R., & Cooper, R. (2009). Unveiling the promise of Community Cultural Wealth to sustaining Latina/o students' college-going information networks. *Educational Studies (Ames)*, 45(6), 534–555. DOI: 10.1080/00131940903311347

Lopez, G. R. (2001). The Value of Hard Work: Lessons on parent involvement from an (im)migrant household. *Harvard Educational Review*, 71(3), 416–437. DOI: 10.17763/haer.71.3.43x7k542x023767u

Lorde, A. (1984). *Sister Outsider: Essays and Speeches*. Crossing Press.

Lorde, A. (2017). *A burst of light: And Other Essays*. Courier Dover Publications.

Lowenhaupt, R., & Reeves, T. (2015). Toward a theory of school capacity in new immigrant destinations: Instructional and organizational considerations. *Leadership and Policy in Schools*, 14(3), 308–340. DOI: 10.1080/15700763.2015.1021052

Lucas, T., & Katz, A. (1994). Reframing the debate: The roles of native languages in English-only programs for language minority students. *TESOL Quarterly*, 28(3), 537–562. DOI: 10.2307/3587307

Machado-Casas, M. (2009). The politics of organic phylogeny: The art of parenting and surviving as transnational multilingual Latinx indigenous immigrants in the US. *High School Journal*, 92(4), 82–99. DOI: 10.1353/hsj.0.0034

Magnan, S. S. (2008). Reexamining the priorities of the National Standards for Foreign Language Education. *Language Teaching*, 43(3), 349–366. DOI: 10.1017/S0261444808005041

Magnan, S. S., Dianna, M., Sahakyan, N., & Kim, S. (2012). Student Goals, Expectations, and the Standards for Foreign Language Learning. *Foreign Language Annals*, 45(2), 170–192. DOI: 10.1111/j.1944-9720.2012.01192.x

Maharaj-Sharma, R. (2022). Using storytelling to teach a topic in physics. *Education Inquiry*, 15(2), 227–246. DOI: 10.1080/20004508.2022.2092977

Mahoney, J. L., Cairns, B. D., & Farmer, T. W. (2003). Promoting interpersonal competence and educational success through extracurricular activity participation. *Journal of Educational Psychology*, 95(2), 409–418. DOI: 10.1037/0022-0663.95.2.409

Marco-Bujosa, L. M., McNeill, K. L., & Friedman, A. A. (2020). Becoming an urban science teacher: How beginning teachers negotiate contradictory school contexts. *Journal of Research in Science Teaching*, 57(1), 3–32. DOI: 10.1002/tea.21583

Martinez-Cola, M. (2023). Understanding demographic shifts in Latino communities: Implications for education. *Demographic Research*, 48(2), 145–168.

Martínez, G. (2003). Classroom based dialect awareness in heritage language instruction: A critical applied linguistic approach. *Heritage Language Journal*, 7(1), 1–14. DOI: 10.46538/hlj.1.1.3

Martinez, J., & Santiago, D. (2020). *Tapping Latino talent: How HSIs are preparing Latino students for the workforce — Covid-19 Update*. Excelencia in Education.

Martinez, M. A. (2013). (Re) considering the role familismo plays in Latina/o high school students' college choices. *High School Journal*, 97(1), 21–40. DOI: 10.1353/hsj.2013.0019

Martinez, R. A., & Fernández, E. (2021). The evolution of Latino education: Historical perspectives and current challenges. *Harvard Educational Review*, 91(3), 331–357.

Martinez, R. R.Jr, Dye, L., Gonzalez, L. M., & Rivas, J. (2021). Striving to thrive: Community cultural wealth and legal immigration status. *Journal of Latina/o Psychology*, 9(4), 299–314. DOI: 10.1037/lat0000191

Matas, A., & Rodríguez, J. L. (2014). The education of English learners in California following the passage of proposition 227: A case study of an urban school district. *Penn GSE Perspectives on Urban Education*, 11(2), 44–56.

Mathes, P. G., Pollard-Durodola, S. D., Cárdenas-Hagan, E., Linan-Thompson, S., & Vaughn, S. (2007). Teaching struggling readers who are native Spanish speakers: What do we know?. https://doi.org/DOI: 10.1177/088840640402700

McNair, J. C., & Edwards, P. A. (2021). The Lasting Legacy of Rudine Sims Bishop: Mirrors, Windows, Sliding Glass Doors, and More. *Literacy Research: Theory, Method, and Practice*, 70(1), 202–212. DOI: 10.1177/23813377211028256

Meade, M. (2016). The genius myth. GreenFire Press. https://www.mosaicvoices.org

Méndez-Morse, S. (2004). Constructing mentors: Latina educational leaders' role models and mentors. *Educational Administration Quarterly*, 40(4), 561–590. DOI: 10.1177/0013161X04267112

Méndez-Morse, S., Murakami, E. T., Byrne-Jiménez, M., & Hernández, F. (2015). Latina/o educational leadership across borders: Learning, growing, and leading together. *The International Journal of Educational Leadership Preparation*, 10(1), 1–13.

Mensah, F. M., & Jackson, I. (2018). Whiteness as property in science teacher education. *Teachers College Record*, 120(1), 1–38. DOI: 10.1177/016146811812000108

Merriam, S. B. (2009). *Qualitative research: A guide to design and implementation.* Jossey-Bass.

Mexican Ministry of Public Education (SEP). (2022). *Educational statistics in Baja California.* Retrieved from https://www.sep.gob.mx

Miciak, J., Ahmed, Y., Capin, P., & Francis, D. J. (2022). The reading profiles of late elementary English learners with and without risk for dyslexia. *Annals of Dyslexia*, 72(2), 276–300. DOI: 10.1007/s11881-022-00254-4 PMID: 35608744

Moats, L. C., & Foorman, B. R. (2003). Measuring teachers' content knowledge of language and reading. *Annals of Dyslexia*, 53(1), 23–45. DOI: 10.1007/s11881-003-0003-7

Moje, E. B., Ciechanowski, K. M., Kramer, K., Ellis, L., Carrillo, R., & Collazo, T. (2004). Working toward third space in content area literacy: An examination of everyday funds of knowledge and discourse. *Reading Research Quarterly*, 39(1), 38–70. DOI: 10.1598/RRQ.39.1.4

Moll, L. C., Amanti, C., Neff, D., & González, N. (1992). Funds of knowledge for teaching: Using a qualitative approach to connect homes and classrooms. *Theory into Practice*, 31(2), 132–141. DOI: 10.1080/00405849209543534

Montiel, G. I. (2017). "Hacerle la lucha": Examining the value of hard work as a source of funds of knowledge of undocumented, Mexican Ivy League students. In Kiyama, J. M., & Rios-Aguilar, C. (Eds.), *Funds of knowledge in higher education: Honoring students' cultural experiences and resources as strengths* (pp. 125–142). Routledge. DOI: 10.4324/9781315447322-8

Montrul, S. (2010). How similar are L2 learners and heritage speakers? Spanish clitics and word order. *Applied Psycholinguistics*, 31, 167–207. DOI: 10.1017/S014271640999021X

Monzo, L. D., & Rueda, R. S. (2001). Professional roles, caring, and scaffolds: Latino teachers' and paraeducators' interactions with Latino students. *American Journal of Education*, 109(4), 438–471. DOI: 10.1086/444335

Morales, A. R., Espinoza, P. S., & Duke, K. B. (2022). What exists and "What I need ": In search of critical, empowering, and race-conscious approaches to mentoring from the perspective of Latina/o/x teachers. *Handbook of research on teachers of color and indigenous teachers*, 441-458.

Morales, A. R. (2018). Within and beyond a grow-your-own-teacher program: Documenting the contextualized preparation and professional development experiences of critically conscious Latina teachers. *Teaching Education*, 29(4), 357–369. DOI: 10.1080/10476210.2018.1510483

Moreno, J. F. (1999). The elusive quest for equality: 150 years of Chicano/Chicana education. *Harvard Educational Review*.

Moslimani, M., & Noe-Bustamante, L. (2023, Aug.). *Facts on Latinos in the US*. Pew Research Center. https://www.pewresearch.org/race-and-ethnicity/fact-sheet/latinos-in-the-us-fact-sheet/

Moule, J. (2012). *Cultural competence: A primer for educators* (2nd ed.). Wadsworth.

Muñoz-Muñoz, E. R., Poza, L. E., & Briceño, A. (2023). Critical Translingual Perspectives on California Multilingual Education Policy. *Educational Policy*, 37(6), 1791–1817. https://doi-org.lib-proxy.fullerton.edu/10.1177/08959048221130342. DOI: 10.1177/08959048221130342

Murillo, E. G. (2017). Critical race theory in education: Review of past literature and a look to the future. *Urban Education*, 52(5), 563–598.

Murillo, E. G., Wortham, S. E. F., & Hamann, E. T. (2002). *Education in the new Latino diaspora: Policy and the politics of identity* (Vol. 2). Greenwood Publishing Group.

National Alliance on Mental Illness. (2021). *Latinx/Hispanic community and mental health.*

National Association of Social Workers. (2015). *Standards and indicators for cultural competence in social work practice*. NASW. https://www.socialworkers .org/Practice/NASW-Practice-Standards-Guidelines/Standards-and-Indicators-for -Cultural-Competence-in-Social-Work-Practice

National Association of Social Workers. (2021). *Code of ethics of the National Association of Social Workers*. NASW Press. https://www.socialworkers.org/About/ Ethics/Code-of-Ethics/Code-of-Ethics-English

National Center for Education Statistics. (2020). *Characteristics of public school teachers*. U.S. Department of Education. https://nces.ed.gov/pubs2020/2020103/ index.asp

National Center for Education Statistics. (2023). Characteristics of public school teachers. *Condition of Education*. U.S. Department of Education, Institute of Education Sciences. Retrieved [date], from https://nces.ed.gov/programs/coe/indicator/clr

National Center for Education Statistics. (2024). *Achievement gaps and Latinx students in U.S. public schools*. U.S. Department of Education, Institute of Education Sciences.

National Center for Education Statistics. (2024). *English learners in public schools. Condition of education*. U.S. Department of Education, Institute of Education Sciences.

National Center for Education Statistics. (2024). *English learners in public schools*. U.S. Department of Education. https://nces.ed.gov/programs/coe/indicator/cgf/ english-learners

National Reading Panel (US), & National Institute of Child Health and Human Development (US). (2000). *Report of the National Reading Panel: Teaching children to read: An evidence-based assessment of the scientific research literature on reading and its implications for reading instruction: Reports of the subgroups.* National Institute of Child Health and Human Development, National Institutes of Health.

National Science Board, National Science Foundation. (2021). *Elementary and Secondary STEM Education. Science and Engineering Indicators 2022.* NSB-2021-1. https://ncses.nsf.gov/pubs/nsb20211/

NCTE. (2021, August 31). *Supporting linguistically and culturally diverse learners in English education.* National Council of Teachers of English. https://ncte.org/statement/diverselearnersinee/

Nieto, S. (2018). Language, culture, and teaching. Routledge. https://www.routledge.com/education

Nieto, S. (2010). *Language, culture, and teaching: Critical perspectives.* Routledge.

Nieto, S. (2010). *The light in their eyes: Creating multicultural learning communities.* Teachers College Press.

Noe-Bustamante, L. (2020, August 11). *About one-in-four U.S. hispanics have heard of Latinx, but just 3% use it.* Pew Research Center. https://www.pewresearch.org/race-and-ethnicity/2020/08/11/about-one-in-four-u-s-hispanics-have-heard-of-latinx-but-just-3-use-it/

Nsengiyumva, D. S., Oriikiriza, C., & Nakijoba, S. (2021). Cross-Linguistic Transfer and Language Proficiency in the Multilingual Education System of Burundi: What Has the Existing Literature so Far Discovered? *Indonesian Journal of English Language Teaching and Applied Linguistics,* 5(2), 387–399. DOI: 10.21093/ijeltal.v5i2.770

Núñez, A. M. (2017). What can Latina/o migrant students tell us about college outreach and access? In M. E. Zarate, P. Perez *Facilitating educational success for migrant farmworker students in the US* (pp. 82-93). Routledge.

Ocasio, K. M. (2019). A Review of Literature Surrounding the Latino Teacher Pipeline. In E. G Murillo Jr (Ed.), *Critical Readings on Latinos and Education* (62-79). Routledge.

Ocasio, K. M. (2019). Nuestro camino: A review of literature surrounding the Latino teacher pipeline. *Critical readings on Latinos and education,* 95-116.

Office of Disease Prevention and Health Promotion. (n.d.). *Social Determinants of Health*. Healthy People 2030. https://odphp.health.gov/healthypeople/priority-areas/social-determinants-health

Olsen, L. (2014). *Reparable Harm: Fulfilling the unkept promise of educational opportunity for California's long-term English learners*. California Together.

Open, A. I. (2024). Story generated by ChatGPT in response to a prompt provided by author. Retrieved [August 29, 2024], from https://chat.openai.com/

Ordoñez-Jasis, R., Dunsmore, K., Herrera, G., Ochoa, C., Diaz, L., & Zuniga-Rios, E. (2016). Communities of Caring: Developing Curriculum That Engages Latino/a Students' Diverse Literacy Practices. *Journal of Latinos and Education*, 15(4), 333–343. DOI: 10.1080/15348431.2015.1134538

Ortmeyer, D. L., & Quinn, M. A. (2012). COYOTES, MIGRATION DURATION, AND REMITTANCES. *Journal of Developing Areas*, 46(2), 185–203. https://www.jstor.org/stable/23215369. DOI: 10.1353/jda.2012.0038

Ovando, C. J. (2003). Bilingual Education in the United States: Historical Development and Current Issues. *Bilingual Research Journal*, 27(1), 1–24. DOI: 10.1080/15235882.2003.10162589

Padilla, A. M. (1994). Ethnic minority scholars, research, and mentoring: Current and future issues. *Educational Researcher*, 23(4), 24–27. DOI: 10.2307/1176259

Paris, D., & Alim, H. S. (2014). What are we seeking to sustain through culturally sustaining pedagogy? A loving critique forward. *Harvard Educational Review*, 84(1), 85–100. https://doi-org.proxyiub.uits.iu.edu/10.17763/haer.84.1.982l873k2ht16m77. DOI: 10.17763/haer.84.1.982l873k2ht16m77

Paris, D., & Alim, H. S. (2017). *Culturally sustaining pedagogies: Teaching and learning for justice in a changing world*. Teachers College Press.

Parker, K., Morin, R., Horowitz, J. M., Lopez, M. H., & Rohal, M. (2015, June 11). *Multiracial in America: Proud, diverse and growing in numbers*. Pew Research Center. https://www.pewresearch.org/social-trends/2015/06/11/multiracial-in-america/

Pascual y Cabo, D., & Prada, J. (2018). Redefining Spanish teaching and learning in the United States. *Foreign Language Annals*, 51(3), 533–547. DOI: 10.1111/flan.12355

Patton, M. Q. (2014). *Qualitative research & evaluation methods: Integrating theory and practice*. Sage publications.

Pedraza, P., & Rivera, M. (Eds.). (2005). *Latino education: An agenda for community action research*. Taylor & Francis Group.

Peer, L., & Reid, G. (2014). *Multilingualism, literacy and dyslexia: A challenge for educators*. Routledge. DOI: 10.4324/9780203432372

Pérez Huber, L. (2010). Using Latina/o Critical Race Theory (LatCrit) and racist nativism to explore intersectionality in the educational experiences of undocumented Chicana college students. *Educational Foundations*, 24, 77–96.

Perez, W. (2009). *We are Americans: Undocumented students pursuing the American dream*. Sterling, VA: Stylus Publishing.

Perez, W. (2011). *Americans by heart: Undocumented Latinx students and the promise of higher education*. Teachers College Press.

Perez, W., Cortes, R., Ramos, K., & Coronado, H. (2010). Cursed and blessed: Examining the socioemotional and academic experiences of undocumented Latinx/a college students. *New Directions for Student Services*, 2010(131), 35–51. DOI: 10.1002/ss.366

Perez, W., Espinoza, R., Ramos, K., Coronado, H. M., & Cortes, R. (2009). Academic resilience among undocumented Latinx students. *Hispanic Journal of Behavioral Sciences*, 31(2), 149–181. DOI: 10.1177/0739986309333020

Perreira, K. M., Fuligni, A., & Potochnick, S. (2010). Fitting in: The roles of social acceptance and discrimination in shaping the academic motivations of Latinx youth in the US Southeast. *The Journal of Social Issues*, 66(1), 131–153. DOI: 10.1111/j.1540-4560.2009.01637.x PMID: 22611286

Piñón, L., Carreón-Sánchez, S., & Bishop, S. (2022). *Emergent bilingual learner education – Literature review*. Intercultural Development Research Association. https://files.eric.ed.gov/fulltext/ED629281.pdf

Planned Parenthood Action Fund. (n.d.) "Health Equity Issues for the Latino Community". *Planned Parenthood Action Fund*. Retrieved from https://www.plannedparenthoodaction.org/communities/latinos-planned-parenthood/health-equity-issues-for-the-latino-community

Planned Parenthood of Greater New York. (2024, October 3). "The Importance of Reproductive Health for Latinx Communities". *Planned Parenthood of Greater New York*. Retrieved from https://www.plannedparenthood.org/planned-parenthood-greater-new-york/blog/the-importance-of-reproductive-health-for-latinx-communities

Poehling, C., Downey, M. M., Singh, M. I., & Beasley, C. C. (2023). From gaslighting to enlightening: Reproductive justice as an interdisciplinary solution to close the health gap. *Journal of Social Work Education*, 59(1), 36–47. DOI: 10.1080/10437797.2023.2203205 PMID: 38606421

Polinsky, M. (2014). Heritage Languages and Their Speakers: Looking Ahead. In Fairclough, M., & Beaudrie, S. M. (Eds.), *Innovative Approaches to Heritage Languages: From Research to Practice*. Georgetown University Press.

Potowski, K. (2018). Virtual Q&A. In Webinar Series Center for Language Instruction and Coordination. University of Illinois at Urbana-Champaign. https://mediaspace.illinois.edu/media/t/1_uds5wrkd/90905681

Potowski, K. (2004). Student Spanish Use and Investment in a Dual Immersion Classroom: Implications for Second Language Acquisition and Heritage Language Maintenance. *Modern Language Journal*, 88(1), 75–101. https://www.jstor.org/stable/3588719. DOI: 10.1111/j.0026-7902.2004.00219.x

Potowski, K. (2005). *Fundamentos de la enseñanza del español a hispanohablantes en los EE. UU*. Arco Libros.

Potowski, K. (2012). *Identity and Heritage Learners: Moving Beyond Essentializations. Spanish As a Heritage Language in the United States: The State of the Field*. Georgetown University Press.

Pour-Khorshid, F. (2018). H.E.L.L.A: A bay area critical racial affinity group committed to healing, empowerment, love, liberation, and action (Order No. 10935583). Available from Ethnic NewsWatch; ProQuest Dissertations & Theses Global: The Humanities and Social Sciences Collection. (2128055672). Retrieved from https://www.proquest.com/dissertations-theses/h-e-l-bay-area-critical-racial-affinity-group/docview/2128055672/se-2

Pour-Khorshid, F. (2018). Cultivating sacred spaces: A racial affinity group approach to support critical educators of color. *Teaching Education*, 29(4), 318–329. DOI: 10.1080/10476210.2018.1512092

Price, J. (2010). The fffect of instructor race and gender on student persistence in STEM Fields. *Economics of Education Review*, 29(6), 901–910. DOI: 10.1016/j.econedurev.2010.07.009

Puente, K., Starr, C. R., Eccles, J. S., & Simpkins, S. D. (2021). Developmental trajectories of science identity beliefs: Within-group differences among Black, Latinx, Asian, and White students. *Journal of Youth and Adolescence*, 50(12), 2394–2411. DOI: 10.1007/s10964-021-01493-1 PMID: 34518982

Pugh, K., & Verhoeven, L. (2018). Introduction to this special issue: Dyslexia across languages and writing systems. *Scientific Studies of Reading*, 22(1), 1–6. DOI: 10.1080/10888438.2017.1390668 PMID: 30718941

Pullen, P. C., & Lane, H. B. (2013). Teacher-directed decoding practice with manipulative letters and word reading skill development of struggling first-grade students. *HEX, 22*(1).

Pullen, P. C., & Lane, H. B. (2016). Hands-on decoding: Guidelines for using manipulative letters. *Learning Disabilities (Pittsburgh, Pa.)*, 21(1), 27–37. DOI: 10.18666/LDMJ-2016-V21-I1-6797

Quezada, M. S. (2016). Proposition 227 and the Loss of Educational Rights: A Personal Perspective and Quest for Equitable Educational Programs for English Learners. In *Latino Civil Rights in Education* (1st ed., pp. 158–169). Routledge. https://doi.org/DOI: 10.4324/9781315672526-15

Quiocho, A., & Rios, F. (2000). The power of their presence: Minority group teachers and schooling. *Review of Educational Research*, 70(4), 485–528. DOI: 10.3102/00346543070004485

Ramos, D., & Wright-Mair, R. (2021). Imposter syndrome: A buzzword with damaging consequences. *Diverse Issues in Higher Education*. https://www.diverseeducation.com/tenure/article/15109066/imposter-syndrome-a-buzzword-with-damaging-consequences

Ramos, D., & Chavez, M. (2022). Family engagement strategies in Latino communities. *Hispanic Journal of Behavioral Sciences*, 44(2), 145–168.

Randolph, L. J. (2017). Heritage Language Learners in Mixed Spanish Classes: Subtractive Practices and Perceptions of High School Spanish Teachers. *Hispania*, 100(2), 274–288. DOI: 10.1353/hpn.2017.0040

Reardon, S. F., Weathers, E. S., Fahle, E. M., Jang, H., & Kalogrides, D. (2019). Is separate still unequal? New evidence on school segregation and racial academic achievement gaps (*CEPA Working Paper No. 19-06*). Retrieved from Stanford Center for Education Policy Analysis: https://cepa.stanford.edu/wp19-06

Revelo, R. A., & Baber, L. D. (2018). Engineering resistors: Engineering Latina/o students and emerging resistant capital. *Journal of Hispanic Higher Education*, 17(3), 249–269. DOI: 10.1177/1538192717719132

Richards-Tutor, C., Baker, D. L., Gersten, R., Baker, S. K., & Smith, J. M. (2016). The effectiveness of reading interventions for English learners: A research synthesis. *Exceptional Children*, 82(2), 144–169. DOI: 10.1177/0014402915585483

Riley, K. (2022). Schools where belonging works. In *Compassionate Leadership for School Belonging* (pp. 61–72). UCL Press., DOI: 10.2307/j.ctv20rsk8p.13

Rios-Aguilar, C., & Kiyama, J. M. (2019). Funds of Knowledge: An Approach to Studying Latina(o) Students' Transition to College. In E. G Murillo Jr (Ed.), *Critical Readings on Latinos and Education* (pp. 26–43). Routledge.

Robert Wood Johnson Foundation. (2024, June 1). "Advancing Solutions for Reproductive Justice" *Robert Wood Johnson Foundation.* Retrieved from https://www.rwjf.org/en/insights/our-research/2024/06/advancing-solutions-for-reproductive-justice.html

Rogers-Ard, R., Knaus, C., Bianco, M., Brandehoff, R., & Gist, C. D. (2019). The grow your own collective: A critical race movement to transform education. *Teacher Education Quarterly*, 46(1), 23–34. https://www.jstor.org/stable/26558180

Roorda, D. L., Koomen, H. M., Spilt, J. L., & Oort, F. J. (2011). The influence of affective teacher–student relationships on students' school engagement and achievement: A meta-analytic approach. *Review of Educational Research*, 81(4), 493–529. DOI: 10.3102/0034654311421793

Rosa, J., & Flores, N. (2017). *Paris, D., & Alim, H. S. (2017). Culturally sustaining pedagogies: teaching and learning for justice in a changing world.* Teachers College Press.

Roseberry-McKibbin, C. (2002). *Multicultural students with special language needs: Practical strategies for assessment and intervention* (2nd ed.). Academic Communication Associates.

Roseberry-McKibbin, C., & Brice, A. (2000). Acquiring English as a second language. *ASHA Leader*, 5(12), 4–7.

Ross, L., & Solinger, R. (2017). *Reproductive Justice: An Introduction.* University of California Press.

Rubinstein-Avila, E., & Lee, E. H. (2014). Secondary teachers and English language learners (ells): Attitudes, preparation, and implications. *The Clearing House: A Journal of Educational Strategies, Issues and Ideas*, 87(5), 187–191. DOI: 10.1080/00098655.2014.910162

Saad, L. F. (2020). *Me and white supremacy: Combat racism, change the world, and become a good ancestor.* Sourcebooks.

Sadovnik, A. R., & Coughlan, R. W. (2016). *Sociology of education: A critical reader.* Routledge. DOI: 10.1007/978-94-6300-717-7

Salva, C., & Matis, A. (2017). *Boosting achievement: Reaching students with interrupted or minimal education.* Seidlitz Education.

Samuels, S., Wilkerson, A., Chapman, D., & Watkins, W. (2020). Toward a Conceptualization: Considering Microaffirmations as a Form of Culturally Relevant Pedagogy and Academic Growth for K-12 Underserved Student Populations. *The Journal of Negro Education*, 89(3), 298–311. https://www.jstor.org/stable/10.7709/jnegroeducation.89.3.0298

San Diego County Office of Education. (2023). *Student demographics.* Retrieved from https://www.sdcoe.net

San Miguel, G. (1999). The schooling of Mexicanos in the Southwest, 1848–1891. In Moreno, J. F. (Ed.), *The Elusive Quest for Equality: 150 Years of Chicano/Chicana Education, Harvard Educational Review:31–52.*

Sánchez-Connally, P. (2018). Latinx First Generation College Students: Negotiating Race, Gender, Class, and Belonging. *Race, Gender & Class (Towson, Md.)*, 25(3/4), 234–251. https://www.jstor.org/stable/26802896

Sánchez, P., & Machado-Casas, M. (2009). At the intersection of transnationalism, Latina/o immigrants, and education. *High School Journal*, 92(4), 3–15. DOI: 10.1353/hsj.0.0027

Santamaría, L. J. (2020). Culturally responsive educational leadership and advocacy: A transformative agenda. *Educational Policy*, 34(1), 7–29.

Santamaría, L. J., & Jean-Marie, G. (2014). Cross-cultural leadership in school settings: Critical perspectives on race, ethnicity, and gender. *Multicultural Education Review*, 6(1), 39–54.

Santos, S. J., & Reigadas, E. T. (2002). Latinos in higher education: An evaluation of a university faculty mentoring program. *Journal of Hispanic Higher Education*, 1(1), 40–50. DOI: 10.1177/1538192702001001004

Scarborough, H. S. (2001). Connecting early language and literacy to later reading (dis)abilities: Evidence, theory, and practice. In Neuman, S., & Dickinson, D. (Eds.), *Handbook for research in early literacy* (pp. 97–110). Guilford Press.

Schwartz, A. I. (2020). *Spanish so white: Conversations on the inconvenient racism of a 'foreign' language education.* Multilingual Matters.

Self-Care & Marianismo: Tending to Mental Health in Latino/x Cultures. (n.d.). Inclusive Therapists.https://www.inclusivetherapists.com/blog/self-care-marianismo-tending-to-mental-health-in-latino-x-cultures

Sleeter, C. E. (1995). An analysis of the critiques of multicultural education. In J.A. Banks & C. A. M. Banks (Eds.), Handbook of research on multicultural education Macmillan. https://www.christinesleeter.org

Sleeter, C. E. (2005). Un-standardizing curriculum: Multicultural teaching in standards-based classroom. Teachers College Press. https://www.christinesleeter.org

Smith, B. D. (2017). Reproductive justice: A policy window for social work. *Social Work*, 62(3), 221–226. DOI: 10.1093/sw/swx015 PMID: 28444300

Solari, M., & Martín Ortega, E. (2022). Teachers' professional identity construction: A sociocultural approach to its definition and research. *Journal of Constructivist Psychology*, 35(2), 626–655. DOI: 10.1080/10720537.2020.1852987

Solórzano, D. G., & Bernal, D. D. (2001). Examining transformational resistance through a critical race and LatCrit theory framework: Chicana and Chicano students in an urban context. *Urban Education*, 36(3), 308–342. DOI: 10.1177/0042085901363002

Solórzano, D. G., Villalpando, O., & Oseguera, L. (2005). Educational inequities and Latina/o undergraduate students in the United States: A critical race analysis of their educational progress. *Journal of Hispanic Higher Education*, 4(3), 272–294. DOI: 10.1177/1538192705276550

Solórzano, D. G., & Yosso, T. J. (2002). Critical race methodology: Counter-storytelling as an analytical framework for education research. *Qualitative Inquiry*, 8(1), 23–44. DOI: 10.1177/107780040200800103

Sonubi, C., Flores, E., & Spalluto, L. (2022). How should US health care meet Latinx community health needs? *AMA Journal of Ethics*, 24(2), 261–266. PMID: 35405051

Spencer, M. B. (2006). Phenomenological variant of ecological systems theory: Development of diverse groups. In Damon, W., & Lerner, R. M. (Eds.), *Theoretical models of human development* (pp. 829–893). Handbook of child psychology. John Wiley & Sons.

Starrs, A. M., Ezeh, A. C., Barker, G., Basu, A., Bertrand, J., Blum, R., Coll-Seck, A. M., Grover, A., Laski, L., Roa, M., Sathar, Z. A., Say, L., Serour, G. I., Singh, S., Stenberg, K., Temmerman, M., Biddlecom, A., Popinchalk, A., Summers, C., & Ashford, L. S. (2018). Accelerate progress - sexual and reproductive health and rights for all: Report of the Guttmacher-*Lancet* Commission. *Lancet*, 391(10140), 2642–2692. DOI: 10.1016/S0140-6736(18)30293-9 PMID: 29753597

Stepler, R., & Lopez, M. H. (2016, September 8). *U.S. Latino population growth and dispersion has slowed since onset of the Great Recession*. Pew Research Center. https://www.pewresearch.org/hispanic/2016/09/08/latino-population-growth-and -dispersion-has-slowed-since-the-onset-of-the-great-recession/

Stewart, M. D., García, A., & Petersen, H. (2021). Schools as racialized organizations in policy and practice. *Sociology Compass*, 15(12), 1–13. https://doi-org.kean.idm .oclc.org/10.1111/soc4.12940. DOI: 10.1111/soc4.12940

Suarez, V., & McGrath, J. (2022), Teacher professional identity: How to develop and support it in times of change, *OECD Education Working Papers*, No. 267, OECD Publishing, Paris, DOI: 10.1787/19939019

Suárez-Orozco, C., Suárez-Orozco, M., & Todorova, I. (2008). *Learning a new land. Immigrant students in American society*. Harvard University Press. DOI: 10.4159/9780674044111

Suárez-Orozco, C., & Todorova, I. L. (2003). The social worlds of immigrant youth. *New Directions for Youth Development*, 2003(100), 15–24. DOI: 10.1002/yd.60 PMID: 14750266

Substance Abuse and Mental Health Services Administration. (2014). *Trauma-informed care in behavioral health services* (Treatment Improvement Protocol (TIP) Series 57). U.S. Department of Health and Human Services. https://store.samhsa .gov/sites/default/files/sma15-4420.pdf

Sullivan, A. L., & Proctor, S. L. (2016, September). The shield or the sword? Revisiting the debate on racial disproportionality in special education and implications for school psychologists. *School Psychology Forum*, 10(3), ●●●.

Sung, K. K. (2017). "Accentuate the Positive; Eliminate the Negative": Hegemonic Interest Convergence, Racialization of Latino Poverty, and the 1968 Bilingual Education Act. *Peabody Journal of Education*, 92(3), 302–321. DOI: 10.1080/0161956X.2017.1324657

Taggart, A. (2022). The Influence of Educación on Latinx Students' Academic Expectations and Achievement. *Journal of Latinos and Education*, 22(4), 1728–1743. https://doi-org.lib-proxy.fullerton.edu/10.1080/15348431.2022.2043864. DOI: 10.1080/15348431.2022.2043864

Taylor, J., & Udang, L. (2016). "Proposition 58: English Proficiency. Multilingual Education. "California Education for a Global Economy Initiative," California Initiative Review (CIR): Vol. 2016, Article 9. Available at: https://scholarlycommons .pacific.edu/california-initiative-review/vol2016/iss1/

The National Standards Collaborative Board. (2015). *World-Readiness standards for learning languages* (4th ed.).

The Reading League. (2022). *Science of reading: Defining guide.* https://www.thereadingleague.org/what-is-the-science-of-reading/

The Reading League. (2023). *Understanding the difference: The science of reading and implementation for English learners/emergent bilinguals (ELs/EBs)* [Joint statement]. The Reading League. https://www.thereadingleague.org/wp-content/uploads/2023/09/TRLC-ELEB-Understanding-the-Difference-The-Science-of-Reading-and-Implementation.pdf

The William Benton Museum of Art. (n.d. a). What is an Arpillera? University of Connecticut William Benton Museum of Art. https://benton.uconn.edu/web-exhibitions-2/arpillera/what-is-an-arpillera/

The William Benton Museum of Art. (n.d. b). View Arpilleras. University of Connecticut William Benton Museum of Art. https://benton.uconn.edu/web-exhibitions-2/arpillera/images/

Tompkins, M. (2002). Sign with your baby: Opening the doors to communication. *Infant Development Association of California News, 29*(1).

Torres, V. (2003). Influences on ethnic identity development of Latino college students in the first two years of college. *Journal of College Student Development*, 44(4), 532–547. DOI: 10.1353/csd.2003.0044

Turner, C. S., Cosmé, P. X., Dinehart, L., Martí, R., McDonald, D., Ramirez, M., & Zamora, J. (2017). Hispanic-serving institution scholars and administrators on improving Latina/Latino/Latinx/Hispanic teacher pipelines: Critical junctures along career pathways. *Association of Mexican American Educators Journal*, 11(3), 251–275. DOI: 10.24974/amae.11.3.369

Tyson, A., & Hugo Lopez, M. (2023, October 30). "5 facts about Hispanic Americans and health care". *Pew Research Center.* Retrieved from https://www.pewresearch.org/short-reads/2023/10/30/5-facts-about-hispanic-americans-and-health-care/

U.S. Census Bureau. (2000). *Census 2000, demographic profile data for California.* https://www2.census.gov/library/publications/2003/dec/phc-2-6.pdf Retrieved from https://www.census.gov/data/"

U.S. Department of Education. (2021). *EDFacts Data Warehouse (EDW): IDEA Part B Child Count and Educational Environments Collection, 2019-20. OSEP Fast Facts: Race and ethnicity of children with disabilities served under IDEA Part B.* U.S. Department of Education.

University at Buffalo. (n.d.). "SW 725 Reproductive Justice" Syllabus University of Southern California. (2018, February 27). *Do you know the difference between micro-, mezzo- and macro-level social work?* USC Suzanne Dworak-Peck School of Social Work. https://dworakpeck.usc.edu/news/do-you-know-the-difference-between-micro-mezzo-and-macro-level-social-work

US Census Bureau. (2000). *Population and Housing Unit Estimates.* Retrieved from www.census.gov/popest/

US Census Bureau. (2010). *Population and Housing Unit Estimates.* Retrieved from www.census.gov/popest/

Vaandering, D. (2013). Implementing restorative justice practice in schools: What pedagogy reveals. *Journal of Peace Education*, 11(1), 64–80. DOI: 10.1080/17400201.2013.794335

Valdés, G. (2001). Heritage language students: Profiles and possibilities. In Peyton, J. K., Ranard, D. A., & McGinnis, S. (Eds.), *Heritage languages in America: Preserving a national resource* (pp. 37–77). Delta Systems.

Valdés, G. (2019). *Transnational students and schools: The borderlands of education.* Teachers College Press.

Valencia, R. R. (2012). *The evolution of deficit thinking: Educational thought and practice.* Routledge. DOI: 10.4324/9780203046586

Valencia, R. R., & Black, M. S. (2002). "Mexican Americans don't value education!"—On the basis of myth, mythmaking, and debunking. *Journal of Latinos and Education*, 1(2), 81–103. DOI: 10.1207/S1532771XJLE0102_2

Valenzuela, A. (1999). Subtractive schooling: U.S.-Mexican youth and the politics of caring. State University of New York Press. Chapter 3 The politics of caring

Valenzuela, A. (1999). *Subtractive schooling: U.S.-Mexican youth and the politics of caring.* State University of New York Press.

Varelas, M., Segura, D., Bernal-Munera, M., & Mitchener, C. (2023). Embracing equity and excellence while constructing science teacher identities in urban schools: Voices of new Teachers of Color. *Journal of Research in Science Teaching*, 60(1), 196–233. DOI: 10.1002/tea.21795

Vaughn, S., Mathes, P., Linan-Thompson, S., Cirino, P., Carlson, C., Pollard-Durodola, S., Cardenas-Hagan, E., & Francis, D. (2006). Effectiveness of an English intervention for first-grade English language learners at risk for reading problems. *The Elementary School Journal*, 107(2), 153–180. DOI: 10.1086/510653

Vega, D., & Martinez, R. (2020). Latino male mentoring: A review of best practices and call to action. *Journal of Hispanic Higher Education*, 19(2), 164–182.

Villalpando, O., & Bernal, D. D. (2018). Latino/a students in higher education: Understanding their transitional experiences. *Journal of Hispanic Higher Education*, 17(3), 223–236.

Wadlington, E. M., & Wadlington, P. L. (2005). What educators really believe about dyslexia. *Reading Improvement*, 42(1), 16–33.

Wagner, M., Cardetti, F., & Byram, M. (2019). *Teaching intercultural citizenship across the curriculum: the role of language education*. ACTFL.

Walls, L. (2016). Awakening a dialogue: A critical race theory analysis of U. S. nature of science research from 1967 to 2013. *Journal of Research in Science Teaching*, 53(10), 1546–1570. DOI: 10.1002/tea.21266

Walls, L. (2018). The Effect of Dyad Type on Collaboration: Interactions among Heritage and Second Language Learners. *Foreign Language Annals*, 51(3), 638–657. DOI: 10.1111/flan.12356

Washburn, E. K., Binks-Cantrell, E. S., & Joshi, R. M. (2014). What do preservice teachers from the USA and the UK know about dyslexia? *Dyslexia (Chichester, England)*, 20(1), 1–18. DOI: 10.1002/dys.1459 PMID: 23949838

Washburn, E. K., Joshi, R. M., & Binks-Cantrell, E. S. (2011). Teacher knowledge of basic language concepts and dyslexia. *Dyslexia (Chichester, England)*, 17(2), 165–183. DOI: 10.1002/dys.426 PMID: 21290479

Wilson-Lopez, A., & Hasbún, I. M. (2023). Countering science as White property through linguistic justice. *Journal of Research in Science Teaching*, 60(3), 675–677. DOI: 10.1002/tea.21838

Wortham, S., Clonan-Roy, K., Link, H., & Martinez, C. (2013). The new Latino Diaspora: The surging Hispanic and Latino population across the country has brought new education challenges and opportunities to rural and small town America. *Phi Delta Kappan*, 94(6), 14. DOI: 10.1177/003172171309400604

Wortham, S., Hamann, E. T., & Murillo, E. G.Jr., (Eds.). (2002). *Education in the New Latino Diaspora: Policy and the politics of identity*. Ablex Publishing.

Wright-Mair, R., Ramos, D., & Passano, B. (2024). Latinx college students' strategies for resisting imposter syndrome at predominantly white institutions. *Journal of Latinos and Education*, 23(2), 725–743. DOI: 10.1080/15348431.2023.2180366

Wright, R. L., Bird, M., & Frost, C. J. (2015). Reproductive health in the United States: A review of recent social work literature. *Social Work*, 60(4), 295–304. DOI: 10.1093/sw/swv028 PMID: 26489350

Wright, S. C., & Boese, G. D. B. (2015). Meritocracy and tokenism. In James, D. W. (Ed.), *International Encyclopedia of the Social & Behavioral Sciences* (2nd ed., pp. 239–245). Elsevier., https://doi.org/https://doi.org/10.1016/B978-0-08-097086 -8.24074-9 DOI: 10.1016/B978-0-08-097086-8.24074-9

Wright, W. E. (2019). *Foundations for teaching English language learners: Research, theory, policy, and practice* (3rd ed.). Caslon Publishing.

Yang, M., Cooc, N., & Sheng, L. (2017). An investigation of cross-linguistic transfer between Chinese and English: A meta-analysis. *Asian-Pacific Journal of Second and Foreign Language Education*, 2(1), 1–21. DOI: 10.1186/s40862-017-0036-9

Yosso, T., Smith, W., Ceja, M., & Solórzano, D. (2009). Critical Race Theory, racial microaggressions, and campus racial climate for Latina/o undergraduates. *Harvard Educational Review, 79*(4), 659-691. Yosso, T. J., & Solórzano, D. G. (2006). Leaks in the Chicana and Chicano Educational Pipeline. *CSRC Latinx Policy & Issues Brief, (13)*.

Yosso, T. J. (2005). Whose culture has capital? A critical race theory discussion of community cultural wealth. *Race, Ethnicity and Education*, 8(1), 69–91. DOI: 10.1080/1361332052000341006

Younes, M., Goldblatt Hyatt, E., Witt, H., & Franklin, C. (2021). A call to action: Addressing ambivalence and promoting advocacy for reproductive rights in social work education. *Journal of Social Work Education*, 57(4), 625–635. DOI: 10.1080/10437797.2021.1895930

Young, J. L., & Easton-Brooks, D. (2022). The Impact of Teachers of Color on School Belonging: A Conceptual Framework. In Gist, C. D., & Bristol, T. J. (Eds.), *Handbook of Research on Teachers of Color and Indigenous Teachers* (pp. 637–644). American Educational Research Association., DOI: 10.2307/j.ctv2xqngb9.52

Yule, G. (2010). *The study of language* (4th ed.). Cambridge University Press., https://www.cambridge.org

Zabin, C., Kearney, M., Garcia, A., Runsten, D., & Nagengast, C. (1993). *A new cycle of poverty: Mixtec migrants in California agriculture*. California Institute for Rural Studies.

Zhai, Y., Tripp, J., & Liu, X. (2024). Science teacher identity research: A scoping literature review. *International Journal of STEM Education*, 11(1), 20. DOI: 10.1186/s40594-024-00481-8

Ziegler, J. C., & Goswami, U. (2005). Reading acquisition, developmental dyslexia, and skilled reading across languages: A psycholinguistic grain size theory. *Psychological Bulletin*, 131(1), 3–29. DOI: 10.1037/0033-2909.131.1.3 PMID: 15631549

Zong, J., & Batalova, J. (2019). Mexican immigrants in the United States. *Migration Policy Institute.* Retrieved from https://www.migrationpolicy.org

Zúñiga, V., & Hernández-León, R. (Eds.). (2005). *New destinations: Mexican immigration in the United States*. Russell Sage Foundation.

About the Contributors

Angello Villarreal, a nationally celebrated and acknowledged New Jersey educator, has been recognized on a national and state level for his transformative contributions to education and leadership. Named a National K-12 Champion on Equity by the American Consortium on Equity in Education and one of the Top 5 Latino Leaders in New Jersey by the United States Latino Affairs. Dr. Villarreal continues to redefine the role of educators in promoting inclusivity and excellence. Dr. Villarreal was born and raised in Lima, Peru. Previously, Dr. Villarreal taught Spanish and ESL at an urban school. He has utilized his experiences working with different types of demographics and educational needs to serve students better. Advocacy is a center of Dr. Villarreal's philosophy as all his research, work, community service, mentorship, and leadership are towards serving the students and their families needs. From creating after-school programs to leading different projects, Dr. Villarreal believes working with the community is critical for the student's success.

Ramon Benavides is the son of migrant farmworkers who dropped out of school at a young age, only to return and become educators in South Texas. He followed in his parents' footsteps and entered the education profession. For the last 12 years, he has taught in the Ysleta Independent School District. He teaches high school biology, AP biology, and dual-enrollment biology at Del Valle High School in El Paso, TX. He is also a part-time biology adjunct instructor at El Paso Community College. Ramon holds multiple degrees – a Bachelor of Science in biology from the University of Texas at San Antonio, a Bachelor of Arts in chemistry from the University of Texas at Brownsville and Master of Arts in teaching science in biology from the University of Texas at El Paso. He is in the midst of completing his doctorate from Texas Tech University in education leadership and policy. His passion for education and serving his students is not limited to the classroom. He sponsors the school's anime, medical sciences, and environmental stewardship clubs.

Additionally, he oversees a new chapter of the Science National Honor Society at Del Valle High School. He is a member of several professional organizations and has two publications. During his summers, he usually participates in Research Experiences for Teachers, which has allowed him to conduct scientific research with Rice University from 2017-2019 and the University of Texas at El Paso in 2015 and 2021. Ramon's goal is to create as many opportunities as possible for his students in every position he serves. From being a biology teacher to a club sponsor, all that he does is for his kids. His objective is never to be satisfied with who he is as a teacher. Teaching is his passion, and the classroom is his refuge, but he acknowledges all that he does would not be possible without the love and support of his wife and son

Melissa A. Campesi is a Children's Author, ESL Educator, and Founder of the Cross-Cultural Storytelling Project. She is based in New Jersey and has a passion for promoting cultural awareness through the power of storytelling. Her notable works include "I am an English Language Learner," a children's book which shares stories of immigrant children in America, and "Imagine Song," which explores a child's journey of creativity through music. Melissa's favorite things to do are write poetry and music, host gatherings with family and friends, and travel to new places around the world.

Norma I. Gómez-Fuentes is a bilingual literacy and dyslexia specialist with extensive expertise in Spanish-English education. She holds a Master's degree in Curriculum and Instruction with a focus on Literacy Studies and is a Certified Academic Language Practitioner. With years of experience as a bilingual classroom educator and dyslexia lead, Norma has developed and led district-wide professional development for educators, families, and staff. Her passion for promoting bilingualism, biliteracy, and biculturalism drives her work in ensuring equitable access to literacy for struggling readers and individuals with dyslexia. Norma is committed to fostering educational excellence through evidence-based practices and a deep understanding of diverse learners' needs.

Vivian Gonsalves is a Clinical Associate Professor in the School of Special Education, School Psychology and Early Childhood Studies at the University of Florida. Her research focuses on early literacy development, teacher education, mentoring, and reading instruction and remediation. She is currently an instructor of special education and literacy development courses in various programs in the College of Education and provides professional development to in-service educators and other related service professionals in implementing assessments and designing instruction for struggling readers. Additionally, she is one of the assistant directors of the University of Florida Literacy Institute (UFLI) and the program coordinator for the Dyslexia Certificate program at UF.

Amanda Goodwin, MSW, LCSW, is a Licensed Clinical Social Worker and psychotherapist with several years of experience in the mental health field. She currently practices as a psychotherapist in a group private practice and has prior experience working in case management, IOP/PHP levels of care, and continuing education coordination, specializing in compassionate and trauma-informed care. Amanda earned her Master of Social Work (MSW) from Monmouth University in 2017 and is currently pursuing her Doctor of Social Work (DSW) at the same institution. Amanda was inspired to focus on reproductive justice in social work following the overturn of Roe v. Wade, deepening her passion for advancing reproductive rights and driving policy change. Her work centers on addressing the intersections of systemic barriers, resource inequities, education, and mental heath that impact reproductive autonomy. Through her practice, research, and advocacy, she is committed to empowering individuals and promoting equitable access to reproductive healthcare and related social services.

Alex Guzmán is an assistant professor at the College of Education at Kean University, Department of Educational Leadership & Secondary Education. His research focuses on diversifying the teacher workforce, educational leadership, and the intersection of bilingual and science education. He has 25 years of experience in K-12 education and higher education as a High School Principal, Director of Curriculum, and Assistant professor.

Caelin McCallum holds a Master of Social Work with a specialization in Global and Community Practice and a post-graduate certificate in Advanced Clinical Practice with Families, both from Monmouth University. She is a licensed social worker and has also earned a professional diploma in Social Innovation from the University for Peace. Additionally, she is a certified DEI Manager, accredited by Rutgers University, and a certified Confidential Sexual Violence Advocate. As a doctoral candidate in Monmouth University's inaugural Human Rights Leadership DSW program, Caelin's academic pursuits focus on integrating reproductive justice into social work education. Her capstone project involves developing a comprehensive repository of resources to streamline the integration of reproductive justice principles into social work curricula, empowering educators to adopt this vital framework. Caelin formerly served as a Board Member for the National Association of Social Workers – New Jersey Chapter (NASW-NJ), where she contributed to advancing professional development and advocacy efforts for social workers statewide. She has also worked as an adjunct professor at Monmouth University and

Georgian Court University, teaching courses in social work and women and gender studies, reflecting her dedication to mentorship and education. In her professional practice, Caelin brings extensive experience in the nonprofit sector, particularly in grant writing and management, having secured over $35 million in funding. Her work is driven by a commitment to addressing the social determinants of health to enhance community well-being. She has been instrumental in developing programs to combat housing insecurity and poverty, as well as establishing systems to support LGBTQ+ individuals and implementing harm reduction strategies for individuals with substance use disorders. Caelin's global perspective, honed through her studies at the University for Peace, and her extensive leadership and advocacy work, continue to inform her mission to create equitable and inclusive systems that improve lives and uplift communities.

Concepción Moncada Cummings is a bilingual/biliterate Mexican American doctoral student at the University of Florida. Her current research consists of emergent bilingual students, dyslexia, evidence-based literacy practices, early literacy/foundational reading skills, dis/ability, and education policy. Concepción's experiences as a former bilingual teacher in public education in the United States have steered her focus in graduate school to bilingual children with dis/abilities, families of multicultural children, and stressing their stories so that their abilities can be highlighted, and their needs can be met. Her interests are rooted in equity, cultural, and linguistic diversity. Concepción es mexicana-estadounidense, es bilingüe, y está en su doctorado en la Universidad de Florida. Su investigación actual consiste de investigaciones con estudiantes bilingües, dislexia, prácticas de alfabetización basadas en la evidencia, alfabetización temprana/habilidades básicas de lectura, discapacidad y política educativa. Las experiencias de Concepción como ex-maestra bilingüe en la educación pública en los Estados Unidos han dirigido su enfoque en la escuela de posgrado a niños bilingües con discapacidades, familias de niños multiculturales, y enfatizando sus historias de las familias para que sus habilidades puedan resaltarse y que reciban ayuda para sus necesidades. Sus intereses se basan en la equidad, la diversidad cultural y lingüística.

Lee Perez is a 9th-12th grade English as a Second Language (ESL) teacher at Omaha Benson High School in Omaha, Nebraska. Perez holds an Associate of Arts degree from Mid-Plains Community College, a Bachelor of Science degree in secondary education from the University of Nebraska at Omaha, and a Master of Science degree in Teaching English to Speakers of Other Languages (TESOL) from Concordia University in Seward, Nebraska. He holds two teaching endorsements in Nebraska: grades 7-12 social sciences and pre-K-12 ESL. Perez has taught for 18 years in the diverse, urban Omaha Public Schools district. He started his career at Marrs Magnet Middle School teaching seventh-grade world studies for the dual language program. He then taught ESL at Alice Buffett Magnet Middle School and Omaha North High School. Currently, he teaches ESL at Omaha Benson High School. Additionally, Perez is an adjunct professor for Bellevue University in their Teacher Education Department. Perez was featured in a professional development series through EdPuzzle, where he did five Professional Development videos on working with English Language Learners (ELLs.). Perez has received several recognitions for his work as a teacher. He was the recipient of the 2021 Award for Teaching Excellence through the Nebraska State Education Association and named a Cox Communications Education Hero for the Omaha area. In 2022, he was named the Nebraska Teacher of the Year. Perez was the first ESL teacher and person of color to receive this award in Nebraska's history. He is also a member of the Commissioners of Education's teacher advisory committee; the Hispanic/Chicano representative for the Ethnic Minority Affairs Committee; and a member of the National Education Association's Teachers of Color cohort. In 2023, Perez received the national Horace Mann Award for Teaching Excellence award through the National Education Association (NEA) Foundation. He is the first person from Nebraska to receive this recognition.

Autumn Rivera is a sixth-grade science teacher at Glenwood Springs Middle School in the Roaring Fork School District in Colorado. She holds a BA and MAT from Colorado College and an MA from the University of Colorado, Colorado Springs. She is currently working on her EdD at Walden University. She is also an adjunct professor at Colorado Mountain College in the Education Department. During her more than twenty years as an educator, she has worked with students from elementary to postgraduate. Rivera empowers her students and strives to provide them with common background experiences. She was named the 2022 Colorado Teacher of the Year and a Finalist for National Teacher of the Year. She is a 2022 PAEMST State Finalist and the 2023 Association of Middle Level Education Educator of the Year.

Françoise Thenoux is an accomplished educator and advocate with nearly two decades of experience in anti-bias and anti-racist education. A proud Latina and racialized immigrant, she specializes in equitable world language curricula. Known as "The Woke Spanish Teacher," Françoise shares resources and best practices for integrating social justice into language education. Her influence extends beyond the classroom through presentations at national conventions, including ACTFL. She has also written scholarly articles for ACTFL. Based in La Serena, Chile, Françoise engages with educators globally to foster inclusive and socially aware educational environments. Follow her on social media for more.

Anthony Villarreal, PhD is the Latinx Faculty Scholar in Student Affairs and Campus Diversity at San Diego State University (SDSU). He earned a bachelor's from Portland State University, M.Ed. in School Counseling from Lewis & Clark College, and Ph.D. in Education from Claremont Graduate University. His research employs asset-based perspectives and centers Latinx students' community cultural wealth in college access/completion. He is an alumnus of the Chancellor Doctoral Incentive Program (CDIP), American Association of Hispanics in Higher Education (AAHHE) Fellows Program, and Association for Public Policy Analysis & Management (APPAM) Equity & Inclusion Fellows Program. He has served on various National Science Foundation grants such as the Mathematics Educators Engaging English Learners in Discussion (MELd) project with the SDSU Center for Research into Mathematics and Science Education and several projects with the Research and Equity Scholarship Institute.

Index

A

acculturation 57, 61, 64, 283, 323
ACTFL 106, 110, 111, 115, 126, 138, 143, 188
Affinity Spaces 190, 191, 192, 215, 216
Audre Lorde 175, 176, 180, 186, 191

B

bilingualism 37, 72, 98, 123, 157, 162, 169, 170, 190, 191, 216, 225, 226, 227, 237, 244, 253, 269, 273, 275, 276, 280, 281, 282, 283

C

Collective Liberation 190, 191, 192, 194
college access 145, 146, 147, 154, 155, 161, 162, 164, 211
Community Cultural Wealth 60, 73, 88, 89, 98, 103, 145, 146, 147, 151, 153, 154, 155, 161, 171, 174, 229, 241, 242, 252, 256
coyotes 36, 53
Creativity 16, 17, 24, 25, 109
critical consciousness 61, 219, 236, 239
Critical Language Awareness 108, 109, 126, 129, 134, 138, 141, 143
Critical Reflection 85, 95, 99, 111, 116, 143
Cross-Cultural Storytelling 1, 23, 24, 25, 26, 28, 29
cross-linguistic transfer 257, 261, 279, 285, 286
Cultural Awareness 15, 20, 109, 111, 119
culturally competent 165, 289, 292, 297, 300, 303, 305, 307, 309, 310, 313, 319, 325
culturally relevant 49, 50, 51, 53, 76, 88, 94, 141, 159, 164, 201, 205, 211, 228, 229, 231, 233, 234, 246, 254, 278, 305
culturally responsive mentoring 100
culturally responsive teaching 26, 30, 50, 52, 88, 220, 257, 279
Culturally Sustaining Pedagogies 110, 113, 139, 142, 143, 228, 254, 255
cultural navigation 63, 68
Curiosity 1, 5, 12, 16, 25, 26, 27, 29, 55, 78, 143, 203, 209

D

deficit mindset 108
Diversity 22, 26, 29, 45, 75, 76, 77, 78, 80, 90, 91, 96, 99, 124, 139, 140, 148, 176, 187, 189, 192, 198, 205, 210, 216, 218, 246, 249, 251, 262, 271, 273, 278, 280, 311
dyslexia 257, 258, 259, 260, 261, 262, 264, 266, 268, 269, 270, 271, 272, 273, 274, 275, 276, 277, 278, 279, 280, 281, 282, 283, 284, 285, 286, 287

E

educational equity 48, 202, 211, 212, 214, 223
Emergent Bilingual 234, 236, 237, 238, 240, 242, 247, 248, 259, 263, 265, 285, 287
evidence-based practices 220, 258, 280

F

familismo 161, 171, 180, 295, 299, 325
full linguistic repertoire 242, 273
funds of knowledge 66, 72, 94, 100, 134, 149, 150, 163, 171, 173

G

Gloria Anzaldúa 181

H

heteroglossic 231, 238, 246, 247, 248
Hispanic Serving School District 212

I

identity 5, 15, 26, 28, 37, 41, 42, 44, 52, 55, 56, 57, 59, 60, 62, 63, 65, 66, 67, 68, 69, 70, 73, 76, 78, 79, 80, 84, 85, 86, 87, 88, 91, 98, 100, 101, 102, 103, 107, 108, 109, 111, 124, 125, 126, 127, 131, 134, 141, 142, 143, 148, 149, 157, 159, 160, 162, 163, 168, 169, 170, 172, 174, 176, 177, 182, 186, 191, 193, 195, 197, 198, 199, 200, 201, 203, 208, 209, 210, 218, 220, 221, 223, 226, 232, 233, 234, 236, 237, 239, 243, 248, 249, 251, 262, 282, 294, 325

identity development 55, 56, 57, 60, 63, 66, 68, 69, 70, 73, 85, 86, 87, 88, 148, 157

immigrant students 57, 147, 148, 167, 173

immigration 35, 36, 57, 58, 64, 148, 149, 152, 158, 161, 171, 174, 176, 182, 183, 184, 185, 187, 188, 189, 244, 245, 252, 296, 297, 298, 299, 301, 303, 304, 307, 308, 309, 310, 312, 316, 318, 319, 320

Inclusion 1, 29, 81, 90, 112, 114, 120, 166, 176, 178, 179, 192, 205, 218, 219, 238, 299, 318

Intercultural Citizenship 105, 106, 110, 111, 112, 118, 139, 140, 143

Intercultural Competence 105, 106, 110, 111, 143

Intersectionality 172, 181, 183, 219, 226, 249, 293, 294, 322, 325

L

language 2, 5, 6, 7, 10, 11, 12, 15, 16, 18, 19, 20, 21, 22, 26, 28, 30, 31, 34, 35, 36, 37, 38, 39, 40, 41, 42, 43, 44, 48, 49, 52, 53, 58, 59, 65, 70, 72, 77, 81, 85, 96, 105, 106, 107, 108, 109, 110, 111, 112, 113, 114, 115, 116, 117, 118, 119, 120, 121, 122, 123, 124, 125, 126, 127, 128, 129, 132, 134, 135, 136, 138, 139, 140, 141, 142, 143, 147, 153, 154, 155, 156, 157, 158, 159, 162, 176, 180, 182, 187, 188, 190, 191, 195, 200, 202, 205, 206, 207, 208, 210, 213, 214, 216, 217, 220, 225, 226, 227, 228, 231, 232, 233, 234, 235, 236, 237, 238, 239, 240, 241, 242, 243, 244, 245, 246, 247, 248, 249, 250, 252, 253, 254, 257, 258, 259, 260, 261, 262, 263, 264, 265, 266, 268, 269, 270, 271, 272, 273, 274, 275, 276, 277, 278, 279, 281, 282, 283, 284, 285, 286, 287, 291, 296, 298, 300, 303, 305, 306, 307, 308, 309, 310, 312, 313, 317, 318

language-based disorders 262, 264, 268, 279, 287

language differences 257, 262, 263, 264, 265, 266, 268, 269, 279, 283

Language loss 35, 36, 37

Latino immigrant youth 55, 56, 57, 58, 59

Latinx 33, 75, 76, 78, 83, 88, 93, 94, 95, 96, 98, 99, 100, 101, 102, 106, 109, 113, 114, 115, 116, 117, 119, 123, 126, 130, 134, 145, 146, 147, 148, 149, 150, 151, 152, 153, 154, 155, 156, 157, 159, 160, 161, 162, 163, 164, 165, 166, 167, 168, 169, 170, 171, 172, 174, 175, 176, 179, 181, 185, 186, 187, 190, 191, 192, 193, 195, 197, 198, 199, 200, 201, 202, 203, 204, 205, 208, 209, 210, 211, 212, 213, 214, 215, 216, 217, 218, 219, 220, 221, 222, 223, 224, 225, 227, 228, 229, 231, 232, 233, 234, 235, 236, 237, 238, 239, 240, 241, 242, 244, 245, 247, 248, 249, 250, 251, 252, 254, 255, 256, 324, 325

Latinx educators 75, 76, 88, 95, 163, 175, 185, 186, 190, 192, 193, 202, 203, 204, 224, 231, 232, 233, 234, 235, 236, 237, 238, 239, 240, 241, 242, 247, 248, 250, 254

Latinx student success 197, 210, 212, 216, 217, 218, 219, 221, 222, 223

literacy instruction 257, 269, 270, 272, 279, 280

M

male mentorship 55, 56, 59, 60, 69

masculinity 56, 64, 177, 237

Mentors 48, 55, 59, 64, 75, 76, 88, 89, 92, 93, 96, 97, 160, 163, 212, 228

monolingual 37, 108, 190, 233, 237, 243, 247, 248, 260, 269, 271, 272, 273, 275

multilingual 5, 6, 7, 12, 15, 18, 19, 20, 30, 44, 84, 108, 112, 120, 123, 129, 136, 138, 139, 140, 141, 143, 154, 171, 192, 193, 195, 216, 217, 220, 225, 226, 239, 246, 249, 252, 254, 256, 257, 258, 259, 260, 261, 262, 265, 266, 268, 269, 270, 271, 272, 273, 274, 275, 276, 278, 279, 280, 285, 287

Multilingual Education 123, 216, 254, 256, 285

multilingual learners 5, 7, 12, 19, 30, 108, 260, 268, 271, 274, 276, 279, 280

N

New Latinx Destination 145, 152, 153, 154, 155, 166

P

Paulo Freire 176

S

Science Educators 80, 94

Self-Care 175, 182, 184, 185, 186, 191, 196

SisterSong 290, 294

social determinants of health 291, 307, 309, 310, 323, 326

systemic barriers 83, 89, 95, 163, 185, 204, 209, 223, 291, 292, 293, 294, 296, 299, 301, 303, 304, 305, 307, 308, 314, 315, 317, 319, 320, 326

T

teachers of color 33, 34, 52, 76, 78, 87, 88, 95, 98, 99, 100, 102, 165, 227, 229

Texas Senate Bill 8 296, 326

Tokenism 77, 102, 175, 193, 217, 218

Translanguaging 24, 72, 108, 126, 128, 143, 227, 253

W

Wage Disparities 193

World Languages 123

Y

youth development 62, 173

Printed in the United States
by Baker & Taylor Publisher Services